LINCOLN CITY FC

A SEASON REVIEW

2018/19

BY GARY HUTCHINSON

First Published June 2019

Copyright Gary Hutchinson

All rights reserved. No part of this publication may be reproduced, stored in a retrieval system or transmitted in any form, or by means electronic, mechanical, photocopying, recording or otherwise without permission in writing from the publisher

CHAMPIONS

For Peter Newton & Dave Mundin

Introduction 11

Summer 2018 13

"Beep Beep" – Raheem Sterling's inspiration Andrade arrives at City 13

Chairman Bob Dorrian stands down 14

Clive Nates elected Lincoln City chairman 15

Harry Toffolo signs two-year Imps deal 16

Michael O'Connor arrives – what this means for Lincoln City 17

Grant Smith becomes arrival number four 19

Goodbye, Ollie Palmer 19

Danny Cowley: working tirelessly but still finding time for the Stacey West 20

Lincoln's record transfers examined, taking inflation into account. 24

John Akinde signs – analysis and opinion 26

Welcome to Shay McCartan 27

Boston United 1-4 Imps – McCartan takes the headlines, but there's further cause for optimism 28

Panic over: Scunthorpe 0-1 Imps 30

August 33

It's a start: Northampton 0-1 Imps 33

Luke Waterfall's Shrewsbury switch; why it isn't the end of the world 35

Confirmed: Imps sign Jason Shackell 37

City strike it Luque as Joan pens six-month deal 38

Empire Rising: Imps 4-1 Swindon 39

Another rampant Lincoln win: Port Vale 0-4 Imps 41

Derby Day Deadlock: Grimsby Town 1-1 Imps 43

Get Out of Jail Free: Imps 2-1 Bury 45

Highly-rated youngster joins Imps youth ranks as Academy grows 48

Top of the League: Imps 3-1 Notts County 49

The Imps secure Derby wide man on loan 50

Reserves outclassed: Blackburn 4-1 Imps 51

Bernard Mensah could be an intelligent signing for City 52

September 54

Indomitable City win again: Exeter 0-3 Imps 54

28 seconds: Imps 1-2 Mansfield 56

- Back to earth with a bump: Imps 0-1 Crawley 58
- A lesson in class from Danny Cowley 61
- That's what good teams do: Macclesfield 1-2 Imps 62
- Joan Luque joins Bromley on loan 64
- Feet on the ground: Imps 2-1 MK Dons 65
- The Cult of Football 69
- Routine: Cheltenham 0-2 Imps 73

October 76
- Remain focused: Tranmere 1-0 Imps 76
- Four points clear: Imps 1-0 Crewe 78
- Priorities, priorities 80
- Still in it: Scunthorpe 1-1 Imps (1-3 Pens) 82
- It's a Pett and Shackell double as Tom scoops Player of the Month 84
- Cowleys linked with another job – Seriously? 85
- Super City with Six Appeal – Port Vale 2-6 Imps 86
- Matt Rhead reflects on Port Vale win and Imps FIFA competition 90
- Frustrating afternoon at the Bank: Imps 1-1 Cambridge 91
- John Akinde – Whatever your opinion of Big John, you must read this 95
- Watergate – Imps 2-2 Carlisle 98
- Don't panic just yet – Colchester 1-0 Imps 101

November 105
- Daylight Robbery: Imps 2-1 Forest Green Rovers 105
- Now that's what I call a cup tie: Imps 3-2 Northampton 108
- Friend or foe? Imps face a two-week break 111
- The future's bright, the future's red and white 113
- Lincoln City going soft? That is up to you 114
- A taste of our own medicine: Imps 1-1 Mansfield 117
- Kevin Austin – A tribute 120
- Two points dropped: Oldham 1-1 Imps 121

December 125
- Into the bag: Imps 2-0 Carlisle 125
- 'Simply can't wait' – Some fan reaction from the Imps FA Cup 3rd round draw .. 128

Over and out: Accrington 2-2 Imps (4-2 Pens) 129

Hosts pay the penalty: Stevenage 0-1 Imps 132

Interesting comments from Danny ahead of the transfer window 135

Winter Warmer: Imps 3-1 Morecambe 138

'Always worked so hard for the team' – These Imps fans react to Matt Green's departure 142

A slightly merrier Christmas than most: Imps 3-2 Newport 143

'There are no corners cut' – Lee Frecklington on intense Christmas schedule 146

Boxing Day Blues: Crewe 2-1 Imps 147

How are we faring? The Imps half season review 149

Character Tested: Cambridge 1-2 Imps 151

January 156

Sucker punch: Imps 1-1 Port Vale 156

Another departure as Joan Luque leaves Sincil Bank 159

Everton Build Up: I'm not excited at all and it's a good thing 160

It was special after all: Everton 2-1 Imps 162

Showing what we have: Swindon 2-2 Imps 166

Imps closing in on first transfer deal of the window 169

He's back: Danny Rowe signs for City once more 170

Joey Barton Issue Contradictory Bolger Statements Following Imps Deal 171

We've won the battle, on with the war: Imps 1-0 Grimsby 172

Plastic Fantastic: No shame in the rise of Lincoln City 176

Sorry to disappoint you League Two: Yeovil 0-2 Imps 178

Two more join the fight: City strengthen even further 181

A great advert for League Two: Bury 3-3 Imps 182

Welcome back to Sincil Bank: Lee Angol 186

Second signing of deadline day is complete 187

February 188

Opinion is one thing: The Lee Angol situation 188

58 Hours: Notts County 1-1 Imps 189

£1m loss – Why the figures don't give cause for alarm 193

Ellis heads out on loan: Reaction 194

Put the anger to one side: Let's remember what made us strong 195

Together Again: Imps 1-1 Northampton 197

Smells like team spirit: Why the Imps are still promotion favourites 200

Two more points dropped: Imps 2-2 Stevenage 203

'Very intelligent footballer' – Chesterfield boss delighted with Imps' youngster 207

On Track: Morecambe 0-2 Imps 207

96th minute goals don't happen by luck: Imps 1-1 Exeter City 210

Dispelling the myths: Why these common-held fan opinions are not accurate 214

March 217

Questions? Answered: Forest Green 1-2 Imps 217

Breathe with me: Imps 1-0 Yeovil 220

The mysterious case of the transfer window 'invisibles' 224

Playing like Champions: Imps 2-0 Oldham 225

Danny Cowley praises squad players as Imps enter final stages of title chase 229

One Step Closer: Mansfield 1-1 Imps 230

Reasons to Relax 234

The Perfect Away Day: Crawley 0-3 Imps 236

EFL Team of the Year 'snub': Let's keep our hair on 239

5,000 to MK Dons? The Imps remarkable support could break new ground 241

Bittersweet Point: Imps 1-1 Macclesfield 243

April 247

Another remarkable night of League Two action – what it means for us 247

Lincoln City Women's side are back 248

Champions Elect – MK Dons 0-2 Imps 250

Imps on Tour – MK Dons 254

The Final Comedown; Waiting for Saturday 258

The Imps Are Going Up 260

Rubber Stamped – Imps 1-1 Cheltenham 261

An Open Letter To Staff & Players Of Lincoln City FC 266

The not-so Good Friday: Carlisle 1-0 Imps 268

League Two Champions 270

Mission Accomplished: Imps 0-0 Tranmere 272

A Trio of new deals 276

Season Ticket Announcement: Fears Unfounded Once More 279

Missed Chances: Newport 1-0 Imps 281

Matt Rhead reveals his Player of the Year and which opponents impressed him the most 283

May 285

'Consolidate? I want to try to establish' – Danny Cowley dispels any notion of mismatching ambitions at Sincil Bank 285

Bittersweet Symphony (Champions Edition) – Imps 0-3 Colchester 286

Four awards in two days for Imps' stalwart 291

The First Day of the Summer: Never Forget the 56 292

The Squad 293

    Josh Vickers 293

    Grant Smith 294

    Matt Gilks 294

    Neal Eardley 295

    Harry Toffolo 295

    James Wilson 296

    Scott Wharton 296

    Cian Bolger 297

    Michael Bostwick 298

    Jason Shackell 298

    Ellis Chapman 299

    Lee Frecklington 299

    Mark O'Hara 300

    Tom Pett 300

    Michael O'Connor 301

    Harry Anderson 301

    Bruno Andrade 302

    Kellan Gordon 302

    Bernard Mensah 303

    Jordan Roberts 303

    Danny Rowe 304

    John Akinde 304

    Matt Green 305

Shay McCartan 305
Matt Rhead 306
Squad Details 307
League Table 308

Introduction

It's been a phenomenal season to be a Lincoln City supporter and I picked just the right time to pen a series of season review books. My first, in 2017, charted our return to the Football League. Last season's book caught us at Wembley and now the trilogy has been completed with a Football League title. It might not be the Twilight trilogy, but it's certainly one most Imps fans will find more entertaining.

Before we continue, if you're new to the series, this book is a collection of the best work from 'The Stacey West', my website dedicated to all things Lincoln City. It's a bit like a 'best of' album. All the hits and no filler.

The articles have been lifted straight from the site with minimal editing. There are two reasons I do it like this. The first is authenticity; I want these books to be a true journey, told through the eyes of a fan as the events unfolded in front of him. The first book tracked a remarkable rise, from the early indications we might win the National League to people's reaction in the ground as Altrincham pulled a couple of goals back in the FA Cup. It felt real and that's the core principle of the book. These articles were written and express a snapshot of time, something that I feel is important to retain if the books are to tell a true story.

The other reason is that it's much easier for me to put the book together. It's how I've managed to publish this just days after launching my other book, 'Suited and Booted', which has always been the main focus of my writing efforts.

One thing that has struck me during the compilation of this book is the amount of articles I've penned defending the players, the manager or the club. It seems with unparalleled success comes an expectation that I would never have accounted for. Fans want not only to win title, but to be entertained as well. I feel the book ends on a cliff hanger, with us being presented the title but numerous fans booing at half time of the game and then leaving before it had been presented. It's like the season end of your favourite series; you know the narrative is left hanging to be picked up next time out.

Can Danny and Nicky turn around the home form that apparently 'isn't good enough', despite us winning the league? Will they even be at the club at all? The articles don't carry on to the recent furore over the links between our management team and West Brom, nut I read some startling social media reaction to that link, with some lashing out at the manager. This being a manager who hadn't courted the other club, hadn't responded negatively and had delivered three pieces of silverware in as many season. Do you know how long it had previously taken us to win three trophies? 36 years (1952, 1976, 1988).

There are significant challenges ahead, that much is for certain. Football is a game which constantly moves, no sooner are you crowned champions than people are looking forward to the next challenge, the next set of obstacles and almost forgetting what a wonderful achievement has just be witnessed.

Three years; that's all it has taken to convert Lincoln City from a side without a trophy in 29 years, to a club with a bulging cabinet full of silver. It's taken just 36 months to turn us from a mid-table National League side that signed off with a 3-2 defeat against Woking in 2015/16, to a club welcoming Sunderland, Ipswich and Bolton on equal terms next season. When all is said and done, that's a great achievement and whatever the future throws at us, that can't ever be taken away.

Summer 2018

"Beep Beep" – Raheem Sterling's inspiration Andrade arrives at City
May 24, 2018

This summer Raheem Sterling will hopefully thrill England fans in Russia, maybe even firing us to a last eight place with his electric pace. This evening, Lincoln City have signed the player who taught him how to use his speed.

In an interview in 2015, Sterling told how he used to watch Andrade knock the ball past a defender and then 'beep beep', he was off like Road Runner. The Manchester City winger stopped the step-overs and tricks and did exactly what Andrade did. It's taken him to Russia, but for his former team mate, it's brought him to Lincoln, via Woking at Boreham Wood.

Let's not underestimate the size of this signing, nor how once again it breaks down a Lincoln City taboo. When have we ever picked up the absolute cream of the crop from the fifth tier? Once upon a time we wanted George Boyd, Aaron Maclean and Craig Mackail-Smith from teams in the division below us, but we missed out. Last summer it was Ollie Hawkins we coveted and failed to get. This time, Danny's got his man and he's in on a two-year deal.

I can imagine the presser tomorrow. We'll be told that Bruno is quick, versatile and has had a great two years at Boreham Wood, he was wanted by many clubs and he can be whatever he wants to be. He can too, he might have struggled since leaving QPR but at one point he played a Premier League game for them and he's matured like a fine wine. It was clear from his two matches against us in 2016/17 that the boy had ability, a confidence on the ball that comes from being schooled at a big club. He's comfortable with it at his feet, not just quick but also effective in possession. He can set goals up and score them himself. If I were to liken him to someone who damaged us recently, I'd say he's a Hiram Boateng figure. Okay, physically there's a difference and Boateng might play a little deeper, but he is a game changer. If Andrade picks up our style, he's a game changer too.

What I've liked about him whenever I've seen him is how down to earth he is. After beating Fylde in the National League play-offs, a match which he scored one and set up another, he was incredibly down to earth, praising the efforts of the whole team. It was his corner that enabled Jamie Turley to head his side into the lead and his own finish on 18 minutes which knocked the stuffing out of Fylde. I watched the whole game and Andrade was man of the match by a mile.

He can play wide, he can operate behind the striker or he can play up front. I would imagine Danny will be able to use him in all of the formations he's trialled this season. In the lesser used 4-2-3-1 he'd play right or central in the attacking midfield three. In the 4-4-2 he would be a conventional wide man and in the 4-3-3 he'd play off a centre forward. My gut feeling is Danny likes the 4-3-3 and sees Andrade on the left and Green on the right of whoever our new striker is, say Tom Hopper.

Whatever the situation, this signing is huge and has come very early indeed. Andrade will have been coveted by lot of clubs and if we hadn't got a training ground being built, we would have been a tougher sell. He will know about the Cowleys though, their reputation within the game is growing by the hour and Tom Champion would have doubtless told him of their methods, even though the move didn't work out for him. It is the infrastructure that also excites players though. They can see where we're going, how we've retained the squad from last season and players know that can only mean more of the same. Lincoln City will be fighting in the top seven again next season, make no mistake at all about that.

I would proclaim this the marquee signing of the summer, but I feel we're in for an exhilarating and frantic pre-season and as good as Andrade is, I believe we've a few more rabbits waiting to be pulled from Danny's hat. However, Andrade is 24-years old and bang on form right now. He's 'proven' as many people wanted, he got 26 goals in all competitions last season, just what people wanted. He's ticked all the boxes without us even getting out of May. There's much more to come this summer, I can feel it in my bones, but few will excite me as much as this guy. I sang his praises a year ago, I desperately wanted to see him come in January but when I saw he'd been off training with Portsmouth I thought the game was up. In my mind, he's League One quality which I firmly believe is where we'll be in twelve months time, especially if the summer recruitment lives up to this opening signing.

Chairman Bob Dorrian stands down
June 4, 2018

Bob Dorrian has chosen to stand down as chairman of Lincoln City, taking up the role of associate director.

The news hasn't come as a great surprise after he hinted at such towards the end of the season, but it brings to a close one of the most turbulent and successful periods of Lincoln City's history. Once labelled 'chicken Bob' by the more salacious websites and fans, Mr Dorrian has since proved himself to be the saviour of the football club, a man who took the wheel of a battered and sinking ship, sailed her through choppy waters filled with rocks and come out on the other side laden with silverware and a crew capable of carrying us onwards.

In short, Bob Dorrian is a hero.

He took control of the reigns at Sincil Bank in 2010 from his predecessor Steff Wright. That administration hadn't served the club as well as we'd hoped, Goal 2010 never materialised and a club consistently in the play offs had found itself battling relegation with Chris Sutton in charge. Steff got out whilst the rain clouds formed, leaving Bob to start patching up the holes in the roof and handing out umbrellas.

Were it not for Bob, the club would have folded. He put in £500,000 of his own money to keep us moving forward and set up the controversial holdings company, controversial at the time because many saw it as a conspiracy to bleed the club dry. He appointed Steve Tilson, a man not one of us thought was a poor appointment. When he failed and we turned to David Holdsworth, we actually turned to a man who saved the club money. I believe Holdsworth was a good appointment by the board, he served his remit and left once the job of plugging a few gaps had been done.

More recently, the holding company helped attract Clive Nates to the board and from there, the club has kicked on significantly. With Bob at the top of the tree we've come out of the six years we spent in the non-league a much more solid club, progressing every day and taking huge strides towards maybe, just maybe, becoming a third-tier club before 2020. Having sat in a board room in November 2011 knowing the club wouldn't be able to pay wages after Christmas, his tenure has seen us arrive at building a new £1.3m training complex. That's the sign of a good spell as chairman.

Bob has now considered that now is the right time for someone else to steer the club forward to even greater progression and there is every reason to be optimistic about the club's future. The club's official statement includes the following:

"The board, on behalf of everyone at Lincoln City Football Club, would like to put on record their thanks to Bob for all his dedication, hard work and financial support during his time as Chairman."

Well Bob, the fans want to do the same and trust me if you're ever in the same boozer I am, you won't need to ever buy another drink. You saved our club, you faced demonstrations, EGMs and all manner of abuse and stood firm and steadfast. Whilst all around you fell apart, you clung to the last remnants of the club and, together with a group of other hardy souls, began to rebuild. They should name a stand after you at the new ground, or maybe call the new bar 'Dorrian's Last Chance Saloon', because I swear you drank in their enough times post 2011.

The board have already elected a successor to Bob and I would speculate it is one of three people. Clive would be an obvious choice, but I'm not sure being based in South Africa he'd accept the role. Maybe Greg Levine, he's closely aligned to Clive and has the skills to carry us forward from his extensive and varied business life. The other shot, a long shot perhaps, might be Roger Bates. What a story that would be, from fanzine editor to club chairman inside three decades.

Whoever it is, they have huge shoes to fill.

Thank you Bob Dorrian.

Clive Nates elected Lincoln City chairman
June 6, 2018

The ushering in of the 'next phase' begun in earnest today as Clive Nates was elected to chair Lincoln City.

He will be assisted by a new vice-chair too, Roger Bates. Despite it being very much 'business as usual', any change in chair brings a new era with it. We've looked at the Bob Dorrian era, a time when distrust became trust whilst on the pitch abhorrent became exciting. The long wait fir trophies ended in style with two in a year and we regained our Football League status. That's quite a tenure.

Much of the revival did coincide with Clive's announced arrival at the club in December 2015, attracted by Bob's enthusiasm and passion as well as our own association with Everton, albeit a brief one. That was rubber stamped in February 2016, after which our fortunes certainly changed dramatically. The official press release states that Clive and his partners will continue to invest in the club through Sportvest and a further injection of funds will be made ahead of the forthcoming season.

Commenting on his appointment Clive said, "I am honoured to have been elected as Chairman of this fantastic club and I will continue to devote much of my time and efforts towards helping us make further progress. An inclusive, collaborative and open management style has been adopted and I will work closely with the Board and especially my fellow Executive Committee members Roger Bates and Kevin Cooke, as well as Liam Scully, Danny and Nicky Cowley in taking the club forward for the benefit of our fans, the community and the city. I especially want to thank our fans for the incredible sup-port I have received since joining the club and hope this will continue long into the future."

Whilst Clive has been around for a couple of years, Roger Bates is part of Lincoln City heritage, one way or another. He was the co-founder and driving force behind Deranged Ferret, the institutional fanzine that often spoke out against the board and club. A lifelong Imp, Roger joined the Board of Directors in 2011 having previously been an Associate Director. It wasn't an ideal time to join the board of the football club and he too has endured the rocky ride captained by Bob Dorrian.

Since that time he has been the director responsible for the club's Youth Academy, tirelessly raising money to plug gaps left by our relegation from the league. Under his leadership, the Future Imps Fund raised over £300,000 to ensure the Academy survived during the non-league years. I've had the pleasure of donating on occasion as well as helping out with the recent Away Days book and believe me, Roger's hard work and enthusiasm is as intense as anyone else connected with the club.

Commenting on his election Roger said, "Having contributed to the running of the club in a number of ways over the past seven years, I feel honoured to have been chosen as Vice Chairman by the Board of Directors."

Today's announcement won't mean anything different at first, but it is a marker in the sand. The change from Rob Bradley to Steff Wright wasn't meant to mean huge changes, but it did. Bob simply took the mess handed to him and rebuilt as best he could, but each chairman's spell is defined by something. I believe, firmly, this change will be defined by further success and an ascent of the Football league.

Also, from fanzine editor to Vice Chairman…. Rob Bradley went from fanzine editor to Chairman. It's about time I started earning a few bob to continue the fine tradition isn't it?

The Stacey West wishes Clive and Roger every success in their new roles, at this moment in time there are no two better people to fill those positions.

Harry Toffolo signs two-year Imps deal
June 12, 2018

The Imps have secured a deal for former England U20 left back Harry Toffolo on a two-year deal.

The defender spent most of his career at Norwich City, signing as an Under-14 in 2008. He is regarded as a solid left-sided defender with an inclination to get into advanced attacking positions.

After two years with Norwich's academy, Toffolo was called up to the England Under-18 squad for the clash against Belgium in March 2013. In August 2014 he was on the bench for Norwich in the Capital One Cup win over Crawley.

In October 2014 he was loaned to Swindon Town, initially for a month but later extended to the end of the season due to his good form. He was a huge hit at the County Ground and his form saw him called up into the England Under-20 squad. He made his three lions debut in a win against the USA. He helped Swindon to the play off final, appearing at Wembley as they lost to Preston.

Much was expected the following season and he made his Norwich first team debut in August 2015 in a 2-1 League Cup win at Rotherham.

In October 2015 he was on international duty yet again, playing the full 90 minutes in a 3-0 win over Holland.

In October 2015, he was loaned to Rotherham on a one month loan deal, again extended until January 2016 but he made just seven appearances for the Millers. After returning to Norwich, he was loaned to Peterborough in January 2016 until the end of the season.

He was then surprisingly loaned to our County rivals Scunthorpe in August 2016. He made his Iron debut in a 4-0 win over Southend on 10th September and once again impressed in the third tier.

Norwich activated a one year extension to his deal in May 2017, loaned Toffolo out again to Doncaster Rovers. Injury ended his loan early, with Toffolo having played 17 games for Rovers.

On 29th January 2018, Toffolo was released by Norwich, joining Championship side Millwall on a free transfer. He was then released on 18th May 2018 without making a single first team appearance.

His capture is something of a coup for City, with Swindon fans certainly jealous a player of his calibre has chosen Lincoln City.

Danny Cowley said: "He's a 22-year-old who already has vast experience having played in the Championship and League One, while doing very well in those loan spells away from Norwich."

"He was a big part of Norwich's team that won the FA Youth Cup, and he's a really bright young player with a fantastic future in the game ahead of him. To have 10 England Youth caps, it shows we've got one of the best left backs at his age."

"He had lots of options, and lots of offers in League One, and the fact he's trusted us to continue his development is something we should be really pleased about."

The defender, who turns 23 in August, is delighted to make the move to Sincil Bank and can't wait to get started.

"It's exciting, it's a club that once you're given an opportunity from, everyone would say yes," Toffolo said.

"The first thing Danny Cowley said to me was that coming to Lincoln would give me the opportunity to play in front of 10,000 people, and to do that with Lincoln City is fantastic."

"The focus is on Lincoln City, and you don't understand how much I'm relishing this opportunity. I want to be part of it."

Michael O'Connor arrives – what this means for Lincoln City
June 20, 2018

Michael O'Connor this evening signed a one-year deal at Lincoln City after turning down a similar offer from Notts County.

The former Northern Ireland international's capture is something of a coup for the Imps, with him not having turned down one offer at Notts County, but two. They made extra funds available to match the deal Lincoln offered, but to no avail.

His arrival offsets the departure of Alex Woodyard as a roving midfielder, always there with a tackle or a pass. He'll be a like for like replacement, but that is by no means the only thing this transfer signals. After all, Bozzie could easily play the Woodyard role too.

Firstly, O'Connor is no stranger to the Imps. He arrived on loan for the final couple of months of the 2008/09 season, debuting as a sub in the 5-1 mauling we suffered at Grimsby.

First time around, O'Connor was a real class act, a battler with a smart touch and a trick or two up his sleeve. Rather ironically, he arrived as a short-term replacement for the departing Lee Frecklington. Had our business with Peterborough been a little more fruitful for Lincoln we might have had an opportunity of signing O'Connor permanently. He certainly warranted it.

However, it was apparent from his performances that our chances of signing him back then permanently were virtually zero, especially as he was rated highly at Crewe. He only arrived on loan by virtue of a 'breach of discipline' that made him unpopular with then-Crewe manager Gudjon Pordarson.

He scored in our 3-2 defeat at Barnet and was ever present until injury forced him out of the final fixture of the season. On conclusion of his time at Lincoln he earned a Northern Ireland call up, lasting 62 minutes of a 3-0 friendly defeat by Italy. His international career stalled in 2015 and he's not been selected since, although he did amass 11 caps.

He later signed for Championship side Scunthorpe, with the Iron paying £250,000 for his services. He's also played for Rotherham and Port Vale, only once dropping into League Two aside from his County stay. His solitary season in the basement division saw Rotherham promoted, a feat they replicated the following season with both O'Connor and Frecklington in the midfield. The notion that one day the two might reunite at Lincoln would have been ludicrous as recently as last summer.

In total O'Connor has 400 senior games under his belt, two promotions and a Player of the Year from Port Vale in 2015.

Let's not get this wrong, this isn't a coup of Michael Bostwick proportions. O'Connor has been injured all season and although his fitness is now not in question, the one-year deal 'with an option' suggests he's got some time to prove his ability following the long lay off. In that respect, it is prudent business for City, getting a League Two / League One quality midfielder with minimum risk.

Something else he brings is a good delivery, his set pieces are well-renowned and lets face it, our free kicks haven't been the best for a while now. O'Connor, if he starts, does have a wicked delivery.

With Bostwick, Frecklington and O'Connor in midfield, as well as Andrade and maybe even Pett, there is a pattern emerging. We seem to be acquiring ball players, a transfer policy starkly different from last season. Our first foray into the Football League saw us load up heavily on wide players, looking for balls into the box. I'm wondering if, with these passing midfielders being recruited, we might be in for a change of direction?

Michael O'Connor is a good, solid signing. Unlike our other two summer recruits he is a proven article, steady and perhaps with some of his best football behind him. He's part of a balanced and measured transfer policy, blending exciting youth (Toffolo) with exciting non-league prospect (Andrade) and now vastly experience.

Grant Smith becomes arrival number four
June 25, 2018

City have today secured the signing of former England C international Grant Smith, the second former Boreham Wood player to join the club.

The former Hayes and Yeading keeper played 51 times for Boreham Wood as they just missed out on a spot in the Football League. He joins Bruno Andrade as the second former Wood player to link up with City this summer.

In 2017, the 24-year old represented his country against Slovakia after being a part of England C's three-day training camp at Lilleshall, and was rewarded for his impressive performances with a full call up. He signs a two-year deal with the club.

Danny Cowley told the club's official site; "He has a fantastic attitude and has a real desire to improve and get better and he's going to make it a really good fight for the number one spot. That's what we want, we want competition in all places, that competition is so important."

Smith has previously had spells with Reading and Fulham before signing a deal with Championship side Brighton & Hove Albion. Following that he moved to Bognor which is where Luke Garrard snapped him up from in July 2016.

The Imps were in the hunt for a keeper, amongst others, following the departure of long-serving stopper Paul Farman to Stevenage.

Goodbye, Ollie Palmer
June 27, 2018

Striker Ollie Palmer today left the club for an undisclosed fee, joining Crawley Town as their new number nine.

The long-rumoured move was announced a little after six o'clock, bringing to an end the striker's one-season stay at Sincil Bank. It comes a year and a day after he was unveiled as our new signing.

It is fair to say Palmer polarised opinion, many felt he didn't get a fair crack of the whip, others questioned his aerial ability and selfishness that plagued his early season efforts.

I was a critic, credit where it was due I thought he picked up the pieces of his Imps stay very well in the second part of the season. His late goals and cameo appearances from the bench caught the eye, but as a starter he never really had an impact. The one exception to that game was Coventry, but after 65 minutes he looked absolutely knackered.

I'm afraid I was never totally convinced and two of the players I have been critical of, Whitehouse and Palmer, have both left the club. Whereas Whitehouse laboured and often didn't get the rub of the green, Palmer was a one-man show who was less predictable than lightning.

We joke about him being unpredictable and that was both his strength and his weakness. He could amble through three defenders and score a worldy, or he would come on and wander around looking like a lost child. One imagines he was a nightmare to manage tactically because it often looked like he had no awareness of the world around him.

I have this image of Palmer wandering around and, every so often, a ball lands at his feet. His brain engages and the only thought is 'run towards goal'. sometimes that resulted in a great goal, other time he lost the ball and failed to find a team-mate with a pass. As the season went on he did get better, but clearly not enough.

I can't write an enthusiastic goodbye, I've tried but I can't. I did apologise to him in a blog for being critical and I did appreciate what he added at times, but the truth is if Ollie Palmer is your number nine, you're not a top seven team. His virtually anonymous outings in the play offs only confirmed that. For a big fella, his physical impact was negligible.

I liked his attitude, at least what I heard of it. His determination to remain an Imp in January and his assessment of Mansfield fans in March, but a few soundbites and a couple of goals couldn't convince me entirely he was worthy of a start. He might have been a good squad player, but now there's more wages freed up to bring someone else in.

I guess I'm being a little too negative, but I just never 'got' Ollie Palmer. I liked the idea of him, I loved the player bagging against Chesterfield, Exeter and Mansfield, but I could never understand why anyone believed he was a better choice up front than Matt Green.

Also, despite improving, he couldn't head for toffee. When 1,000 fans travelled to Crewe and sung; "We've got Ollie Palmer, he can't win a header, we've got him on a two-year deal", you know there are weaknesses in his game.

I'll leave this by thanking Ollie for his efforts and wishing him, and Crawley, the best of luck in the future. Most Imps fans are perhaps a little more positive than I, with lots of love on Twitter for the big bugger.

Danny Cowley: working tirelessly but still finding time for the Stacey West
July 1, 2018

The unconfirmed news that we're chasing John Akinde has brought a somewhat unusual raft of excitement and euphoria. Maybe, just maybe, we're going to sign a 'top' striker.

Now, I don't want to ruin anyone's Sunday, but those expecting an announcement in the next couple of hours are going to be very disappointed indeed. Having an offer accepted for a player, if indeed it is us, is not the tail end of the process. In fact, it is only the start.

I don't know John Akinde, but let's assume he isn't a bachelor living in a dingy flat in London. Let's assume he's a regular 28-year old, living with a long-term girlfriend or wife, maybe even with a young child. His wife might have a good job too, you never know. He's settled in the south and, just because Barnet have agreed to sell him, he has a big decision to make.

Agreeing personal terms isn't as simple as us saying 'here's some wages' and him going 'it isn't enough' or 'cheers, I'll get the car keys'. There's factors to consider such as relocation; does he or doesn't he? If he does, what about his family?

My gut feeling is we are in for John Akinde, but I can't see anything being decided right now, certainly not before the lads go to Spain. Ask yourself this; would you decide to up and move sticks just like that? Ditch your current job for one that is paid similar or slightly better, but move your entire family away, your girlfriend away from her family and job, just for a two-year deal?

Why do you think Lyle Taylor chose Charlton Athletic over Sunderland? The latter will bounce back, will most likely win League One and guarantee second-tier football next season, but Lyle Taylor is London-based.

The truth is, London clubs can get the same players we can with a smaller budget. That is fact, you may not think it is, but it is. Barnet do so well because they're in London, young players wanting to go out on loan can stay in the M25 and professionals looking to drop down the divisions can do the same.

Lincoln City is a ball ache to get to from everywhere other than Newark and Lincolnshire and that brings with it problems. We got Michael Bostwick because he was settled in his home and could commute here easily. There's a reason we've done so much business with Posh over my lifetime, because of location. There's a reason we don't do much with Exeter or Carlisle, the same reason..

One of the most beautiful humans on the planet (after my Fe), once sang the immortal words 'A Pessimist is Never Disappointed' and this article may seem very pessimistic, but it isn't, it's just real life. Sometimes fans have a blinkered view of the market, they think because they signed Akinde on Football Manager, he should be easy to sign in real life, or because he's requested a transfer he should jump at a move to Lincoln. Real life doesn't work that way and sometimes I wish we viewed football the same as any other business or career.

It's like Danny's insistence that we will be fishing in the loan market, a source of much consternation and anger amongst some. Us, the great Lincoln City who got to an FA Cup Quarter Final, picking up freebies? We deserve better, we're not bargain basement now, etc etc. Do you really, honestly believe Danny won't pay for a player? Think about it, before we even had a cup run he bought Elliott Whitehouse for a nominal fee.

However, do you think he's going to shout it from the roof tops? Do you think he's going to hang a sign outside his door letting agents know they can start screwing us over for a few more grand? Of course not. Knowing Danny as I do, I imagine it is a source of great discomfort for him, telling the media we're fishing in the free agent pond. Anyone who has chatted to him properly for half an hour or so knows he's as candid as they come and even misleading people for a second wouldn't sit well with him.

I spoke to Danny a few days ago, he rang me for a catch up and just to let me know how things were going. Contrary to popular belief I don't have a direct line to him and we perhaps chat every couple of months because I'll rarely bother him. I feel he's got enough on his plate without me ringing him up asking what was happening. Anyway, he called whilst he was driving from one player to another, probably a six-hundred mile round trip. He doesn't tell me names, I don't ask. If I guess a player we're after or follow the breadcrumbs that is one thing, but I wouldn't want a top-secret move to be scuppered by me gobbing off on here.

Anyway he asked how I thought pre-season was going, honestly. Perhaps I give the impression of being hugely pro-club, if so I make no apology because I am. I'm honest about what we need, a new striker and I'll always be critical where I feel there's a need (new kit). I told him I thought the current new signings were very good, I thought the players who had left were fringe players but that everything hinged on who the new striker was.

Without going into details, Danny knows what he needs. He doesn't sit on his hands a home blindly thinking everything will be alright. He spends every hour of every day bettering this football club, every second he is awake plotting how to get an extra ten points next season, an extra ten goals that will see us jump into the top three. He lives and breathes Lincoln City, his happiness depends on three precious points every Saturday. After all, he has the lovely wife, wonderful kids and the job he loves so the only thing left to covet is success.

When a man is that driven, that focused on achieving what he wants to achieve, do you honestly think he does things by halves? Do you truly believe we miss out on players for something within his control? Danny has a budget to work with, a good budget for this level, competitive but not astronomical by any means. We won't fork out silly money for Tyler Walker, not because we can't or because we lack ambition, but because it doesn't fit the model of the club.

Danny said something in the conversation which I had to ask him if I could quote. He said; "2016/17 was a great season, a special time for Lincoln City fans. I don't want to look back in ten years and think what a great season it was or how it stood out above everything else. I want that season to be more than just a special season, I want it to be the start of a journey where everything changed for this football club, the point where we went from being one level to another for good. I won't make silly decisions that might jeopardise that, I will spend Lincoln City's money like it is my money but, where I need to, I will spend the money."

Essentially, the board have backed him and he will spend on the right players, but he will not settle for second best. He will not throw thousands at a player who could bankrupt the club, nor will he throw loads of money at the one season, et promoted and for want of a better word, fuck off to Ipswich and better himself. He's here for the long haul but he's building a legacy, not a one hit wonder. If Mansfield don't go up, they've spent around £275k on wages and fees for Tyler Walker and have nothing to show for it. Danny won't do that, not with the club's money.

He wants to bring a player to the club with the right attitude as well as ability, but I see a problem he faces. Take Tom Hopper. If he wanted to sign Hopper, he would have met the boy and sold the club. He will have wanted to see ambition in his eyes and hear it in his voice. However, what message would it send if the same player then turned down a League One offer in favour of League Two? A player hungry to play at a higher level choosing not to? It would render his words pretty hollow, would it not? The same goes for a League Two player choosing moves up over a move sideways. Does Tyler Walker want to play for Mansfield for the betterment of his career? Last season he turned out for Forest and Bolton, do you truly believe he thought the next career move was a season playing for a team with three sides to their ground?

The point I'm trying to make here is the way many view the transfer market, me included at times if I'm entirely honest. everything seems so very cut and dried doesn't it? I know in January we didn't get a target because of location, purely that. He would have been perfect for the club, linked up with Matt Green and provided the big man support. He would have been able to add perhaps six or seven goals after Christmas and maybe, just maybe push us a place or two higher. We didn't miss out because we were cheap, because we didn't work hard enough or because Danny and Nicky are naïve in the transfer market, all that sort of talk is utter rubbish. We missed out because of where he was based. He lived in a town where his wife had a great job in a hospital and he needed to do the school run every day. Simple. We weren't offering life changing money, he wasn't young, free and easy and he had to go elsewhere.

Danny and Nicky are not suffering from a lack of transfer window experience, they just put the long-term future of the club before an immediate hit. It baffles me how anyone questions their methods when we've had two seasons of previously unparalleled success. That isn't to say they're infallible, I'm sure in a darkened room with a nice single malt, Danny would open up and confess JMD didn't work out, but there's been very few permanent deals that haven't either impacted the club or brought a fee at the end of the deal. We've not been lumbered with a wage we don't want. Okay, we missed out on a striker in successive windows, but we still won at Wembley and made the play offs.

Similarly, do you believe Danny waits until the end of the summer to do his deals on purpose? Don't you think maybe, just maybe he'd like to smash them all out in early June and bugger off to the Cape Verde Island with the family for a week? Of course he would. This summer things are even tougher because of the World Cup. The Premier League moves aren't happening because all eyes are on Russia, meaning that all the subsequent links in the chain are experienced stagnation. We might well be looking at a couple of young players on loan, but until stuff dies down in Russia, much of the market is going to remain calm and flat.

Please, trust me when I say Danny is working tirelessly, endlessly and incessantly to better this club. The 'failure' t land a striker isn't entirely true anyway, a year ago we beat five or six clubs to 17-goal Matt Green who had a good season for us and will again. Landing Green, Bostwick and even Frecklington and now Andrade tells me they're far from naïve and inexperienced in their dealings. Hopefully, things will pan out this summer and hopefully, we land the targets we need. If we do, the squad will be immense come the big kick off, maybe we'll be at 21 or 22, but it will be 22 players who would grace any other squad in this division without doubt. How many other sides will be able to say that? How many of Forest Green's squad would grace ours? Ten? Fifteen?

If we get everyone we want, I wager every single one of our players would walk into their match day squad, or indeed every match day squad in League Two. If we don't get everyone in we need, rest assured we'll still be every bit as competitive as last season.

Danny reads Twitter, Facebook and all that. He sees some of the utter drivel written about his policy, the club's reticence to sign strikers and how we're apparently changing for the worst. Before you type just think for a second' would I really want Danny to read this? If the answer is no, put the phone down and go sit in the sun with a good book.

Let Danny do what he's good at, yeah?

Lincoln's record transfers examined, taking inflation into account.
July 4, 2018

News that the Imps have made a club record offer for Barnet striker John Akinde has led to discussions about our previous record holders.

Whilst speculation rages on at the real cost of Michael Bostwick, the undisclosed fee is the bane of the football fan. If rumour is to be believed, Harry and Bozzie arrived for a combined fee that, if split down equally, did NOT match the current record of £75k shared between Tony Battersby (pictured top courtesy of Graham Burrell) and Dean Walling.

Whilst Tony Battersby is the current holder of the record transfer fee, or certainly the latest having arrived after Dean Walling, is he the true record holder? Considering inflation, who is actually the Imps' record signing?

I've scoured our previous records and using the Bank of England inflation calculator, I've worked out what each of the previous holders might be worth in today's market. The result is quite surprising, showing two strikers sharing the accolade.

The Imps first notable transfer fee was paid in 1933 for John Campbell. In 184 appearances Campbell smashed 104 goals, including seven hat tricks. That would seem to be money well spent, with us paying Leicester City £1250. In 2018 terms, that would equate to £85,047, already breaking the so-called record.

In 1952 our record fee of £6000 was matched when we paid Manchester United that sum for Brian Birch £164,122 considering inflation. He scored 16 times in 56 outings before moving to Barrow in 1956.

Aside from one move we'll come on to later, our record fee wasn't shattered again until the mid-1970s. It was 1974 in fact, when Lincoln City fans clubbed together to help fund a move for west Ham keeper Peter Grotier. His transfer fee was £16666, equivalent of £165,123 in today's money. He delivered too, picking up a Fourth Division winner's medal just two years later.

By the end of the seventies, City had fallen on hard times again, certainly in terms of points. To stop relegation from the third division, we paid Sheffield Wednesday £33,000 for Tommy Tynan, a player who averaged a goal every three games at Hillsborough. He averaged a goal every nine games at City, although he only appeared nine times. That disaster set us back £179,984 in today's money.

Colin Murphy arrived looking to get the Imps back into the third division and in truth, he spent big. Back then, the money might not have seemed a lot, but he bought Derek Bell from Barnsley for £36000. Bell went on to score 33 times from 69 starts during an injury hit spell at Sincil bank. The move, in today's terms, cost us £173,154. Frustratingly for City, Bell was a local boy, born in Wyberton but snapped up by derby County as a youth.

Two other players arrived around the same time, Tony Cunningham, Trevor Peake and Steve Thompson. Both cost fees that would be described as modest by today's standards, £15,000 for Peake and Thompson, £20,000 for Cunningham. In today's terms, Peake cost £72,000, Thompson cost £61,000 and Cunningham almost made six figures, £96,196.

Around the same time, we also made another signing, one of the top three outlays, taking inflation into account.

By the end of the 1980's we were breaking records again. Paul Smith joined whilst we were a GMVC side, costing £47,000 from Port Vale. That would equate to £125,684 today. A year later, almost to the day, Gordon Hobson switched Division One side Southampton for Sincil Bank in a £60,000 move. Today, that would have cost us £152,952.

As the years draw on, the prices get smaller. We paid Leicester a club-record £63,000 for Grant Brown in 1990, £136,130 in today's money. With 458 starts for the club, that proved to be a decent investment. In the late 1990s both Dean Walling and Tony Battersby set us back £75,000. Walling's fee would be worth £129,768 today, whereas Tony Battersby would cost us £125,466.

So, who are the three players who tops our record signings chart, taking inflation into account? Find out below.

3. Ephraim 'Jock' Dodds - £207,395

In 1948 we paid £6000 to Everton for 33-year old Jock Dodds. It was an ambitious bit of business by City, reflected in the fact it would be worth £207,395 in today's money.

Dodds scored 113 goals in 178 matches pre-war for Sheffield United and was capped eight times during war time for Scotland, scoring nine goals. Just before the outbreak of hostilities he moved to Blackpool where he bagged 13 in 15 matches. Hitler put paid to that run though and in 1946 he switched to Everton where the goals kept coming, 36 in 55 games.

After his move to City, Dodds scored 38 goals in 60 outings before retiring in 1950, partly due to his involvement in player procurement for the Colombian league. He tried to recruit players to go to Bogotá, to play in a new league outside FIFA control. He was banned by the Football Association in July 1950 for bringing the game into disrepute but was later cleared.

2. George Shipley - £216,442

In the late 1970s, the moves for Tynan, Thompson, Peake, Cunningham and Bell, the biggest move of them all was for tricky winger George Shipley. We paid a then club-record fee of £45,000 to Southampton, £216,442 by today's standards.

He went on to play 229 games for City between 1980 and 1985 and became an integral part of Colin Murphy's wonderful side of that period. Along with Phil Turner and Glenn Cockerill, his skill and guile created endless chances, with him bagging 42 goals in the process.

He teased and taunted full backs, often described as a winger, but by others as attacking midfielder. He twice finished the season as the club's leading scorer and missed only eight matches in five seasons with City.

When Shipley left Lincoln, he did so for just £15,000 or £43,207. He briefly returned in 1989 without making a competitive appearance.

1. Andy Graver - £349,187

Graver netted 150 goals in almost 300 appearances across three spells with the Imps. He was fast, opportunistic and above all, a natural goal scorer who showed a passion that would be unheard of today. One of his moves, in June 1955, would be worth nearly £350,000 in today's money.

Bill Anderson brought him to the club from Newcastle United for £3000 in 1950 (just over £97,000 today). He enjoyed immediate success for the Imps scoring on his debut against Halifax and quickly established a fruitful partnership with inside-forward Johnny Garvie. He played a key role in City's record-breaking 1951/52 campaign scoring 36 goals in 35 League games as the Imps won the Division Three North title. He even earned a call up to the England B side, but injury prevented him from getting international honours.

In December 1954 he was sold to First Division Leicester City for a record fee of £27,500 plus Eric Littler, making the deal worth around £28,000. That figure today would be the equivalent of around £728,000.

The following season Andy returned to Sincil Bank for £14,000 which is still the Imps record signing in real terms at £349,187. Rather ironically, he moved again in November, this time to Stoke City for £12,000 or £299,303. He finally returned to Sincil Bank for two more seasons in 1958, costing £2500 from Boston United, or £55,256, before retiring from football at the end of the 1960/61 season.

In total, Andy Graver brought Lincoln City almost £1.2m of fees by today's standards and we paid around £500,000 for him. The move that holds our record wasn't fruitful at all, he played 15 times and scored just four goals. How ironic that perhaps our greatest ever player was actually a big money buy that flopped. I think we can forgive him that.

John Akinde signs – analysis and opinion
July 6, 2018

Finally, John Akinde has become an Imp. You might have seen it on social media already, unless you've been asleep for the last hour. Like I have.

It brings to a close a week of speculation, a week of worriers worrying, ex agents lying and others secretly hoping. Personally, I always had faith we'd capture him if it was at all possible, now we have. As Helgy keeps posting, Nevermind the B0ll0cks, here's Big John Akinde.

The signing marks something of a watershed moment in my Lincoln City supporting life time. never before have I known us to go out and buy a player of such huge repute, not one with a proven track record of scoring goals. One might point to Phil Stant or Joe Allon, but Akinde is different.

He's powerful, quick and has a natural instinct for scoring goals. From what I've seen of him, he's a born finisher, from the Liam Hearn mould in that respect. The goal he bagged against us in January was pure brilliance, utilising his close ball skills as well as his deadly finishing. I didn't appreciate it at the time, nor for one second did I think he'd be in red and white seven months later.

Once again, Lincoln City have turned heads, just like last season when Michael Bostwick signed. There isn't a club in League Two who wouldn't have wanted Akinde, there's not a first team in the division he wouldn't walk into. Kane Hemmings and Kristian Dennis would be split up to accommodate him, that is how good he is.

There's also the personal circumstances that had to be negotiated, I know his partner has a good job and they've got their dream house in Kent. This wasn't a straightforward move, not a free and easy Josh Ginnelly type who can bunk down with three other lads and live the life of Riley. It's no Bozzie either, living an hour down the road and moving through convenience. Akinde has moved here for ambition, pure ambition. That is exciting and in the story of Lincoln City, it is unique.

Even when we signed Gary Taylor-Fletcher, a superb player who lit up Sincil Bank at times, he was rebuilding a shattered career. Akinde might have had one season without a double-digit goal tally, but he will now enjoy a pre-season with Lincoln, serve time in the friendlies and hit the ground running.

I saw one happy person's immediate response was effectively 'who we signing next'. Take a day off chap, we've finally got the striker everyone thought we couldn't get. The one signing that has eluded us for too long. Why not, for once, enjoy the moment?

Tactically Akinde joining City means we can change our pattern of play significantly. We won't just have to go long now, although the effective diagonal ball will still be used. He'll bring more out of Tom Pett and Lee Frecklington, maybe looking to get the ball into feet and have them overlapping too. He'll then offer a double threat, either as a creator or a finisher. Remember, 22-goal Bruno Andrade has to fit in there somewhere and 17-goal Matt Green will almost certainly be Akinde's partner. That's a scary array of attacking talent.

Has there been a more impressive signing in Lincoln's recent history? Maybe, it could be argued Michael Bostwick or even Lee Frecklington were pretty big deals for us. Has there been a bigger statement made by the club in the whole time I've been following them? I'm not so sure. The fee is thought to be around £150,000 to start with, doubling our record purchase, then there's bound to be a clause or two in there. This is a big investment and I would imagine it is a decision the board have not taken lightly. The presence of a three-year deal proves that.

Last summer someone asked me about Akinola, getting him mixed up with Akinde. I laughed and said the difference was Simeon Akinola might be affordable for us, John Akinde never would be. What a difference a year makes. I don't think my feelings could be any clearer on this, it was almost a fortnight ago I identified Akinde as the one forward I'd love to see in a Lincoln shirt. I've got my wish.

Welcome to Shay McCartan
July 24, 2018

Who is the player we've blagged on a season-long loan from Bradford City? Twelve months ago he was hot property, but a tough season at valley Parade has left him surplus to requirements.

He switched Accrington for Bradford for £200,000 in June 2017, but struggled to settle at Valley Parade and started just 13 times last season, scoring four. Luton and Accrington were amongst nine clubs to express solid interest in him in the transfer window and I wouldn't mind sticking a tenner on it we were amongst the other seven. He stayed put though, eager to work his way into Simon Grayson's plans. He failed and now he's been loaned out by Michael Collins.

He's not a big lad, under 6ft, but he's earned international honours for Northern Ireland and was seen as the next 'big thing' after finally breaking through at Accrington. He hasn't had a great scoring record, 10 in 39 in his last Accrington season and just four in 19 for Bradford. That doesn't mean he isn't a good player though and at 24 he's come to an age where it is now or never.

The change of manager at Bradford has led to a mass of incomings and outgoings and I've no doubt Danny is delighted to secure his man, the elusive 'fourth man' we lacked last season. Interestingly, McCartan won't be here to sit on the bench, he'll increase pressure on Matt Green. Danny only signs players who improve our current offering, don't forget that.

In my time working for FLW I've seen a lot of football, lots of clips and heard a lot of reports on players and McCartan's goal return doesn't do him justice as a player. He's a real live wire, stocky and strong with good ball retention and pace. He's also a dead ball specialist, hitting six free kicks in one season during his time at Accrington.

You might not have heard of McCartan, but this is a big move by the club. He looked destined for a much bigger future when he left Accrington and with two years left of his deal, he could still have a big future there. His immediate future is in red and white, which is of immense benefit to us.

Welcome Shay, you'll like it here. We're good people.

Boston United 1-4 Imps – McCartan takes the headlines, but there's further cause for optimism
July 25, 2018

The criticism of the Imps pre-season was that we hadn't scored enough goals so, right on cue, we hit Boston United for four.

Fresh from our challenging games against Norwich and Blackburn and well prepared after not sparking a 22-man brawl against Sheffield Wednesday, City showed what threat we will carry against opposition we should be beating well. Just like turning on a tap, City turned on the style.

It wasn't a full-strength side, but we still put together some slick moves to easily dismiss the ex-Imps XI wearing amber and black. Okay, maybe that's pushing it a little, but Nathan, Jonny Margetts and Adam Marriott all featured against a side they'd fired to National League glory 14 months ago. How times change.

The big news was Shay McCartan, his superb goal and his likeness to an Imp of old. Few will remember Ben Tomlinson fondly, purely because of when he played, but I thought McCartan had shades of Tomlinson about him. He's not the biggest but he played with that cockiness that made Tomlinson a hero for a brief time. Whether it's a friendly, Braintree away or a home game at the Bank, a debut goal will always help endear you to fans and McCartan has given Danny a real selection headache up top.

There's so many options it is unreal. We could go all out, 4-3-3 and play Akinde, Green and McCartan. That might frighten the bejesus out of other sides, but it is a bit too gung-ho for Danny.

The likelihood is a 4-4-2, meaning one of those three misses out. As for the big man, he's going to be a late sub in most matches but his starts will rapidly diminish. He still has a big part to play though.

The big shout is playing Akinde and McCartan, vastly unfair on our leading scorer and arguably hardest worker from last season, Matt Green. From having a forward line devoid of real talent, we've suddenly got an embarrassment of riches going forward.

I was delighted to see McCartan arrive, I know Danny has been an admirer for a while and had circumstances been different doubtless he would have been an Imp in January. He stole the headlines last night, but that does a huge injustice to the player I still feel is the signing of the summer: Bruno Andrade (pictured top courtesy of Graham Burrell).

Andrade hit two last night but his constant running, ability on the ball and confidence in his passing sets him apart from anything we've had in recent years. There was a split opinion when Elliott left, but honestly who would you rather have playing behind the front two? An uncomplicated grafter like Elliott, or a proper baller, a man with pace, tricks and an eye for the spectacular?

Bruno Andrade hit 22 goals last season and got 15 assists and no matter what anyone tells you, the standard in the National league isn't that far behind ours. there's a clear step, that I grant you, but Andrade owned the National League and he could easily have found himself playing for Portsmouth or another League One side. I know we forked out for Akinde, I know Scott Wharton should be higher up, I know Shay McCartan is a coup, but none of those trump Andrade for me.

Some names write themselves onto the team sheet, others are open to debate. Up front it is two from three, at the back probably the same. from what I've seen left back is still up for grabs, only Neal Eardley and Michael Bostwick are 100% guaranteed a start if they're fit. Maybe it would be hard to leave out Wharton or Akinde, but the reality is if they're not fit we can cover adequately. In my opinion, Bruno Andrade is a 100% cert to start whenever he's fit.

It was nice to see Anderson on the mark too, he's not been the same since he was dismissed against Luton and how he's going to be accommodated depends on the system we use. If we are planning a 4-4-2 I can't see why we haven't brought in more wingers, Andrade could play out wide but would be wasted, leaving just Pett and Anderson. There's a chance we'll go 3-5-2 or a variation thereof, but again where does Harry fit in that? His goal will give him confidence but he's going to have to adapt if he's nailing down a starting place in the side.

After the occasional panic from some on social media, the side is panning out nicely. There's any one of six trialists I wouldn't be disappointed to see join and flesh out the squad and I expect two more loans as well. I'm still utterly convinced we'll be raiding Bournemouth, but Danny has assembled the permanent players before the loans. I like that approach, we got burned in January with the loan deals we placed a lot of emphasis on and although we still finished top seven, there were implications when Dickie and Ginnelly left and JMD flopped. this year if there's anyone letting us down it will be one of the permanent players, but with the quality we've signed I get the feeling we'll not have a flop. There's one I'm not entirely convinced of, but I won't start picking at players before they've played ten or fifteen games for us.

Ten days to go and the squad is coming along very nicely indeed and finally, we have our goals. It's also nice to know we understand what 'friendly' means because I guarantee when clubs start looking at some League two side's behaviour, they won't be in a rush to loan them players or arrange friendly matches next year.

Panic over: Scunthorpe 0-1 Imps
July 28, 2018

I recall a few weeks ago reading a raft of messages fretting around Lincoln's transfer business, but after defeating League One play-off side Scunthorpe in the final pre-season friendly of the summer, I think we can safely assume the panicking was all for nothing.

I've had to follow events from a beach on the Isle of Wight, hence the low number of articles over the last day or two. There's worse places to be, although as an aside you can perhaps blame me for the weather change. The last time it rained I was on holiday on Lindisfarne, we come to the IoW for a weekend and it rains again. I'll keep you informed when we go away in future so you know not to.

I've seen a bit said about the Imps starting line up and, in the absence of any views from the game, that is what has driven me to get the laptop out whilst I'm away. All summer I've been utterly convinced Danny is planning a three centre back tactic, with wing backs and then a flexible approach further up the field. We haven't seen it all summer, but I think there's a reason.

I suspect there is a degree of subterfuge, a reluctance to play in the formation against the bigger clubs we've faced to retain the element of surprise for visiting scouts. Danny has been very good at diversion, misdirection and the like, whether it was the Ben Nugent saga drawing attention away from the likes of Juan Luque, to his reticence in press conference's to give anything away. I'm still of the belief his preferred approach this season involves more across the back and better players pushing forward.

Tactically we're blessed with a manager who not only tries different set ups, but uses them regularly once he does. He makes the team fit the players to a degree, he certainly did when he first arrived. Last season we started without Rheady as a focal point remember, but the recruitment in the summer was all about wingers. The JMD experiment didn't work and slowly but surely we resorted back to the diagonal ball because we needed to, This summer how many wingers have we been linked with, and I mean out and out wide players? None? That suggests the 4-4-2 of last season is gone, but will there be a 3-4-3, a 4-3-3 or something more exotic like a 3-1-2-1-1-2 (that is a joke btw)?

I think Danny liked the way we started last season, conceding few goals but the offshoot was we struggled to score. With Bozzie and Woodyard protecting the back four we looked strong and the goals against only really flowed once we upset that partnership, around the time Josh Vickers got injured. This season we seem to be looking at the same number of players in the middle of the defensive third, but set up differently. With either O'Connor or Bostwick protecting a flat back three, with more emphasis on the wing backs to get forward.

That relies on us having a rich array of attacking talent and on paper we have that. McCartan's capture was a real bonus so soon after John Akinde, but along with the likes of Green, Pett, Andrade and Rhead we have more options that at any point under Danny's tenure. It's exciting to see, there's no two people who will name exactly the same starting line up and tactics at the minute. I'll be doing something along those lines later this week, offering my opinion, but with such a great mix and more to come in, the personnel shouldn't be an issue.

I would imagine Danny would like another defensive player, whether that is in the middle of the park or possibly right-sided. It looks very much as though Juan Luque is on the verge of earning himself a deal too, which is the interesting 'project' I had hoped for earlier in the summer. I know I'm a little fixated on the whole Mo Eisa thing, but you don't find a player like Eisa if you don't take the odd risk. Luque looks to have a certain physicality that will be an asset, a bullish build along the Harry Anderson lines, he's direct and he will offer versatility too.

To go to a League One side fielding a strong starting XI and win 1-0 is noteworthy, not so much at the beginning of July but certainly as a final warm up match. I'm not a fan of friendlies as you know, not as a competitive spectacle, but the final one is perhaps a little more fiercely contested than the rest. To all intents and purposes it is the most intense game of the summer and therefore the result is perhaps more important than the rest.

Of course, a Scott Wharton header shows we've retained some approaches from last season, we'll certainly be a threat from set pieces and signing Scott on a season-long loan was another piece of astute business. He's going to be a top player when he's served his time with us, Blackburn are incredibly lucky to have him, as are we. Not being there today means I can't pass judgement on his performance, but I reckon 'd be on safe ground to say it looked as though he'd never been away. To think, I was underwhelmed when he signed on deadline day, thinking he was no more than cover.

I appreciate it wasn't a 'proper' game, I know that things will be very different in a week's time but still, this was a nice way to round off a very challenging set of games. City played just one side they were expected to beat in a pre-season more focused on finding faults than a winning formula. I believe that Danny knows the formula, he knows what the players can do and he wanted to see what they couldn't do and where their limitations might be. There's never going to be a glut of wins when you open against a side featuring a £10m forward, then face a Hull side only out of the top flight for a short while, a promotion winning side from last season and a Championship play-off side two years out of the last three. Even the final game today was against a successful side from 2017/18. This was never going to be a summer about winning games, but a fact-finding mission for a manager hell-bent on improving each and every single day.

When I look at the squad from that Norwich game and the squad today, I can't help but be impressed with the summer business. However, the comings and goings have also been accompanied by Ellis Chapman's run in the side. His start this afternoon suggests he's going to get much more game time this season than last. I noted the D3D4 podcast had him as one to watch in our division, which is a wise pick. from what I've seen he's first team quality, but I know Danny will manage him carefully. I don't expect Ellis to start against Northampton, but I do expect him to be on the bench and perhaps play at Port Vale in the EFL Cup. As he comes of age, he'll be as important as any player we've signed this summer, I'm sure of that.

August

It's a start: Northampton 0-1 Imps
August 4, 2018

It's a start and in truth, it's a bloody good one. By that I mean it is a good result and I'm a big believer in the result being the only thing that truly matters.

That's probably for the best because on another day we could have lost 4-1.

I'm not being critical, football being the game it is dictates that at the end of 90 minutes the only thing that truly matters is the result. We weren't terrible and on the opening day against a squad comprising of League One quality players in extreme heat, we were never going to give the best account of ourselves, especially when half of our team were new and playing a system they looked ill at ease with.

I know some might think I'm going to be too critical, all I'm going to do is tell you how I saw the game, a game we won 1-0 and a game that left me thoroughly delighted on the way home. One thing I know you want from me is honesty, is that not right?

For the first 15 minutes we may as well not have been on the pitch, Northampton looked full of ideas, we looked uncomfortable and edgy. Across the back we made rudimentary mistakes, two of which left Josh Vickers with big saves to make. I remember glancing up at the clock with 18 minutes gone wondering what we were going to have to do to force their keeper to make a save.

As the first half wore on it was clear both sides were struggling with the conditions, Northampton ran out of ideas whilst we didn't seem to have any from the get go. My presumption is we'd come to contain, not to settle for a point but to let them have all the possession they wanted in front of our final third, but limit them to just that. It worked, to a degree, they passed it sideways and got little joy, in fact their only real route to goal, other than our errors, was a big boot over the top.

The 3-5-2 that we set out with did seem to leave Neal Eardley and Toffolo exposed at times, maybe in cooler conditions Wilson and Wharton would be out quicker to cover, but Northampton got joy on the flanks. Sam Hoskins impressed me, he looked lively and quick and had the beating of Toffolo time and again.

In patches you could see what we're going to be about though. The Matt Green and John Akinde partnership wasn't evident today, but for me Green was only beaten to man of the match by one rather obvious candidate. Last season's leading scorer looked full of running and was often found in the channels where he spent most of last season. Once or twice we knocked a nice 20-yard ball from inside our own half and in-between the full back and centre half. Both Green and Akinde latched on to a couple and although little came of it, it deviated from the usual diagonal we've enjoyed so much joy with before.

From a neutral point of view, there wasn't much to cheer in those first 45 minutes. Toffolo showed his attacking prowess with a vicious strike that fizzed just over the bar, but that was the closest we came to testing their keeper. At the other end, we've got a new orange superhero who was alive and alert when his defence sold him short. Dean Austin had done his homework and the Northampton forwards knew all about balls back to the keeper. Still, Josh Vickers is the best keeper in this division and he proved it today.

Immediately after half time everything burst into life. I'd just bought my third tepid bottle of Coke (don't they have fridges in Northampton) for £2.40 each and taken my seat when Neal Eardley picked up where he left off last season, creating goals. Matt Green did the same, finishing the cross in from the right with a stooping header to steal the thunder on John Akinde's competitive debut. In truth, his all-round game had outshone our record signing anyway.

That sparked rather crazy scenes as a Lincoln fan in the home end suddenly cheered, sparking a bit of a brawl. At first it seemed as though they were fighting amongst themselves, before the truth became apparent. The police chucked our boy out, then went in for the Cobblers fans too, one of them a 50-something woman with more aggression than any of the 22 players had shown.

Once we'd scored then the game plan became clear. We had the bank of five and then a three, clearly happy for them to dominate possession in the belief they wouldn't hurt us. Green came off, a move designed purely to save him from doing any more running as he'd covered as much of the pitch as anyone and we saw Bruno Andrade come on.

Football is a results business and the second we got the goal, the result became the only important thing. From a paying fan's point of view it ruined the game, from a manager's point of view the plan worked a treat. They're not paid to entertain us, they're paid to win matches and we did whatever it took to win the game. The Cobblers threw everything forward, but they didn't get anything clear-cut at all. We're best defending in numbers, few teams will turn around a one goal lead against us and so it proved today. Mark my words; Northampton Town will be around the top seven come May and if I didn't predict it in my 1-24 then I stand corrected now.

I have seen some criticism of the officials, I thought they did a good job too. There wasn't anything too contentious that I saw, the odd wrong decision but you get that every game. It is easy to bash the referee and his assistants, but on the whole they coped well. I was disappointed to hear some remarks aimed at the female assistant referee, the sort of 'Viz' humour more at home in a Carry On film or the 1970s. There's no need for it but sadly amongst 1453 you still get the odd one who think it is hilarious to shout lewd requests at women. I'm not a snowflake either, I just respect everyone regardless of gender and think behaviour like that belongs on a VHS video of Roy Chubby Brown, gathering dust in the loft.

On the opening day of last season we drew 2-2 with Wycombe and on reflection, that was a great result against a side promoted automatically at the end of the season. Today, we beat a side 1-0 in a result that might seem much more impressive in seven month's time.

It might have been very different, a long punt over the top caught us out at the end, weary legs perhaps, but we were certainly caught short. Andy Williams should have scored, there's no doubt about that, but Josh Vickers made himself big, stopped the shot and even cleared up the bits and pieces. It was as good as a goal, if Vickers were a striker his contribution would be classed as a hat trick today.

That's it. I could go on about the things I thought weren't right, but why would I? We won, it is the first game and the conditions weren't ideal. The 3-5-2 system was relatively new and it looked like it, like a new pair of shoes that didn't quite fit right and caused blisters. If we persevere I'm not saying it won't work, I'm never going to judge anything on the opening day of the season, especially not when we won.

I feel as though this has been a barrage of negativity, but really it isn't. It was just a scrappy game of football between two teams settling into a rhythm and a purpose. We got three points and they didn't, they had enough chances to take all three but didn't. They'll be sound this season though, I spoke to some of their fans on the way out and they were a bit concerned, but they've no need to be.

As an aside, I found their whole set-up very warm and friendly. All the stewards I spoke to were helpful, friendly and spoke to you like a person. The car park attendants were good, their fans were decent and all in it was a good atmosphere. Aside from the silliness after the goal it was a good afternoon all round. Last season we experienced Barnet, Stevenage and Port Vale where the staff were assholes, aggressive, spoiling for a fight and treated us like animals. That wasn't the case today, so respect to Northampton for that. They do need to sort that stand out though, it is a bit atmosphere sapping to have a building site running down one side of the ground, even if you have glued a few seats to it. At least they've made an effort, Mansfield Town should take note.

Also, £2.40 for warm coke? With that sort of mark-up I reckon a fridge or two is in order, surely?

Anyway, we'll wake up in the morning having kept pace with the early winners, but the league table won't take shape for a few weeks, form won't emerge until September and essentially all that has happen is one hurdle has been negotiated. I want to get five or six games on the board, that is when the sediment starts to settle and the cream begins to rise.

We have more points now than we had after the first three games last season and as far as I'm concerned that is a great start, no matter how we came to the end result. The record books will always show Northampton Town 0-1 Lincoln City, with Matt Green's name up in lights.

It should have the name Josh Vickers in bold, highlighted in yellow marker with five stars next to it, because he's won us the points today, plain and simple. Him and 42 minutes (plus stoppages) of sheer game management.

I'll end with a 'new feature where I'll give my Imps' Man of the Match, and name a player from the opposition who really caught my eye too. Today, I've gone for Matt Crooks as I thought he showed real class in the middle of the park. They couldn't find a breakthrough because we were tight, but he'll get assists and the odd goal this season if he plays like that every week.

As for us, if we win 1-0 when we're far from our best, I stick by my prediction earlier this week. One down, 45 to go.

Luke Waterfall's Shrewsbury switch; why it isn't the end of the world
August 6, 2018

It looks suspiciously like captain Luke Waterfall is on the verge of a shock switch to League One side Shrewsbury Town which will give Imps plenty to discuss over the coming few days.

In terms of trophies won, Luke is the most decorated skipper in Lincoln City history, lifting as many trophies in twelve months as any other has done in their entire tenure. He will always command respect and a certain amount of adulation and a move away from Lincoln certainly wasn't to be expected at this stage.

If you look back to my first team prediction of last week, you'll perhaps notice something rather pertinent. Luke wasn't named. This isn't me turning on a player who may be leaving, I've got loads of time for Luke both as a person and a player, but I don't think he's suited to a three at the back, nor do I think in a two he's one of our best two players.

Being captain means very little in my eyes, not when it is given to you, but when it is not taken off you. Luke would never have been stripped of the captaincy, he did nothing to warrant such an action, but had we been picking a captain for the squad without anyone having held it before, do you think Luke would have go it? Or would Michael Bostwick and Lee Frecklington be having a bare knuckle fight instead, while Luke sat at the side happy with a squad place?

What Shrewsbury will be getting is a committed defender who will fight every single step of the way for them as they struggle against relegation from League One. That is where they are, forget the cup final and the play off race, their team has been ripped apart and they've not replaced key players. Luke's going from a potential promotion fight to a relegation battle, albeit in the division above. He's probably earning more money too, so there's no complaints from me about loyalty.

There will be a fee, one would imagine upwards of £50,000 which will be nice. It might even be a bit more, I'm not really sure, but whatever it is remember; last season Luke had to win his place back and , had it not been for Rob Dickie leaving unexpectedly, he might not have been here at all. If he'd spent the second half of last season on the bench, perhaps he may have left in the summer. Instead, circumstance thrust him back into the side and as you'd expect from a fighter, he took his chance well.

The one thing we will miss is his prowess at the other end of the park, perhaps more so than his defensive contributions. He was a behemoth in the opposition area and that perhaps was never as evident as when we beat Colchester last season (pictured top). He always weighed in with a goal or two and certainly had me on my feet a few times more than most.

I know there will be those who think we're selling off our best players, but every club is a selling club. The only reason Shrewsbury are even in for him is the sale of Toto Nsiala to Ipswich, opening up a space in their squad. Therefore, don't be fooled into thinking Danny brought in Adam Crookes knowing this was going to happen, up until the middle of last week Shrewsbury probably didn't know it was going to happen.

Also, don't think that there's a big name replacement coming in either, not just yet. I wouldn't imagine Danny expected to sell Luke Waterfall and any planning to replace him will have begun before the weekend which is when I'm led to believe this first came to people's attention. Our squad is developing nicely and there's always going to be set backs in that process, such as this news.

Ask yourself this; if we get promoted this season, do you think Luke would have been a regular for us in League One? If we didn't get promoted, would Luke be one of the players you'd look at and wonder about replacing, especially once his contract ran out? He wasn't the only one to sell

Vickers short on Saturday, but he did make a horrible back pass that could have cost us the game. Granted, when we won promotion he won us as many points as anyone, but was he as commanding last season? He didn't break into the team until before Christmas, then suffered the ban for Mansfield and perhaps benefitted from lifting the Checkatrade Trophy in more ways than one.

I'm gutted because this summer I had Alex Woodyard, Paul Farman and Luke Waterfall signed pictures on my wall, two of which I've already replaced. I wont tell you who I've got in their place because it seems like a kiss of death right now!

If this does happen my honest assessment is there are no real losers. Luke gets a wage rise and a stab at League One, we get a fee and a bit of time to replace him and everything is friendly and on good terms. There's no panic, no reason to start fretting about the squad or where we are as a team, it is just a transfer deal that was unexpected, but not surprising. That is football, you roll with the punches and adapt on the move. In terms of how I feel this will hit us, far less than the loss of Alex Woodyard, about as much as the loss of Adam Marriott last season and a little bit more than losing Ollie Palmer. All in all, we'll live.

I'm not convinced Danny had a replacement lined up on Saturday afternoon, but I guarantee you right not he's on the phone, cajoling someone into loaning us a player or enquiring as to whether another target is free. It might be one of the trialists, it might be someone such as Sam Hughes from Leicester, but we'll have cover whatever happens.

If you do leave, best of luck Luke and thanks for the memories.

Confirmed: Imps sign Jason Shackell
August 9, 2018

The Imps have secured the services of 34-year old Jason Shackell following his release by Derby County earlier this summer.

Shackell played seven times on loan at Millwall in the Championship last season, but that is just the tip of his extensive experience in the upper reaches of the Football League. In fact, in all of his 19 seasons in the game, Jason Shackell has never dropped out of the top two divisions.

He's played Premier League football twice, making 38 appearances for Burnley in 2014/15 and 11 for Norwich a decade before.

The bulk of his career has been spent with Norwich, Wolves, Burnley and Derby, although his last full season of football came when he appeared 46 times for the Rams in 2015/16. Since then he's struggled to get regular football at that level, although he has made 484 senior appearances in his extensive, career.

At least two of his moves, from Norwich to Wolves and from Derby to Burnley, were for fees thought to be around £1m.

Shackell is an 'old-school' defender, with strong leadership qualities and has captained Norwich City, Derby County, Barnsley, and Burnley during his career. He's also a two-time Championship winner, lifting the title with Norwich in 2004 and Wolves in 209. He also earned a runner's up medal in 2014 with Burnley.

Shackell joins on a one-year deal and is likely to play a significant role over the coming weeks as the Imps adjust to life without Luke Waterfall.

"There's a lot of younger players in the squad and some really good experience here, but hopefully I can add to that and help pass on anything knowledge wise, or in tactics," Shackell said.

"That's something I look to do. I like to help others where possible and help develop the squad that is already here."

"I think this is the right move for me. I've always played Championship or higher, but this club has been quite successful in the last few years," he added. It's on the up and the management team and the staff all seem great when I spoke to them. I received a lot of positives and I'm thrilled to be joining."

Shackell will wear the number five shirt at Sincil Bank, and is available for Saturday's Sincil Bank opener against Swindon Town

City strike it Luque as Joan pens six-month deal
August 9, 2018

The Imps have today secured a deal for Heybridge Swifts forward Joan Luque, on a six-month contract.

Luque started out at San Pedro Lumen and UD Bon Pastor and at the age of 10, he had the football world at his feet. Catalan giants Barcelona wanted to have a look and Guillermo Amor, head of Barca's youth system, telling the youngster that he was convinced he could be a Barcelona player if he really wanted it.

He spent two years at Barcelona but didn't make the grade, dropping down to play youth football for Damm, Gramanet, Europa and Cornellà. He featured in the Copa del Rey Juvenil for Cornellà as they beat Real Madrid in the first leg of the second round, with Álvaro Morata, Pablo Sarabia and Dani Carvajal all lining up against him.

He made his first senior appearances for Gramenet B, scoring 8 times in the Primera Catalana. At the end of the season was selected by NIKE as one of the 100 best players of Catalonia.

Since then, he has played for numerous clubs, including CF Montañesa, Vilassar de Mar, FC Santboià, Sabadell B and Heybridge Swifts.

He found his way over to England after former Gramanet team mate Guillem Ramón suggested a trial for a group of Spanish players on English soil. he impressed, earned a deal and set about making a name for himself.

Despite his trial, he recently extended his Heybridge contract to the end of 2018/19, but with his dream of playing in the Football league, the Imps trial was too good of an opportunity to turn down.

His arrival comes after Heybridge accepted a bid from another unnamed League Two club, but it would appear that was never a consideration as he signs for the Imps. He takes the number 19 shirt and is in contention to be involved this weekend against Swindon.

Empire Rising: Imps 4-1 Swindon
August 11, 2018

9th August 2016, two years and two day's ago. I remember watching Lincoln City under Danny Cowley for the first time, we dismantled North Ferriby 6-1 by playing slick, attacking football. It was joyous, a night I labelled as 'the night something changed'.

I came home that night enthused, it was the first home game of the season, the second we'd played in the campaign and I'd witnessed something that I felt was fundamentally different from the norm. What I'd seen, what everyone in Sincil Bank had seen, was the start of the new era. Lincoln City's Empire was on the rise.

Since then, things have changed. We've had the cup runs, the trophies and players come and go, but I haven't seen us dismantled a side like we did North Ferriby. They could deal with us that day, we passed them off the park. Within weeks Danny had realised to beat Tranmere, Forest Green and Dagenham, we needed to be tough, resilient and use Matt Rhead as best we could. We were labelled long ball, unfairly in some respects, but then again accurate in others.

That is a hard tag to shake, especially when you're winning matches. Other clubs love to blame the so-called 'moon ball' we play, or they perceive that we play. I wont deny we have spent two years going long as well as playing a bit, but we haven't been like Wimbledon of old, nor are we a John Beck side.

Today, I saw a Lincoln City performance that, in the main, harked back to the North Ferriby match. I'm not saying we utterly dominated Swindon, that wouldn't be accurate, but we won the game by passing, moving and letting the ball slide across the grass. There wasn't a long ball team on the field today and anyone who says there was is either bitter, misguided or both.

Danny pulled a surprise pe-match, no sooner had I been telling everyone I thought we'd go three at the back than he announced a flat back four again. In his interview after the game Harry Toffolo called it a 4-4-2, on the team sheet it looked very much like the 4-2-3-1 that we first trialled away at North Ferriby later in the National League season. Maybe we're getting hung up on formations, but there was nothing predictable about how we set up at all. Matt Green, 17-goal leading scorer last season and scorer of the winner last week, sat out.

Bruno Andrade and Harry Anderson, two player who have been on the fringes of the first team in pre-season, two players who started the midweek friendly against Doncaster, both started. Who saw that coming? I know they scored all four goals between them, but genuinely who would have put those two in the first team today?

It was a surprise, make no mistake, but perhaps not as much as the opening half an hour was. It was a joy to watch, I know many Swindon fans felt they were really bad, but there was a case for us just being that good. John Akinde was giving a masterclass in how to be the one up front, Bruno and Harry were scintillating, not giving their full backs a chance and McCartan was pulling all the strings just in behind. I've singled them out, but there was a player who wasn't pulling his weight and everything flowed wonderfully.

There's an argument that perhaps the foul for our penalty started outside the area, but let's face it the referee had a horrible afternoon and had we not won 4-1, I might be spitting bile about him right now. I couldn't see, I was up the other end of the pitch, but we got the spot kick and Akinde scored perhaps the most nonchalant penalty I've ever seen.

We've been known to shut up shop after a goal, maybe look to defend our one-goal lead. Not today. If last week we could have been 3-0 down on 30 minutes, our second after the same period of time could have been our fourth. It was classic Lincoln, a well-worked set piece that ended up being bundled home by Michael Bostwick, many fans Man of the Match. At 2-0 those around me said we would go on to win by four or five nil. Just seconds before we'd hit the crossbar, Michael O'Connor close to opening his account on a great afternoon for him.

When Swindon did get a lifeline, it was harsh. The referee had seemed shaky, he'd given them a corner after one of their players dribbled the ball out of play unchallenged, but he seemed eager to give something, anything to even up the Anderson decision. When he did give it, it was the softest penalty you'll see in a long time. A drive from outside the area caught Michael O'Connor on the knee, deflected up passed his arm and into the hands of Josh Vickers. The referee gave a penalty.

I've watched it back and I saw it from perhaps the best angle in the stadium and at no point can I see the ball's trajectory altered as it passes O'Connor's hand. If it touched it, nothing changed and it came after the shot had the sting taken out of it by his knee. I won't write here what I said at the time, but it gave Swindon a route into the game. They scored their fourth of the season, the third penalty they've had, Michael Doughty levelling for them.

It knocked us for six I think and for the first twenty minutes of the second half, they looked like they might get into the tie. Doughty is definitely the boy, he pulled the strings for them and perhaps deserves better players ahead of him to receive some of his endeavour. I said ahead of the game the difference might be the front players for both sides and Swindon don't have the quality wearing 9 and 10, whereas we do. They put up a good fight until the hour mark though and although they didn't seriously threaten the goal, they controlled play.

I felt safe though, Bozzie and Scott Wharton were both on form and the full backs looked much happier in the 4-4-2 than in a 3-5-2. Toffolo had the best game I've seen him play and as for Neal Eardley, he is certainly a full back over a wing back. We lost the midfield battle for a short while though and with the players Swindon have, it didn't surprise me. Maybe if they had a Matt Green or John Akinde it would have been a different story.

The game shifted again with a change in midfield, the excellent McCartan was replaced by the equally as excellent Tom Pett. City immediately looked energised again, with Andrade and Anderson absolutely terrorising their opposite numbers and getting balls in and around the area. Andrade drove at goal himself once or twice, Harry was a bullish and defiant in possession as I've seen him. He's one who can go on and be a great player, but since his New Year's Day dismissal at Luton he's struggled. Not today.

O'Connor swapped for the new boy Jason Shackell on 73 minutes and a short while later Akinde came off for Green. Let that sink in, we brought on Matt Green and Jason Shackell. What other team in our division wouldn't have started those tow players? None, that's how many.

Bozzie stepped effortlessly into midfield and we turned the dominance back on. For a moment, I thought we might never stop scoring, we rained down on their goal again, firstly Green set up Toffolo and then it was last year's leading scorer himself getting the fourth. Matt Green changed the game, 13 minutes on the field and he weighed in with a goal and an assist. That is where things have changed, we can now affect things with the players who come on just as much as those who start the game. It's frightening that at 2-1 up looking to defend a lead we can have such big players coming on to take advantage of the other side's fatigue, quickly making a tight looking score line seem like a hammering.

Such was the display that I heard several names mentioned for Man of the Match, Bozzie, McCartan, Anderson and Andrade all got a shout, Scott Wharton got a mention as did Matt Green! I have to go for Harry Anderson, I thought he was back to his unplayable self, direct and physically strong but playing with confidence once more. Bruno Andrade wasn't far behind though, he's a different winger, packed with flair and flicks and maybe a touch more guile to Harry's battering ram. What a pair they might turn out to be.

That said, special mention to Freck and Michael O'Connor who won the midfield battle in the first half hour, something that was never going to be easy against Swindon's quality. They laid the foundations of today's result.

I've kept it relatively brief tonight as I have to go out (Shakesby's in Horncastle, looks like posh nosh so I'll be a bit lost. Hope they do chips), but when the final whistle went I had the same elation as that day two years ago as North Ferriby made their way off the field having been hammered 6-1. What we saw today was the starting point for the next chapter, the blueprint for how things are meant to be. The new philosophy isn't look for the big man, it isn't diagonal balls and managers 'knowing what they get with Lincoln'. It is a first team full of surprises, line-ups nobody can confidently call, strength in-depth and impact from all of the match day squad, those who start and those who do not.

This, Ladies and Gentleman, is the Cowley Empire rising once more, evolving and changing to adapt to the new pressures and challenges. I scoffed last season as we made the play offs and Danny talked about 'work in progress' and all that. I thought he wasn't far off with what he'd got, but if the first thirty and last thirty of today or anything to go by, in the words of Bachman Turner Overdrive, you ain't seen nothing yet.

Another rampant Lincoln win: Port Vale 0-4 Imps
August 14, 2018

For the second time in four days, City have smashed four goals past a League Two rival, albeit in the Carabao Cup.

It was another comprehensive display of controlled, attacking football, once more played on the deck much to the surprise of the opposition. Not only that, but the Imps made seven changes from the side that won on Saturday and there was no break in their stride. The tactics were switched, again, and nothing changed.

Before I go on to the game, I've got an observation that, even after three games, I can't keep to myself. Every season I've been a Lincoln fan watching League football, there's been a side who are simply better than everyone. I remember Rushden and Diamonds and Yeovil dominating at one point, I remember it being Notts County, MK Dons and Chesterfield. However well we did under Keith, there was always one team you watched and thought; that is the benchmark.

Anyway, Port Vale found that out with aplomb. It was out first win in this competition since August 2005, our first win at Port Vale in nine years and the biggest victory at Vale Park ever. They're the numbers.

The facts are for the second match in succession we've been significantly better than the side we've faced, even with a so-called reserve side of sorts out. Young Ellis Chapman made his debut and looked every inch a seasoned professional, Matt Rhead did what Matt Rhead does and at the back, Jason Shackell looked as good as the pundits have told me he is.

The big performance, the really standout performer, has to be Tom Pett. I'm delighted with that too, he's another I championed a lot before he signed and vigorously defended after some quiet displays last season, but since his goal against Yeovil he's got better and better. Tonight he played in the central midfield position and bossed the game, getting on the ball and pulling the strings.

City had the game wrapped up as early as the fifth minute, Port Vale switched off at a corner and against the best sides, the very best in the division, you can't do that. Scott Wharton nodded the ball across goal and Shackell netted with virtually the first touch of his first start for the club. That ended the game right there, Vale were never going to fight back, it is that simple.

The rest of the first half was Lincoln's, Vale did look to get back into the game but City controlled as much of the play as they needed to. Did Vale look like scoring? Not really, but in 270 minutes of football nobody has. Swindon got the penalty on Saturday, but from open play we've not conceded as yet. It is going to take a good side to put the ball in the net at the moment, or a special atmosphere which Grimsby might be able to create.

In the second half, Port Vale folded like an ordinance survey map. City were 2-0 up within minutes of the restart, a clear-cut penalty despatched by Matt Green who makes it three in three. Is he going for Gary Taylor-Fletcher's record of scoring in the first six games of a season? I wouldn't be surprised, especially given how many chances we're creating.

Vale didn't look dangerous at all, the atmosphere was flat and their efforts were tame at best and lame at worst. The one player who did look like he might be able to produce something was Ricky Miller, but when he did conjure up a shot, Grant Smith marked his debut with a fine save.

Danny proved me wrong towards the end of the game, instead of blooding Luque and Crookes he gave minutes to Michael O'Connor, John Akinde and Bruno Andrade. All three came on to great effect, just as the subs did on Saturday.

O'Connor showed his awareness with a stunning strike, again poor marking saw him stride forward but still have plenty to do from 25 yards. he did it anyway, a superlative strike put the game beyond any doubt at all.

Minutes later John Akinde got his second in as many games and his first from open play with a smart finish after dispossessing their centre half. It was classic Akinde, a strikers goal created himself and finished succinctly.

Pett was an undoubted Man of the Match, but only because he was incredibly good, whilst the rest of the side were just very good. Ellis had a debut he'll never forget, the biggest Imps win ever at Vale Park, both Matt Green and John Akinde bagged as they're paid to do and Matt Rhead got to wind up his Stoke City rivals.

Shay McCartan deserves a word too. He was billed as a striker, but since his arrival he's reminded me of a Paul Gascoigne type player, picking the ball up from deep and carrying it forward to create openings. as O'Connor gets more game time it is evident he'll be a massive player for us too. There wasn't a bad player in an Imps shirt tonight, it is that simple.

Our opponents never looked like scoring, every time we surged forward we threatened and that came against a virtually full strength Port Vale side, a team managed by Neil Aspin and Gary Brabin, experienced football men, featuring decent players. They're not this season's cannon fodder, they're not heading to the National League and anyone saying this is 'just the cup' are mistaken. This was an example of what we should expect this season.

Danny Cowley is keen to ensure they don't get carried away, he'll look to dampen the excitement in order to keep the pressure off his players, but here is a fact: we are close to being the best side in League Two. We know, as long term Imps' fans, this season feels different. this squad is remarkable in its depth and quality. W know what good looks like and what shit looks like and I guarantee you, this is good. If it keeps on like this, it will be beyond good. It'll be beyond very good.

When we get into our flow, it is fluid and we look unstoppable. The trick is keeping everyone happy, all those talented players must feel included and utilised. Do you think our management team can foster team spirit and the like? they only sign the right characters, I've got no doubt. Remember, Danny said the lads won't hit method until October time. Swindon, 4-1. Port Vale away, 4-0. we're not even on method yet. I apologise to Danny now for going against the 'we're a work in progress' rhetoric, but I tell it as I see it. Sorry.

Whoever we draw this Thursday, Middlesbrough, Manchester City, Mansfield, not one of them will want to face us in this form. We're indomitable, insurmountable and inspiring when we're on form. Danny just has to make sure that continues.

Derby Day Deadlock: Grimsby Town 1-1 Imps
August 19, 2018

Lincoln City are still top of the early League Two table after an entertaining but evenly balanced derby-day draw with Grimsby Town.

I'll confess yesterday I was pretty distracted, our annual family party took place and although I had the game on the radio ahead of the guests arriving, there was no iFollow feed, so I'm not in a position to comment too much. That may be disappointing if you've got on this for some sort of assessment, but I'm not going to blag you, especially when half of you were probably there anyway.

What I do know is that the draw is being treated like a defeat in some parts of Lincoln, whereas up the A46 you'd think they had won the league. Both sets of fans would be doing their side a disservice: a draw at Grimsby isn't a bad result for us and they shouldn't be shocked at getting a point because from what I've seen and heard, they're a decent outfit who are only a couple of players away from a proper play off push.

Here's the thing: you win your home games, draw your away games and you're going up. If you occasionally play below-par and get points, you're going up. Yesterday we weren't at our best, but we got a point and that is as much as anyone can ask. My understanding is we got a bit of an awakening in parts of the game, out-manoeuvred by a team whose opening day defeat looks like being an anomaly, rather than the norm. Maybe we're not going to have it all our own way, maybe we're all getting carried away with the bookies making us favourites and Swindon letting us score four. Sometimes, sides are going to give us a run for our money because football is eleven against eleven and anything can happen.

Whilst I won't comment much further on the game, I do feel well placed to smile at some of the social media reaction. Put simply, some fans seem to be going into melt down already. I see John Akinde (three goals in four games, that John Akinde) is the latest scapegoat. Apparently he's lazy, looks disinterested and should be replaced. Right. Tell me, have you ever had to take a late penalty to level the scores in a huge local derby? Every had to settle into a new club, a new style of play and alongside new players? Ever scored three in four games whilst being 'below par' and lazy? No? Thought not.

I get that people can offer opinions, it is all I do here, but sometimes I despair at what I read, to a point where I stopped reading. I know we drew and we were expected to win, but are we not top of the table, unbeaten and having scored nine in three games? If Akinde keeps scoring at the rate he has been doing, penalty spot or not, he'll get 32 goals this season, yet he's lazy and disinterested? I don't buy that a penalty is an easy goal, you have to put them in the net when presented with the chance and as a team, you have to be in the area and attacking to win one.

I see Freck is coming in for some stick too. Honestly? I don't think we've seen the best of him yet and after six months, maybe that is a concern. I didn't see him yesterday so I can't comment, but what I do know is he was excellent against Swindon last weekend. Again, this side is settling down and at this early stage I don't think last seasons form should be brought into the equation.

Danny spoke in the fan's forum about managing expectation, mainly in the playing squad, but maybe we should also take heed. What do we expect? To win every game 4-0? All of this 'lets smash the cods' on social media is fine, but the reality is Blundell Park is becoming a tough place to visit again and with the added pressure of it being a derby, a draw is a decent result.

That is going to be my last word on yesterday. It would be remiss of me to say too much more having not been there, but don't underestimate the result. I always say the opening day throws up results that are odd, look at the 1995/96 season when we beat Preston 2-1. They ended up winning the league and we ended up getting through three managers and almost got relegated. Grimsby won't lose many at home this season, not in the style they lost against Forest Green and when everything is said and done, a point there will be a decent outcome.

We're still top and we're still unbeaten.

Get Out of Jail Free: Imps 2-1 Bury
August 21, 2018

There's a collection of clichés used to describe football and tonight, I've heard plenty. Game of two halves, you make your own luck, the trick to being successful is winning when playing badly.

Only one of those truly describes Lincoln City in the aftermath of the 2-1 victory over Bury, the last one. Successful sides win games in which they have been below par and for at least fifty minutes of this game, I thought we were below par.

this was never going to be an easy game, Bury have good players and their performances ta both MK Dons and Forest showed they're resolute away from home. Anyone who thought they might come here and shut up shop was sorely mistaken though. Still, there is an air of expectancy around our fan base and the fact is very few people would have expected anything other than a win this evening. That wouldn't be arrogant or disrespectful, but our early form and recruitment makes us favourites at a packed Sincil Bank for virtually any game we play at the moment.

There's only so much tinkering one team can take though and in having flexibility, we perhaps have an Achilles heel too. I was incredibly surprised to see Matt Rhead start and for us to set up in a 4-3-3. Last season, when the players were tired and we needed to be strong and direct, 4-3-3 worked. Right now, with McCartan, Akinde, Anderson and Wharton on the bench, I'm not sure it would be my first choice of set up, nor my second. Or third.

4-3-3 is a formation in which width is at a premium, it relies on the players either side of the front man to get into the wide positions, but surely it also relies on that front man being mobile enough to then make use of himself in the space they vacate? Am I wrong there? Whatever the issue was, after fifteen minutes or so, everything went a bit awry.

The first exchanges were good, I don't subscribe to this 'terrible first half, great second half' analysis I'm seeing everywhere. Bury were clearly up for the game, on the ball they looked very good and they weren't afraid to carry it forward and probe at our back four. On the other hand both Tom Pett and Ellis Chapman looked good for us, Ellis made the odd slip, nerves perhaps, but on the whole he looked very comfortable. Their keeper made several good saves, one from a header which looked like giving us a nice lead. Not long after we had a passage of pressure broken up by Rhead getting clattered and that seemed to flick a switch.

After that we were, for want of a better word, woeful. Pett and Chapman were getting on the ball, but there were few options for them to aim for. The more we dropped possession, the more we looked uncertain and at the back we were positively awful. Bostwick and Shackell played like two players who have only just met and the full backs were unable to offer width because Bury kept men forward. I thought the Shakers looked good and when they scored it was no less than they deserved. The goal was sloppy, not once or twice but three or four times. We failed to clear a ball that could have gone out easily, we didn't deal with a corner and then we didn't deal with another. Take nothing away from the visitors, they sensed we were off it and they pressured the right areas.

When the whistle went for the end of the half it was a relief to not have to watch such disjointed football, passing going astray, runs made in the wrong areas and basic errors littering our play. If you were one of the people who booed around me, and it was only one or two, don't come again. Cheers.

Half time was a period of reflection and on the whole the main players who impressed were Pett, Ellis and Matt Green. Green worked tirelessly and I thought if we had got a goal, he would get it. Ellis didn't look like a 17-year old making his home debut and Tom Pett cut a dejected figure trying to pull the strings, but failing. We lacked industry in front of the back four, we lacked an Alex Woodyard mopping up. It's ironic last season we had two, Bozzie and Alex, tonight where they should be there was a huge space.

I didn't like to see their subs land the ball on our groundsman's head at half time, but the lad stood up for himself well. I thought there might be a dust up at one point and as our lad had a rake and the Bury player didn't, it was only going one way.

The group I sit with talked about possible substitutes and I suggested perhaps Ellis should come off, purely as a tactical switch, but I confidently remarked; Danny won't do that because it might affect him adversely. Lo and behold, he did it.

Ellis hadn't played badly, not at all, but the 4-3-3 didn't work and he was the fall guy. Of the two, Tom Pett had the better first half, but Ellis was really unlucky to come off. As soon as Harry came on though, we had width. Tom Pett's commanding display continued.

The analysis I've seen and heard so far suggests we were scintillating in the second half. We weren't. For the first fifty seconds we got at them, but soon those little slips crept back in. I saw Freck and Harry have a little ding dong at one point as a pass got wasted and it made me wonder if the constant changing of tactics had confused one or two.

Slowly but surely we crept back into the game, but we never really looked like scoring. their keeper seemed to be on the end of all our box entries and even when we went all in on the hour mark, things didn't change significantly. I've seen criticism of Akinde, but in terms of contribution he offered exactly the same as Rhead today: little.

We showed great attitude though and kept trying to find a way through. When we did get the little triangles and passes to work, we looked good, but far too often the ball simply travelled across the back four and back again. I thought Harry Toffolo had a good second half, I thought Tom Pett had an excellent one.

I said against Swindon we were punished with a harsh penalty and I've got to say I think that the balance has been well and truly redressed. I couldn't see adequately to say whether or not it was a penalty, but very few of our players appealed for anything other than a corner and had VAR been a thing, I suspect we might have no more than a point, if that. Still, the ref gave it and upset their rhythm by sending a player off too. Harsh? Maybe, but that is football.

John Akinde came into his own to strike his third league goal for us, his third from the spot. My old man is convinced his languid approach and nonchalant strikes will cost us one day, but he made no mistake at all. The fans , who had never stopped singing to their credit, erupted and there was only ever going to be one winner.

The second came from a combination of two players who didn't fill me with confidence tonight. I thought Andrade struggled in the 4-3-3 and had to work hard to get into the game second half, but his raw speed and persistence paid off as he outran two defenders and pipped the keeper to the ball. It squirmed free and Freck, another who hadn't looked comfortable all evening, finished with aplomb.

Afterwards he said he doesn't think in those situations, it is instinct. I'd prefer it if he doesn't think too much because that finish was calmness personified. To not blast the ball was clever, to outwit the defender and make the goal empty was pure class. Say what you want about Lee Frecklington, he has composure and quality when it matters. Two cool finishes of very different sorts won us the game.

I thought our game management was good after that, Grant Smith looked very comfortable and the new keeper might find himself warming our bench for longer than he anticipates. his shot stopping was good, apart from the goal but there was little he could do. Towards the end he took the sting out of the seven minutes, but as a team I felt we reverted back to nervy passes and broken possession. Yes, we showed control to see out the game, but not before giving away silly free kicks and corners when we should have been leaving the ball in block 2, row J.

One of the moments of the game came as the clock wound down, Tom Pett collected the ball in the middle of the park and carried it fifty yards, across the field, constantly under pressure. He was aiming for the corner, but instead drew a free kick. It was classic Woodyard, something I recall him doing early last season and it showed the awareness and composure of the former Stevenage man. Man of the Match? By a country mile.

Maybe I've been critical overall, we're one of two teams in the division with ten points from twelve and yet again we've bounced back from conceding an early goal, this time to win. We've had a helping hand, be it from Will Aimson or Seb Stockbridge....

Yes, that is right. The referee was one Seb Stockbridge, a man who is no stranger to controversy at Sincil Bank. Remember last season, he sent Billy Knott off at Notts County for a high kick, drawing my anger. He then dismissed Farrend Rawson for handball in the area, at the same end of the ground, as we beat Accrington 2-0 in the league. He's been one I'm critical of time and again but tonight, he's certainly redeemed himself in terms of decisions against us.

Did we deserve all three points? Probably not, no. Bury were good in possession, moved the ball nicely and all too often made simple thirty yard passes between our players. They were allowed to receive the ball with backs to goal and turn and perhaps if they'd got decent forwards they might have had three or four. We weren't terrible all night, Joe Murphy made some good saves early on but a draw would have been a fair result.

Still, it wasn't a draw, we won and just like against Northampton, the record books will only ever show this as our third win in four.

Bury will be fine this season, if they play like that all campaign they'll sit around the top ten, no doubt at all. I thought Nicky Adams and Stephen Dawson both looked good on the ball, but in Chris Dagnall they have a striker past his best and in Gold Omoyato they have one who needs someone better next to him to accentuate his ability. At the back they were well-drilled but a little naïve towards the end, but their overall performance deserved something.

We move forward, four games down and ten points on the board. Kevin Nolan brings his side to Sincil Bank this weekend in a game that has a huge meaning for them. They've lost again tonight, conceding seven in two games and the early pressure is one him. If we could perhaps go back to 3-5-2 or 4-4-2 and find width as well as pace up front, we'll be fine.

Just don't go 4-3-3 again because I fear we're running out of our Get Out of Jail Free cards.

Highly-rated youngster joins Imps youth ranks as Academy grows
August 24, 2018

Talented Nigerian Jordan Adebayo-Smith has joined the Imps on a two-year scholarship, according to All Nigerian Soccer.

The move appears to be confirmed on the Imps youth team website, where Adebayo is listed as a player for the U18 side.

The report says that the talented 17-year-old was offered a two-year scholarship following a successful summer trial. It is thought he featured for the first team in the friendly against Derby U23 side, scoring in the process.

Adebayo has previously been on trial at Watford, failing to earn a deal, but was approached by the Imps through the East Soccer Base Academy.

Adebayo-Smith is described as "lightning quick and very skilful with an eye for goal" and plays up front.

If the move is as the report says, it does show the academy growing rapidly in terms of where it sources players, as well as recruiting fresh faces. At the fans forum last week, Danny spoke passionately about the desire to build an academy the club could be proud of, one that offered something very different to the others in the area.

It remains to be seen if Adebayo-Smith is the next face to emerge from the youth team and stake a first team place, following in the footsteps of 'one of our own', Ellis Chapman.

The academy has also been boosted recently by the arrival of David Bridges as Head of Coaching. 35-year old Bridges is a former pro who featured for Cambridge, Stevenage and Kettering amongst others in a career spanning 16 years and 451 appearances. he represented England at C international level and was part of the same Stevenage team as Michael Bostwick, winning promotion from the Conference in 2010.

In the matchday programme for the Bury game, he said of Lincoln City's academy: "The people are very clear where they want to take the club. I've been really impressed with the mentality and the attitude within the environment. "

We might not hear a lot about the development within the academy, but it does seem as though things are progressing at a fantastic speed now we're back in the Football League.

Long may it continue.

Top of the League: Imps 3-1 Notts County
August 25, 2018

There's something about football which always leaves me fearing the worst. It's an inbuilt pessimism that sees a side lose 4-0 to Yeovil and makes me think 'they'll come good against us'.

That's probably why when I got asked about the match before kick off I predicted a win, perhaps 2-1 but a tight game. I thought it would be a challenge, Dennis, Hemmings and Boldewijn are all class players and with Vaughan pulling the strings I thought we might struggle. When I saw the team sheet, a tentative 4-3-3 again, I was equally as fearful. We'd lacked width against Bury and this line up looked to offer the same problems.

It's fair to say I was wrong.

I thought we started really confidently, the patterns of play were nice and it was clear their right back Tootle wasn't quite fit. Andrade scared the life out of him, he probably would have done fully fit but when you're coming back from injury the last thing you want is him running at you. we had pace, movement and fluidity.

None of that can account for the opening goal though, a sumptuous strike from Freck which showed his utter class. He's one that has come in for some undue stick in recent weeks, but that ball was struck so sweetly and instinctively that there was only ever one outcome. He likes a game against County, he scored the last team we beat them (before today), he scored last season and he got the pick of the bunch today.

It was, for twenty minutes, much the same as the Swindon game. we controlled the play through clever midfield work, Frecklington and Pett in particular were impressive. Andrade made their players nervous whenever he had the ball and although we got less joy down the right, we were still causing problems. Their goal came against the run of play, but it sparked some belief in them.

It was a sloppy one to concede and I imagine our lads will be sick of seeing it on the video screen on Monday. It was a decent enough strike and I'm not sure there was much Grant Smith.

From there we drifted for ten minutes or so, a few sloppy passes and a bit of loose play had me wondering if it was Bury in reverse; we score and then fall apart. Instead, we snatched the advantage and once we had, the result was never really in doubt.

I thought Akinde played his part well for the second goal. The joy came from the right, but John was a huge presence in the area and caused panic between keeper and defender. Normally, that ball gets collected comfortably, but he did what he had to do for it to break loose. Bruno still had plenty of work to do, but his finish was smart and clever. At 2-1, there was only one winner.

I don't want to pull County down too much as it may do us a disservice, but they're clearly low on confidence and luck. Losing their centre half and then the right back to injury meant square pegs in round holes and that was evident in the way they defended. I thought we could have taken a wider lead before we got our third, not because we were rampant but because we were comfortable. There wasn't a thought we might get five or six, County are bad but they're not woeful. When the third went in, yet again with Andrade involved, the game was over.

I was surprised at County, they offered little and even Boldewijn was ineffective. You can see why he would be a handful, he's a pretty big lump but moves quickly and with a certain intent, but he was shackled really well. I thought at the back we were solid, Bozzie and Shackell looked far better than they did on Tuesday night and Grant Smith is essentially sticking one finger up at Sam Slocombe. League One starter were you? whatever, you're not having my shirt. Fair play to Smith, his distribution is good and he's a decent shot stopper too.

I have to say that although Freck got Man of the Match, and he was excellent, I thought Andrade would have been a worthy winner. He has terrifying pace, but a nice range of tricks and an end product. When we signed him I said he could be the big signing of the summer, I stand by that.

I thought Akinde had a good game, he gets accused of being lazy but he's one of those lumbering centre forwards who don't look to be doing much, but are. He worked hard, he won lots of balls and he was involved in the second and third goals. What more do we want from him?

I thought Neal Eardley had to work to make things happen today, he wasn't at it in the first half and I noticed him and Harry have a couple of exchanges. I don't mind players having a pop at each other, it shows passion. as long as they don't end up carrying it on, it is healthy. Neal improved second half, maybe the threat diminished somewhat, but he picked up his levels for sure.

As for a player from the County side I'd like in ours, on today's performance I wouldn't take any of them. It sounds ridiculous to say that given their talent, but they were all off the pace. I rave about Boldewijn and on his day he'd be great for us, but they had a bad day at the office. They were unlucky with injuries, they played a Lincoln side with a point to prove after Tuesday (even though we won) and they're lacking confidence.

If someone had offered us 13 points from five games, we would have left them with a stump for a hand, but here we are in second gear and already top of the pile. No, we don't get carried away because we will have a wobble, but today was a professional performance, clinical, entertaining and as comfortable as we'll see against the big teams in the league.

Up next MK Dons and Exeter, albeit with some cup games too, but if we're on 16 points or more once those games are over, I think every single one of us will be forced to suppress little giggles of joy. For now, we'll enjoy being top of League Two which, I think, is the first time we've led outright since Jamie Forrester put us there in the 2006/07 season. I don't think we were top at any point last season, happy to be corrected.

I know one thing, Saturday nights are far easier to enjoy under Danny Cowley than they ever have been before. Long may it continue.

The Imps secure Derby wide man on loan
August 28, 2018

Danny Cowley has secured the services of Kellan Gordon on loan until January.

20-year old Gordon spent time in League Two with Swindon Town last season, making 31 appearances for the Robins, scoring four times. He impressed in the friendly against Derby U23s and will add options to Danny's squad.

Prior to moving to the County Ground, he made his first-team debut as a substitute in the Rams' Carabao Cup Round One tie at Grimsby Town last August. He also featured against Lincoln in the 2-2 draw with Swindon last season. Gordon is versatile and offers options at right back, but is primarily a winger.

It is thought he is available to play in this evenings Carabao Cup clash with Blackburn, having not played for Derby in their first round match against Oldham Athletic.

In his first year as a professional, the winger missed just one of the Rams' U23 fixtures and he capped off a fine personal year by scoring three goals, including a great effort in a 5-3 win over Manchester United and the winner against Chelsea on the final day of the season.

That should conclude just about Danny's business now, leaving no need for a live blog on deadline day. He's got Gordon, Sam Slocombe, Scott Wharton, Adam Crookes and Shay McCartan on loan, meaning we can not pick any more players in the squad. The maximum we can sign is eight, but only five can play at any one time.

We could sign a free agent, up until tomorrow, but only if they've been without a club since the permanent deadline expired earlier this month.

Reserves outclassed: Blackburn 4-1 Imps
August 28, 2018

On the face of things, it looks as though the Imps have been well beaten tonight and in terms of the balance of play, that is the case.

After a tight first half in which City applied themselves well, Blackburn upped the ante after the break and didn't give the visitors a look in. They had many first team players out and scored some good goals to put the game beyond the Imps.

However, consider this. Lincoln City made seven changes to the side that won 3-1 at the weekend, Adam Crookes and Juan Luque made their first starts for the club, Matt Green and Matt Rhead both got a start and there were appearances for James Wilson and young Ellis Chapman who was excellent in the middle of the park.

Blackburn made six. One of their goal scorers was Kasey Palmer, another starter from their Championship win against Brentford this weekend. So whilst they did make use of their squad, we did the same perhaps to a greater degree.

The first half wasn't bad at all, City composed themselves well after conceding the early goal, with Ellis Chapman looking very assured. Juan Luque looked lively, if not a little naïve at times. His link up with Adam Crookes looked to be in its infancy, which is perhaps to be expected. Crookes made amends with a performance in which he improved significantly.

Remember, Blackburn haven't lost this season but we matched them for a period of time. Losing the second goal did kill the Imps off though and after that, there was only one winner.

Danny Cowley explained the changes and his responsibility to the fans in his post-match interview with Rob Makepeace.

"I think it is always hard as a League Two club coming to a Championship club. we made a lot of changes which was a necessity tonight. It's hard when you're playing nine games in 28 days. You have to make the right decisions for the group and for the club long-term."

"It's hard as a manager because we had over 1,000 fans who have travelled hours to get here and that always plays on your conscience. We have to make the right decisions to allow ourselves to get into the best possible positions to compete on Saturday."

"It's really tough because you're exposing young players and inexperienced players to very good Championship players."

Danny talks about learning and there was one big lesson we've learned as fans tonight, something that we haven't seen from Danny before. He's clearly prioritised the league over the League Cup, something that has never been the case. Last season there were some changes, but to drop Luque and Crookes in the side showed that Exeter is a priority.

I know Danny speaks of not wanting to lose and being disappointed. He talks about never accepting defeat and I get that, but if he was given a choice, do you think it would have been a win tonight or a win on Saturday. His team selection suggests Saturday is by far the more important game and honest fans would agree with the decision.

Is there much more point in picking over this match? Is there anything we can truly learn that will help us in assessing our chances going forward? Ellis gets better, he didn't look out of place at all. Luque took his goal well and he's a dirty diamond right now. One or two others maybe didn't impress too much and Rhead did look to be a passenger for long spells. He's a battering ram and will be far more effective from the bench, not from the start.

Danny perhaps summed things up best at the end of his interview with Rob Makepeace tonight,.

"If the EFL want us to value this competition, they've got to rethink their scheduling. If they schedule the second round after we've been Saturday, Tuesday, Saturday, Tuesday you're going to get weakened sides others you'll break players. I urge them to rethink their scheduling."

As for this season's competition, we now sit the rest of it out but if come May we're in the top three, few of us will recall this as the crushing defeat the score line makes it look like.

Bernard Mensah could be an intelligent signing for City
August 31, 2018

The Imps have announced the loan signing of winger Bernard Mensah from Bristol Rovers until the end of the current season.

23-year old Mensah is no stranger to City, having appeared against us a number of times in the National League. He had two loan spells with Braintree in 2013/14 and 2014/15, then with Barnet in 2014/15 as well.

He finally secured a permanent deal, moving to Gary Waddock's Aldershot Town in the summer of 2016. Whilst at The EBB Stadium, Mensah scored 17 times in 63 matches and quickly attracted many admirers. That lead to his move to Bristol Rovers in January of this year.

Mensah can play in a range of positions, as a centre forward, attacking midfielder or a winger, and has appeared nine times for the Gas, including one substitute appearance against Peterborough United on the opening day of the current season.

Why I think he'll be an intelligent signing, apart from the weak play on his name, is the versatility he'll offer. He's clearly an impressive forward, a little in the Andrade mould in that he's come from a London club, dropped out of the league and is now looking to prove himself.

Our strength in depth is provided by having players who can operate in a number of positions, for instance Kellan Gordon, Adam Crookes and Shay McCartan. Our squad isn't huge in terms of numbers, but the different formations up front could be a major advantage.

In an interview with the Bristol Post after his January move, Mensah said: "I play everywhere! On the left, on the right, in midfield, just behind a striker, up top. So I can pretty much play all attacking areas really. But here it's up to the gaffer, wherever he plays me I'll be happy."

I expect Mensah to figure prominently over the coming weeks, he was frightening for Aldershot in the 3-3 draw we had in November 2016, going on to score seven in 11 to secure them a play off place against Tranmere Rovers.

September

Indomitable City win again: Exeter 0-3 Imps
September 2, 2018

There's all manner of plots and sub-plots to out history with Exeter, or at least our recent history. Up until twelve months ago neither side cared about each other at all.

That all changed last season, but I'm not entirely sure why. I get that we met in the play-offs, but I didn't think anything other than the final few minutes of the second leg were particularly bad. Sure, there was one fan captured making gestures and another should have been arrested for knocking our kit man about, but on the whole they weren't bad-tempered games were they?

That's why I was surprised to hear them signing '3-1 to Exeter' before the game. Not only did it seem a little out of context, but it was breaking one of the most sacred rules of football: never crow about a previous win if you're not assured the current one.

I've been away again this weekend, so instead of a hooky iFollow feed I've had some match highlights to enjoy today. I spent my evening in a pub just outside High Wycombe, explaining to three blue-shirted Chairboys how we look forward to joining them, or passing them (after too much vodka) next season. I was buoyed by the result of course, but then again who wouldn't be? Which Imps truly kept their feet on the round last night? Even the cold-hearted fishermen on Banter must have afforded a little leap of delight.

From what I can gather the first half was a tight affair until the goals, there certainly wasn't too many highlights going our way before the quick-fire brace. However, the 42-odd minutes before a double goal salvo really counts for very little indeed, especially when you consider the wider implications of the goals that put us in front.

In the summer, we signed a player who frightens League Two, genuinely frightens them. He's been with Barnet so the fear was limited, he might score goals but they were never going to be a threat. In January this year, as he scored to put them ahead, I remember saying to my Dad 'Imagine if he was in a decent team'. Well, imagine no more.

John Akinde is class, we didn't break the club record to bring him here because of his record, we brought him here because he has all the attributes we needed from our centre forward. On his day, he's Matt Green and Matt Rhead rolled into one. That's no disrespect to either, they have strengths they play to and both are good players, but Akinde can offer a bit of both. He's got the pace and ability to carry the ball the Rheady perhaps lacks, but he's also the target man which Matt Green is not.

The problem was that some of the ne'er sayers seemed keen on writing him off after just four goals (three from the spot). I've read that he is lazy, that he doesn't make an effort and other rubbish along those lines. Yesterday, he looked much like the John Akinde I drooled over in January.

I'll skip straight to his goal because it might not win 'Goal of the Month', but if you study it closely, it's a peach. It's all him, determined and powerful in the middle of the park, tenacious in carrying it forward patient in the opening developing and then clinical, deadly clinical with his finish. That's not just a good finish, it is technically very good too. Pym immediately lambasted his defenders, but he was left for dead with the precision of the shot. I wonder how many of their fans thought the keeper might do better, just as our did with Paul Farman last season. You could say Pym was well and truly Akinde'd.

The opening goal was where he turned provider, taking up an unfamiliar role from out wide to tee up a midfielder who constantly talks about arriving in the box late. I'm not sure Freck arrived late, he arrived bang on time to score his third of the season. Now, correct me if I'm wrong, but doesn't that make him our leading scorer with goals from open play? Again, he's a player who had been called off the pace and lost, yet as every game passes he grows into the new system.

Ah, the new system. Before we broach the second half, let's talk about our system shall we? It is apparently one of two systems. According to one of the BBC Devon guys, the one probably on crack, we're just like Wycombe Wanderers (the side that pipped Exeter to automatic promotion last season). He said (and I quote) "Time wasting, physical, going down for fake injuries at every opportunity. Akinde scored a good goal for them but if this is Lincoln's strategy for promotion then it's very sad." Hmmmm. There may have been some game management, nothing different to any other side seeing out time with a 2-0 lead away from home, or even 3-0 later on. By 'physical' I assume he means going in for tackles, winning tackles and the like. You know, playing football. Honestly.

There's the other side of the coin though, the one that isn't as bitter. For instance there's my Uncle Keith, an Exeter fan since the mid-eighties when he was moved down there aged 15, but an Imp before that and an Imp at heart. He simply said that they were playing terribly, lacking a decent striker and a defence. Manager Matt Taylor was a little more honest, saying: "All credit to Lincoln, they are a good team. They pressed us high up the pitch, they messed us around and dominated us physically, which is a disappointing factor. We just had no real control, certainly in our backline, and it just fed through the rest of the team." He did mutter something about them not dealing with long balls, but having seen Big John pick it up in the middle of the park and strut through like a hot knife through cheese, he can't be talking about us.

That left-sided combination paid dividends again too, with attacking defenders like Harry Toffolo, you hardly need wingers. However, if Carlsberg did wingers, in my opinion they been called Andrade. Between the two of them they brewed up and own goal, but the build up play was exquisite. I'm not sure if the pass was better or the run. Both were worthy of the goal that followed.

So there we have it. Exeter City, one of the better sides we faced last season and early pace-setters this time round, are beaten. We're not just top of the league, we're clear top by three points, with a goal difference nine better than Newport in second and seven better than MK Dons, expected to be around us too. It's early day, very early indeed, but there's already a nagging feeling in my mind that those who sniggered at my pre-season prediction might be eating their words in a few months time.

I wonder when the last time was we went top of League Two and stayed there?

28 seconds: Imps 1-2 Mansfield
September 4, 2018

Why 28 seconds? Why define a game with a number in this way? Well, before I even start to dissect the game there's a stat I liked that I think sums it up perfectly.

Danny revealed in the post-match interview that if you too our time in possession and worked out how often we were fouled, there was an infringement committed against us every 28 seconds. If anything can sum a game up then for me, that is it.

Mansfield didn't come with a plan to manage the game, they didn't come initially with a plan to win the game. They came with one thought only, certainly in the first half. to kick us off the park. There's physical, which we are. Then there's outright dirty, which they were.

The game started well for us, a goal started with a Joan Luque tackle on the edge of the area and finished with a wonderful cross and simple header by Matt Rhead. At that point we looked like we'd go on to grab three or four. Sadly, a poor piece of defending by Adam Crookes led to a quick-fire equaliser. I know Crookes made up for it with a decent display, but that's the second time in a week I've written something along those lines. To be fair to him, he was playing at centre-half which didn't look natural at all. He looked as uncomfortable there as I would in a vegetarian restaurant.

After that we spent thirty minutes watching our futile efforts to avoid being kicked. Mansfield weren't just robust, they were fouling us, on purpose and getting away with it. Sure there was a booking or two from Ross Joyce, a man I remember well from last season, but he didn't have a grip of the game. They'd chop a player down, get booked and we'd win the free kick. It would be launched into the box and he'd blow for a foul the other way. It's familiar, especially if you read the link to our 2-2 draw with County last season.

At one point I recall us playing a pass into McCartan, their lad took Anderson out off the ball and without a second's thought for the advantage, we got a free-kick despite being in a good position. Their player got a yellow and as soon as the ball was crossed in, Joyce gave a free-kick the other way. Textbook Ross Joyce.

I'm not blaming the referee for anything, I thought we got bullied a bit. Usually it doesn't happen and with a couple more experienced pros on the field it wouldn't either, but we had perhaps one too many young players on the field. They picked up something like four yellow cards in the first half, it could have been six. There's not a lot more to say about the first 45 minutes. Two goals, lots of fouls and a weak referee. It didn't bode well for the second half.

I thought we came out with intent and hit them hard for about six minutes, but then they got the upper hand. After kicking us all over for one half, they outplayed us for much of the second. They'd done what needed to be done, they had scored a psychological advantage and I thought it showed. A niggly, broken game wasn't easy on the eye and anyone recalling the goals and thrills of last season's competition would be left to do just that; reminisce. There was to be no more thrills, nor spills.

The game changed in one move, but it also defined the next few months of our season too. Mansfield brought on Tyler Walker and CJ Hamilton. They don't have a game Saturday, so could afford to do that, but also they wanted it more. Us? Not long after we brought on Jamie McCombe, who resembled a pub player with a bit of a paunch, if I may say so.

Walker scored with his first touch as Mansfield looked to press the advantage. On our bench, John Akinde and Lee Frecklington remained seated. Mansfield brought on a couple of their big players, whilst ours were left fit for Saturday.

We could moan about them not having a game, we could make reference to their robust tactics being a result of yellow cards not carrying over, but then we're also beneficiaries of that with O'Connor's late sending off. The truth as I see it is this: as much as I write articles about which cup we should prioritise, there's only one that Danny cares about, the one in which we play 46 games.

What else is there to say? Last week I wrote about the same attitude towards the League Cup and tonight we saw it in the EFL Trophy as well. If we'd wanted the win, really wanted it, we would have replaced one of the midfielders for Lee Frecklington and brought on Akinde for Rhead. Instead, we let the big man have his 90 minutes and settled for a defeat.

I may get shot down for saying that, I'm not one to shout about 'concentrating on the league' after a cup defeat, but that is the feeling I get, to such an extent I might not even bother with the Wolves game. I saw nothing in the latter stages of this evenings game to suggest that this competition is anything other than a couple of friendlies to keep players fit. Checkatrade Trophy? Completed it last year mate, not fussed anymore.

To be fair to them, when they played the ball around they looked a decent side. I suspect they'll suffer the same sort off ate as last season, any success they have will be in spite of their manager, not because of him. They've got some decent players and they played a strong side tonight and when they stopped kicking anything that moved, they weren't a bad side.

As you always get with Mansfield, there was plenty of theatre and aggression towards the end of the game. Some casual observers might say 'typical Lincoln', but look at it this way: both teams played Sheffield Wednesday in a pre-season game, which side play the game in the right spirit, and which side ended up fighting on the pitch with a player on an FA charge?

(I am aware of the racist comment and I do not condone that in any way, but if you're a Mansfield fan telling me Forestieri made that comment out of the blue during a well-mannered and friendly game, I call you out as being untruthful. He should have the book thrown at him, 100%, but there's always a catalyst and I stand by my comments.)

Swindon fans hate Flitcroft and I can see why. Sure, him and Nicky had an argument during the game, but when a hand was offered he had to start shouting and ranting like an angry child. Give it up Flitcroft, you've won the game, keep some dignity. Instead he got carried away with everything, just like Evans used to. Maybe it is something in the water at Mansfield, maybe their culture just breeds behaviour like that. You can ask Fernando Forestieri and Jos Luhukay about it too, the cynical fouls in games where cards don't matter, and how they reacted to it. No need.

In fact, there's no need to be such dicks about it at all. game management, like Wycombe do (or we do at times) I can handle. Time wasting, sure. What I can't stand is where it appears as though an opponent is deliberately trying to injure his opposition number. I felt that tonight, I felt they wanted to rack up the injuries and that doesn't sit well with me at all. In fact, I'm pretty disgusted by it. It's not why we lost, there's no excuses here, nor hiding behind a familiar narrative, I just think it stinks.

Am I hacked off we lost? Yes. Do I feel a little short-changed? Maybe. I know one thing, if you offered me a defeat tonight and three points Saturday, there's only one choice I'd make. I do rate this competition and, if we were taking it seriously, I'd get behind it, but we're not putting as much weight behind it as we did last season. We're prioritising the league and whilst that might not please the born winners who want a victory in every game at all costs, it does show exactly what the club's plan is from now until May.

O'Connor's red card? Definite red. He got caught up in the fouls and lost his cool. At least he rose to the occasion and refused to be bullied.

Last year, we beat them at their place, but not long after they got the league points. If it is the other way around this time, I'll be delighted. I know one thing for sure; Flitcroft isn't anywhere near as adept as winding situations up like Evans. He looked a fool at the end and doubtless his post-match interview will lack the class that Danny will show. What happens during 90 minutes should be forgotten, but sadly the likes of their manager don't see that.

I was in a good mood too, thanks to Barbara Freshney. In KFC before the game she spotted me and came over to tell me how much she loved the site. I get a little awkward in situations like that and may have come across as a mumbling fool, I'm not good with praise from strangers, but I do appreciate it and was really grateful to get some nice feedback. Thank you!

Tonight's lesson is this: Don't book hotels, coaches or whatever, because the plan is not to go to Wembley, not in this competition, nor in the play offs. The club are focused 100% on the League, at least now we know it for certain. Nothing has changed in terms of the 46 game season since Saturday, we're still top, we're still unbeaten and we're still a good side. You'll only truly see it in League Two though.

Back to earth with a bump: Imps 0-1 Crawley
September 8, 2018

It's not often we leave Sincil Bank having been beaten, but are there some early warning signs after it happened twice in a week?

It was easy to be complacent about Tuesday's result, a competition we've already won hardly seemed worth getting worked up over, especially when you look at the changes we made. However, that word complacent takes a whole new meaning on this evening after we were beaten by Crawley.

I'm going to jump straight into the game and look at a rather tepid and half-arsed first half. Is there a better way to describe it? Crawley were decent, nothing more, but we weren't at the races. Ollie Palmer could have opened the scoring, but luckily he showed the sort of finishing ability I remember him having. It was an early warning and the reality is they didn't have a better chance in the next 85 minutes.

Our central defensive pair looked solid, Shackell and Bostwick have to be the best there is at this level, but around them we just looked very flat. The full backs, both of them, looked to be exploited on occasion. Passes from midfield went astray and there was a huge gap around John Akinde. All over the park, bar the two centre half positions, we were sloppy.

In flashes, Harry and Bruno both showed their skills and both had efforts at goal in the first half which were perhaps a little wasteful. It was Harry first, doing the hard work but drilling a tame ball off target. Bruno screamed at him across the box, politely suggesting there was a better option. Within fifteen minutes it flipped the other way, Bruno had a good chance which he chose to take himself rather than share.

Even though we were poor I felt we had the best chances and they don't come better than John Akinde's just before the goal. I champion Akinde as one of the best strikers in this league, but he flashed an effort wide that it looked harder to miss than score. It wasn't a howler, but it didn't demonstrate the quality I believe he has. Against Exeter I felt John took a huge step forward, today he took a couple back.

Then there's the goal, a classic case of not playing to the whistle. Was there a foul on Bruno in the build up? Maybe, but the fact is if you go down there's no guarantee the referee will believe you. I didn't see an infringement, that's my opinion. I don't think anything happened to him that Palmer and Bostwick hadn't been doing to each other all game. However, he went down, a couple of our lads paused and it's 1-0. I'm sorry to say, it was criminal to give that goal away. There's only one noise that should stop you playing and that is a whistle, not a wingers exaggerated scream as he goes down.

I'm not saying Bruno dived by the way, nor that he was at fault. It was those around him who chose to argue and not follow play. It wasn't the first time either, earlier in the half at the other end we had a cracking chance but Harry paused on the ball believing their defender had been fouled. His tame effort earned a corner but I think he felt that play was going to be called back. Danny talks about learning lessons, I'm sure there's a big one there.

On the balance of play I thought we were worth a draw at half time. Crawley are a decent side but they're nothing special. They did their homework though, they isolated Akinde, whether that was purposeful or a failing on our part I don't know. However, it is worth remembering that we did have chances in the first half and could have been in the lead.

The second half looked to start well, but not in the conventional sense. We didn't threaten the goal and our patterns of play didn't come back, but Crawley just retreated in the second half. I still have a problem with our set pieces, aside from maybe one corner we don't make the best of them. We had free kicks in decent positions too, but again made little of them. That 'round the corner' set piece that we did with Matt Green last year has stopped working, this afternoon we tried it and just looked foolish.

Let's talk about the sending off. There was a lot of anger around me, their defender apparently cheated, etc etc. That is utter rubbish. Freck's first touch was heavy and his second was on the man, not the play. His studs were up, it was a red card. You could say the Crawley lads contributed to the card, of course they did. They're looking to appeal those decisions and when it is as clear-cut as that, they're entitled to do so.

By the way, the foul on Akinde later in the game was no comparable either. It was a foul, it was a booking but Akinde was not through on goal and the foul was not serious foul play. Sorry, I call it how I see it and for me, the referee got those decisions spot on. What he didn't do well was general control, stealing yards at throw ins, hurrying up play and spotting handballs, but they're minor infringements. There was a lot of anger being directed at him from the rows in front of me, but it was largely unjustified. I'd say it was maybe frustration.

Even Grant Smith had an off game. He did make a great save in the first half, making amends for almost serving up a goal for Ollie Palmer but luckily he showed all the sharpness in front of goal as our striker and we got away with it. Smith's distribution wasn't great either, but he was kicking into a swirling wind, so he should be afforded a little bit of slack.

After the sending off I've heard it said we looked better, there was only one team likely to score and so on, but let's be frank, we were never going to score, were we? The only time we looked a danger was when Rheady came on, ten minutes too late. I'm all for Rhead getting a run out from the bench, but in games like this afternoon I think it needed to be a little earlier. I expect Danny saw that our play had picked up and he didn't want to upset that rhythm, I can understand it to a degree.

Perhaps I wouldn't have brought Mensah on, I'd like to have seen us throw Rhead and Green on for Akinde and Pett and just go for it. What is the worst that could happen? We concede again?

Maybe I'm missing something with Matt Green, an injury or something else, but he has more energy and movement than Akinde and Rhead put together. That's not a slur on Rhead, nor intentionally on Big John either, but we needed a striker who would chase everything, certainly as Connolly's legs got tired. Instead we tried to batter them without really getting around them or running at them. That was a shame.

That's it really. It was a bad day at the office, it was an afternoon we need to forget, the second is as many seasons against Crawley. It's also an early home defeat for us, something we don't see very often. Danny wasn't happy either, his radio interview started out as a bit of a 'one word answer' session. He was clearly irked and rightly so. I heard talk of a Manager of the Month curse, but I don't believe that at all. there's one reason Danny's side lost today and it isn't because he won an award.

His players let him down, and aside from Shackell and Bostwick, they let us down as well. It was sloppy, disorganised and complacent. Don't expect to see the XI against Macclesfield next weekend anyway, and not just because Freck is suspended.

A lesson in class from Danny Cowley

September 13, 2018

Sadly, I don't get to the press conferences much at the moment, the harsh realities of writing for a living I'm afraid. However, I tune in every week to have a listen and usually, it's much of the same.

Danny plays his cards close to his chest, talks about respect and togetherness in the group, talks about nursing injuries but never reveals who or what. he always says the opposition have good players and always talks up their strengths. If Danny was ill one week, I'm pretty sure I could take one of his pressers and aside from being slightly worse looking and with a better beard, nobody would know.

This week was different though, because this week we got another glimpse of the man, the respectful and measured man who is in charge of our football club. This week he badly burned an opposition manager without even trying, or wanting to.

You may have heard former Imp (two games, rubbish) David Flitcroft paying silly sods in an interview about Danny this week. He didn't quite have the slavering quality of Garry Hill, but it all felt a bit contrived as he said he wouldn't be intimidated by anyone, especially not Danny 'big bad bugger' Cowley. No way, not him. Not Sir Flitcroft. Not going to happen.

Quite why he lashed out a week after or game was a mystery, but Rob Makepeace put it to Danny in his conference this week. Rob's a journalist, he's doing his job and presenting the chance for us all to get a bit of controversial copy to incite clicks and hits. Danny gives us enough though; wins, strong teams, silverware. He won't gift us controversy as well.

"We played Mansfield last week and we play Mansfield again in the coming weeks and months and I'll talk about Mansfield then. Save trash talk for boxing. We've got respect for David Flitcroft and we've got respect for Mansfield, they're a good club and they'll be very, very competitive in the league this year and we look forward to seeing them very soon."

Ouch. genuinely, ouch. Bait ignored, but Rob wanted to know if it was hard not to rise to provocation in the media like that?

"Not really, because we just want to focus on us. I only want to think about things I can control. I can't control David Flitcroft and I can't control Mansfield and I won't get involved in tit for tat. I Love the sport of boxing but I get disappointed on a regular basis when I watch boxers before fights show such a lack of respect for each other. I certainly wouldn't want to see that coming into football and I certainly wouldn't want to be involved in it."

That wasn't it though, Danny's moral compass had been revealed and once it is out, he's not going to put it away again. Mark Whiley of the Echo asked if he felt the likes of Macclesfield would raise their game for a side like Lincoln.

"It would be arrogant for us to think that. Let me just be clear there will be no complacency or arrogance in our dressing room, none at all. We're just down to earth, hard-working boys. Some of us have come right from the bottom of non league to get to this point, we massively value and appreciate the position that we find ourselves in. we'd never, ever take it for granted. We never be arrogant enough to think that anybody would need to raise their game to play against us."

"It would be really disrespectful of me to suggest a team would raise their game just because they're playing a certain opponent. The teams we play against and compete against every week are professional people and part of being a professional person is being the very best version of yourself every single game."

I've been is press conferences and as calm and collected as Danny is, he has a forceful and deliberate way of answering questions without raising his voice. It might be a part of the 'playing down our success' card he likes to produce from time to time, but it is perhaps more a reflection of him not getting carried away, not wanting to project this image of favourites. What he doesn't want is for team to raise their game.

I disagree slightly, I think teams do raise their game for certain fixtures. Take Grimsby the other week. They were a tough side for us to compete against and they gave us a real game, but since then they've been as crumbly as a biscuit. Why? Because against Lincoln they were spurred on, whether it was the atmosphere, the proximity of the clubs, whatever. They looked better and they played better.

What Danny doesn't want is to put that out there for people to pick up on. He wouldn't never insult another team or manager in that way. I wonder, if the question had been asked in a Mansfield presser, what the answer would be.

I just hope David Flitcroft was watching that interview to pick up a few tips, he needs them. I can say this even if Danny can't!

That's what good teams do: Macclesfield 1-2 Imps
September 15, 2018

In the end, the result is all that matters. I've said it after bad performances this season and I now find myself saying it after a decent performance.

It is always hard to go to a bottom of the table side, because to many it's a no-win situation. You're expected to take all three points, anything less is unacceptable. when a side does win you can merely hear people saying 'they should have won', not actually understanding that sides at the bottom fight, scrap and try to beat you too.

City went to Moss Rose and faced a side keen on not being beaten, They had three cross the back with a couple of wing backs, perhaps a very astute move to combat our width, but also with one eye on our attacking threat. The more they had a the back, the less likely they were to score. I'd tole they don't usually have three centre halves and in the first half, it showed. They looked like a side at the bottom of the table, a little ragged and dare I say lethargic before a ball had been kicked.

This wasn't a case of just beating what was in front of us though, because they might not have been an effective unit but they weren't easy to break down. I confess, when Tom Pett scored I thought we might go on and score a few. It was a good goal, James Wilson on a rare start looked comfortable out wide and swung in the cross which Big John nodded down for Pett to score. He's the 12th different scorer in an Imps shirt this season, 13 if you count own goals.

It was no less than he deserved, Pett has become one of our key players. His work rate is incredible and I like him a bit deeper in the midfield, he covers a lot of round and is very comfortable on the ball. Dare I suggest, he could be the player most suited to fill in the Alex Woodyard role.

I was pleased for James Wilson too. I still rate him hugely, but he's been a victim of circumstance, picking up the injury not long after he started and then finding himself down the pecking order. He also took a lot of stick for not being a right back last season, but I thought he did well this afternoon filling in for Neal Eardley. remember, the last time Eardley missed a league game we lost 4-1 at home.

The first half was very much one-way traffic, with Bruno Andrade looking assured and effective on the flank. He's settling into league football with ease and every week he seems better, more equipped for the challenges he faces. He's a handful too, he can cross, shoot and move the ball forward at his feet. I'm a big fan of wingers, my favourite players have almost all been wide men (Puttnam, Ainsworth, Gain) and there's a new name to be added to the list very soon.

If he gets 25 goals, Akinde might be knocking on the door for the not-so coveted title of my favourite player and just before half time he had an effort saved by O'Hara, a common theme that only developed more in the second period.

After the break it remained relatively one-sided, City pouring forward and on another afternoon it might have been 4-0 going into the final minutes. As mentioned, Kieran O'Hara has had a wonderful game, keeping the score down going into the final stages. His save from McCartan's free kick was good, his save from Anderson's header was sublime and then he saves from Akinde too, all three of which would and could have gone in on another day. He's on loan from Manchester United which is perhaps a nod to his ability, but I have to ask what they're putting in the water at United. Sam Johnstone, Dean Henderson and even O'Hara, all incredible keepers being farmed out on loan, or sold.

I don't think anyone can fault Akinde today. Because he's big and at time a little languid, he takes a lot of stick and there's definitely an element just waiting for him to fail, albeit a small one. He's keeping Rhead out of the team, Rhead is a fan favourite and of course, John cost a lot of money. Put all of that to one side though, he's a good striker who we seem to see the best of away from home. On another afternoon, he gets two or three goals and that was a sharp contrast to the tepid showing he put in last week.

Of course, disaster struck when Macclesfield equalised, a goal from Jamie Grimes who was one of the players I picked out on the Podcast this week. There wasn't a lot wrong with the goal but it was galling to know we'd done everything but score and they managed to do so with what felt like their first shot of the game. That's football though, all the usual clichés can be rolled out about 'it only takes a minute to score' or 'you have to take you chances'. Well, in one moment they took one chance and it looked as though we'd be sharing the points.

I'd had a sneaky look at my phone by this point and knew Newport were being humiliated at home, which gave me an inkling that we'd be top with a draw, but teams that win titles, or get promoted, don't simply accept draws, even when it has been presented in the manner this one was. It would have been easy to shrug and make some half-arsed comment about 'that is football for you', but Lincoln City aren't about that.

The winner came, predictably, from a set piece. Let's not play down the Andrade effect in the goal, his jinxing produced yet another save from O'Hara which, on another day, would have restored our lead. The quality of the young keeper could hardly be faulted and he was rightly named Man of the Match, rightly and prematurely. The second doesn't take away from his overall game, but he did make an error, coming for the ball when he should have stayed put. The result? That deadly centre forward and clinical finisher, Jason Shackell, banged home the winner.

Jason Shackell got Man of the Match, but it could easily have been Andrade or Tom Pett. That isn't to say the other lads didn't play well, all in all I thought it was an assured and decent performance. Okay, we didn't win 6-0 like Yeovil did, but we've got a three-point lead back at the top, we're still top and we've got a good goal difference. You don't get any more points for scoring so many and this was a game in which the win was the most important thing.

We had to bounce back from the Crawley game or, as soon Negative Neds would say, three defeats in four games. We know the Mansfield game was a free hit and the Blackburn was a match against much better opposition, but it was still three defeats in four. Now, we've lost one of eight league games. That is a stat I prefer much, much more.

There's got to be an honourable mention for Shackell and Bostwick. They're fast becoming an iconic Imps' pairing at the back, a mix f experience and power but completely without fear. I had doubts about Shackell, not his ability but whether he could play 90 minutes every week and keep pace. He might be 35 but he's incredibly fit and is showing the rest of League Two's defenders how it is done. As for Bozzy if he ever wants to drink beer out of my fridge, watch my TV and take my car for a spin, he's more than welcome. Hell, I'll even pay for his taxi fare here.

Never get too low when we lose, never get too high when we win, right? There's a long way to go but this afternoon we showed three very important character traits that all good teams have: we bounced back from a loss last week, we fought back into a winning position after a late blow and we got our 12th scorer, further enhancing the fact we have goals from everywhere.

Next week it's the big one, MK Dons at home. I'm delighted we're going into that game with a nice cushion between us and them.

Joan Luque joins Bromley on loan
September 21, 2018

The Imps Spanish attacker Joan Luque has joined National League side Bromley on loan in a short-term switch.

Bromley are 18th in the National League and are managed by former Gillingham midfielder Neil Smith. the move is clearly aimed at getting Luque a run of first team games, in much the same way us borrowing Bernard Mensah and Kellan Gordon is.

Luque has appeared three times this season for City, most notably when he scored our only goal at Ewood Park in the League Cup. His chances have been limited and Danny is now sending him out with a view to getting minutes under his belt.

He joined us from Heybridge Swifts on deadline day, but only came in on a six-month deal and therefore needs a chance to get match fit in order to prove his worth.

"The plan is for him to play some games, he's come into the club and done great, he's a boy with top end quality who can score goals and create goals. But he needs to play, and with the team playing so well his chances have been limited and we want to make sure he has a run of games." Danny told the club's official site.

"In the short term as I say, it's about getting him a run of games. Bromley are a really good club, they have an excellent manager and they know about Joan Luque, they know the type of player he is so we expect him to go there and do really well."

It seems a wise move, I've been really impressed with Luque but he has looked raw and if the rest of the squad are getting games, he needs to keep pace with that. He was one I'd like to see in the Checkatrade Trophy, but he'll get better experience from the hustle and bustle of National League life.

If he impresses at Bromley, then he'll be welcomed back with open arms. It really is all over to him now.

Feet on the ground: Imps 2-1 MK Dons
September 22, 2018

Never too high when we win, never too low when we lose, right Danny? That's the mantra isn't it?

Stop winning in such bloody dramatic circumstances then. How can anyone wearing red and white not come home from that absolutely buzzing. I want to record a podcast right now. I want to talk up our performance, our desire and the size of that result. I want to scream 'champions elect' from a rooftop. However, quite rightly, we must keep our feet on the ground. It is one more game, three more points but nothing has been won and lost.

Is that entirely true though? We haven't won the league this afternoon, but we have won some momentum, we've finally beaten MK Dons at the seventh time of asking and we've taken their unbeaten league record. There's a lot to be said for breaking down barriers, smashing through other team's records and simply ploughing on.

Anyway, whatever the result it was a superb afternoon of football. The big team news was Josh Vickers' return, not entirely expected but still very welcome. Josh is a super keeper, a big presence and a comfortable pair of hands. he commands his box well and although I feel bad for Grant

Smith, Josh is our number one. What is testament to our squad is a player who started the season as number one at Bristol Rovers can't get on our bench.

Other than that is was pretty much business as usual. Freck is still suspended and I suspect Michael O'Connor is the player benefitting from that, with Tom Pett pretty much a staple of the first team. Shay McCartan, a wonderful footballer, got a start and sadly Matt Green is still on the bench. I can't speak highly enough of Matt Green and the depth of our squad, having him on the bench, is incredible. Make no mistake, MK Dons would surely have started with Matt Green today, had he played for them.

I think the depth we've got is unparalleled this season. I dare say at no time in history have we had such a rich and varied squad. I know back in the seventies and eighties we had great teams, teams it would be hard to ever talk down, but have we ever had a squad with a bench packed full of players that would play for 90% of our rivals? I think not. There was some discontent at one point this summer that the squad might not be deep enough, that looks hilarious now, doesn't it?

Anyway, on with the game, we all know what miracles we've achieved on what is a competitive budget, but not one unmatched at this level. I thought we came out of the blocks well, playing nice football on the ground, pressing where needed. It was obvious that our opponents knew their stuff though. As we switched play from one side to the other, their defence moved as if on rails, never leaving a gap. It was no less than I imagined Paul Tisdale would demand, but they still have to come and do it. We saw (you saw, I was laid up with my back) the same in the play off semi final last season. I thought it had 0-0 written all over it.

We had a decent chance in the opening few minutes, but then MK started to nudge their way into the game. They have some very good players and I perhaps shouldn't have been surprised to see Dean Lewington looking as fit and agile as he did twelve years ago. I rarely come out and say this, but I admire him greatly. To play for one team for your entire career is commendable, but to still perform to an acceptable level deep into your thirties is impressive.

Mind you, Jason Shackell is still right up there despite being 34. I watched him closely in the first half and he's such a massive influence in the back four. I think he's what we've needed for a while, not just an organiser and a talker but a leader too. Bozzy is a player who leads by example, powering headers and throwing in tackles, but Shackell brings something different. it's a knowledge, a know-how that maybe Bozzy has, but that Shackell delivers. Together, they're quality and perhaps one might argue a better central defensive pairing than Luke and Raggs were.

The best chance of the first half fell to Mk Dons who proved they weren't here to make up the numbers. A rasping drive from 20 yards looked to be going in, but for an excellent save by Josh. Instantly, you felt calm with him back in the side. That isn't saying Grant Smith didn't make you feel that way, but there's something about Josh Vickers that makes me at ease. When he goes for a cross, he's going to win it. His save justified Danny's decision to put him back in the side.

It wasn't as if we weren't creating chances, but nothing really clear-cut came our way. I'm beginning to think that centre forwards are always going to divide opinion, because I thought Akinde was excellent in the first half. His laying off of the ball was a joy at times and he's clearly done a lot of work with the wide players. Time and again his little flick or his hold up play allowed us to advance and whilst he didn't get a decent effort away, he was a real threat all game, certainly more so than Chucks Aneke.

I thought MK Dons were robust, but on the acceptable side of the word. They definitely came wanting to get stuck in, but Stuart Attwell did superbly well. There were two early incidents, one a foul by MK Dons and another where Eardley smashed the ball with his fist after conceding a free kick. Attwell didn't get a card out for either incident, had he done so we might have seen a shambles of a game. Instead, he pulled out the first card for a cynical trip and booked a couple more before half time, but it never threatened to boil over. If Flitcroft's moaning means we get refs of his quality every week, then thank you very much indeed.

It does amuse me that we get labelled as a dirty side when once again, it was the opposition racking up the bookings. What we are is a dangerous side and one or two of the yellows they collected were for fouls intended purely to stop us going forward. Fair play to MK, it wasn't a case of Mansfield-style thuggery, but a managed approach to discipline.

Usually at this point I say something like; 'we came out far stronger in the second half' or 'the visitors seized the initiative after the break', but the truth was it was just end to end once again. Not in a thrilling, chance after chance way, but in an equally matched teams looking for an opening way. Usually, if you're 0-0 at home the crowd get a bit edgy, but Danny's press conference certainly helped the 8900 or so home fans remain in good voice.

Maybe they could have snatched something on 54 minutes with an Alex Gilbey effort across goal. Perhaps we should have scored from John Akinde's 60th minute header. It was engrossing, absorbing and for a short while. MK made a couple of changes which helped them in the short-term Jason Shackell put in a huge tackle on Aneke just past the hour, before John Akinde had an effort deflected wide two minutes later. It was becoming end to end and it was nail-biting stuff too. I thought one goal might win it and on 64 minutes, a goal came.

Considering the balance of play, the goal itself came from nothing. A big boot over the top caught us out and the sub Healey slotted it home. It felt like a sucker punch, like a blow below the belt. These two teams had played some great football and yet it was a big punt that opened the scoring. It was a goal that, last season certainly, we would have been proud of ourselves.

For a second, just a split second, my heart sank. We'd matched the visitors, perhaps been a shade better, but what lay in store for us? Paul Tisdale's teams are always well organised and in Moore-Taylor they had a player epitomised that desire. They had defended resolutely and in numbers and despite our fans cheering as loud as the visitors, trying to egg on the team, it felt like a pin had been pushed into our hopes. For a split second.

Then I heard the growl of four Rolls Royce Merlin engines, right on cue. The Lancaster Bomber, a symbol of Lincolnshire and of our heritage, provided a fly past. The whole stadium erupted, Yes, we were 1-0 down, but we're Lincoln City, not the Lincoln of old, not the side that go 1-0 down and crumble. This is Danny and Nicky's Lincoln City, this is the new Red Imps that never say die and in one fly past, everything seemed to lift once more. I'm sure the performance would have been the same had it not happened, but as a supporter it was a massive moment. To be honest, it was a little moving.

Akinde immediately volleyed wide, Eardley smashed a drive over the bar and Dean Lewington had to resort to another of those 'clever' fouls to stop Big John surging away once more. It was ten minutes of belief, Lincoln looking for an opening. We saw Matt Green warming up as in the aftermath of Lewington's foul the ball drifted across. Instead of heading for goal, Big John nodded it smartly to Shay McCartan who smashed a goal of real quality into the top corner. I've seen those go all over, high, wide, not very handsome and I think one even landed in my back garden once, but this time it tore into the back of the net. Only one team was ever going to win at that point. Sorry MK Dons, but today you were the supporting role.

They didn't give up though, only a linesman's flag prevented them taking a 2-1 lead and full credit to their management, they didn't time waste or game manage, they wanted the win as much as we did. 20% of the season gone, did Tis think he needed the win? Maybe. They ensured it was a competitive and energetic game right into the final minutes.

Our first booking came on 87 minutes, not long after MK Dons' got their fifth. Strong referees? All for it mate.

Those words, 'final minutes' never used to mean much to Lincoln fans. It was usually the time to get out early, knowing that the game was over. I can't remember how many times BC (before Cowley) I used to sit with my head in my hands, knowing that hope had gone around 82 or 83 minutes. By 85 we'd be going through the motions. Not now though. We don't just play to the final whistle, we seem to gain strength from the closing moments. There's a belief we will pull something out of the bag. Today, Sincil Bank fizzed with belief. It was almost visible, bouncing from fan to fan player to player. Today, we were going to with. It was for Tim Smith, the brave man who led the teams out prior to the game. It was written in the stars, I could hear it on the roar of the Lancaster engines. We were going to win.

And we did.

Those final few minutes saw almost 9000 home fans pushing the ball into the net, or those behind the goal sucking it in. Of course, it needs someone to actually put it home and with what was the first decent set piece of the afternoon, Jason Shackell gave us the win. Textbook Lincoln, a set piece delivery that evaded the grasp of the keeper and ended up in the back of the net. Luke Waterfall did it, Sean Raggett did it, Bozzy has, Wharton has, hell even James Wilson got one that way too. This time it was out captain for the day who lifted the lid on a charged afternoon. 2-1 with virtually the final touch of the game.

Did we deserve it? I think we edged what as a very good and competitive game of football, played in the right spirit by two teams who will almost certainly be involved in the top seven for a majority of the season. I thought to a man we were excellent, there wasn't one who let us down. Akinde was excellent, a little eager towards the end to hang on to the ball but certainly a handful. Shackell and Bozzy were excellent again too and the full backs provided some good support. Tom Pett was hugely influential in the middle of the park and his drive and endeavour kept us going all afternoon, as did that of Shay McCartan. Michael O'Connor was full of hard work and Harry Anderson was a constant threat too. In goal, Josh Vickers did what he had to do when called upon.

I know what you're thinking, there's one player I haven't mentioned. I'm going to end my piece today by talking up the qualities of Bruno Andrade. I may be biased, I'm a fan of wingers, players who get beyond full backs, players who drive at goal whenever they can. I love a trick, a well placed one I mean, not a fanciful and decadent trick, one that has a purpose and end product. I want a player to get me off my arse in anticipation and expectation. That is Bruno Andrade all over. He was my Man of the Match today on an afternoon where six or seven had a decent shout at getting it.

So there we go. We've beaten a very good side 2-1, we've had a spine-tingling afternoon which was a credit to League Two football. It is one win, nothing more and nothing less, but right now, typing this, it feels every bit as good as the day we beat FGR 3-2, or the evening after we beat Torquay 2-1. The difference is we played well throughout the game and I don't think we're anywhere near our best yet.

Frightening really.

The Cult of Football
September 29, 2018

I've been reading Ian Plenderleith's rather excellent book 'The Quiet Fan' recently, a meandering tale through his life as a football fan, but not fanatic.

It's well worth a read despite me almost certainly identifying with the type of character he refers to as only wanting to spend ten minutes a time with in the early sections of the book. I'm an obsessive, one who collects, hoards and spends too much time reminiscing and arguing points long gone, never to be settled.

I am a huge collector, I love old programmes, shirts and badges. I have oddities, such as Jeff Hughes call up letter to Northern Ireland Under 21s, and a copy of a player's contract from the early 1920s. Occasionally, when I have a spare hour and want to immerse myself in Lincoln City, I go through this stuff, reading old programmes, photographing shirts or trying to catalogue what I have. My desire to be in front of a spreadsheet wanes long before my desire to root through my Imps collection.

Fe and I even chuckle because she admits he has no idea what any of it is worth if I had some sort of accident tomorrow. Macabre, maybe. I try to educate her though, because if she thought about selling my Limited Edition play-off final shirt for a tenner, or handing over my St Andrews Stand appeal badge as if it were a £3 special from the club shop, I'd come back to haunt her for the rest of her days.

There's no value to be put on these items, not truthfully. To me, it is priceless, because it all builds the mystique and identity of me as a Lincoln fan. Not to you, not to anyone else at all, to me. I want to have belonged, still belong and, when I do finally pop off upstairs to chill with Butch, Keith and my Grandad Hutchinson, I still want to belong.

It's why I write the books, not for monetary value or anything like that, but because as a kid I was enthralled by Ian and Donald Nannestad's books. They brought to life periods of the Imps' history that had been closed off to me, they strengthen my knowledge and passion for the one common cause I've always believed in and fought for. In putting my own material out there, physical and real, I hope it might surface in twenty or thirty years time, in the hands of an Imps not yet born. I want my name to be associated with the club I love in that way, I always have.

As a kid, I wanted to manage Lincoln, but I knew to do so I'd have to become a player first. I tried that, it didn't work as I didn't like to get hurt, no was I the athletic type. In my late teens the solution arrived in the form of a big red suit and from there, I've been linked to the club I consider to be as much a part of me as my pancreas,

That is why, whilst reading Ian's book, I've been trying to formulate what it is about football that means so much, but manifests itself in different ways with different people. I liken being a football fan to being a tropical fish. There's many different types, some that can't be kept together, some that are better in groups, others alone. There are bottom feeders, breeders and all shapes and sizes but they have one thing in common; they need water to survive. They are all brought together by that condition and I see us as the fish, Lincoln City as the water.

I've spoken at length in the past about my start in life as a City fan and over the years I've experienced a transformation of sorts. I began as the little ginger kid with his Dad at the front of the Railway End, progressing through those awkward teenage years where I turned up hoping to avoid trouble and keep my head down. When I started as Poacher I was approaching 18 and I began to get more vocal, to a point where I became the angry ball of rage that I look upon with bemusement now. I'd call the ref all sorts of names relating to genitalia, I spit vitriol and hate at anyone not in Imps colours and I kept the rose-tinted glasses firmly on my face. Between 1998 and 2009 there wasn't a penalty at the Bank justly given against us. True story.

I recall being asked not to drop the 'C' bomb once, I can't remember who we were playing but they were obviously bad buggers because they weren't in red and white. One of our own asked me not to swear and I did it twice as loud next time. Indignant at being told how to support my club. To a degree, that is my bug bear now.

Over time I've developed a calmer streak at the game. I still want Lincoln to win, despite what I say if they fail to do so I still enjoy my Saturday evening and Sunday a little less. I'll drop the odd profanity, but usually in a positive way, such as 'effing get in', rather than questioning the referee's parents or bluntly assessing the opposition left back's tackle. I save my vocal chords for the podcast, my views stored and formulated over an hour's drive home to be expressed via the keyboard not spat in someone's face.

I've even gone from enjoying eight pints before a game to sipping Coke. Change, but one thing remains constant; I still bloody love the club. As do you, I'm sure, otherwise why would you be reading a football blog? I know I have fans of other clubs follow me, Bury, Birmingham and a host of others and over the years I've learned that these people are not the enemy, they just fervently follow a team local to them. They're like me, some of them more so than many of our own fans and yet I'd still identify with the red and white on match day over anything else.

It is the history, the shared experiences of the people for whom it means something more than a game, a rivalry and a cup run. It's the shirts I've been sorting out this morning, the shared memories of goals, players and seminal moments.

But why? What is it about football that captivates and owns me? I suspect many people have different routes by which they arrived at Sincil Bank and of course, some will feel stronger than others about it, but there's a good hardcore of us that have been going, through thick and thin, for a lifetime. There's too many to mention, but Mandi Slater started out around the same time as me, Sam Wray whom I spoke to for the first time this week has seen as much Lincoln City as anyone. Marcus has always been there, leaning to the left of course but backing up his strong views. There's hundreds more, some I know and many I do not, but we know who we are and each season new people come along, tainted or touched by the Imps' bug in a way that nothing else can.

Is it belonging? Is it that mob mentality, that primal feeling you get from being amongst a thousand like-minded people, all wanting the same thing and all erupting with joy at the same moment, united forever by a shared passion for eleven red and white shirts? I've often asked what is a football club, what is the constant from my first game on that cold October afternoon in 1986 and now? Not the players, not the kit, not the staff and not even the structure of the ground. No, it is the history, the shared experiences of the people for whom it means something more than a game, a rivalry and a cup run. It's the shirts I've been sorting out this morning, the shared memories of goals, players and seminal moments.

There's a great clip on YouTube which features David Mitchell playing the part of a pundit, seemingly ridiculing the beautiful game, poking fun at how it is marketed. He goes on about relentless football, huge matches to see who wins until the next time they meet, the never ending football which nobody really ever wins or loses, going on forever. I'm sure it is meant to parody the futility of being a fan as much as anything. For me, it manages to encapsulate it instead.

That constant is what surely brings people to Lincoln and indeed to clubs across the country. There is no end, there is no definite outcomes. You are never truly the outright winner, or loser. A club's fortunes ebbs and flow, completely independent of your life and the things happening to you. I've often spoken of my battle with anxiety and one thing I always relied on was 3pm on a Saturday, where nothing changed. Sadly when I was at the height of my issues in 2011, I wished it had! Seriously though, the ground is there, the fans are there wanting the same thing I want. They might be completely different to me, they might be sinking pints, banging lines and wearing the clobber, or they might be the retired cynics looking back on their heyday with ever-increasing fondness. They might be the newer fans, attracted by Danny's success or they might be people coming back after leaving, for whatever reason. It doesn't matter, they're there. I'm there. You're there.

It's why I get a bit down when I see people criticising each other for different things. Leaving early, not jumping and singing, banners, fund-raising, opinions on players... all these subjects divide us. The only thing that unites every single one of us is moments like last weekend, when the

Lancaster flew over or when McCartan equalised and of course, Shackell's winner. Those moments are the constants. It is those moments I'll look back on in two or three decades time, fishing out a shirt or a programme that reminds me. Hopefully in 2037, I'll still be writing about it and discussing it.

The point about leaving early was raised on the pod earlier this week and I'm going to end this rather aimless ramble by talking about that and fund-raising. I'm trying to adopt a 'live and let live' policy, something very few people seem to. Wouldn't supporting Lincoln be a better place if you could express an opinion and not be called names for it? Wouldn't it be good if you could leave five minutes early to beat the traffic and not be looked down upon as half a fan? If you missed Shackell's winner last week, more fool you. It doesn't make you less of a fan, it was you who missed out though.

It's the same with fund-raising. I read earlier this week on a rare trip over to Vitals that they had pumped £14k into the club via sponsorship since 2011, a fabulous effort whether you like the site or not. I have no issue with Jules nor the site in general, they do good work and it deserves complimenting. However, further down there was a comment from a poster asking what the other Lincoln content platforms had given the club over the years. That grated my cheese.

I'm sure it wasn't aimed solely at me, but I took exception to it. I've never pretended to run the Stacey West to solely raise money for the club and I would hope after 16 years of Poacher I could be forgiven for thinking I'd pulled my weight when it was needed. I feel a little defensive because I got a DM a couple of hours later, the sender of which I shall not disclose, asking the same question. The truth is, I can't put a figure on it. I will say this though; I believe Vitals gets as many hits in a month as I have between January and August, due to the message board in the main. Everything I get is content driven and the sort of revenue my adverts generate is very, very small compared to theirs. What I have done is put money where I feel it is appropriate, the FPS for instance. I sponsored a hole on the FPA Golf Day, I've given to charities such as Mayflower House in Boston too. I've given proceeds of a book to the club too and supported the academy whenever I could.

I feel it is a shame when people who do try to do positive things are almost forced to show their hand by sceptical individuals hiding behind pseudonyms on message boards. Why could that thread not simply applaud Jules' efforts, which it rightly should? Why can we not accept that others have different opinions to ours, or different ways of supporting the club, be it financially or in the stands? Why is it that there's often competition, a 'we're better than you' mentality when in truth, we all want the same thing. We all want late Jason Shackell winners, we all want three points this afternoon and if you're there brilliant but if you're not, it doesn't make you less of a fan.

The same goes for the collectors, the hoarders and the memorabilia geeks. Just because I have fifty (I counted them today) shirts, doesn't make me any better or worse than someone who wears them until they've got covered in paint and then gets rid. Just because one fan shouts and swears, he's no less or more of a supporter than Ian's quiet fan with his Dad, mates or partner. If I sit in the box, I'm not getting less of an experience than those in Block 7, I'm getting a different one but who is to say yours is better, or mine is better? We're all Imps, that awful saying that got over done couldn't be more true. We all hurt when we lose, we all get the endorphin kick when we win and whatever happens, those of us with Lincoln City in our hearts will all be back next year.

Some of us will be there with a few more shirts and programmes. Some of us will be there wanting to hear Sweet Caroline before the game. Some of us won't. Some of the content platforms will have stuck another four-figure sum into the club, some of won't have earned a four-figure sum to stick in the club. Some of us will be writing articles, day in day out to entertain other Imps fans. Some of you will (hopefully) still be reading them.

But each and every one of us will still love this fucking beautiful game and the club we've chosen to call our own. Live and let live, yeah?

Routine: Cheltenham 0-2 Imps
September 30, 2018

There are wins which lift you off your seat, that stay in the mind for a long while and define seasons.

Those sorts of wins happen once every ten or fifteen games, even for the very best of clubs. I look back to 2006/07 and think of Swindon, Walsall, Barnet and Rochdale. I look at the National League and think Forest Green, Tranmere and of course, Macclesfield. This wasn't one of those wins. This was Wycombe at home in 2006, or Maidstone in 2016. It was the sort of win you need to be a success, functional and enjoyable for those who were there, but not one you'll talk about as a season highlight.

Why? Certainly not because of the way we played. I'm a little late with my analysis for several reasons, one being I wanted to watch the whole game back on iFollow. I couldn't be there this weekend, I'd promised my partner a nice meal out and stuck true to my word. I don't want to come on here and write about games I've not seen, hence the lateness.

No, we played well from start to finish, which was as much as a reflection on us at it is Cheltenham. I quite like the Robins, they're a team I admired in the National League and one with which I've never had any real issue. They've never been unfair and although we've struggled to beat them up until recently, I didn't have cause to dislike them. Listen to their manager's comments last night, I still don't. He was honest, truthful and gave us credit for what we are; a good side.

When you're a good side, games like this are almost expected to be won. Not by Danny and the players of course, they know better, but by us lot. The armchair pundits, bloggers and pod cast presenters. The fans, you expect it too, right? Did anybody truly think we'd go to Cheltenham and lose? That wasn't a lack of respect for our opponents, but was it the sort of game Accrington lost last year, the Champions of the division? No. They won 2-0. The year before, second-placed Plymouth won 2-1. Luton and Portsmouth, both promoted in those seasons, drew here.

If you want to win leagues, you get something at Cheltenham.

Which is exactly what we did with a methodical and confident display which is becoming a regular sight now. The slips against Bury, Crawley and Northampton, poor performance which brought six points from nine, have been forgotten. The early season tinkering which saw us play 4-

3-3, 3-5-2 and 4-4-2, has stopped. Even the rotation has ceased. Ladies and Gentleman; Danny Cowley has found his method. The players are getting on board and it's all clicked into place as we lead the table by three clear points.

There's a couple of talking points to cover and I suppose John Akinde has to be the first. I find it amazing that some fans choose to single him out despite the fact we've won (again), despite the fact were top (still) and despite the fact he's top ten in the division for both goals and assists. Yes, he missed a good chance and granted, his goals from open play haven't flowed as yet, but his all round contribution has been excellent. I know people will say 'we didn't sign an all round contributor, we signed a 20-goal striker', but surely if we're top, leading scorers in the division and he plays every week, he's doing something right?

Isn't he? Or is that just me trying to look on the bright side? I just don't understand how some are calling out a player who has been a key figure in our rise to the top of the table. I know y'all love Matt Rhead but here's the thing: he played for 70% of last season and we never went three points clear at the top. I love Rheady, but he ain't a top of the table League Two striker, week in week out. John Akinde is, the proof is the fact he plays, week in week out, and we're top.

Aside from that, three players have got my pulse racing this season but before I move on to them, I think a special mention has to go to Harry Toffolo. He was excellent yesterday, he wasn't tested at full back by a winger as such, but going forward he is a real handful. He's an attacking defender and has potential to play further up the field, but his link up play with Bruno in particular was excellent. We've seen it already this season, but these routine games against sides who don't want to attack us as much are his bread and butter, because his license to get forward is increased.

Tom Pett gets my praise every week and that carries on today. There's talk of who we drop for Frecks return because the captain will get back into the side, but I can't see it being Pett. He offers something in front of both boxes and gets better every single time I see him play. The latter point goes for Bruno too. He's the sort of player we've not had since Dany N'Guessan or maybe even before him; a winger with pace, trickery and an eye for an effort. Here's a stat you might like. Before yesterday's game I took all of the performance data from ESPN's website, put it into a huge spreadsheet and then worked out a few different ratios for the division, stuff like 'shots on target per goal' or 'shots off target per goal' (I do that sort of stuff with my spare time, it's a symptom of being such an anal fan). Bruno has a better shots on target per game ratio to shots off target than any other Imp, coming in at 0.78 on target and 1.78 off. John Akinde manages 0.78 on target per game, but at the expense of 2.33 off.

Not only can he shoot, but he can create too. He's got a bit of everything and I'm delighted he's an Imp. Bruno Andrade will play in the Championship during his career, there's little doubt in my mind about that. I said it about Sean Raggett and he has, I said it about Woodyard (and he will) and I'll nail my colours to the mast and say it about Bruno too. He scared Cheltenham to death yesterday and that is a common occurrence.

Another player who impressed me yesterday was Shay McCartan. It's easy to say that as he scored one and pressured a defender into doing the same, but he's another who is growing into this team more every week. He's been a great capture and we're seeing what prompted Bradford to pluck him from Accrington a year or two ago. He dealt with provocation well too, there was an elbow off the ball he wasn't happy about but instead of reacting, he forced one goal and scored another. One could argue that is a reaction, the very best type.

It is hard to go too much deeper with yesterday's game because even Michael Duff will admit his side will be well away from us by the end of the season. They're not Grimsby bad, they're not top seven good either. He'll keep building and they'll pick up points but they won't be affecting the top of the table. We will though.

I tipped us up at the beginning of the season and eight wins from ten is the sort of form sides who win divisions show. Here we are, just 10 games in and we've got as many points as Grimsby, Mansfield and Notts County combined. We're packing the best goal difference, the joint best defensive record and we're the second-highest scorers. It could be argued we've played five of the bottom six, albeit four away from home, but when you've hammered the side in third 3-0 at their place there's no using ease of fixtures against us. Our next four games are Tranmere, Crewe, Carlisle and Cambridge, three sides in the bottom half and Carlisle one place above it. Realistic to think we might get ten points from 12?

Danny urges players not to get carried away and I'll end with the same mantra. Never too high when we win, never too low when we lose. I said the same last week and then spent seven days waxing lyrical to everyone I could about how good we were against MK Dons. This weekend we were no worse, we probed, passed and picked until the Cheltenham rear guard fell down. We now face a Tranmere side with as few goals conceded as us and the division's leading scorer leading the charge.

That will be another test, a more significant one to the routine win we bagged this weekend. That much, I guarantee you.

October

Remain focused: Tranmere 1-0 Imps
October 2, 2018

 Football is a game that can delight and infuriate, a game where when you're at the very bottom, small victories seem huge and when you're at the top a defeat can feel worse than it is.

 When you lose to one shot on target in a 90 minute game, despite utterly dominating for the first 45, it can be hard to take. However, take it we must. This evening James Norwood scored a breakaway goal for Tranmere after we had piled on the pressure and had arguably the best half of football, proper football, under Danny Cowley.

 Is that not the game? I that not why we love this sport? That unpredictability, even when we're on the wrong side of it. Today's pain is tomorrow's joy and we feel right now perhaps what MK Dons or Macclesfield felt recently. Okay, we played better than our opponents did on those days, but there's still a feeling of being done over. it's hard to take, but teams lose games. Unless you're Arsenal of 2005 or whenever it was, you lose games. even games you dominate for 45 minutes.

 I wasn't going to do my usual post-match article immediately because I fear I would have the same knee-jerk reaction to that of some fans I'd heard on the radio. I was afraid I'd be too pro-club, too defensive of John Akinde and of Danny's team selection. Then I realised what you come here for is opinion, whatever that may be.

 I'm not going to over-analyse the game. we played far better than we have done at any point this season in a first half we could have scored four in. Tranmere came out in the second half shooting towards their own fans and were better, although they still struggled to provide a serious threat. the one chance they got, they scored. There's a few points to pick up after that, all opinion to which I'm entitled. You're entitled to your opinion as well, much of it revolving around John Akinde I'd guess.

 He's somehow become the punching bag for fans and as soon as we draw a blank, he's on the block waiting for the chop. I admit, John Akinde hasn't scored as many goals in open play as I would like to have seen. His all round contribution has been very good, but he doesn't look on course for 20 goals at present. Last season, Matt Green had a tough spell and everyone wanted him out. Now, Akinde is having a similar tough spell and he too is some people's favourite punch bag.

 I respect opinion, I respect your right to express it and I won't tell you you're wrong outright because that isn't my place. I believe John Akinde brings an awful lot to this football club, I believe if we hadn't signed him then fans would have been angry as to why and I believe he will play a major part in our season. I cannot fathom, for one minute, why there is so much hate being directed towards him. Someone on the radio called Anxious Imp texted in (anxious about what? Being top? Get a grip) with a comment about Akinde. It might have been along the lines of 'all the money we've spent and we don't have a goal scorer in the team'. It may have been another texter with that, but I almost spat my Horlicks down my Super Ted PJ's.

All the money we've spent and we have 13 scorers, we have creativity and guile all over the pitch and the strongest 22-man squad that a Lincoln City side has ever seen. I find it gobsmacking that someone, after hearing us lose a game we should have won, felt moved to criticise the recruitment. They also said that we should have gone for someone like Norwood. What, a petulant boy sent off late on for pure stupidity? A player whose goals have contributed to his side being lower mid table before tonight? Yeah, I'd have loved that. Forget being top, forget the great squad, forget the fact that John Akinde, prior to signing for us, has a better record than Norwood.

Jesus wept.

Then there's the anti-Frecklington brigade, those who are free to express their belief that changing the side tonight and bringing Frecklington in cost us the game. You know the ones, those who forget his goal against Bury, against Notts County and the fact that up until his sending off, he was one of the top players this season. We should have started with O'Connor and Pett, we've lost because Freck started.

Rubbish. In the first half our midfield, Pett and Frecklington, owned that game. Why oh why do we need a scapegoat? Why can't we just look at processes, rather than individuals? Why can't people see the bigger picture and realise we didn't lose because of Akinde, nor Frecklington.

If anything, we didn't score because our set piece delivery was poor, as it has been in recent weeks. It wasn't great against MK Dons either, but that is a process isn't it. there's not easy tweet based around that is there? Best get at Akinde instead.

Or, maybe we didn't get back into the game because we went long to Rheady late on, a tactics doomed to fail because McNulty, for being a big bugger and slower than a tractor, had a great game. He had Rhead in his pocket the minute the Big Man came on. The tactic I would like to see, with my solid FIFA 10 career made and some Football Manager successes behind me, would have been Green for McCartan, keep playing into feet and use pace against McNulty, not power. What do I know though, I haven't put Lincoln City on top of the league, have I?

That is where we fell down a little tonight, I still don't know why we can't see Green and Akinde on at the same time. there's a partnership there I believe will bring the best out of both. I don't think we should drop Shay McCartan for one second, but I would have loved the legs of Green along with Akinde, not Rheady. I love the Big Man, I say it every week, but he is not top of League Two standard and in my eyes he offered very little after he came on. some jester will say he won more headers than Akinde, but to what end? If John had stayed on and we'd kept going into feet I think there was joy to be had.

Opinions. I take Umbridge at some I read but I won't tell you outright they're wrong. I'll let you work it out for yourself. I notice nobody is looking at Bozzy playing Norwood onside for the goal, screaming at him to be dropped for Wharton. You know why? He's a good player who made an error. Nobody pointed to Josh's fumble early in the second half, the moment of sheer horror that almost brought him embarrassment, you know why? He's a good keeper. John Akinde is a good striker, he's not scoring as many as we would have hoped, but without him we wouldn't be where we are now. Fact. before any joker says 'no, we'd be further ahead', we wouldn't.

I'm tired and I'm disappointed and I'm going to bed. The words of Danny Cowley keep going round my head though. Never too high when we win, never too low when we lose. I'd have taken this position at the beginning of the season and if we're still two points clear at Christmas, I'll be happy as well. We will lose games, we'll probably lose them by playing worse than we did tonight. We'll win games by playing worse than we did tonight.

It isn't all about the goals, although if you don't score them, you don't win, but the process was right. On another night I'm writing about a 3-0 win. That's football. It's why we love it and sometimes, it is why we hate it as well.

Just don't blame John Akinde, it isn't all his fault you know.

Four points clear: Imps 1-0 Crewe
October 7, 2018

David Artell said in his post match interview that it would have been hard to tell which team was top and which was 17th going into yesterday's game. In truth, he's right.

I don't want that to sound arrogant or anything, but David Artell is right in a way. For large portions of yesterday's tussle it wasn't easy to pick out the table toppers. We were, for want of a better word, poor. Crewe brought their A game, we brought our C game and two evenly matched teams fought out a very uneventful match up. In the end, none of that matters though because we won and as I've written too much already this season, the only thing that truly counts is the score on 90 minutes.

Lincoln City have won more games than any other side in the Football League. We have the third best goal difference of any side in the Football League too. We lead our division by more points than any side... are you catching my drift? Currently, it could be argued we're the best side in the country at our comparative level.

It's why I find it hard to come on here and write much negativity, but I suppose if I were to analyse the game honestly, that is what I would have to do. The first team was largely unchanged, Tom Pett missed out in favour of Michael O'Connor which of course had the experts up in arms because obviously, Freck should be dropped. John Akinde kept his place too, the same John Akinde who, prior to kick off, had been involved in more goals for Lincoln than any other player for any other team. Still, Matt Green wasn't starting so the two favourite punch bags were on display.

Or two of the first team currently the best in the country at their comparative level. I suppose it depends which way you look at it really.

Moving on from the team selection, it was a thoroughly miserable day in Lincoln and I couldn't help but think that there was an element of the Crawley about the afternoon. It was dull and overcast with few in the fan zone. Five years ago that was the norm, but if the rain stays away the area gets packed. I caught a wry smile from Trevor Swinburne when I went and had a listen to Phil Hubbard doing his pre-match bit to the assembled fans. Usually you can't move in that area but thanks to the British weather, only a few hardy souls caught Phil's words.

On to the game itself, we've been widely criticised on social media for the first half performance and to be fair to Danny, he's even had a bit to say about the first half. We weren't really 'at it' and anyone playing Danny Cowley bingo post match would have heard all the old favourites 'lacking in intensity', 'no purpose to our play' and 'couldn't get our rhythm going'. I don't think it was all down to us playing badly, Crewe were a well organised side from the midfield back. They made sure they doubled up on our wide players, cutting off the triangles that have bamboozled Cheltenham and Tranmere. It made our play look very disjoined, Bruno and Harry struggled to get into the game and as a consequence much of our possession was fruitless.

Shay McCartan struggled to get on the ball with any purpose and John Akinde looked isolated, although I thought he worked hard again. I'm not going into the debate again on here, you have your opinions of John as does everyone. He certainly wasn't the worst Imps players on the pitch.

We had chances, at least one. Harry Anderson came the closest, but Ben Garratt saved smartly. If it had gone in, Crewe's Chris Porter could have had an assist, his header from a free kick setting up Anderson. That was about it for the first half, an uninspiring, tepid performance from a side who looked as though they'd played two away games in the week leading up to the match. That's not an excuse, but it looked tired. Crewe fought well, rarely threatened and only contributed by stopping our flow of play.

On the plus side I thought the centre halves both did well, not quite as well as previous weeks but well enough to make sure Josh Vickers wasn't troubled too much.

In to the second half and the game did improve, not to a point where it could have been classed as entertaining, but enough to prove that the players wanted it. The first ten minutes or so were just more of the same, so Danny tweaked things. Tom Pett came on, Harry Anderson came off and we seemed to go to a 4-3-3, tucking Bruno and McCartan in around Akinde. After all, it hadn't really happened for us from the flanks, so why not try something new?

There was an instant impact and if you want the goal back, which I urge you to do, you'll see Akinde involved twice. Crewe didn't clear their lines after an initial effort and courtesy of a couple of won headers, the ball fell to Pett who rifled an effort at goal. Garratt, who had been in excellent form all afternoon, got a hand to the effort but such was the venom it had been hit with, it trickled over the line. Sincil Bank erupted and the game presented itself for us to take.

That wasn't what happened though. Not long after a stinging Crewe volley called Josh Vickers into action, but the stopper was alert to the danger. They had resorted to having pop shots from 25-yards, failing to find a way through our packed defence. Again, the two centre halves were dominant, allowing us a certain wastefulness up front. That isn't complacency, but we know that we can rely on the back two in most situations, even if I did think Bozzy looked a bit like a dog who had gone for an operation and come back partially shaved and partially shaggy.

The warning was there and as expected the game began to open up a bit. Bruno Andrade had a stinging drive that tested the keeper from nowhere, but Garrard was equal to it. At the other end, Neal Eardley got caught out by a bouncing ball and Charlie Kirk found plenty of space, but his shot was tamer than my Mum's cat. Had that not been the case, it could have been 1-1 but Eardley turned and trotted away as though little of note had happened. Lucky let off.

Bruno had found some space in the latter stages of the game, maybe the Crewe legs tired, maybe the game became stretched as Crewe chased an equaliser some felt they deserved. Either way, he skinned Kevin O'Connor and the 23-year old dragged him to the floor. It was as cynical as they come, but there was no card produced. I guess rookie referee Paul Marsden felt a 2-0 deficit would be punishment enough. Lee Frecklington likes to live dangerously, so he passed a Gareth Southgate-esque penalty at Garrard to set up a tense final few minutes.

City hung on, as much a testament to Crewe's lack of attacking power as to our own play. I'm trying to subtlety say it was one to forget, one where picking a Man of the Match was almost like picking the lesser of thirteen evils. Michael O'Connor got it, fair enough. Tom Pett was nominated by the caller on BBC Radio Lincolnshire by virtue of the goal, which is usually the sponsors method of picking it. Me? I would have plumped for Jason Shackell, purely because him and Bostwick looked the most composed of all our players.

I don't think we were terrible, but make no mistake we weren't good. Crewe did very well, they were robust, organised but they lacked anything up front at all. If they had a striker, maybe Matt Green or John Akinde, they'd be on the fringe of the top ten on that showing. I've heard at times this season they've been excellent, then on the flip side they've also been incredibly poor. Yesterday they were alright.

As for us, as soon as the whistle went I wanted to forget about how we got the three points and concentrate on the elation of seeing a league table with four points separating us and the nearest challengers. It's a nice feeling, not only being safe for the next game no matter what, but knowing that we've been on top for six weeks or so now. We're the team to catch and whilst the top side changes every week in the Championship and looks like doing the same in League One, in League Two we're setting the pace. okay, we lost in midweek when we should have won, but in the main we're winning when we play badly, winning when we play well and all the other times, finding ways to win.

Just imagine when this team clicks properly, when our corners begin to land on player's head again, when the wingers get free rein, when the patterns of play become second nature and of course, when Big John Akinde gets his eye in. If we're four points better than everyone else right now, imagine what we could be like.

That'll get you through until next weekend's trip to Port Vale.

Priorities, priorities
October 9, 2018

Not so long ago I wrote an article where I suggested we ought to focus more on the EFL Trophy than the EFL Cup. For those who get confused about the two, the trophy is the one we won, the Cup is the one Blackburn stuffed us in.

I concluded, correctly, that the financial rewards lie with the EFL Trophy, whereas a League Cup run would cost us unless we got to the quarter-final or so. I wrote that in good faith ahead of our game against Mansfield in the group stages, a game we lost for a couple of reasons. Firstly, Mansfield were bloody awful that night, booting us all over the place and picking up bookings that they wouldn't have risked in the league.

Secondly, they didn't have a game on the following Saturday and played a strong side whereas we didn't and thirdly, we didn't want it. When chasing the game we left Matt Green on the bench and brought on Jamie McCombe. That is why I'm not heading to Scunthorpe tonight because I know, deep down, despite being a born winner and all that, Danny doesn't care about this competition.

He's even said it. I know few of you read the programme these days, but for the likes of me who still cherish the printed product, there's the odd nugget of gold in there. Prior to the Crawley game, Danny wrote: "Our intentions in the competition are different from last year. We will use the competition to learn about our young players while keeping our senior players that have not been in the starting XI match fit and match sharp."

"That doesn't mean that we won't be ultra-competitive and doing all we can once we step over the paint. it is just that our objectives this year are different and consequently so is our planning for these games."

In other words, we ain't going out to win it because we want to be promoted to League One. I know there will be a group of you (Craig Robertson) who will immediately point to us winning it last year as a reason for failing to get promoted. It isn't, but this year we don't just want to scrape in third, do we? We want to win the league and that means making sure our key players are not injured by some over enthusiastic Scunthorpe third-choice left back.

Danny does go on to explain how it isn't an easy decision to make as he wants to win every game, but that there is a bigger picture. Yes there is, the chance to maybe play away at Hull next season or even meet Ipswich in league competition. That's more important than retaining a cup that we've already saved once.. Let some other mugs beat the Under 21 side in the semi final, or at least try to. If they don't the competition loses the last of the integrity we ensured it still retains today.

Is that it? Do we not bother about the FA Cup either? It's clear we weren't too bothered about the League Cup, fielding a second-string against Blackburn and Danny himself essentially says the Trophy is a sideshow, so what of the grandest cup competition of them all?

Don't expect us to step aside in that.

Knowing Danny, there's no way he'll risk the same strategy in the FA Cup as the other two. It is the greatest club competition in the world, forget that Champions League rubbish, the FA Cup is where anyone can make a name for themselves, where real fairy tales are written and where a club's fortunes can change overnight. You want an example? Us. That cup run gave us the money to recruit in January 2017 and become push on through the final straight to win the National League. That readers, is fact.

We won't improve on our cup run of that year, we won't make the quarter-final again because events like that happen once in a lifetime. Just thinking about what we achieved gives me goose bumps as I write this. Stood in silence at Turf Moor as Sean Raggett's header was adjudged to have crossed the line. Literally in tears as Nathan Arnold did it (oh yes he did) in the 90th minute against Ipswich. Even listening to such utter tripe about us needing a replay to beat Altrincham in the first round proper from fans around me in a half-empty Sincil Bank. That run was special and because of that alone, we'll never take that competition lightly.

No, Danny will happily see Kellan Gordon and Adam Crookes run out against Scunthorpe tonight, but I can't see him ever doing the same in the FA Cup, even if we did draw Spennymoor or Dunston UTS (both still in it btw, I've checked). He would still go for broke, not least because the games are on a Saturday and therefore not interrupting with the league schedule.

Tonight is a write off. If you're going, fair enough, but just remember what to expect. It is admirable wanting to cheer the lads on, but having won it once and knowing the club's stance I can't get myself enthused at all. It'll be the same when we play Wolves and as things stand, I'm not going to that game either. It isn't a boycott as such, but if Lincoln City are focused on one competition, then so am I.

None of this is bad news, anyone who thinks we need the revenue from the EFL Trophy or who believes not fielding a strong side is affecting the winning mentality is, in my eyes, wrong. I happy for them to hold that opinion but a part of me is pleased that we're focusing on the league. Yes, I'd like a cup run but knowing that the club is so pointed towards promotion excites me too. Knowing Danny is a winner, someone who is likely to put £300 in one of those teddy grabbing machines at the sea-side just to say he got something, makes me comfortable that the decision hasn't been taken flippantly. This isn't an Evans quoting 'we're concentrating on the league' when his Mansfield side are eighth or ninth. This isn't a post-match excuse after a defeat. This is ambition, beyond the EFL trophy and even the League Cup. It is a club wanting one thing and one thing only, promotion.

Knowing Danny and Nicky, if that is what they really want, what everything is focused on, then the likelihood is that it'll happen. Nobody will give a flying rat's ass about Scunthorpe in the EFL trophy in May if we're crowned champions.

Still in it: Scunthorpe 1-1 Imps (1-3 Pens)
October 10, 2018

I guess last night had it all, an end to end game, a dramatic equaliser after a goal of the season candidates was ruled out incorrectly and finally a penalty shoot out win in which both keeper and players were heroes.

Before we go on I'd like to set the record straight. I'm happy we won, I didn't boycott the game nor did I want us to lose to get it over and done with. I didn't go because I feel we're only interested in staying in the competition if it has minimal impact on our season. That is a message conveyed by Danny in his programme notes of another game.

To message me directly and say 'you're wrong, he brought Akinde on' might make you feel superior and by all means feel free to do so, but I was not wrong. I quoted Danny. I didn't say he wasn't going to try to win the game, I said it had been prioritised. I'm perfectly happy at spending my money on going to port Vale rather than to Scunthorpe. If you chose last night's game over Vale then doubtless you've been thoroughly entertained. I'm glad, paying fans deserve that.

I'm a little upset I wasn't there but it was my choice. I half expected a repeat of Mansfield, a Lincoln team that had a go but ultimately got let down by subs. Maybe Danny's reticence in bringing on the big guns against Flitcroft's hit squad was a result of the challenges being put in, maybe not. The precedent set by that game suggested we wouldn't be taking last night as seriously as perhaps we did later on.

It sounds as though it was a good run out for the lads, Sam Slocombe made some morale boosting saves which is nice. He's not been overly impressive on the field since his arrival and I've been told that isn't reflective of how he is off the pitch, so for Imps fans to see him play well is a big positive. We've got enough scapegoats already.

I'm informed Bruno turned the game, but then I could work that out for myself. He's a top talent and without a doubt one of the best signings of the summer. I haven't seen his goal but again I'm reliably informed it was onside and should have stood. Last season we saw two cracking games against Everton and Notts County, both with super goals in them and I guess last night was a rerun of that. Players feel they have a certain freedom in the EFL Trophy, just ask the Scunthorpe winger Colclough. He got their Man of the Match but hasn't been impressive in their side otherwise.

I'm delighted Ellis got a good run in the side last night and by all means he acquitted himself well. Pett starting suggests to me we'll go O'Connor and Frecklington at the weekend and Harry Anderson obviously impressed with his goal which again, is great. I would have liked to see Matt Green get the goal his all round display deserved, but must offer congratulations to him on the birth of his child too. He didn't look as though his mind was elsewhere but I suspect any goal he did score would have been dedicated to them.

I'm not going to insult you all by writing my usual analysis of the game, I wasn't there, I wouldn't have paid to watch it on iFollow and I realise a majority of you will fail to understand this. It might even lose me a few readers. The honest shout is I felt very bitter coming away from the Mansfield game, I felt we were going to simply hold our hands up and admit we weren't fussed at all. You can't tell the excellent Kellan Gordon it wasn't important, a player who is definitely a winger not a full back, but if Danny had to choose between a win tonight and win Saturday then I know which he'd go for. For that reason, I picked Port Vale.

Sadly, or maybe not sadly, Danny Cowley is a winner and he just can't help himself, can he? When the game went to 1-0, he couldn't bring himself to leave it alone like he did against Mansfield. I wonder if he had sleepless nights about losing a game we should have won? I wonder if perhaps he thought that the scalp of a League One side was too much to resist. The winner in him just couldn't let this competition go, not when the chips were down.

Will I be at Wolves? Maybe, yes. I said previously no but sat at home listening to the game, avoiding the various iFollow streams on principle, I felt like I was missing out. I wont lie, as their penalty hit the scoreboard a part of me wanted to be there, I wanted to have experienced that drama and elation for myself. I wasn't though, I turned my radio off, put another log on the fire and read a book.

Sometimes we make decisions we're glad to have made, other time we would change things if we could. Would I subscribe to iFollow given my time again? Absolutely not. With hindsight, knowing how we went at it last night, would I go to the game? Would I see a Lincoln City victory at the finish of an end to end game of football between two committed sides?

Yes, of course I would. I'm a Lincoln fan. To suggest I'm anything other is lunacy.

It's a Pett and Shackell double as Tom scoops Player of the Month
October 12, 2018

For the second successive month, a Lincoln City player has scooped the PFA Player of the Month award.

Between them, Pett and Shackell shared 49% of the vote, with the industrious midfielder taking 28% and the veteran defender weighing in with 21%. The rest of the field was Sam Surridge (15%), Byron Moore (13%), George Edmundson (12%) and finally Luke Norris on 11%.

Tom Pett is a worthy winner of the award and a player who is growing in stature with every game he plays. At the beginning of the season Imps fans could have been forgiven for overlooking the central midfielder, he played in some of the warm up games that may have been classed as fringe player matches.

Instead, he's used the extra games to build fitness and strength and has given Danny and real selection headache in the centre of the park. In a recent poll on this site, he was the player with the most votes over a three-way question as to our midfield pairing.

What he brings to the side is versatility. He can operate in front of the back four looking forward, or behind the strikers looking backwards. He's devious on the ball, tenacious and creative but retaining possession well. Considering many felt he was coming as a winger, I think he's rewritten his own biography since settling into the middle of the park.

Could there be a more worthy winner than Pett? Even when he was dropped he came on and scored with his first touch, no moods, no dropped head just application and endeavour.

As for Shackell, it is becoming increasingly obvious we pulled of a real coup when we signed him. There's always a fear when you sign a 35-year old that you're not getting the best version of someone. As a Lincoln fan we only have to think of names such as Foley, Hebberd, Phillips or Hamilton to know what can happen when a talented veteran drops down to the basement division. That isn't Jason Shackell at all.

He's keeping Scott Wharton on the bench, no mean feat at all, and he's established himself as one part of a ferocious centre back pairing which has to be as good as 95% of the division above ours, let alone League Two. A successful side are not just a threat going forward, but are also stubborn to break down. I don't think our defence is as drilled as MK Dons for instance, I think we rely as much on hard work as we do natural understanding. Harry Toffolo is an attacking full back and on the left we occasionally look exposed, but Toffolo's hard work and Shackell's reading of the game means we're as tight at the back as anyone.

These awards don't win you any points and doubtless Pett would point to his team mates and say they deserve it as much as him. Having spoken to Tom he is a very humble and grounded player and on a personal level I'm delighted for him. He'll take heart from being recognised by the fans, as will Shackell, but both would swap any accolades they receive as individuals for a place in the top three come May.

With them in our side, we stand a better chance than most, that is for sure.

Cowleys linked with another job – Seriously?
October 12, 2018

I've held my silence on the latest links between Danny and Nicky and a job in the Championship, but as I've been asked a few times to respond I suppose I'd better.

Not going to happen.

There, good enough?

No?

Okay, how about this. Brentford have a set up that means whoever is in charge of the team is not the sole manager. Dean Smith was not Brentford's manager, he was their Head Coach. Yes, he was responsible for tactics and matchday, but not player recruitment. He didn't bring in Thomas Frank, the man tipped to replace him internally. They do things differently at Brentford. Can you imagine Danny Cowley being told that amongst the things he couldn't control was player recruitment?

They have two directors of football, Rasmus Ankersen and Phil Giles, as well as a technical director. Danny and Nicky cover those roles themselves, forging Lincoln City into what they want with the support of the board. Why on earth would they move somewhere that takes away that autonomy?

Here's why they're being linked with a move to Brentford; because we're doing well. Book makers want your money and they see a great opportunity to make some by giving odds on them moving. The news spreads, questions get asked in press conferences and it all begins to snowball. Badly.

The Ipswich job I thought maybe might appeal, but the manner in which that was denied and having seen them around that time as well I became utterly convinced they're here until one of three things happen. 1) They take us to the Championship and realise that is perhaps our ceiling. 2) Their contracts run out and they've completed their self-imposed project. 3) West Ham get hold of their numbers.

It's that simple. The Brentford links are, in my eyes, ludicrous. It's odd saying that, what with them being Championship promotion contenders and us being in League Two, but I believe Danny and Nicky when they talk about Lincoln City, the project, the direction we're heading in and all that. I have no fear at all about Brentford and although it is the job of the press to ask questions, I was actually dismayed to hear it put to Danny yesterday.

The Echo need a few clicks so they run a headline which in my eyes was sensationalist and more shameless than a ten page gallery outlining my first team preferences. Anyone with advertising is competing for clicks, but I won't do it by creating nothing news. I might get a few pictures spread over a few pages, but link our managers with another club when deep down I know there's no base to it at all?

That really isn't the direction I want to take my site it. I respect them more than that and I respect you more than that.

There, that is my final word on this subject.

Super City with Six Appeal – Port Vale 2-6 Imps
October 14, 2018

I said in my preview I fancied us to break a streak yesterday. I thought it might be Vale scoring first and us to win. Instead, rather than break a streak that's lasted a few months, we broke one than has lasted 88 years.

Scoring six away from home is no mean feat and yesterday our club once again surprised us by turning in a comprehensive display that matches the margin of our biggest ever win at Vale Park, a record we set in August. It's our biggest ever league win there, the first time we bagged six away since we won 6-0 at Darlington on January 2nd 1932. Anyone who still harbours a grudge at Vale's failure to beat Barnet on that awful day in May 2011 can probably call it evens now.

I'm going to be doing two articles today, this is the match one, analysis and opinion, but there will be another charting the away day from start to finish later. After all, a 6-2 win away from home dictates a fan experience too I feel. It wasn't just a good day on the field, but a great one away from it.

The early team news startled some people. John Akinde missed out through injury, there was no Michael O'Connor and before the game kicked off we lost Jason Shackell too. That's a pretty big group of players to lose and last season that leaves us looking threadbare, losing players of that calibre. This season it just means able-bodied replacements come in and fill the gaps.

Whilst no footballer would ever wish harm on another, I can't help but feel devout Stoke City fan Matt Rhead would have relished the opportunity to start against the other half of the Potteries derby. Likewise, Scott Wharton has been knocking hard on the door recently and he will have relished a shot at the first team in the absence of Shackell.

I thought the first goal was always going to be important in this game, and whilst the other five added the gloss and shine the game was essentially wrapped up inside three minutes. Had they scored first we would have faced a tense affair, them trying to keep it tight but us looking to pick them apart. I wouldn't be confident they could 'keep it tight' though because their defending was the worst I've seen in a League Two match for an awfully long time.

As it was we got the first goal and as soon as they needed to chase the game it was basically over. That isn't arrogance, it is merely an observation. If they needed to get players forward and come at us then there would be gaps and on a big pitch like Vale Park, with players like Harry Anderson and Bruno Andrade, we had goals in us. I didn't think it would be six of them though.

The warning signs were there with that early corner. Harry was unmarked from Toffolo's delivery and he swept the ball into the area the keeper shouldn't be exposed; the front post. The man on the post, there to defend that exact type of shot, was ineffective. I could use the term woeful time and again to describe the Vale defending but I'll try to find different terms meaning the same thing.

The odd thing is for the next 35 minutes we got a pretty standard League Two game. The officiating was patchy at times, Vale offered a little, not much and we got forward when we could. It was clear they missed Tom Pope, he's the focal point of their attack and without him it looked blunt. Ben Whitfield, the player we have been linked with who joined them from Bournemouth, looked a possible threat but delivery from the back wasn't good enough to pick him out. If they did, our full backs dealt with it easily.

The big talking point of the first half hour came when Lee Frecklington was, in my opinion, assaulted on his way through on goal. He broke through as he likes to, flicked the ball passed the keeper and was unceremoniously taken out. Brett Huxtable, a referee I've been highly critical of in the past, gave nothing. The more I watch the tackle, the worse it looks. However, with perspective, many people felt the same about Matt Rhead's collision with Dean Henderson in the cup final. The difference is that was given as a free kick and Rhead was booked. Scott Brown got away lightly.

It wasn't a red card, the ball had gone and Frecklington wouldn't have caught it, but anywhere else on the field that is a foul. He's made contact late, sent our player flying and it is a 100% stonewall penalty. The fact Freck went off injured highlights the severity of the challenge.

Four minutes later Bruno was felled in the area and again, Huxtable gave nothing. Being at the far end of the pitch my view wasn't great (best get an email off, eh Crewe fans?) but it looked a penalty. However, if it isn't, surely Bruno should be booked for diving? I won't say we were hard done by as they're sometimes given, sometimes not and I don't want to make outlandish comments without seeing it properly.

That led us to the 38th minute and the moment everyone around me said we needed to see; the second goal. When it came, Shay McCartan was the scorer, a wonderful footballer whom I sincerely hope doesn't fancy going back to Bradford in January. His run and finish provided us with the only goal of the eight to come direct from open play, not a set-piece, throw-in or dead ball. Of course it ended the game as a contest but I felt that was the case from minute three.

It looked like being three in the minutes afterwards as we laid siege to their goal, Harry Toffolo looking particularly impressive during that phase of play. McCartan was then pulled down by Legge who was rightly booked as we entered four minutes of injury time. Legge was a player I'd identified as one with experience but he was utterly appalling.

Those frantic few minutes were end to end. Scott Brown saved Bruno's free kick but Vale broke and Josh Vickers saved Luke Hannant's header. If they'd scored that and gone in 2-1 at the break it might have swung the game their way. As it was, the hapless Legge nodded Rhead's flick on into his own net before Huxtable could get the whistle blown to give us an unassailable 3-0 lead at half time.

Watching the third goal back it really is a terrible goal to concede on their part. Legge, a seasoned professional, should have done much better but his supposed clearing headed appeared to be a great back post finish, if only it was at the right end.

They trudged off in their quite fetching 'Escape to Victory' style kits looking like beaten men, perhaps hoping the dressing room floor would open them up and provide a route out of Vale Park. As for City, it seemed job done.

The game was over at 3-0, very rarely is a side going to surrender a 3-0 lead and if they do, it isn't going to be one managed by Danny Cowley. In terms of game management we took a rather different approach in the second half, we passed, probed and look very impressive indeed.

All through the game there was little triangles emerging which had us drooling in the stands. The full backs and wingers swapped the ball with ease, occasionally joined by McCartan or one of the midfielders who would make up the three. Vale were chasing shadows for much of the game and although everyone in the away end would have settled for 3-0, this was going to be much more than just an impressive victory. It was going to be another Rochdale moment, another day that in ten or twenty years you'll be telling your kids 'I was there'. Or 'I watched it at home on iFollow'. Whatever.

If 3-0 was comfortable, 4-0 was a rout, plain and simple. It came from a corner yet again and again it was deplorable defending which allowed Michael Bostwick to stab the ball home from close range. For the 1165 behind the goal it was a dream start, wonderland as someone close to me said. It just seemed that everything we touched was turning into goals.

Vale's back four were bad, but they had decent players elsewhere on the pitch. Ricky Miller came on having endured a torrent of abuse from the Imps' fans as he warmed up and he did very little. Ben Whitfield and Luke Hannant looked decent but there was a lack of solidity to everything they did. 4-0 maybe painted the game as more one-sided than it was, but if you can't get the basics right then sadly it's going to happen against the likes of us.

Besides, they had Huxtable to thank for an inconsistent and one-sided display in the middle of the park. He was quick to give free kicks their way and one of those led to a truly tremendous goal from Tom Conlon. It was the pick of the strikes from the afternoon, evading Vickers in the top left-hand corner of his goal. 4-1, game on?

Not really. We'd already lost Freck for James Wilson, but the centre back who hasn't had the opportunities his ability deserve was playing comfortably in the middle of the park. He looked a natural and despite being patched up our side was coherent and controlled. Mind you, it is easy to be when you're 4-1 up.

Ricky Miller got himself a booking too, he cuts a frustrated and petulant figure at times and that was evident throughout his cameo.

On the hour Wilson eclipsed the former Dover man and got a yellow for a foul on the edge of the area. Similar distance to their first goal, similar position and full marks to the taker, similar quality. This time our pair of safe hands clawed the ball away and with that went any lingering hopes of a Vale comeback.

We closed the game down nicely, began taking a little more time over dead balls, not so it could be construed as negative but just disrupting the flow of the game. We forced corner after corner, every one of them causing complete panic against the lamentable white-shirted defenders. On 64 minutes Scott Wharton made a nice near post run after three deliveries from Bruno and couldn't quite get his effort on target. he wasn't tracked and perhaps one of those centre backs could have heeded the warning.

They didn't and shortly after the live wire Matt Green came on, it was 5-1. Scott Wharton with a near post run and a thumping header. Don't say you weren't warned Vale.

Matt Rhead came off for Ellis Chapman and gave the captain's arm band to Neal Eardley. I wonder when the last time was that we had three different captains on any given match day? That demonstrates the leaders we have in our side. It doesn't matter who has the band around their arm, they're all leading in their own way. Bruno and Harry leading the attacks down the lines, even Vickers watching and bawling from the back. Ellis came on and looked just as competent and comfortable as anyone on the pitch. Why wouldn't he though? He's 17 going on 27 in terms of maturity and he set up Matt Green for a shot at the sixth, only for Scott Brown to make a decent save.

That led to a corner and somewhat predictably by now, the sixth goal. Same as before, whipped corner from Bruno headed in, this time by James Wilson. Mad isn't it? Wilson and Wharton don't get a look in for weeks and both come into the side and score. Selection headache Danny? Lovely.

There was still time for Huxtable to get himself off with a penalty for the home side and the more I watch it the more I have to laugh. If we hadn't been 6-1 up I'd be fuming, not because it was or wasn't a spot kick, but because it looked identical to Bruno's. Not only that, Huxtable didn't hesitate, he puffed himself up even bigger than he is anyway and was beaming as he pointed to the spot. Look Mum, look at me....

Ben Whitfield scored to add no respectability at all to the score line. What I would say is credit to them for continuing to attack and look for something when the game had been long over. If their back four hadn't been so feeble, they might have bagged a point. Maybe.

After the game Danny pointed out that there was lots of excuses his side could have made but 'excuses don't win you points'. No, six goals do. It was a resounding win, one that will have had all the other teams sighing and muttering 'Lincoln won again' as they got back into their dressing rooms. In real terms the win gave us little more than everyone else got, Newport, Exeter and Colchester all bagging three points. What it does give us in a much better goal difference than everyone else, it gives us more goals against Port Vale in two matches than most of the division have managed in all of their away games and it gives us a memory to take away.

Remember though, never too high when we win. It is a step forward, a great result hat sends a message to everyone and gives us confidence, not only in our own ability but in the depth of the squad too. Of the scorers, Harry Anderson wasn't meant to start, James Wilson didn't start and Scott Wharton has struggled for starts.

This was the game where we truly accentuated what is great about this squad, the depth and control we have from those waiting for a chance as well as those doing it every week. It was the game when we finally made the corners pay, one after the other. How many times have we come away from games this season lamenting that delivery? Yesterday was the game we all talk about when leaving a 1-0 win saying 'one day we'll batter a team'. Today we did and I've no doubt that we'll bag five or four against this season.

As for getting six, maybe. Who knows? This side has such professionalism and organisation about it that much depends on the opposition as it does us. We turn up most weeks (Crawley aside), do relatively well, put balls into the box and do our thing. How the opposition handle that dictates whether we win 1-0, 6-2 or draw, or even (on rare occasions) lose. Port Vale didn't handle it at all and yet on the balance of play, I can't see them being in the bottom six come may.

Frightening. Are you watching League One? We're coming for you.

Matt Rhead reflects on Port Vale win and Imps FIFA competition
October 19, 2018

Burly striker Matt Rhead is well on his way to becoming a Lincoln City legend.

Indeed, the billing of Rhead as a legend prompted debate on the recent Stacey West podcast, with my assertion being he is an Imps legend. Winning at Wembley, earning promotion from the National League, getting to an FA Cup quarter-final and remaining at the club from the dark days to the bright ones.

I have, at times, questioned his first team role and the limited approach it gives us now, but there's no questioning his application, impact nor his huge personality. Rhead is a nice guy, always ready to say hello and always open when chatting in an interview.

This week I caught up with him on his day off in Stoke in readiness for the club programme piece against Carlisle. He was, as ever, chatty and upbeat and someone you can have a laugh with as well as chat openly too. We've covered all manner of subjects, his days at home, the long journey and social media trolls. You can read about that in Tuesday's programme.

You can read some of the interview right now though, starting with a reflection of the club's win last weekend. As a Stoke fan, the 6-2 victory over Port Vale delighted Rhead, but he paid tribute to the manager after the squad adapted to lots of late changes.

"That (the win) is testament to the gaffer. Everyone is on the same page, whether they're coming on as sub or starting the game. Look at Harry Anderson, he wasn't in the side before kick off but came into the side and scored straight away. Everyone is heading in the right direction which is only positive for the rest of the season."

With the Imps top of the table, I asked Rhead if their approach changed at all, was there one eye on the points gap or was it simply business as usual.

"Nothing changes. We're just enjoying the run of results, we're playing well and getting results which means we're top of the league. We just go into the Cambridge game, that's our focus and after that we go on to the next one. I think if we keep performing well then, we'll have success this season."

Finally, the boys had been taking part in a FIFA tournament, won by Bruno Andrade. Oddly, Andrade didn't mention it during my chat with him for the Cambridge programme, but Rhead confirmed that he doesn't think any of them are any good anyway. When asked if he'd taken part, he laughed and said;

"No, I'm too old for that! To be fair the boys take their computers on away days when we stop over and have a bit of a competition, but I don't think any of them are any good to be fair. I'll keep away from that, I don't like losing which doesn't help."

If you ever need proof that Rhead is too old for playing FIFA, remember he referred to the consoles as 'computers' Proper old school is our Matt.

Frustrating afternoon at the Bank: Imps 1-1 Cambridge
October 21, 2018

I'm going to have to jump straight into the topic on everyone's lips aren't I? The red card for Ellis Chapman.

I made my feelings very clear in last night's blog and in the main I stand by those comments in general. Yesterday's official was terrible, he typified the lack of consistency and the arrogance being shown by a percentage of lower league referees at the moment. His decisions were clumsy, incorrect and at times baffling. It wasn't just against us either, he denied our visitors what looked to be a clear-cut penalty in what looked like an attempt to 'even things up'.

As it transpires, the popular opinion is he need not have bothered because Ellis Chapman's red card seems to be the right decision.

I'll stand by my initial thought that it isn't a sending off, just. I can't see any way at all it will be rescinded, there's evidence aplenty that it was a studs up challenge. Still photographs have highlighted it as a so-called horror tackle, the slow motion replay suggests so too.

Both can easily make something happening in real-time look far worse than it is. For me, their lad slides in under Ellis' foot as the youngster goes to block the ball. In doing so it appears as though Ellis is coming down with his studs on Gary Deegan. The point to understand is very few players appealed for it and in terms of force, Deegan got up almost immediately. If there had been intent or if the real-time incident had any significant force behind it, then there could have been an injury.

Sadly, for that reason alone, an appeal will not be successful. However, that doesn't change the fact that he made the decision quickly, without consultation and I still do not believe it is a red card. I respect everyone else's right to an opinion, I hope that you afford me the same. My final comment is that the Cambridge bench told Danny they'll help with an appeal, so all the still photographs in the world haven't convinced them it was a malicious or dangerous challenge.

When making your assessment, remember the challenge Matt Rhead made on Dean Henderson, a challenge that looked far worse in slow motion than in real-time. Also, remember the precedent last weekend where Lee Frecklington was taken out, injured and there wasn't even a free kick coming our way.

If these things even themselves out, I feel sorry for Carlisle on Tuesday.

I'll park the decision and the fall out for now. I was so incensed yesterday I genuinely intended to write about the game up until the 21st minute and leave it there. Of course, the cold light of day has calmed me somewhat and there's so much to analyse I'd be taking the easy way out in doing so.

We're under a bit of an injury crisis at the minute, aren't we? No O'Connor, Frecklington or Shackell. Some suggested Akinde was carrying a knock too, hence Matt Rhead starting. I'm not sure that was the case, I think Rhead impressed against Port Vale and retained his place on that basis. Still, to have the three players missing that we do cannot be easy to accommodate. At least last weekend we had Freck, but to have to start with Ellis and Tom Pett wasn't ideal. No disrespect intended to either by that, but it heaped pressure on the two from the off.

Not that it mattered as we tore into Cambridge early doors. The first ten minutes suggested a scintillating game of football. They looked ropey at the back, edgy and nervous, and our goal came from the usual persistence of Bruno Andrade and then a smart header by Rhead. To see the big man with the armband on and scoring stings a bit, it means I have to give more money to charity!! Seriously though, it was a quality cross and goal. I blamed their keeper for being out of position a little, but it was a good finish nonetheless.

Not long after my Dad leant forward and said 'I can't believe this lot behind me, saying already we need a second goal. They're never happy'. Within thirty seconds Cambridge were level, proving that for once, the moaning buggers were spot on. Let's be honest, it wasn't a good goal to concede, their lad seemed to have plenty of time and my own assessment is we weren't screening the back four in the manner we usually do. If Michael O'Connor is on the pitch, they don't score that. I'm not directly having a go at the players who were on the field, but a dedicated defensive midfielder stops the shot coming in or forces a pass rather than a pop.

It reminded me a lot of the Swindon goal last season when we drew 2-2. Olly Banks (I think) hit it after we left their lad with time thirty odd yards from goal. On that occasion the shot was parried by Farms for a tap in, but the Cambridge lad left Josh with no chance at all.

It looked like game on then, but the 21st minute happened and the complexion of the game changed. If you go down to ten on 70 minutes then there's a whole different approach, but we didn't. We had too much football left to play at that point and it meant Danny made changes, changes that haven't been well received by a large portion of the commenters on social media.

Firstly James Wilson came on in the centre of defence with Bozzy pushing into midfield and Harry Anderson sacrificed. It was harsh on Harry, but if you're down to ten against a team with pace in attack like Cambridge, you can't keep your wide players on and leave holes in the middle of the park. We had looked a threat and with that change our chances of winning the match diminished. I don't think we threw in the towel, but at that stage the first intention was not to get beat. A point is better than none and if we average two points per game between now and May we'll win the league. That is fact and you average two points a game by being sensible with changes when you have to be.

That brings us to John Akinde. As soon as we made the first change, the second was inevitable. It doesn't matter than Matt Rhead was playing well, it wasn't about performance, it was about set up. John Akinde was always going to come on, pure and simple. Why? Because he can carry the ball at his feet, chase balls down and generally offer more mobility than Rheady. Did he do that? Yes and no.

I'm not getting into the John Akinde debate again, I'm a little sick of it. There's a section of support wanting to get on his back just as they did with Frecklington at the end of last season and Paul Farman at the start. This anger and desperation to have a scapegoat upsets me a bit. I'll be the first to admit John Akinde didn't appear to have a good game yesterday. Perhaps he was carrying the injury that kept him on the bench, maybe the constant barracking has left him low on confidence. Maybe he heard the so-called fan somewhere up behind me who booed him coming on. I kid you not, I heard one man boo. I accept it was one voice in amongst many, but that in itself made me incandescent with rage. I suppressed it though, by tutting and telling my mate Matt that it wasn't on.

What I will say is that at one point Akinde picked up the ball in the middle of the park, ploughed his way into the area and ended with a cross which resulted in a corner. It wasn't a goal, it wasn't an assist but it was a glimpse of what he can do. He doesn't look confident at present and I just hope he gets the same break as Matt Green got last season.

From there until the end of the half I thought we settled into the game, we always looked like conceding but also offered a threat ourselves. The back two of Wharton and Wilson looked composed, Wharton was a contender for Man of the Match in my eyes. Considering their lack of game time together and the extra man Cambridge had roaming around up front, they defended well.

The game was being lost in the middle of the park, as you'd expect with three of our four central midfielders out of the picture. Tom Pett didn't have a bad game, but struggled against the sheer volume of players he was up against. It seemed as though they had two or three extra at times. That was either down to their excellent organisation, or the fact we remained committed to having numbers back, rather than pushing on. Oddly, our fans were getting angry with their keeper taking his time, when it played into our hands. Ten against eleven (or twelve) always meant a draw would be a decent outcome.

It might not have been, had Bozzy been sharper in front of goal. His could have put us 2-1 up and had that gone in, I think we would have won the game. It sounds obvious, we drew 1-1 so if we'd scored one more of course we would, but I mean had we bagged it the balance of play swings back in our favour, Cambridge have to come at us more and we could always hit something on the break.

After the break they brought on David Amoo and I noticed something about him; he seemed to want to please our fans. He scooped a ball back to Josh Vickers at one point and out fans cheered him, to which he raised a hand in acknowledgement. He's a tricky wide player with a good delivery and he currently plays for a club from which we have a couple of back room staff. January window anyone?

Anyway as the second half went on I felt there was a winner in it somewhere. If Cambridge had a decent striker I think we would have been beaten. Ade Azeez, linked with us once upon a time, looked the part but didn't play the part. He had a swagger, a good physique and looked like he should be a danger, but when the chips were down he didn't have it in him. They applied pressure, making lots of box entries which were all dealt with, eventually. It wasn't concise but it was typical Lincoln City, dogged and resilient.

When we got a chance to break we took it, more often than not through Bruno Andrade. He had to be a contender for our Man of the Match too, he was a constant thorn in their side and was unlucky not to create more. His corners caused some problems, Scott Wharton might have scored from one of them. throughout the game Bruno looked dangerous and if anyone was going to create a chance for us, it would be him.

Lee Collins wasn't up for letting the game take its natural course though, he was shocking for both sets of players. His decisions did seem to favour Cambridge at times, but having denied them a stonewall penalty in the first half it wasn't all one way. He overruled his linesman twice for throw ins, he definitely got a blatant corner wrong and right at the end of the first half he incensed Bozzy to a point where Danny had to come on the pitch and pull him away. In the second half he continued in much the same vein. Something needs to be done, but it won't be. Red card or not for Ellis, Lee Collins is not a consistent, measured or fair referee.

As the game ebbed away, Matt Green came on and we finally got to see that Akinde / Green partnership we've all wanted. I wanted it, I thought they'd play off each other well. I was wrong.

They went for the same ball on two or three occasions, giving us less width and attacking threat than before Matt Green came on. Unbelievable as it may sound, it seems like Danny Cowley, the man who works with them every day, every week, knows them better than you and I, people who see them on a Saturday afternoon. who would ever have thought that?

Towards the end Danny began to get the crowd lifted and the atmosphere went through the roof. To be fair to the visiting fans they tried to add to that too, making it a loud and passionate finish. The sight of Danny and Nicky trying to rev up the crowd was inspiring and it was hard not to get caught up in it, but the on-field action did their motivational efforts an injustice. Whilst we were all off our seats willing the ball into the net, Josh Vickers was taking an age over goal kicks knowing perhaps that a point was a decent result.

That was pretty much it. Despite a late corner delivering a bit of hope we might snatch another unlikely victory, the delivery didn't quite work and we ended up with a point.

I was impressed by Cambridge up to a point. Their midfield won the battle, although having an extra man allowed them time and space to play the ball. They were well organised across the back and I liked George Maris whom we know well anyway. David Amoo added some width in the second period, but they were let down by the lack of a decent striker. I thought their keeper was a clown too, came out far too often and if we'd kept all our players on the pitch I suspect it could have ended up 3-1 purely by virtue of his erratic behaviour. We didn't and that is that.

Tuesday will soon be here and if we can get a victory there it will be back to business as usual. It was a shame to see Newport losing and Exeter drawing, knowing we could have pulled further away, but those two are not going to be our main challengers. Tranmere, Colchester and MK Dons are the ones to watch. Although it will certainly be worth watching which referee we find ourselves lumbered with each week as well, because they're seemingly as important as anything or anyone, red card or no red card.

John Akinde – Whatever your opinion of Big John, you must read this
October 22, 2018

Much of the talk about red cards and the like seems to have eroded the negativity towards John Akinde over the weekend, although I've seen it bubbling away under the surface.

John has become the latest target for the social media experts, the fans who watch a handful of games and can immediately assess a player. I'm not sure why Danny doesn't just appoint 39-year old lorry driver Steve or 54-year old care assistant Tina to the scouting staff because they're clearly much more informed than him, a man who lives and breathes football.

Sarcasm aside, people are entitled to opinions and (regrettably in this instance) I respect that right. However, opinions should be formed on more than 45 minutes against Cambridge or a couple of headers he failed to win in another game. Opinion should be based on fact and in some cases backed up by statistics.

There's a saying about statistics and lies which is relevant when talking about how many times we've beaten Carlisle since 1954. However, performance statistics don't lie, not the sort that football clubs are collating and analysing every day. Think about it, why would clubs bother with GPS vests, performance analysts and the like if they were all pure folly? They wouldn't. They accrue this information and build these statistical overviews because they're relevant.

If only someone could get hold of some in-depth John Akinde stats eh? Maybe compare them to other players? Well, I have. I've not got everyone's, but I do have the John Akinde stats and I can compare them to players in the Championship or Premier League using the website Whoscored.

If you are one of those fans knocking John Akinde, one who sees him on a Saturday and thinks our other forwards are better, you need to read this. Please.

What I would say, before we go into the numbers, is this shouldn't even be a thing. Whilst John hasn't scored recently from open play, we're top of the league and he's been a major part of that. Look at the last ten years or so, remember when we were top of League Two for this long in the past? No? You know why? Didn't happen. yet as soon as it does, we want a scapegoat for not being further ahead.

The reason John came on at the weekend was simple; you can't leave Matt Rhead alone on his own up front after having a man sent off. If you asked the big man he'd tell you pretty much the same thing. Whatever you feel about John Akinde, he's more mobile and will chase lost causes. You couldn't bring Matt Green on because there's little chance of playing long to him if we needed to. John Akinde, despite carrying a knock, was the only choice. He's half Rhead / half Green, better than both in their weaker areas but not quite as good as both in their strong areas, as well as having his own attributes that bring something different to both players.

He's unique in that respect and I guarantee you Cambridge United would have happily taken John Akinde this summer. If they had, they'd not be in the bottom three whether he scored goals or not. Anyway, the rhetoric is all well and good, but you want the numbers, don't you? these figures are correct up to the Cambridge game, but not including.

Shall we start with a few numbers and comparisons? What about dribbles? I appreciate a forward is judged on goals, but that is very one-dimensional If a striker is not scoring, yet he's playing regular and the team are winning, is his all round involvement not important? Of course it is. Therefore dribbles, passes etc are all factors that should be considered.

This season John Akinde has made 151 dribbles in matches he's been involved in. On average per game he makes 9.6 successful dribbles, which is around 65% success rate. The method by which Whoscored collate dribble information doesn't make this comparable, but I'm reliably informed that this success figure is the highest in the side. Remember, Bruno Andrade is the wing wizard whom we all say is good on the ball and yet John Akinde is the joint best in the side according to the stats.

What about passes? He's made 156 short passes in games he's been involved in this season, averaging 15.9 per game with an 83% success rate. Shall we compared that to some bigger players? I'm not saying John Akinde is as good as Billy Sharp here, nor the other players I compare him too, but the point is their impact to their respective sides.

Billy Sharp, talisman of Sheffield United and part of the reason they're looking to the Premier League, makes 14.3 passes per game with a 70.9 success rate. Lewis Grabban, last year's leading Championship scorer, makes 14 per game with an 81% success rate. In fact, only 35 players in the Championship have an 83% pass success rate or higher, midfielders and forwards. When you consider every full match day features around 330 players, that gives an impression of what a good return 83% is.

There's other stats too, Akinde has been involved in a defensive one on one situation 21 times this season, or 2.1 times per game. He's made 18 defensive headers, 1.8 per game and (believe it because this is 100% fact) made 306 offensive headers, averaging 30 per game., Thirty headers. I know that raises a question about us not being long ball, but it also perfectly demonstrates his involvement. His success rate in aerial challenges is 65%, making him successful (on average) 19.5 times in a game. The leading winner of aerial duels in the Championship is Lukas Jutkiewicz with 12.2.

We'll move on to Akinde's shot data too. There's no secret he's struggled for luck in front of goal, there's been a couple of games where his finish has just let him down. He's had 25 shots at goal this season, 2.5 per game. Kemar Roofe has the same shots per game for Leeds. Dwight Gayle has fewer, 2.3 for West Brom. Sadio Mane has 2.3 per game for Liverpool, Romelu Lukaku 2.1 for Manchester United. His touch won't desert him every time, but John Akinde is getting into the positions and finding chances on a regular basis. What is it Danny says? He'd rather have a forward miss ten chances than only get into position for one or two? A player of John's quality, no matter what Tina from the chip shop says, will find his touch. In the mean time, his overall involvement speaks for itself.

You want more? Okay, here's more.

John Akinde has been directly involved in 13 of our 27 goals this season, more than any other player in any other side at this level. He's involved in a Lincoln City goal every 57 minutes. Think about that, every hour of football you've watched, John Akinde has been involved in a Lincoln City goal. That is four more than any other player.

With John Akinde in the team, Lincoln City pick up 2.8 points per game, which would give us a season total of 128.8. Without him in the side we average just one point per game, or 46 over a season. Yes, stats can be made to tell a story, but seriously, 46 is relegation numbers, 128.8 is record numbers. It is a team effort and those figures aren't solely hinging on the impact Akinde alone has, but it's more than coincidence.

You want more? What about key passes? Short passes to and from a team-mate are all well and good, but John Akinde has made 27 key passes this season, 2.7 per game. A key pass is one that leads to a chance for a team-mate. Only five players in the Premier League have a better key pass ratio than that, with the likes of Christian Eriksen and Mo Salah way behind on 1,9 per game. In the Championship only Oliver Norwood has a better key pass average. That is ONE player in the whole second tier making as many key passes for his side as John Akinde makes for Lincoln City.

Jack Grealish, £25m rated at Aston Villa, makes two key passes per game. Samu Saiz, the Leeds United magician, makes 1.9. Eden Hazard is only marginally better on 2.8 per game. I know Akinde isn't as good as these players, but his contribution to Lincoln City is better than their contribution to their sides, bar Hazard, Just.

With him on the pitch, not necessarily directly involved in play but as part of the team, the numbers are impressive. We shoot every 408 seconds, the highest amount of shots with a single player on the field. We create a clear-cut chance every 34 minutes and we score every 48 minutes. Nobody has a better set of figures than that this season. Nobody. Yet he still gets abuse on social media.

Here's perhaps my favourite stat, one that should make people sit back and think for a minute. We're top of the league and in terms of minutes played, John Akinde is one of our key players, our number nine. Without him we would not be where we are right now. That, Ladies and Gentlemen, is almost certain. There's no conjecture, no opinion, no 'but he looks lazy' or 'he missed this chance or that'. It is almost certain.

If we were eighth or ninth I could understand the opinions, within reason. If we weren't scoring or if a lack of goals was letting us down, I could understand it. The numbers don't lie, performance data doesn't tell porkies. These numbers are 100% correct up to the evening of the Cambridge game and although you may doubt that, I'm sure there's someone at the club who would verify it if they were allowed.

Where did I get them? Never you mind. Just know this; John Akinde is not on 'ropey ground', he's not 'on his way out' or whatever rubbish is being spouted right now. Booing him when he comes on, half fit, to fill a lonely role up front is moronic. I'll admit he didn't look fantastic against Cambridge, but it wasn't an easy game to come into and perform, not carrying a knock. He had to plough a lone furrow and it didn't work every time, but even with that data in these figures he would still be the massive influence he's proven to be.

Still, we all need a scapegoat right? Personally, I choose referees after the last two we've had, but for some reason a section of fans think it must be the case of our centre forward who has some incredibly impressive statistics to his name already.

These numbers are 100% correct as of Friday evening and are absolutely reflective of the data collected and used on a daily basis by the club. I guarantee it.

Watergate – Imps 2-2 Carlisle
October 24, 2018

I'm going to start in the unlikeliest of places this morning, because I want to talk about Carlisle United first of all.

There is going to be some mild ranting later on, it turns out a night's sleep doesn't help one bit with the anger, but I don't want that to seem like an excuse, nor a slur on the opponents last night.

I thought Carlisle turned in a professional performance, one that saw them play a striker at centre half and pair him with a defender that made Matt Rhead look like he was malnourished. However, Gerrard and Bennett kept our threat at bay significantly better than a player I've billed as comparable to Sean Raggett and the indomitable Michael Bostwick kept them out.

Not only that, but Carlisle broke quickly, always looked a threat and managed to completely unsettle us and disrupt the rhythm and continuity of our play. Perhaps, had we not given away two goals, we might have been more assured, especially as Andrade had his full back on toast for most of the first half.

I thought their fans deserve a mention for coming all this way on a Tuesday night and I sincerely wish them all the best in all their fixtures from now until May, bar our trip to Brunton Park. I have no issue whatsoever with them. Not one bit.

I especially rated the boy Nadeson up front, lively and energetic and I thought Neil Hair had a tremendous game for them denying two stonewall penalties. Mind you, given everything else we got wrong there's no guarantee we'd have scored them and Hair did deny them one too. They say these things even themselves out over a season and at last count I reckon we're owed three penalties and two red cards. Here's hoping we get Seb 'Homer' Stockbridge at the Bank sometime soon.

That's got Carlisle out of the way, now we'll move on to the goals we conceded shall we. The first one was a mistake by Matt Rhead, granted, but when a striker loses a ball there should be a defence behind him capable of at least trying to intervene, should there not? To watch him run between our two centre backs, neither of them cutting the ball out nor alert to his run, will give me nightmares for ages.

Then their second goal, a simple hoof up field which bounced once and should have been dealt with. Back when I played (badly) for Wragby Under 13s I remembered my Dad telling the defenders a simple mantra that has always stuck with me: if in doubt, kick it out.

I don't know if Wharton was to blame or if Josh has to shoulder some of the criticism but I do know one thing; as they're watching that back in training tomorrow there is going to be red faces and a lot of apologising. Danny has already apologised to the supporters for the quality of defending, not just one the goals but all night. We never got to grips with their attack, they looked threatening whenever they came forward and the one positive to take from the game is we didn't lose.

We did score goals of our own of course, one a great effort by Michael O'Connor who won our Man of the Match. The other has been described by Sky Sports as an intended cross, maybe it was but it brought a howler out of the Carlisle keeper. I felt he had a few in him if we'd challenged him enough, but we didn't.

Lets move on to the other big bit of news shall we, the post-match rant by Danny about the state of the pitch and specifically, the fact we had no water on it. I've never heard Danny quite that angry before but similarly, I've never heard him quite as upset at a referee as I heard on Saturday evening. I get the sense Danny is beginning to get frustrated and I also believe had Rob asked the question of the referee, Danny would have refused to answer because there was no point at all.

Anyway, the water. I don't understand plumbing but I have never heard of their being no water in a stadium. Did that mean the toilets won't flush and the showers won't work? Or do we just draw the water from the pitch from somewhere else? If I want to water my garden I go to the hose pipe, turn on the tap and 'boom' I'm in. Water. Is that not how it works?

I was genuinely shocked at that post-match interview, as were a lot of people. I know Danny Cowley as well as you do and he's not a man to look for excuses, nor to apportion blame when there isn't any, so it leads me to believe someone at the club has messed up, big time. I was also very surprised at Tom Pett then coming out and contradicting his manager, saying it was the same for both teams and they needed to deal with it better. I would pay to be a fly on the wall in tomorrow's video session. Danny, if you're reading this, please can I get an invite?

Anyway, we've got no water, abysmal defending and a decent opposition side, so under usual circumstances we'd lose the game. we didn't, there's a blessing and we're still top, albeit by just three points now. MK Dons are coming good, but had a referee not handed them a lifeline we'd still be four points clear. Still, I'll steer clear of that subject. For now.

Water aside, there was plenty to pick out of the performance that warranted both credit and criticism. I truly believe in the first half we were the better side. They hit us on the break, twice with success but several times with no success, but overall I genuinely believed we were the better side. Bruno Andrade may as well have gift-wrapped his full back and given him away as a Christmas present he owned him so much, and the patterns of play between him and Harry

Toffolo were a joy to watch. I like Harry as an attacking full back, but his defensive attributes still need work.

On the right we got joy too, not as much, but Neal Eardley's injury put paid to that. James Wilson came on and had a decent game, but he's not an out and out right back and you could sense he doesn't have the sort of chemistry with Harry Anderson that Eardley does. Don't take anything away from Wilson though, that is three games now he's played in different positions every time. He's becoming a bit of a versatility man, but he is competent in a couple of roles, rather than outstanding.

We can't moan about injuries at all because Carlisle had a centre forward playing in defence, so us moaning that we had a left-sided centre back covering for another left-sided centre back would be ludicrous. They don't help of course, losing Shackell and Frecklington is a huge blow, both are key players in this side. No matter what anyone says I believe Freck is a huge loss for us in the advanced midfield position.

Case point, whenever the ball fell behind the strikers last night I felt we were second best. I know O'Connor got Man of the Match and he did play well, but often we lacked a challenge on the second ball. That just invites pressure and in years gone by, Alex Woodyard would be the player on the spot. Certainly last night, nobody truly took up the challenge and often we gave away possession from those bounces far too easily, wet pitch or not.

I'm on a roll upsetting people this week, so let's wade straight in on big John shall we. Genuinely, if you think he had a bad game last night I suspect you see things very differently to me. He offered far more running than Rheady did, but instead of playing into his feet we went long. That isn't his game. He's a big unit, yes, but he isn't an out and out target man. He proved that with the surging run that drew arguably the Carlisle keeper's best save of the night and technically, everything about that was perfect. He used his power and strength to get away down the channel, cut inside and put the shot in the right area, where the keeper had a chance of parrying it into the path of someone else.

He challenged his headers, chased what he knew he'd get and should have had a penalty. when we played into feet in the dying embers of the game him and Green worked well together and I can't for the life of me figure out what he did wrong last night that would warrant being picked out as a villain ahead of Wharton, Rhead, Bostwick, or McCartan.

Plus he's barely trained as he currently has a sick child. I'll say no more, I get accused of being an Akinde lover and whilst I'll freely admit he hasn't been as prolific as I imagined, his performance last night doesn't warrant criticism in my opinion. I'm nearly done now because I can feel all sorts of anger rising in me again.

Neil Hair.

There we go, anger levels increase by fifteen percent. I'm sorry to all those who want to protect referees, but he got three huge decisions wrong last night. There was a handball in our area by our defenders which should have given Carlisle a penalty, as there was by one of their lads. On neither occasion did the assistant referee flag, which was a surprise given some of the offside decisions, but the referee was no more than twenty yards from either.

Also, did anyone tell Hair he wasn't meant to get in the way? I counted at least two occasions where we lost possession due to him being right in the way of the ball, one of which led directly to a chance for Carlisle.

Finally, try to have a look at the video of Akinde being fouled below please. All I ask is how that is not a penalty? Put the two handball incidents to bed, that is a foul on a player by the keeper in the area, how is it not a penalty? Has there been a rule change recently? Are keepers allowed to do that now?

There's going to be recriminations after this result, a draw that earned us a point when literally everything conspired against us, including our own inept defending. In my eyes, if you score twice at home you should win, especially if you're top of the table. Watered pitches and bad referees aside, had we not pressed the self-destruct button twice we'd be five points clear right now. Those other factors didn't help and if the pitch had been watered and Neil Hair hadn't bottled the big decisions, we would probably have won the game.

Is that the sort of luck, the sort of point that might pay dividends at the end of the season? I'm not saying it is a good result, far from it, but given everything that happened and the uproar it has caused, let us not lose sight of the fact we didn't lose.

I despise the saying 'we go again', but perhaps right now it is apt. We travel to Colchester knowing we need to pick up a win because if we do, we will have eight points from four games. Just because the draws came at home and the wins away is irrelevant, two points per game gets you promoted. don't ask me to predict the scores though because with variables like watered pitches and erratic officials you just never know what is going to happen.

Don't panic just yet – Colchester 1-0 Imps
October 28, 2018

I always feel less inclined to write about a defeat, not because I believe everything is rosy or I refuse to accept our failings, but because I'm a mardy bugger who doesn't like losing.

I certainly feel that in the event of a defeat, the best thing to do in terms of an article is pause and reflect, rather than be overly reactive. Too many people go to social media immediately berating anyone and everyone once we've lost a game and it would be easy to do the same after yesterday's game.

Then, when you take a step back and reflect, there's a bigger picture which the cruel sting of a defeat often masks. Some people can't see it at all of course. Others don't want to.

I'll be honest, yesterday wasn't good at all. It's the second season in a row we've gone to Colchester and not turned up which is disappointing, especially with such a great set of fans in terms of vocal support. We take 1,000 away and yet sections of the side don't turn up for the game. I'm not going to be reactive and say things like 'unacceptable' or 'not good enough' because it was only a fortnight ago I was on here praising a 6-2 away win at Port Vale.

There's not an awful lot to say about the game is there? Danny, in my eyes, got the team selection right, but even Jason Shackell coming back didn't help out with a sloppy goal we conceded. I do know lots of people want Kellan Gordon given a run out at right back instead of James Wilson and they're entitled to ask for that. What I do know is there's a world of difference between playing Scunthorpe stiffs in the EFL Cup and Colchester in the league.

I'll confess I don't think James Wilson is a great right back, but I do think he's more suited to the role than Gordon. The Derby lad is clearly a winger, an attacking force whom, given the performance from the wide players yesterday, might be getting a chance in the coming weeks. If he does get his first team opportunity, I sincerely hope it is pushing forward so we can see what he's capable of. All the plaudits coming his way from the Scunthorpe game are around making runs forward, but our right back needs more defensive qualities than anything else.

Away from the goal it was just a poor match between two sides who seemed to be doing their best to not win the game. Colchester offered little of the threat I expected, their goal was perhaps a little fortunate and they got all three points which I'm sure they're delighted about, but they played us on one of our worst days. We've seen this performance a few times from City, first half against Crawley, 75 minutes against Bury and the whole match at Northampton. We're not adverse to looking poor and nor is it one man's fault.

You know where this leads me don't you? Big John of course. Immediately after the final whistle social media was flooded with anti-Akinde stuff, calling him everything and anything that people could think of. He had a bad game. No doubt. So did McCartan, Andrade and Anderson, yet why are they not being hammered? Anderson was, up to Akinde arriving, involved in a club record deal albeit for two players, why is he not being questioned as heavily?

The problem I have is I don't feel I can say when John Akinde hasn't played well because I'm afraid of being lumped in with the fans who delight every time he doesn't. I don't get why we have to have a scapegoat and here's a thing; Danny doesn't either. I don't often reveal my conversations with Danny and I will never, ever quote him directly from our personal chats, but he's told me in recent weeks he doesn't get why some of the fans have to identify one player whom they want to call out, all of the time.

What really upsets me is the 'fans' who wait on social media to get their bile in quickly. It happened with Farman last season, some supporters were delighted when Paul dropped a cross or cost us a goal because it vindicated their ridiculous witch hunt. there's an element of that with John, one or two people are actively looking for him to fail. When you do that, you don't see the positive in what he does. Okay, there wasn't much to see yesterday, but that wasn't just Akinde was it? Why wasn't there a call for McCartan to be dropped? He's a forward, he's scored fewer than John Akinde, why isn't he coming in for stick too?

I feel as though our defeats and failing these days are almost always hinging on Akinde, people see both the wins and the losses as a symptom of his performance alone and it isn't fair on the player. I got called out by people for doing a worst XI vote the other week and for constantly berating Drewe Broughton, yet some of the same people who did so are openly having a pop at John every game. He didn't deserve stick against Carlisle, but when he had the run and shot in the second half, people were critical he didn't score, not positive that he'd got on the ball and created our only real chance of the second half. Glass half full, or half empty? Sadly, in the case of John Akinde, some fans will never be convinced.

That said, he was poor yesterday. I won't lie nor do I have rose-tinted glasses on, but he wasn't the worst imp on the pitch. You wouldn't know it though.

I think our only real chance came from the foot of Michael O'Connor didn't it? He scored the goal that caught the eye on Tuesday as well and it's clear what he brings to the side. What he can't do is bridge the gap between midfield and forwards like Lee Frecklington does and in recent weeks Tom Pett hasn't been able to either. For my money, we're missed Freck and we're desperate to get him back in the advanced midfield role.

By the way, having to name him on the bench due to FA rules is utterly ridiculous.

Anyway, lets look at a couple of others who didn't do well yesterday, Anderson and Andrade. The latter has terrorised full backs this season, but not yesterday. Are teams getting wise to their threat? it's be easy to say yes, but Carlisle weren't on Tuesday and Port Vale certainly were not. Some teams do their homework, others do not. Colchester did.

Anyway there's no making excuses, we lost. We lost fair and square against a team who had a game plan and stuck to it. That is as much as we can say, there's not pointing the finger at the referee as (for once) he had a good game. It shows what a difference a professional referee makes and whilst both sides have cause to question the odd decision, his management of the game overall was good.

I came away looking at social media and got incredibly disheartened. Apparently it isn't good enough, we don't have the minerals to sustain a promotion challenge and if we want to go up then there has to be change. Our players are not good enough either and we need a proven striker in the January window.

Thing is I then looked at the table and we're top, two points clear of second, four points clear in the automatic promotion spots and eight clear of eighth. Now, I understand these 'still top' arguments wear thin when we've given up a big lead over MK Dons, but we are still top. People say it is only because teams below us are losing, but that argument is odd. If we're in a division where everyone can beat everyone and we're dropping points the same as everyone but we're still top, doesn't that demonstrate we've done something right?

If we're doing so badly, what must the other sides be thinking too? They've failed to capitalise on our blip, haven't they? We might not have steamed into a bigger lead, but we're still top of the pile. Yes, we were poor yesterday and yes, we could have won Tuesday too, but we didn't and yet we're clinging on courtesy of beating MK Dons at our place. We were good enough that day weren't we?

Apparently, two points from three games is not good enough. I wonder how Accrington fans felt when they lost four on the spin last season? Or won one in seven? Portsmouth, champions in 2017, got two points from their opening three games and at two different points in the season lost three in four. In 2016 Northampton had a spell where they got one point from 12, then picked up just four from 12 at the end of the season but finished on 99 points to win the league.

You might be bored with the history lesson, but in 2015 Burton Albion won the league despite losing eight in twelve in all competitions between September 16th and November 9th. I could go back further but I'm sure you get the picture. Even champions have bad runs.

As for needing a proven goal scorer, there's plenty to say on that. as things stand, we've scored 30 goals, matched only by Colchester who, incidentally, looked poor in front of goal too. The next highest scorers have four fewer than both of us. In that case, do we need a goal scorer or is the current method simply producing goals from all over the pitch, not purely one man?

Also, what is a proven goal scorer? A man who scored 20 goals in three of his last four seasons? If so, that's John Akinde. If not, what is a proven scorer? Leo Fortune-West? Joe Allon? Simon Yeo, who signed for us with no Football League experience?

I'm not pretending there isn't a part of me worrying about where the run might go, but that is as much based on the 2006/07 season as anything. In that campaign we changed from being direct to playing a passing game, caught everyone unawares and then were found out to have no plan B. Is that happening now? I don't think so, I believe there is a plan B or that we can change things.

For now, we're top of the table, still clear of the chasing pack and still setting the pace. We've had defeat in four, dropped points at home as everyone will but it isn't time to write of the manager, the players or our aspirations. To do so is completely ridiculous in every way.

I can't sugar-coat the result yesterday, I won't try to but please, for the love of God, have some perspective. If we don't win at all in the next three or four games then maybe there's cause for concern, but to collect two points from nine when, all things being equal, we could have as easily had six from nine, isn't the end of the world.

November

Daylight Robbery: Imps 2-1 Forest Green Rovers
November 3, 2018

They say luck evens itself out over the course of a season and going into today's game I felt we'd not had much.

Luck, along with hard work, has seen us get on the right side of a win today, but it was by no means comprehensive. However. I am not one to look on the dark side of things. What I do want to do, before I go any further, is mention I believe FGR were denied a stonewall penalty for handball in the second half. These things even out though, right?

Anyway, jumping straight in, the game started at a frenetic pace. Predictably we set up to combat their style of play with a packed central midfield and John Akinde up top on his own. The formation would rely an awful lot on Akinde getting on the end of long balls and the others getting around him. Without any shame we went much longer today than we have been doing because we know that Forest Green usually struggle to deal with it.

In the first few minutes I thought we might run riot, their keeper looked as nervous as any I've seen this season and their centre halves seem unsettled by Akinde. I've waited four paragraphs, but with him scoring the opener I'll mention Big John now; he was excellent today. He clearly frightened the hell out of their defence and he was full of running, chasing the balls he needed to. The goal came from a long punt up field on which he gambled and won.

We saw the 'real' John Akinde today, lively, able to create a chance or two and strong as week old cheese. When his goal went in I just felt huge relief for him and I think many in the ground felt the same. I hope that it sparks a good run for him now, but I don't think he'll do what Matt Green did last season and bang in eight or nine in as many games because we're employing him in a marginally different capacity.

In fairness to Forest Green, they didn't let that upset them and they stuck to their task. They were excellent today, they move the ball around stylishly and with purpose and pace. I can usually pick out one or two players I like from an opponent, but with them it was far more. Joseph Mills was outstanding on the flank, Carl Winchester controlled the midfield, Theo Archibald was a constant threat and whenever they came forward it was with purpose and vigour. It didn't take long for them to get level either.

I haven't had the benefit of a replay so I may be wrong, but I think James Wilson got caught out by a neat ball behind and from there they queued up for a finish. Reece Brown got it, another player who impressed me. I know regular readers of my blog might be surprised to hear me praising FGR but I will always give praise where it is due.

The first 20 minutes or so were incredibly entertaining with two sides approaching the game differently but both getting chances. Harry looked bullish and committed and although he faded, there was a steely determination in him. We had opportunities, not least the smart free kick routine which Bruno might have done better with. It baffles me how we worked it because I watched, looking for the runner and nobody seemed interested, then Bruno sprang up from nowhere. His work rate is phenomenal and he never runs out of energy although on that occasion, the end product was lacking.

Sky Sports have described the game as an 'even contest', but I can't agree with that at all. Yes, we had chances but as the half progressed I believed only one team would score again and they were playing in the Hi-Viz shirts. Our best threats came from Bruno and Harry Toffolo combining on the left flank, or when Lee Frecklington got around Big John.

The last 15 minutes of the second half were nerve-wracking to say the least, they were in the ascendency with a ball hitting the bar and shots flying over. They enjoyed possession, seemingly unchallenged until the edge of the 18-yard at times, plus as the half wore on they were first to the second balls too. We began to get sloppy, one slip from Michael O'Connor had me swearing loudly, not ideal in the directors box with Bob Dorrian behind me, Liam Scully in front of me and the FGR contingent not far away. Mind you, I imagine Bob felt like dropping an 'F' bomb too.

The half time whistle brought respite from their increasing dominance and perhaps came just at the right time. We'd lost our way a little after a great opening twenty, but the truth is whenever the visitors went forward they looked dangerous. Speaking of dangerous, Reece Brown might be a cracking player but his challenge on Jason Shackell was not nice at all, going in at groin level. I would imagine a still photograph might have seen him banned for three games.

Having said that I didn't think the referee was having a bad game, he let things flow and although I didn't agree with all of his decisions, he was right in the main. The early penalty shout for Harry Anderson was a foul, but it was also outside the area.

In the second half I expected much of the same from the visitors and they didn't disappoint, although I wish they had. They moved the ball around wonderfully, at times we chased shadows as they made neat triangles, overlapping runs and positive one twos.

We could have been ahead after just three minutes of the half, Lee Frecklington's wicked volley went just over, but it showed fans a glimpse of what happens when we play football. I know some say we should do it more often, but the game plan was laid out and our lads stuck to it. One chance fired over doesn't prove we're not doing things right, but a final result does.

Michael Bostwick was very good in the first half, but in the second he was utterly dominating. Tahvon Campbell is a very good player, at just 21 he almost matched Bozzy for strength and won a few headers. They say you can't put men against boys but I'd take Campbell here all day long. Still, our main man was back on form, solid as a rock and putting in crucial tackles. I lost count of the times he flew in, safely of course, but with the sort of ferocity that gives forwards nightmares.

They kept playing their football, retaining possession and looking for openings, but what they did not do was threaten from inside the area. For all the nice football, they couldn't find a way past our defence and that, in the main, was down to our centre half pairing. I know Wilson gets some criticism for his performances at right back but when you consider it isn't his natural position, I think he does well. He won't bomb forward like Neal Eardley because he's not that sort of player, but he's steady and reliable.

As the game wore on it became clear if we were going to get anything it was going to come from the left flank, because Bruno was, as always, virtually unplayable. Whilst we praise the two defenders for their contribution, Bruno constantly offered an out ball and seemed to have the beating of his full back too. One slip is all it takes and when we got that break we seized on it.

I'd been talking up Kellan Gordon as a winger and when his number came up I'll confess I was delighted it was on the flank and not at right back. One minute later I was bloody ecstatic. Right place, right time, 2-1.

As they came out hunting the equaliser I felt we got some of our best football in, Akinde was terrifying them, dispossessing players, running at the keeper and being a proper nuisance. It was fitting that he got such a wonderful ovation when he came off, because he had worked his socks off, literally on the back of his calves. I felt today was his moment, his time to get the confidence and kick on. Like Greeny against Port Vale last season, this was the day that he felt the love at home and that we saw what he is all about. I hope it continues because if there's one thing they lacked that we didn't today, it was John Akinde.

Genuinely, if you look at their play, their approach and their style, the only thing missing was the big centre forward bullying and harassing. Campbell played well for them but he wasn't the Akinde figure, the man looking to break the last line of defence and win things he had no right to win. If they had a Big John, it might have been different.

They don't and we won the game, despite the six minutes of stoppages.

The relief around the stadium was evident, not just for John but for us all. The roar that greeted the final whistle was almost as loud as for the goals, such was the pressure that the three points lifted from us. Make no mistake at all, we've beaten a very good side today, not the Forest Green of last year that struggled, not the one form the National League season who lacked character and resilience, but a team who I predict will be top four. They're good.

The fans were excellent too, the noise coming from the Coop was incessant and impressive. I rarely get to watch and listen from the other side of the pitch and I'm glad I've had the chance to do so. There's nothing better than seeing our fans doing what they do, 617 in one corner, right the way across. Maybe it was a different perspective, but I thought the noise levels were the best this season and the reaction to them scoring has to be something the players find positive. Shay McCartan spoke in the programme of the great relationship between fans, players and club and it was brilliant today. You should all be proud of playing your part.

I'm going to pay a slight tribute to Mark Cooper now, much as it sticks in my throat doing so. He doesn't harass the fourth official, he wasn't the bully boy figure I've got him down for with his players either, he was reserved and calm on the bench. I'm not going to go as far as say I have any respect for him, but his team stuck to their principles, they played the game in a good spirit and were worthy adversaries. Let's be honest, we won a game we really shouldn't have done. Anything he says to that effect in his interviews is right, whatever context it appears on social media. I don't like the man, but he's got them playing good football, big budget or not.

This result was huge for us today. If we'd drawn, perhaps what we deserved at best, we would have got three points from 12, the same as winning one and losing three. Draws are no good, ask Mansfield and our opponents todays. It's alright saying 'we've lost fewer games than you', but you don't win titles by not losing, you win titles by winning. That might sound obvious, but fans and pundits go on about being unbeaten, it's no good if you don't win. It's better to win two and lose two than to draw four.

That's why one defeat in four is manageable, but three draws around it would not be. To win today gave us that edge again, that little leg up that I think we need to kick on. It puts the blip behind us and with a cup break, it might allow us to settle and compose ourselves for the winter period. Not for the first time, a game against Forest Green could well be seen as a turning point.

I know we weren't pretty today and it's drawn criticism. I heard a caller on Radio Lincolnshire who baffled me by saying he'd been massively disappointed by the game. How can you be disappointed? We beat Forest Green, one of the best sides in the division and we did it by playing to our strengths, by battling and fighting and showing proper character. People said to me after the game we have to play better if we want to go up, I asked why? If we play like that and win like that every week, we'll go up. I'm not saying we played well, I'm not saying we shouldn't look for improvements, but I am saying the there's a time to be critical and a time to just say 'we won against one of the top teams and we're still on course'.

So I will. We won, against one of the top teams and we're still on course.

Now that's what I call a cup tie: Imps 3-2 Northampton
November 10, 2018

The magic of the FA Cup is still alive and well in Lincolnshire, our hopes of another cup run are too after a scintillating and hotly contested first round victory at Sincil Bank.

If we're going to kick off with a cliché or two, it truly was a game of two halves, with one half showcasing the very best of Lincoln City, whilst the second proved to be a topsy-turvy affair which had enough drama and excitement to fill a whole game on its own. Once the floodlights have powered down and the doors are locked for the night, we're in the second round.

It was far from straightforward, it wasn't always pretty but once again, Danny Cowley's Lincoln City showed resilience and fortitude when it mattered against a very good side. Northampton might be in the bottom half right now, but if they're not top ten at the end of the season I'll be gobsmacked.

I had been vocal prior to the game about how I felt we should treat this as a league match and play our full strength side and so it came to pass. I'd seen plenty of calls for Matt Green to start after his brace in mid-week, but I ask you where? Who do you drop? John Akinde, arguably one of the best players on the park last week? Shay McCartan, a different type of striker who currently fits our system? I feel as bad as anyone for Matt Green, he's a player I've championed since the minute he joined the club. Right now, he's showing great attitude but our first choice pairing is John Akinde and Shay McCartan.

It's testament to how far we've come when a crowd of 6,000 is considered a poor effort and I'm not going to start fan shaming on here. It is a shame we couldn't break 7,000 or more, but with so many games in close proximity it's no surprise we struggled for a gate. Before anyone on social media does think to moan about the numbers, remember today's 'poor' crowd was three times our National League average. Across the country, FA Cup first round weekend shows a down turn in attendances, not just at the Bank.

Those who didn't go, or indeed those who couldn't, missed a cracking first half from City. The football was slick, free-flowing and at times Northampton looked like a side who deserved to be in the bottom half. Their big lump at the back, Aaron Pierre, looked nervy and we probed down both flanks hoping to expose a weakness. The wingers were exceptional, the full backs similarly as effective. Before anyone calls out James Wilson, for a centre half he was once again functional at right back. On the other side, the Toffolo and Andrade combo was brilliant to watch at times.

It was those two who combined wonderfully to open the scoring on 15 minutes, not long after Akinde had fired just wide. A smart exchange of passes set Toffolo free and his cross was inch perfect, right across goal at pace. Harry Anderson still had a job to do, stealing in from the flank to finish emphatically. With John Akinde effectively playing as a lone striker, the wide players have to get in where they can and the goal had an element of our winner against Forest Green. We're dangerous from the flanks, however we manage to work the space and a quality delivery causes problems.

Harry Toffolo is someone I've occasionally thought could do better defensively, it would be harsh to levy that this afternoon as he was exceptional. When he's running at defenders and combing with Bruno it's like we've got two wingers on the field, going back to the days of having an inside left and an outside left. The tactic relies on them working hard tracking back and I'd love to see how many miles the full back ran today, not just around his goal, but all afternoon.

On the other flank Harry had a bit more running to do, but James Wilson turned in a solid display, functional as I believe I've already said. In the middle of the park both Pett and O'Connor were working hard and we should really have scored more.

Shay McCartan was up to his usual tricks, making penetrating runs, one from the left hand side caused the Cobblers all sorts of trouble. Like a blowtorch through ice cream, he found himself right on the edge of the six yard box and needing a smart finish to make it 2-0. His smart effort was low, but forced a great save from David Cornell.

Northampton rarely troubled at the other end, but on a rare foray forward Josh Vickers was forced into a superb stop. His shot stopping is first-rate, 99% of the time and his instinctive fingertip save kept the game at 1-0. As the first half drew to a close that one chance was perhaps all the opposition had to show for their 45 minutes work, whilst in truth we could, and should have been leading by more.

We came out in the second half looking just as dangerous as the first and within five minutes I felt we should have had a penalty. Andrade and McCartan, both looking exceptionally dangerous, combined well. The Irishman moved into the area and appeared to be felled by a Cobblers defender, only for referee Graham Salisbury to wave appeals away. A challenge on Akinde in the first half drew some shouts, I thought it was soft, but from my angle we should have got a chance from 12 yards.

McCartan nearly made it 2-0 minutes later again, looking as lively as ever he linked up excellently with Akinde who was again putting in a solid display as the lone striker. Shay fed off him, rounded the keeper but couldn't slot the ball into the net. City were looking rampant, pushing and probing at will.

The second did come, again Akinde was involved as he knocked down a James Wilson ball for Tom Pett to lash home a wonderful low drive. It was one of those shots that is impossible for a keeper, hard and low with just a slight bend away from his right hand side. As it nestled in the back of the net there was a feeling we'd go on and score four or five, such was our dominance in the game.

That didn't happen though, Keith Curle's side found their feet and showed that the early Josh Vickers save hadn't be a one-off, but a glimpse of what they might be capable of. They grew in stature and got a goal back within three minutes. I praised Josh Vickers for being a great shot stopper 99% of the time, but on 53 minutes we saw the other 1% as a relatively tame effort from Jack Bridge beat him on his right hand post.

That goal fired the visitors up and we began to make sloppy passes and poor choices. Big John drifted out of the game as the Imps became disjointed, but lets not forget this Northampton side had won six of the last seven games. They have been full of confidence and they began to show why. They could have easily levelled on 64 minutes, a looping effort appeared goal bound before Vickers made amends for their goal with a save of genuine world-class quality.

The second half had become a nervy affair, City were in the game but certainly not as confident in possession as the first half. Michael O'Connor was working incredibly hard and both Tom Pett and Shay McCartan could have extended our lead, but at the other end Northampton looked increasingly capable of getting something from the game. Sam Hoskins, a player I rated in the season opener at Sixfields, looked a danger as did Kevin Van Veen.

It was Van Veen who broke Imps' hearts with less than ten minutes on the clock, some weak football from City saw them break down the right flank, Bruno losing his man in a rare lapse of concentration. It was a smart turn and finish from the cross, but from a defensive point of view it was a touch naïve. We'd gone from being 2-0 up to drawing 2-2 in a game we should have put to bed in the first 45 minutes. That's cup football, right?

There should have been nine minutes left for the visitors to hold on for a replay, but somehow we ended up playing for another 18 minutes.

The next ten were uneventful, the board went up for five minutes injury time and many started to make their way towards the exits. Those who did try to beat the traffic missed a typically feisty end to a thrilling game.

Firstly, any notion that Bruno had cost us the second goal was erased by the sort of strike you see once or twice a season, a wonderful rocket that surely claimed to be the pick of the goals. It's rare to see City score three from open play, especially three of such quality, each one possibly better than the last. A great team goal opened the proceedings, a typically Lincoln goal and pile driver finish put us 2-0 up and Andrade then served up the best of the bunch, making it 3-2.

It might have been harsh on Northampton who deserved something from their organised second-half showing, but over 90 minutes the winner was deserved. Just. There was still time for a bit of controversy though, sub Junior Morais got his marching orders although I must confess I wasn't watching what he actually did!!

Oddly, ahead of the game I called it as a 3-2 City win. I felt it would be an open game, both sides knowing they weren't going to lose league points and wanting to give it a go and that led to a good game of football between two committed sides. Keith Curle always builds teams that are organised and work for each other and you can clearly see the improvement from the opening day of the season. They'll be fine under his careful management and we should be proud at having stopped their fine run of form.

Danny wasn't happy with the goals we conceded and I can understand why. As much as I've praised the Cobblers, we shouldn't have let either in. The two efforts that did deserve goals brought wonderful saves from Josh Vickers, but the two we did conceded will doubtless be replayed on Monday morning in the privacy of the training ground. There's always points to develop and us being a bit too easy to break down will be the hot topic, no doubt.

Personally, I think we're missing Neal Eardley, James Wilson is a good professional but he's also a centre back. He's doing very well under the conditions, but he doesn't have the natural inclination to get wide as Neal does. Kellan Gordon is a winger and I'm not going to hear an argument for him to play right back.

Now we enter a two-week break where hopefully Neal Eardley and Lee Frecklington can get back on the grass and some of those who we've been patching up can work towards a recovery.

I wanted to pick a Man of the Match tonight, because I've seen Harry Toffolo mentioned as well as Bruno Andrade, but I thought it should have been Shay McCartan. He was exceptional, beating players with ease and unlucky not to bag a brace. That's harsh on Bozzy and Jason Shackell too, both put in great displays at the back, making it even harder to believe we conceded such soft goals.

We're in the bag for the next round, bring on Monday evening!

Friend or foe? Imps face a two-week break
November 12, 2018

The Imps face a two-week lay off thanks to the international break, with opponents Yeovil (rather loosely) having three internationals and obtaining a cancellation of the weekend's fixture.

Whether the break is a good thing or not is all down to opinion, as it would be easy to argue a case for both. I suspect most footballers would tell you that after a morale boosting win like the one we just had, another game would be a positive. We're on a roll remember, two wins in two matches both against decent opposition.

Make no mistake, our win against Northampton was excellent. We conceded two sloppy goals, but at times in the first half we looked excellent and when you've got the wind in your sails you want those games coming thick and fast. Whilst I'm sure the lads are delighted there's no EFL trophy action to come up and a cup replay wouldn't be welcomed, a League two encounter next Saturday wouldn't be a bad thing.

Then you consider that we're patched up at the moment, with injuries to Neal Eardley and Lee Frecklington ruling them out at the weekend. The injury to Neal is significant, because we don't have a right back in the squad to cover. That is fact, I know some will say it isn't, but Kellan Gordon is a winger who can play right back, James Wilson a centre half who can do the same. It is the only position we don't have adequate cover, although right now with Sam's injury I'd say the same on the left.

Therefore a break to get Neal fit might not be a bad thing, but you have to consider the level of opposition. Yeovil are on their arse at the moment, beaten by National League North side Stockport in the FA Cup and falling down the division like a mafia boss in concrete wellies. With our without Neal Eardley and Lee Frecklington, I suspect we could have bagged three points.

In not playing we are likely to be knocked off the top spot this weekend, with that little blip finally coming home to roost. MK Dons might have been hammered by Grimsby in the FA Cup, but they've got Macclesfield this weekend, as home. They will win that game and take a one-point lead over us at the top of the table. In reality, little will change as we'll have a game in hand and an advantage which comes against Yeovil, but psychologically there will be a big step backwards. We'll be playing catch up, we won't be the team to beat. Whatever you believe went wrong against Carlisle, Cambridge and Colchester, the impact is going to be felt.

The week after we host Mansfield Town and MK Dons travel to Stevenage for a local derby of sorts. Again, the possible implications of our break could be felt. Mansfield have to play three matches in the period we have none, namely the Checkatrade game against Scunthorpe which, lets face it, they won't be too bothered about. I heard some people saying we're not out yet, trust me, we will be. Mansfield might not throw the game but with all the games they have coming up, they'll be fielding a reserve side.

They then host Port Vale on Saturday before a possible replay against Charlton Athletic in the FA Cup before their trip to Sincil Bank. it's very ironic that it has panned out like this, they benefitted from cancellations after both of the Checkatrade games earlier in the season allowing them to play full-strength sides, but now it is their fixture congestion causing them issues.

They could feasibly come into the game against us having played 210 minutes of football in the previous seven days, with us as fresh as a daisy. It is possible they'll pick up knocks, players might be getting tired and that could give us an advantage, but is it really such a big leg up? We faced Forest Green with players patched up and knocked about and won 2-1, so although we will get a slight edge, it isn't the sort of head start that gives us a clear path to victory.

What will be interesting is the clash of styles. Mansfield don't play wingers which interests me, our wide boys will be fresh and rested and that is one area of the field where we'll be hoping to press home the extra fitness levels gained by a fortnight on the training ground. The break also gives Danny and Nicky an extra week to focus on the Stags, to analyse their videos, give players specific roles and find those small margins which win games. It might even give them time to put their finger on exactly why we're conceding so many silly goals at the moment.

There is no definitive answer to whether the two-week break is a good thing or a bad thing but you can guarantee the Mansfield Town camp will spin it one way, possibly MK Dons the other. In the meantime our boys can get on the training ground and look to build on two thrilling, nervy home wins that have put us back on track.

The future's bright, the future's red and white
November 14, 2018

Last night the young Imps despatched South Shields with relative ease in the FA Youth Cup to secure a huge third round tie with West Brom.

It was a great night at Sincil Bank, with several people reporting back to me today. I'm still carrying some germs and had it been a warm summer's night it wouldn't have stopped me attending but what can I say? I'm as soft as warm cheese.

Still, plenty of people had their beady eyes out for the Stacey West and everything fed back to us is good. It seems that there's a real collection of talented boys playing for Lincoln City Academy right now, several of which caught the eye.

Ellis Chapman played and although he had a good game, he wasn't the player most people I've spoken to picked up as Man of the Match. If that doesn't get your pulses racing for the youth we're harbouring, nothing will.

The evening undoubtedly belonged to one lad who has already been in the first team but has yet to make his debut, Jordan Adebayo-Smith. He bagged a hat trick, the difference between losing 2-1 and winning 4-2, but his performance has earned rave reviews from everyone watching. He's been likened to Matt Green by some, others say he's a natural finisher without comparison in the current squad.

With his pace, his eye for goal and his apparent dedication to lost causes, one fan last night told me he was 'as close as I've seen at Lincoln' to Gareth Ainsworth in his prime. That's high praise indeed and his goal scoring exploits certainly suggest he's one to watch.

His pace certainly terrified the opposition and he was as comfortable turning creator as he was finisher. He almost teed up Ellis in the first half, showing an unselfish streak in pulling the ball back. There's no doubt at all you'll be hearing lots more from him.

Tim Akinola caught the eye too, he operated in midfield last night but looked 'commanding and strong' according to one fan. We've been burned with an Akinola before, but this one looks to be on a fast track to the first team. Gianluca Bucci also stood out on the left, he was on a run prior to being fouled in the build up to Adebayo-Smith's second goal just after half time.

Duncan Idehen had given the Imps the lead with a header from a set piece, proving that to a degree, the method is trickling down throughout the club!!

Aside from the positives for the future, the highly competitive nature of the Under 18s proves that the investment at that level of the club is paying off. The players who have been attracted to Lincoln are clearly talented, with 'one of our own' Ellis Chapman right at the head of that queue. Undoubtedly, the current jewel in the crown is Adebayo-Smith, but there's enough quality to suggest that several could emerge, not just the one or two that we know.

One thing is for certain, last night's game and win has put the youth on the map, certainly awoken some elements of the fan base to the great work that has gone in. It could be that South Shields on a cold November night was their equivalent of Oldham at home on a foggy December night.

Both were FA Cup games, both were at home, both were won in stylish manner and both set up big matches in the third round. From hereon in, it is imperative you keep an eye on these boys because they're the Imps' stars of the future. Think Keith's class of '92 all over again.

Lincoln City going soft? That is up to you
November 21, 2018

I've been away for a few days as you may have noticed, but I seem to have come back to a social media storm surrounding our SLO's and the club going soft.

Firstly, thank you to everyone who took the time to stop by on my various social media outlets to wish me happy birthday. So far, being 40 is much the same as being 39.

I wanted to get back on the horse with a short piece about this ridiculous notion that Lincoln City have gone soft, as if we're some sort of poster club for modern football that others are not following. There's a train of thought that suggests we shouldn't be welcoming Mansfield fans to the ground this week, their trip shouldn't be pleasant and on the whole we're some sort of soft touch. There's so much wrong with the argument, I fear a short piece may turn into a long on.

Let's start with the role of Supporter Liaison Officer shall we? It seems to me that Alan and his team have come in for a lot of stick recently, but I do assume those criticising realise that it is a nation wide role? The SLO isn't something dreamed up by the club, it is an FA requirement. Some teams do it better than others, or different to others depending on your viewpoint, but we haven't cooked it up ourselves.

When it comes to the 'supporter experience' I know there are a few doubters. It tends to be fans who cannot accept football is changing. It's been changing ever since the early nineties and it continues to do so. There is an unwillingness (in my opinion) for some to accept that change as well as for some of the newer factions to accept the old guard too. Just because someone likes to have a few beers and chant songs, doesn't make them a hooligan and it is a shame when that accusation gets made. Likewise, the families, disabled supporters and minority groups are permanent fixtures at the club and want a different experience. They shouldn't be excluded and Lincoln City are, in my opinion, doing everything they can to accommodate everyone.

That isn't us being too corporate, it is the changing face of football. A crowd of 9,000 will now not just be 8,500 white males and 100 women and kids. That isn't what the game is developing into, the days of the eighties have gone, for better or for worse.

As for us making Sincil Bank too welcoming for the away fans, surely that is down to those in the stands as much as the club's media? Do you really believe the SLOs and media team would be allowed to do anything other than welcome travelling supporters by the FA? Those who think we're being too soft, what is it you want from the club? You want them to tell Mansfield fans to f*ck off and too not bother coming? To direct them to the home pubs so they get a kicking, or to parking areas that don't exist? You want them to serve cold tea, out of date Mars bars and burned pies? Ok, maybe the last one will be applicable, but they club cannot, under any circumstances, treat visiting fans with contempt. We'd get hammered by the FA.

I was at the front of the queue moaning about Forest Green last season, keeping our fans out in the rain and I believe that a club has a responsibility to treat away fans with a degree of dignity and respect, whether you like it or not. When I go away I expect certain standards and I know full well our supporters do too. When we don't get those standards (Barnet and Stevenage spring to mind) then people kick off, fighting and arguing. I've been to many grounds in the last twelve months and aside from the two mentioned I have found helpful stewards, decent facilities and value for money. I expect it, so do you and don't pretend otherwise. If you went to a ground and were forced to sit in the rain, were dealt with by rude, heavy-handed stewards and denied basic facilities, you'd kick off. I know I would. The hosting club, be it Lincoln, Mansfield or Forest Green, have to provide a proper welcome. If they don't, you can complain. Look at Crewe, they complained for absolutely nothing at all.

Remember Wycombe on the opening day of last season? The huge fan zone serving beer for us? What a great day that was. Are the fans moaning about us being too welcoming suggesting we shouldn't have been afforded that courtesy? Because I'm damn sure that some of the names I've seen complaining were enjoying a pint or two that day.

In saying we've gone soft, have you considered last time we were in the Football League there was no strict control over social media because in the main, clubs didn't have active accounts on Twitter? The use of sites such as Twitter is something that sprung up in our absence, as are SLOs and as such I fail to see what parallels those complaining on social media are drawing? I believe wholeheartedly that had we had social media in the days of Keith, Colin and Graham the message to opposing fans would have been exactly the same. We haven't particularly changed our approach in welcoming visiting supporters, but the methods by which the message is delivered have certainly varied.

You see, it isn't up to the club to make Sincil Bank imposing and unwelcoming, it is up to you. The club are expected, by the FA, to welcome away fans as guests. Ok, granted the social media welcome occasionally makes it sound like we're bringing family friends into the fold and that is a bit far, but in the main the club are doing exactly what is expected of them by the powers that be.

In the eighties it became common place for programmes to have write ups welcoming the visitors and since then it has been the norm, whether that be managers, officials or Alan on the pitch. That hasn't changed, the manner in which the welcome is delivered has gone from printed to social media, but we have done it for years. I have a pile of programmes to the side of me, Keith and Rob Bradley welcome Doncaster in the top one. Peter Daniel welcomes Aldershot and John Schofield welcomes Walsall. In 1967 our programme for the match with Workington opens by offering a 'hearty welcome' to all visiting officials and fans. It is nothing new.

If we want Sincil Bank to be intimidating then don't expect the club to break FA protocol, instead you make the noise. You make it intimidating. Gilbert Blades didn't spray 'this is your last chance to run' on the stand in the eighties did he? No, the fans did. The club don't pipe the songs in through the speakers, you sing them. As a modern football club, Lincoln City will welcome visiting supporters, but the noise and vitriol from our own fans is what makes it a proper fortress, not Alan ignoring them on the mic. We have 8,500 dedicated home fans almost every single week and any advantage we are to glean will come from them, from you and I, not from social media.

Don't get me wrong, I think modern football has lost a certain edge, whether that is a bad thing or not is down to perception, but games in the eighties are very different to today. For instance, we get more fans than we did at the end of the eighties and through the nineties, we're treated like human beings with no cages or heavy police presence. Is that a bad thing?

Do I hope Mansfield fans come here and feel welcome? Not especially, but I wouldn't want it to be because our club were being petty, I want it to be the noise from our fans, the people who create a derby atmosphere and make the cauldron of Sincil Bank what it is. Then I want it to be because Danny and the lads hand out a proper hammering.

There seems to be a distrust of some of the different groups at the moment, be it the SLOs, the Supporters Board, even the 617 in some quarters. Every fan has a different approach to supporting the club, a different experience they want to have. Some feel they want to be a part of a group such as LISA, others want to come to the ground at 2.45pm after having beers with their mates on the High Street. Some want to help shape the experience from within the club and have a voice, others want to help their fellow supporters enjoy the games. Some want to organise banners and displays, others want to hire boxes and sip wine during the match. None of those groups are wrong or right, but they have as much of a right to do their thing as any of the others. Quite why one camp feels the need to dig and probe at the other is beyond me, especially when they rarely tread on each others toes.

You want to needle someone, criticise and nibble away? Do it to the opposition fans, make Sincil Bank intimidating yourself. Don't expect the club to stray from the guidelines but once you get into the ground the atmosphere is up to you. Banners, songs, bouncing and noise. That is what makes or breaks a derby, not a tweet from the club's SLO or Alan ignoring fans on the mic.

Incidentally, in 2011/12 Alan and I were told by the club NOT to welcome away fans to the Bank during a game to make it more intimidating. Did it work? Of course not. Why? Because we had less than 2,000 home fans in the stadium and the 15 or so that travelled from Bath City deserved a mention for their dedication. If you don't like Alan welcoming their supporters, chant over the top of them when he does so. The power lies with you, the Lincoln City fans.

A taste of our own medicine: Imps 1-1 Mansfield
November 25, 2018

Football is a cruel mistress. When the board went up yesterday for an inexplicable five minutes of stoppage time, I felt I'd be enjoying my protracted 40th birthday celebrations with a fine Imps win followed by a vodka chaser. Or six.

That late Jacob Mellis strike knocked the wind out of our sails and the feeling walking away from the ground was one of deflation. We'd thrown away three points, or that is how it felt. In the ground, the vociferous cheers from Mansfield supporters made me wonder if they'd perhaps won some silverware I hadn't been aware of.

Such is football, the visiting side had the elation of the late goal inside them, we had a feeling of defeat, despite the draw. It is only with the passing of time and a Stevenage win that things become clear. In truth, we had more to celebrate than David Flitcroft's side as we remained five points ahead of them. I said it before the game and I'll stand by it now; a draw was a decent result for us. it wasn't the preferable result, of course I wanted us to win, anyone suggesting otherwise is deluded, but I called a 1-1 draw and I'm happy with it. Ben Kennedy's goal helped of course.

Anyway, before all the late drama and inevitable shenanigans at the final whistle, there was a football match, a local derby / rivalry / whatever. It's the first time this season we've seen the ground with a decent away following in one end, with the pre-match atmosphere ramped right up. I was pleasantly surprised to find the High Street very low on police in the morning, Wetherspoons had a few dubious looking characters in it, but the boys in blue had a low-key presence. There's no need to antagonise the atmosphere with lots of visible police, but they were there, in the background. From what I've heard there was no trouble either, happy to be corrected of course. Last year I recall some clashes after the game, but hopefully things passed off peacefully yesterday.

There was little surprise in the team selection, Neal Eardley coming back was a big boost and it was pretty much business as usual in the starting XI. It's sad to see Freck still struggling, but in Tom Pett we have a more than adequate deputy.

I felt the first half was a huge anti-climax. There had been lots of build up, lots of talk about the size of the game and how the teams were evenly matched, plenty of tactical analysis and speculation but what we got was 45 minutes of football few will remember with any fondness. That isn't to say either side were playing badly, but we definitely cancelled each other out and my thought was that the visitors were the only side who would score.

We had a chance or two, Bruno looked to catch Bobby Olejnik out of his goal but scooped a decent effort wide, but credit to John Akinde who harassed the keeper into slicing in to Bruno. At the other end Josh Vickers made a decent save too, but there's not a fan on either side who will be petitioning the club for a highlights package from the first 45 minutes.

I felt John Akinde was having a good half and Chris from Running Imp agreed. He's not sold on big John as I am, so to hear him say he'd played well means he must have. I know there was the inevitable negative feedback on social media for him after the game, but in my opinion it is unwarranted. I did see a post claiming he's not scoring enough for a lone striker, but his role isn't simply front man getting on the end of things. He's working hard to get the ball, then make things happen. He looked isolated, but is that his fault? No.

I thought Tom Pett had a strong first half too, both Bozzy and Shackell at the back looked as solid as ever. I'd been worried about Tyler Walker before the game and threatened with the pace of CJ Hamilton on the radio, but I thought both were thoroughly underwhelming. If I had to praise the visitors, which I do, I'd say their back three are as good as any defence we've seen this season, MK Dons included. I also liked Neil Bishop in the middle of the park, he was commanding, hard-working and showed his experience whenever he got on the ball.

There was some criticism of the referee and before I go any further I'd like to clarify; a retweet on Twitter is not an endorsement from me. My podcast colleague Ben felt the ref was having a poor game and I retweeted it for comment, not because I necessarily agreed, so the Mansfield fan who DM'd me might like to rethink his words. I didn't think Gavin Ward was having a brilliant game, but given the magnitude of the occasion and the commitment from both sides, he was keeping a lid on things. I heard plenty of comment about how things could explode on the pitch, but he did a good job keeping everyone in check. There will always be the odd decision we criticise or disagree with, that's football. He got nothing major wrong for me, he rightly admonished Danny for his touchline antics but he did seem to have a rapport with the players. I saw him sharing a joke with Neal Eardley at one point, a sign of a calm and approachable referee.

The D3D4 podcast guys had come to the game and they felt it was a committed first half between two good sides. I felt it was tepid at best, even in the stands. The early efforts of our boys to get the atmosphere ramped up seemed to die away with the pace of the game and the Stags fans, from where I was sitting, were on some sort of silence vow. I feel that a big away following can be more important than three or four times as many home fans, 1,600 all pumped up and signing is often better than 1,000 or so vocal home fans and the other 7,000 joining in occasionally. Not yesterday, not in the first half.

I feared for the second half, I'd seen little to suggest we'd win the game and plenty that made me wonder if they might. I commented that something had to change, even if it was just the ferocity with which we went at the Stags. From minute one of the second half, it did.

I'm not going to claim we tore them to shreds, it would be inaccurate, but we started to make our mark on the game. The wide men got into proceedings more and as we stretched their midfield opportunities began to present themselves, albeit half-chances and openings. I've seen this morning Harry Anderson got a lot of stick yesterday, even he has tweeted to say sorry, but at one stage I suggested he might be a potential Man of the Match! I got that his end product wasn't the best, but until he tired he gave a good account of himself.

I'm genuinely surprised at the clamour to offer negative opinion after a game. Look, I'm all for opinion and I know mine will differ to yours sometimes, but there does seem to be a mentality that after any game we look for the negatives, not the positive. I'm not telling anyone they can't offer critique, but I would like to know why some are so keen to do that and never give praise when it is due? Why, when we've got a decent point against a top side in the division, are we instantly texting into BBC Radio Lincolnshire to say Harry Anderson was shit? What about praising O'Connor or Pett, Bozzy or Shackell? Why must analysis always, always focus on the negative. It truly galls me.

On the other flank, Bruno was causing his usual menace and Harry Toffolo put in another good performance too. I had feared we might get done from that flank and although their equaliser came from their right hand side, overall the two players linked well. If we're going to be promoted, Bruno Andrade is sure to be a deciding factor. He's got a bit of everything, a trick, a cross, pace and belief he can strip a full back.

As the game wore on I felt we were going to settle for a point, but the atmosphere truly developed as the game wore on. The visiting fans found their voice (no doubt read my tweet), plus our own support were driven passionately too. It felt like a completely different game to the first half, a flying Lincoln City desperate to grab a win, with the Stags keen to eat up time and hold on for a point.

There was the free kick excellent saved by Olejnik, John Akinde brought a long ball from Bozzy down superbly and was eventually thwarted by two defenders and the keeper and Bruno Andrade jinxed into the area only for his effort to be saved. Chances, not clear-cut but all that might have led to something. Anything.

The changes did make a difference, but again I've seen criticism for them being made too late. There's little point in bringing devastating pace from the bench after 50 minutes because the players we're looking to expose won't be tired. Isn't our habit of scoring late goals testament to the fact we get those changes right, not wrong? When Rhead came on the defence were so tired he even went on a run with the ball! I know that it isn't easy for Matt Green to make an impression in ten second half minutes, but to make changes on the hour when, in the main, our game plan is working would be baffling.

I do agree that Kellan Gordon needs more game time and if that comes at the expense of Harry it only underlines our strength and depth. I've said all along Gordon isn't a right back and that is evident whenever he comes on. I don't buy the argument he played well their against Scunthorpe reserves either. League action is different and I know a right winger when I see one. Gordon injected fresh pace and endeavour on the right and along with Green and Rhead gave Mansfield a different problem to solve.

They failed.

Gordon took his goal well but if you watch it back, all the subs were involved. Fresh legs, late on, working their magic. Who is to say if they'd come on ten minutes earlier they would have been able to cause the same trouble? Who is right, the manager who made the switch that brought the goal, or the fan who just thinks if it had happened earlier we would have got two? My money is on the man in the dugout.

I made reference to five minutes injury time which I thought was a little over the top, but Jacob Mellis only needed three to bring the visitors level. Danny believes the ball was well out before Danny Rose kept things alive, I couldn't comment and the video I've seen of it is inconclusive. If it was we could have a bit of a moan, but on the whole the officials did well and that sort of decision will, hopefully, even itself out. It isn't a blatant handball like the Carlisle game, nor a foul on an advancing players like at Port Vale or (again) Carlisle. It's contentious, sure, but it's not blatant and in those circumstances you get some and not others.

It hurt though. A win would have been just the thing to give us a kick going into the festive period, but seeing the visitors celebrating so passionately was a real kick in the love eggs. Our joy turned to desolation, not at losing the game, but at failing to secure the win. That said, how many times have we done the same to others? How many times have visiting fans sat in the Stacey West and watched 8,000 Imps celebrate a last-gasp winner, deserved or not? MK Dons and Northampton spring to mind, but Bury fans will have felt the pain too, even if it wasn't late. That is football.

The little bit of argy bargy at the end wasn't needed. I think the Mansfield bench celebrated a bit too close to Danny and when he took it up with someone they stuck their chest in looking for a response. That is how David Flitcroft and his team conduct their business, much the same as Evans and Raynor did. Danny and Nicky are no saints, they're not the sort to get involved in embarrassing scenes if they can help it, but their touchline demeanour isn't without its controversy. Still, I'd like to see everyone shaking hands once the whistle is blown, not some fitness coach or other wanting to make a name for himself by going for a future Premier League manager like Danny. Needless.

Coming out of the ground I had to placate my mate Dave who feels we don't score enough goals (most in League Two) and that we need to win our home games. It was a typical response from someone who had been elated one minute and seen victory snatched away the next. By the time our car got back to Wragby the mood had changed to us getting a decent point, still being five points clear of arguably an automatic promotion contender and having a game in hand. Stevenage taking the lead against MK Dons helped the mood too, even though by the time I was back in Withcall Tisdale's side were winning.

Football deals you surprises though and at 5pm we were all delighted with the point that put us back on top. One late equaliser had left us feeling empty, but a late winner elsewhere put that into perspective. From joy, to dismay and back to joy in just two and a half hours.

I love football.

Kevin Austin – A tribute
November 25, 2018

This weekend is an incredibly sad one for Lincoln City and for football, with former player Kevin Austin losing his battle against cancer at the age of 45.

'Super' Kevin Austin, as he became known, was one of the finest defenders to grace the Imps' turf in recent memory. In his pomp he was quick and strong, best described as a 'specimen', physically impressive but as athletic as any that went before him.

Austin joined us from Leyton Orient where he'd been seen on TV in the infamous John Sitton rant. Few Imps fans will have registered it at the time, but if they missed his name on TV, they certainly knew it following John Beck's arrival at Sincil Bank.

The controversial manager knew Austin had all the attributes he needed in a defender and turned to us for help. He asked the crowd to buy him a player, we responded with coins in buckets and donations to the club. Back then, before the ski trips, expense claims and sleeping in the office, everyone trusted Beck, and we backed him. In return, he brought Austin to the club.

The powerful defender made his debut in a 2-1 defeat at lowly Torquay in a season where Lincoln missed out on the play-offs by just a point. In that season Austin showed he had a little bit of everything, pace and power with a fearsome tackle to match. He was a key player in the Coca Cola cup success over Man City and he was part of the team that took Premier League Southampton back to Sincil Bank.

The following season he was a major factor in our successful bid for automatic promotion. John Beck built his teams on strength, aggression and the ability to defend as if their lives depended on it. That was Kevin Austin to a tee, every inch the leader and inspiration.

Whilst in the third tier he scored what turned out to be the winning goal in our 2-1 home win over Manchester City, but could not stop the Imps sliding back into the basement division. As we floundered financially, having lost Beck and our place in what we now call League One, Austin's ambition was beginning to outstrip our own.

He made 146 appearances for Lincoln, every one of them all-action and full of effort. He was a marvellous individual, a defender of such immense promise I often wondered how he'd rocked up at Lincoln. He could, and should have gone on to play top flight football.

It came as no surprise when his contract ended and he secured a move to Barnsley. After three impressive seasons in red and white, many fans felt that he'd quickly ascend the divisions in the same way Gareth Ainsworth did.

Disaster struck in only his third game for Barnsley, ironically back at Sincil Bank in the Coca Cola cup. He suffered an Achilles tendon injury in a challenge that ended his season and he never returned the same player, leaving Barnsley after only three outings. He had a plethora of clubs, most notably Swansea, and he even earned seven caps for Trinidad and Tobago, but was never able to recapture the scintillating form that had him voted at number 56 in the Imps all-time top 100 legends.

Kevin Austin: 12/02/1973 - 23/11/2018

Two points dropped: Oldham 1-1 Imps
November 28, 2018

Playing away against Oldham Athletic isn't usually a game you expect to come away from carrying three points. Prior to this evening's encounter, we had gone just under sixty years without a win there.

That run is now going to get longer.

There's going to be a lot of social media feedback bubbling about after this one, there's no doubt about that. It was an engrossing game of football between a tough, organised home side and at times a disjointed Lincoln City. The obvious punch bag is going to be everyone's favourite scapegoat John Akinde, wrongly.

I'm going to launch straight in to the argument because I am baffled by both the criticism of John and his awful luck in front of goal. His recent run reminds me a lot of Matt Green last season, a player now widely described as a natural goal scorer but a year ago castigated as the cause of our poor form. This year, John Akinde is the one getting the stick and in truth, he's turned in two good performances.

He missed a couple of chances this evening and his honesty probably cost us early on, but overall he was one of our better players. I'm not sure he's as sharp in front of goal as he once was, but hopefully his time will come, just as Matt Green's did last season.

My personal opinion is we should have won tonight's game. To play against ten men for an entire half should yield a win, especially when you consider we asserted some degree of dominance in the second period. However, we couldn't break down a wonderfully resilient home side and when we did, their keeper was in good form. We fluffed some chances, not just Akinde either, and in certain areas our usual approach broke down. I believe, if you read my preview, I called us not getting as much joy from the flanks and it seems I was right.

We didn't get a lot of joy anywhere, but not through a lack of trying.

If I was putting my negative hat on I'd say our two attacking players are still too far from each other, I'd ask if we're missing Frecklington with Tom Pett turning in an average performance. He's gone off the boil the last game or two, but players come in and out of form all the time. It led to a frustrating evening in which John Akinde did 95% of his job right, missed a decent chance or two but was otherwise very isolated. There wasn't a great deal of supply from out wide, McCartan was too far away and that somehow reflects badly on John and not anyone else.

The first half was all a bit shambolic towards the end, Danny Gardner's injury prompted a spell in which little football was played. I felt for Gardner, he's clearly a talent and when he went off I thought we could get the upper hand. then there was the obscenely long wait for an injured linesman to be replaced, before the red card.

I've been told by some it wasn't a sending off, others think it was. I heard the line 'evening things up' in relation to Lee Frecklington's injury against Port Vale, but that wasn't the case. Miller went in high and reckless on Josh Vickers and in my mind, it's a red card. If it was the other way around I couldn't defend it either and the letter of the law these days is all around having control. Miller was high and had little control so it is a sending off. Fair play to Josh he didn't stay down and I even saw some Oldham fans criticising him for getting up and the card still being shown. Stay down and he's a cheat, get up and it isn't a foul? Logical.

The best chance fell to Akinde in the early stages and depending on your outlook he was either unlucky or wasteful. He could and maybe should have gone down when his shirt was tugged, but he saw a goal scoring opportunity and went for it. He was close, hitting the bar, but in truth he should have scored. He's lacking a sharpness in front of goal which I find upsetting because that is what he's being judged on, nothing more. His all round play is superb and yet he misses a chance and everyone wants him replaced.

Still, at 0-0, 10 v 11 and with Gardner off as well, it did seem as though we were in the driving seat. League One last season, big club, good players, 59 winless years, none of that should have mattered. This is 2018, we had more players, we're above them in the league and from this point on we should have won the game. It is that simple.

If you have a numerical advantage then you want to press that home early in the second half. What we needed was to come out of the blocks fighting, punching wildly and swarming all over the home side. We saw Oldham collapse in the FA Cup two years ago and if we'd been first to score in the second half I firmly believe we would have gone on to win the game handsomely. I had every confidence we'd do just that and even hearing 'Saturn 5' at half time didn't upset me too much.

Instead, we got hit with a super effort and apparently had the wind taken out of our sails. We needed to do anything but concede and yet once again, the clean sheet eluded us. We've now kept just two clean sheets in 17 matches, but yeah, the problem must be Akinde.

In fact, we've kept just five clean sheets all season, one of those coming in the EFL Cup, so if we're truly looking for a scapegoat perhaps we have to look at the defence. That said, we only kept six clean sheets in the first 25 games of last season, but good sides don't leak goals as we do. MK Dons for instance, have kept 11. John Akinde still the problem here?

It was the first punch of a frenetic and entertaining second half, levelled quickly by Michael O'Connor with another of his trademark strikes. He's been a top player for us since joining and he highlighted one of the positives in our play; we rarely draw a blank. In fact, we've only failed to score in a game on three occasions this season, the same as MK Dons.

From there we should have gone on to win the game, but we were always susceptible to an attack as well. We had chances, I admit Akinde missed a couple he should have scored and Bruno had a great effort that on another day, he too would have bagged. We didn't lay siege as such, but as in the Mansfield game I thought we were comfortably better in the second period. We should be though, they only had ten men.

Our main route to goal in the last two seasons, set pieces, have been woeful recently. Our corners offer little threat, our free kicks are wasted far too often and for some reason we've lost that little bit of magic from the dead ball situations. Maybe the Port Vale game was a millstone around our neck rather than a bonus because it's certainly ensured teams defend far better from our set pieces. Mind you, with delivery like we had this evening, there's not a lot to defend. Short corners; just no. Why do it? We've got big lads, why not get it into the box? We score from corners when they're right and when they're cleared, we usually pick up the pieces outside the area. Tonight, as on Saturday, we tried short corners and ended up completely wasting the opportunity.

I understand there's method behind what we do and I understand as a fan, I don't see the work on the training ground, but against Port Vale both Harry Toffolo and Bruno Andrade got assists from corners. Why is Michael O'Connor on them now?

It always felt like we might get a goal, when we did get something away their keeper made a save, but then again on the break they looked dangerous. I thought Surridge coming on was a brave move by them, but he turned out to be one of their best players. For every half chance we missed, they conjured up a quarter chance and drew a round of 'oohs' from the home support, which by the way was significantly lower than a 'big' club like them should be getting. Their performance and desire certainly deserves more fans watching, especially in a ground like Boundary Park.

As injury time approach I expected us to really go for it, but we didn't. The subs didn't make a big impact, having seen Kellan Gordon bag twice form the bench recently I was surprised to see Rhead come on for Harry Anderson. Given that we desperately needed to stretch ten men in the second half I was very surprised to see Matt Green with less than ten minutes of normal time left in the match. I'm not the manager, he sees the players every day and has a method, but I know I'd liked to have seen Gordon for Harry in a straight swap and perhaps McCartan off for Matt Green with at least 25 minutes left to go. We're all armchair pundits though, are we not?

Still, I didn't expect them to look most likely to get the goal in stoppage time, but they did. Credit to them, they played very well, but I stand by my assertion that if you're top and playing a team in 13th place with ten men, you should be winning the game. Sadly, and you know I struggle saying something like this, that result is simply not good enough, whatever Oldham used to be.

Where do we go from here? What I'd like to think is after the constructive criticism, which is entirely justified, and once the anti-Akinde lot have put their keyboards to sleep as well, we can all pull together and turn this blip around. By the way, one defeat in eleven isn't a bad blip to be having, nor is still being second in the league when you've only won once in six league matches. However, if we're to void this turning into 2006/07 all over again then we have to stick together as a fan base, keep supporting the lads and remain behind our own players.

We're still in a promotion challenge, we're still in a great position and whether others are catching up or not will be irrelevant if we can reach the same heights as the start of the season. I wonder if we've become predictable again and maybe Danny needs to look at some of the formations from earlier in the season and try dusting them off for the element of surprise.

I do feel we need some fresh faces against Carlisle. I've always said the FA Cup is a priority and we shouldn't experiment but if we would have dropped players for the league, then the same should happen in the cup. There's one or two changes I'd make but leaving out Akinde isn't one of them. I'd like to see a much flatter 4-4-2, akin to last season, when Rhead and Green fed excellently off each other. I'll be doing a piece on the side I'd like to see before the weekend but in the meantime let us not start falling out, blasting players with harsh words or tearing into the team and tactics when we're at the highest point we've been at in over a decade, we've sustained a place in the top three for perhaps the longest time since the early 1980s and we're only a month away from being able to shake things up with a few new faces.

This is still a good season, even if we're going to be waiting for that elusive win at Boundary Park.

December

Into the bag: Imps 2-0 Carlisle
December 1, 2018

The Mighty Imps made it to the third round for the second time in three years with a strong and organised win against a decent Carlisle side.

After all of the discussion this week around various subjects, there was a superb togetherness in the ground, reflective of the Lincoln City we know and love. The game started with a tribute to Kevin Austin and I think it only right for me to do the same. I was behind glass for the match today, courtesy of my good friends at Running Imp, but the poignant minute's applause was still as moving. To hear one last chant of 'Super Kevin Austin' brought a lump to my throat and, if I'm honest, I had to stifle a tear.

Prior to that there had been much discussion about the starting line up and, as predicted on the podcast this week, Rhead and Green started up front. I'm not sure it was to take anyone out of the firing line, rather a chance for a couple of good League Two strikers to stake a claim for a first team place. It was also great to see Lee Frecklington back in the side, a player as important to us as anyone.

Other than that it was business as usual and rightly so. The prize money for today was £60k I'm told, a January transfer fee maybe, or just a nice boost for the coffers. We're not bathing in money, contrary to public belief and anything we spend has been earned the right way, on the pitch and by player sales. When there's a pot of gold like that waiting for the winner of a game, there's a strong inclination to take it seriously.

Besides, it is the FA Cup and we were 90 minutes away from round three, maybe another Ipswich clash or something similar. If we weren't going to play a strong side for this game then something was wrong.

What we needed to do was come out punching, fly out of the traps and give Carlisle a bloody nose before they knew what the situation was. If we could do that, it shakes their game plan and gives us the momentum to grab that money and that place in the draw. It is fair to say we took the initiative.

One of the attributes we showed in the National League season was early goals, something I feel we lacked last season, so to see us with (and I'm sure Danny will have said this at some point) an energy, intensity and purpose was refreshing. The two recalled players had a hand in it too, Matt Green laying the ball to Bruno, his whipped cross nodded home by Matt Rhead. It was a classic Lincoln goal, the sort of open play goal that resembles a set piece, delivery into the box.

What that did was put Carlisle right off their stride and for the next 25 minutes or so I thought we might go on and get two or three more. there was a zip to our play, not scintillating or as refined as we have been but a real desire. You could say we wanted it more, but I'm sure it was more a case of us feeling the pressure building on the visitors.

When we didn't add the second though, they came back into it and perhaps for the next twenty minutes we rode our luck a bit. Bozzy and Shackell were excellent, but behind them Josh Vickers was showing why he's our number one keeper. He made a couple of very good stops, not only that he made sure anything loose into the box was picked up and dealt with.

We do like to sit off the opponent and occasionally that seems to invite pressure on, but Carlisle's spell didn't end in anything really clear cut. They showed they were a decent side, their movement from right to left hoped to open us up but, like a bad TV series, we weren't easy to get into at all.

I was in the executive boxes with Chris and Josh Illsley of Running Imp and they were tasked with picking today's Man of the Match. It was hard because despite us playing well, nobody truly stood out. Bruno and Harry Toffolo looked good on the left, but for the final twenty minutes not much went out that way. I thought the visitors did a good job of keeping everything very narrow, nullifying the threat. Had we not hit them early and bloodied their nose I suspect it would have been frustrating, but whilst they subdued us they didn't get anything meaningful away of their own.

I thought Freck was having a good game, my old man tells me he rated Tom Pett in the first half; Neal Eardley made some good deliveries and Harry Anderson was his typical bullish self. Nobody grasped the game by the scruff of the neck and demanded to be noticed, but everyone was putting in a shift. It was, for want of a better word, a functional first half.

The best way to sum up the opening 45 was that the goal defined it. After we scored we didn't need to throw caution to the wind and they didn't want to be opened up and go two behind, so neither side pushed forward too hard. There were chances at both ends, it was engrossing, but both sides knew the crucial period was after the break.

The second period promised to be better, with it being a cup tie Carlisle had to come at us and we knew that could leave them open. To be fair, they did have best of the opening ten or fifteen minutes of the second half. Josh Vickers was once again big and strong and I suspect Chris had made his mind up on the Man of the Match before the hour mark. That's not to say it was a closed shop, but Vickers had, at times, kept us in it.

We weren't hanging on for dear life, but a keeper is rarely praised just for doing his job, yet Josh did his superbly. When asked to deliver it forward he used both feet equally as comfortably, he received the ball in some tight positions but remained cool. I'm saying this now because post match several people questioned why he got the award and asked if we'd only done it because it was his birthday. No, we didn't. we did it because on balance, we feel his performance was worth at least a goal.

Now that's out of the way, and the first ten minutes of the second half were put to bed, we get to talk nothing but positive because I felt the final half hour we saw some great stuff from City. The wide players got much more of the ball, the midfield spread it nicely in either direction and both Green and Rhead were busy. Matt Green might have had the goal everyone was wanting him to get on 55 minutes, Pett worked the ball to Freck when he might have had one of his low, hard drives. It was a neat move though and the captain's ball just evaded Greeny at the back stick.

I wanted him to core today, desperately. I'm a big fan of Matt Green, always have been and his hard work definitely tired the opposition defence. He plays a lot with his back to goal, looking to turn and run the channels but a good striker has instinct and the position he took up showed that. He was millimetres from it, but alas no cigar.

Neal Eardley found himself in some space in the area and his drive could easily have made it two as well. Neal was another who played very well today, always willing to whip in a cross but, when he sees a little glimpse of goal, he's on it. I remember his strike against Cheltenham last season and I back him to get another at some point, although today he was just thwarted by the block.

The temperature was rising in the Bank as Freck had a couple of efforts in the space of a few seconds, and when Greeny and Rheady were replaced minutes later we got a glimpse of how things should be. The two players departing were given a great ovation, the two coming on even more so. There's a lot of focus on John Akinde at the moment, but the huge cheer that went up when he came on must have been heartening to hear. It shouldn't need highlighting, he's got the support of 99% of the fans, even those who feel he needed the break today.

The changes just ensured we kept the momentum going and Lee Frecklington, whom I can exclusively reveal was our other pick for Man of the Match, had a cracking drive saved by Collin in the Carlisle goal. Is it fair to say it was all one way traffic? I think so. There was only ever going to be one side score again at that point.

It would be remiss to say we poured forward at every opportunity, but we were by far the most lively side. Carlisle looked short of ideas in the absence of Ashley Nadeson and their little flurry at the start of the second half seemed to be as much as they had in the locker. Akinde simply took up the channel running, with McCartan the man linking the midfield and attack. He does it well, perhaps on occasion he carries the ball too far, but him and Bruno have got to be the most effective dribblers we've had at the club in many a year. The ball sticks to their feet and whilst they do get crowded out at times, it is nice to see them asking questions of defenders with runs, especially late on in the game.

Eventually, the goal had to come. We'd knocked on the door enough and whilst Carlisle hadn't rolled over, but for the early flurry they'd offered little. Shackell and Bozzy had both been commanding at the back and the changes gave us some fresh legs up front. 1-0 had everyone wondering about a repeat of Mansfield, but 2-0 ended it.

I'm not sure what I cheered more, the goal or the scorer. I think we know 95% of Imps fans are behind big John, some of the talk around him has been silly. I'm not going over old ground, I thought he'd answered his critics against Forest Green and again with commanding performances against Mansfield and Oldham, but today he gave everyone what they wanted to see, a goal. He could have had one before, pulling a smart save from Collin, but there was no doubt about the one that went in.

Again, Bruno Andrade was provider, he's a beast of a player who I believe will net us a big transfer fee in the future, but right now he's providing assists and lots of them. His ball was perfect, right across goal to where the danger man was lurking. It was the same goal we scored against Forest Green and Mansfield, a ball that is becoming as reliable for us as a set piece. This time, John Akinde was on the end of it and the smile on his face said it all.

I also liked the celebration between him and Matt Green, a huge embrace on the touch line told a thousand stories in itself. Togetherness.

It wasn't just the win, nor the goal for big John, but also the clean sheet that will be important. It was a shame to see Josh Vickers head off the pitch in tears, even worse to know he had to go straight in the ice bath and couldn't collect his champagne from me, but hopefully the injury isn't serious. He was a big part in that '0' next to Carlisle in tomorrow's papers and it'll be a nice platform to build on against Accrington and certainly next week against Stevenage.

What more is there to say? We're now in the hat for the second round and any little rumblings will have been dampened down. I would call for everyone to keep their feet on the ground, not to indulge each other in 'I told you so' tit for tat comments because none of it has any point. Today, in the stands we were together, on the pitch the players were together and we showed how powerful that really is.

I only hope our endeavour gets the draw it deserves, Lee Frecklington wants Leeds United, some bloke on the radio wants a Manchester club, my Dad wants (and I quote) 'a shit club' in round three so we can progress further and me, all I want, is for us all to have a week of smiling and remembering exactly what it is that makes this football club so strong from the top right to the bottom.

We're all Imps.

'Simply can't wait' – Some fan reaction from the Imps FA Cup 3rd round draw

December 3, 2018

Lincoln City are the side who never do well in the cup, the team who get to the third round but never pull out the big boys.

Last time we got Ipswich, away. The time before that we got Sunderland, a Championship club at the time, at home. No disrespect, they're both bigger clubs than us, but when is it our turn?

Even when we drew a top flight club in the third round, back in 1994, it was Crystal Palace away, arguably not as big as the Sunderland game. When we did finally get one of the big clubs, we had to fight to the quarter-final for the right.

Not no more.

Today, the football gods smiled on us. Back when I was growing up there as a 'big five', Everton being one of them. They're going great guns in the Premier League right now and have been members ever since it began in 1992.

In fact, they've been members of the top flight since 1954. They're winners of European trophies and league titles. They're a huge draw. The fact Clive Nates is a fan is a great story, but the real story here is Lincoln City.

Finally, we get to go to a Premier League ground without having to battle through energy-sapping rounds. we can have our big day and get it out of the way in January, then concentrate on the league having been to Goodison.

Unless.... well, you know. The magic of the cup.

It's great to get a decent draw and hopefully it will help unite the fan base, not least because there's around 6,000 ST holders and a similar allocation. Still, that can all be decided in time.

Tonight, like the fans below, I'm just delighted to get a good draw and have a top day out.

Nick Procter
@nickprocter27
Wow wow wow!!!! Everton away, almost as if the football god's have smiled on us for the sake of our super chairman @cliven7 who found Lincoln through his support of the toffees. LCFC Takeover of Liverpool and a last minute winner to send us through please. I simply can't wait.

Craig
@ValentinoMossy
What a draw. @LincolnCity_FC away at Everton. The boss @cliven7 dream tie and one hell of a day in prospect for the imps. Predict big big numbers for this

Dan Norton
@Dlnorton150879
Absolutely buzzing about this . Cannot wait for January now. Should get 15% as Everton won't sell their home allocation. Clive Nates will be a happy man tonight.

Clive Nates
@cliven7
Oh dear, now I have to come over. And it's likely to be cold

Over and out: Accrington 2-2 Imps (4-2 Pens)
December 4, 2018

18 months after we first kicked a ball in the Checkatrade Trophy, we're finally eliminated from the competition. In another bizarre night of football we've found ourselves on the wrong side of a second successive penalty shoot out.

We were never going to Accrington to win the game, not in the conventional sense. If you think we should have played a stronger side and given the travelling supporters something to cheer, you're missing the point. We've already had our day at Wembley, we've already won this competition and unlike the FA Cup or promotion, there's no glory in winning it in successive seasons.

Last year, it was the consolation prize. It was a bloody good one and of course, we had a great day out, but football isn't only about days out. The excitement that comes with a Wembley trip or a Goodison Park trip isn't what football is all about, not at all. Promotion, aspirations of improvement, achieving things you've not achieved before; they are what this beautiful game is all about. Tonight, the only thing we were ever going to win was pride. Going to Wembley again in this trophy wouldn't further the club in the way we want to. Last year, it gave us what we needed from it and we all enjoyed London, but if you ask me would I risk the top three for another stab at that, I'd say no. Been there, done that. let someone else have to worry about beating the kids and protecting football's integrity. We've done our bit.

Danny told us all what his intentions for this competition were after the Mansfield result. There was no hiding it, no pretending we'd go hell for leather. We did the same in the FA Trophy two years ago and to an extent, we did the same in this competition last season. Okay, the team selection was perhaps a little more 'out there' this time around, but there was never any pretence of anything else.

I'm not going to insult anyone's intelligence and pretend that being eliminated was what we wanted on the night, of course we didn't. Young Jordan Adebayo-Smith didn't go out thinking he wanted to lose the game on his professional debut, did he? Matt Green wanted goals to prove his points, Ellis wanted to show his talents in midfield. The players we selected wanted the win, but we just selected players who haven't been featured as much in the league.

On Saturday, Swindon did that in the FA Cup against Woking. That, in a competition with such history and glory, is criminal. For us to do it in a competition we won earlier this year and that comes third in our current list of priorities, is acceptable, justifiable and in my opinion, the right thing to do. Had we done it in the FA Cup I wouldn't have been outraged.

Danny will have learned more about the fringe players from 96 minutes of football this evening than he will have done in a month of training sessions. He will have seen first hand the spirit and resilience some of the lads have, the sort of attitude that players who haven't been able to affect the season so far have. One excellent example would have to be Joan Luque, on the bench for Bromley in recent weeks but turning in a tricky and unpredictable display in the middle of the park. He's raw, very raw, but he put in a good shift after a busy couple of days. We needed to see him in action and we did.

Jordan Adebayo-Smith will have relished his chance too, he didn't look out of his depth at all and I suspect his is a name you'll hear much more over the coming years, just like Ellis Chapman. The younger players playing tonight did well and will be pleased with their contribution. Scott Wharton and Kellan Gordon will have given Danny food for thought and Adam Crookes will have been happy to get some game time under his belt.

It was always going to be gung-ho, a wonderful spectacle for those who thought that a combination of iFollow and Checkatrade represented something other than a degrading of the soul. I didn't watch it, I can't give you the usual analysis because I had little interest in the tactical battle. It wasn't Danny against John Coleman, it wasn't a measure of how far we've come or got to go. It was a one-off, almost an exhibition match as unpredictable as it was unimportant. I didn't feel a defeat would be a bad thing but, curiously, when Matt Rhead missed the penalty my heart did sink a little. I'm a Lincoln fan and if they were playing the board game Hero Quest with David Flitcroft and his kids, I'd be a bit gutted if we lost. It's my make up, my nature.

That said, within about 30 seconds it had subsided and whilst I committed to the game, I didn't feel the worry going into the final minutes. I was a little dismayed we didn't win on penalties after reaching them seemed to be the game plan in the last thirty minutes, but I wasn't 'kick the cat and shout at the missus' angry*. We turned in a good performance against a decent side but, when push came to shove, they brought on top first team players and we brought on back room staff. I half hoped to hear Alan Long was in a tracksuit on the touchline.

Some might think in bringing on Jamie McCombe and Tom Shaw we were devaluing the competition; the FA think we're the same level as an Under 21 team so who is devaluing it really? We used it in the same way they do, giving players who wouldn't usually play a run out, only we played some of our over 32s as well as our under 21s. I would imagine Tom Shaw will go down in history in some way, the youth team coach making a debut, but he's 32 and played for Chester as recently as last year so his inclusion wasn't all that odd. As for big Jamie McCombe, we all got the story we wanted when he bagged our second, didn't we? Go on, how many Imps fans who remember him from the Keith era weren't a little bit delighted he scored? It was like a blast from the past, with a little voice inside saying 'gwon Jamie', knowing how delighted he'd be to show he's still got it. It might earn him some extra kudos in training too.

It's pointless dissecting the match any further. They wanted it, we didn't. It's not because we're defeatist, not because we have a losing mentality but simply because Danny doesn't want to keep rolling out a patched up team for relatively meaningless games when we could come up against Manchester City Under 21s with a couple of £30m teenagers in and end up getting beat. Last season we hadn't been to Wembley, but now we have. Now it isn't such a big thing and the money we'll get from the Goodison Park game in January will more than compensate for not being in this competition until the end.

I wonder, had we not progressed in the FA Cup would we have perhaps played a couple more first team players? Maybe, but the fact is we are in the FA Cup third round, we are second in the league and if we go to Everton, get beat and end up being promoted automatically, not one person will start moaning about tonight's fixture.

When Rob Makepeace is about to interview Danny and he calls it a 'great night for Lincoln City', despite going out of the competition, you know we got out of the game exactly what we wanted. Youngsters got minutes, fringe players got a chance to showcase their talents and the squad gave a battling performance that might just make a few first team regulars sit up and take note. Also,

Danny knows that ahead of the Everton game it might be wise to practice penalties. Say what you want about John Akinde, but he doesn't miss from 12 yards.

The Checkatrade Trophy; a competition in which we progressed from the group stage without winning a game and then were eliminated after remaining unbeaten in 90 minutes against three sides, two from League One and another full of kids. You couldn't make it up.

I don't have a cat to kick and if I shouted at my missus she'd kick my arse. Besides, she's in Cambridge so probably wouldn't hear me.

Hosts pay the penalty: Stevenage 0-1 Imps
December 8, 2018

If ever there was an indication that the standard of teams in League Two is closer than you think, today was it. You only need to look at the clash with Stevenage to see what fine margins separate the top teams and those on the fringes of the top ten.

This afternoon wasn't one we'll be writing home about at the end of the season, it's not one for a highlights DVD and aside from the 1350 travelling fans, who will I'm sure have it down as a top away day, it will be instantly forgettable if judged on quality alone.

However, if one is to judge the game on effort, character and commitment, this could be the win of the season. It's not so long ago we drew away at Oldham and were seemingly on our arses, criticised in some quarters for not being good enough. I'm not going over old ground again, the fact is we're second in the table, we were at the start of play today and we are at the end of it. Things do seem much different after a win though, do they not?

I'm quite happy because a couple of pre-match shouts came to fruition. I did call a penalty for us at some point in the game, and so it proved. I also said much would depend on our central midfield players and Michael O'Connor was named by Steve Thompson as Man of the Match. In truth, there were a lot of brave performances out there today, Bozzy and Shackell were excellent as ever, Neal Eardley looked like the player we saw consistently last season and Harry Toffolo was excellent despite the heavy knock he took. Four defenders all being praised should tell you how tough the win was.

Stevenage are very much like us last season, big and strong with a direct approach and a mix of experience and skill. Cuthbert at the back was Luton captain last season, Ben Nugent was a Gillingham player too, so they're recruiting a certain quality. They've even got Paul Farman on the bench, just like we had for most of the season (sorry Farms). What they lack is a striker, a big and burly man who puts himself about and causes a nuisance. You see, those strikers do not come along all that often and if we're being honest, the fact we have one was the difference today.

Say what you like about John Akinde, many have, but he's a handful who proves a wonderful outlet away from home. We needed to hit them on the counter to some extent today and when we had Green and Rhead up top it wasn't easy. Rhead, for all his qualities, cannot be the target and carry the ball forward, but John can. Games like today are where his 'two in one' attributes come in handy and once again, he showed that to a tee.

Aside from McCartan's struggles this week it was very much business a usual for City. It would have been interesting if Shay had been fit, would Tom Pett have played against his old side? Or would Michael O'Connor, a player suited to the fight in the middle of the park, have been missing? Either way, with Shay not fully fit it saved Danny the only big decision he'd have to make. I know many want to see Kellan Gordon get a start, but one thing Harry gives you is fight. I'm not saying Gordon doesn't, but he's not as robust as Harry. Right now, if we're at full strength, Harry plays for me. Kellan Gordon has had an impact from the bench and in the right circumstances will be worth a starting place, but in a blood and thunder League Two game it has to be Harry.

Nothing is ever straight forward with City and the first few seconds of the game proved that. Grant Smith must have had injury nightmares after his collision with Alex Revell, having only just come back from his loan spell. After the lengthy break he was back on his feet and I thought he put in a strong display considering the early knock. He didn't have a lot to save, but he has a good command of his area. It's testament to our recruitment that the keeper deemed as our back up is able to step up so confidently. I have little doubt he'll be an important player in the coming weeks as Josh Vickers continues to battle his own injury worries.

Tom Pett could have had the goal he was no doubt dreaming about last night with a smart drive on nine minutes, but sixty seconds later the game was effectively decided. It was a goal entirely of John Akinde's own making, his direct running frightened the experienced Cuthbert into a silly challenge and we got our third penalty in as many visits to Stevenage. In midweek we struggled to put the ball in the net from 12 yards, but if there's one player who is going to score from the spot it's John Akinde. I read earlier in the season that his goal record wasn't as impressive because some were penalties. Well, when you win it and then score it as far as I'm concerned it's worthy of adding to the tally. 1-0 and although we didn't know it, that was game over.

I thought after that we controlled it until the 30 minute mark. The wind was behind us which certainly helped, but Stevenage hadn't come out of the dressing room, they were playing long balls into the wind and getting no joy at all. One the other hand, we moved the ball around nicely an attacked with a certain zest. Akinde could have had a second on 29 minutes, but after Tom Pett set him up he drilled into the side netting. He was the difference for me though, he chased the scraps and fought for everything, whereas Stevenage didn't have that up front.

It was as if the hosts suddenly woke up after that and we began to weather the storm a little. The two centre backs were immense, Jason Shackell is a player with no right to be as low as League Two, not only for what he does with the ball, but his overall management of the game and organisation of his peers. He was a real gem we unearthed on Deadline Day. I wouldn't ever like to play Danny at poker because he's always hiding an ace up his sleeve when push comes to shove.

Stevenage's game plan changed, they toughened up no end and started targeting key players. Harry Toffolo took a big knock and like Grant Smith, played on regardless. Bruno was coming in for some heavy treatment too, as was Harry. To be fair, the tackles were strong but I couldn't say it was a thuggish approach (like, say, Mansfield in the Checkatrade). It was robust, typical League Two reducers full of venom but always on the right side of the law. Just.

The saying 'game of two halves' always amuses me because although it is right, it is also staying the obvious. In the second 45 minutes they had the wind behind them and were able to retain possession much more. Dino Mammria, a no-nonsense manager whom I have a bit of time for, clearly changed things around a little and approached the game differently. It wasn't enough to affect the result, but it left us under the cosh. Of course, we react in those situations and decisions made in-game are often the reason we win matches.

It's not always a sub either, sometimes it's the little things, shifting a midfielder deeper, dropping a player further back or marking someone a little tighter. Often, as fans, we won't see the change immediately but when you're close to Danny on the touch-line you can hear the little tweeks he makes, with the advice of his ever-expanding backroom staff. There's blood and thunder on the pitch, but a game of chess going on off it.

Grant Smith made his first save five minutes after the restart which set the scene for the second period. We weren't truly threatened as such, but it became tougher for us to get out, with a gale holding the ball up and Stevenage finding a rhythm. I liked Campbell-Ryce, I thought he offered a great out for them and had pace to burn. Maybe it was because he came up against Harry Toffolo and his injury, but I thought he looked dangerous. I was disappointed with Revell, he's a strong lad but he wasn't able to impose himself on our back two. Maybe that is because they're so bloody strong. Who knows?

What you do need in a game like this is an extra leg up and the travelling support certainly made sure they were heard and effective. The Lamex rang out to Lincoln City songs and it clearly spurred the lads on. Tom Pett might have had his goal in the second half, firing over, but then the hosts surged forward but couldn't find their way through. It wasn't end to end in the traditional sense, it was a fight, not too easy on the eye but certainly with enough in it to hold the attention of a neutral, if there was one in the ground.

It was nice, in a way, to see Scott Wharton get a run out. It's never good for a player to go off injured, but Harry Toffolo had looked at 65% for most of the game and that meant a reshuffle. Wharton isn't a left back as such, but he's composed and can travel with the ball. One surging run in particular remind me of what he looked like last season, making it all the more difficult to see him on the bench so often. He's the big loser in the Jason Shackell signing, which is a shame. Still, he played his part today and didn't let us down when he came on.

The last twenty minutes or so didn't carry any real threat for City. There was a little mild peril perhaps as Stevenage hunted the goal, but this wasn't the Lincoln City of recent weeks, likely to leak at the back. There was a resilience today, that togetherness that Danny lauds off the pitch was as evident as ever. Bodies were put on the line where they needed to be, but the game was managed well. Not by time-wasting I might add, but by shepherding players into less effective positions, by keeping the ball out of the danger areas and by keeping cool heads.

The big chance came in the last-minute for the hosts, the one they wanted came from a free kick courtesy of Joel Byrom. His curling effort was saved superbly by Grant Smith, a player who wasn't called into action enough to be Man of the Match, but did everything right and was reliable and strong.

That was pretty much that. Six minutes of injury time brought little more danger and City were able to hold on, having blocked, tackled and manipulated the game in increasing amounts. As I've said, the back four were superb, including Scott Wharton in that when he came on. Michael O'Connor screening in front was excellent too and at times late on made it a back five. After the first thirty minutes it wasn't a big attacking game for City, but even so players like Bruno, Harry Anderson and Lee Frecklington played their part. John Akinde was excellent, he gave a solid performance in the lone striker role and even tracked back hard when he needed to.

It wasn't pretty, it wasn't straightforward but it was a great win for the Imps. Credit to Stevenage, they make a formidable opponent and are sure to be around the top seven by the end of the season, especially as they've already avoided defeat at home against MK Dons and Colchester.

They didn't avoid defeat against Danny's Imps though and whilst the win is great, lets not get carried away. We've got Morecambe up next, a side likely to sit with ten men behind the ball and hit us on the break, a game we have to go out and win not just by fighting like today, but also by showing creativity and guile.

Ten days ago I was arguing against us being something like 19th in the form table, but stats can be made to say what you want. Here's a good one for you: we've lost once in 14, counting Checkatrade games as draws. We're unbeaten in eight matches too and have two clean sheets in three.

We're back on track, but if we're to stay there we'll need the walking wounded to recover quickly and we'll need to show the same fight in the next 26 league games.

Interesting comments from Danny ahead of the transfer window
December 14, 2018

I've been doing a bit of catching up with comments and articles from the past week and two different bits from Lincolnshire Live caught my eye.

There's obviously going to be lots of build up towards the transfer window and as such, the Echo have been talking to our manager about transfer window strategy.

The two articles I'm going to refer to are here and here, if you want to check them out. One is recent, the other is from August and will hopefully provide some background information.

Essentially, Danny is saying that keeping the squad together, in its current guise, would be an achievement in itself as we're doing so well. He's keen to point out he wouldn't stand in a players way, but at the same time he wants to keep much of the side intact. If he manages that, then it'll be a largely successful window.

Of course, much of the fan opinion is different, the need the strengthen is, as always, top of everyone's priorities. It always interests me that there's such a focus on bringing players into a club at this stage of the season, just because you're allowed it seems to be expected. I find that odd, but not as odd as the mainstream media found it that Spurs didn't buy anyone in the summer. Imagine, not buying a single player!

Only we can, almost. At the end of the 74/75 season Graham Taylor made one addition to the squad. Worked out well for him. Anyway, this isn't 1975 and there demands on the players are tougher.

I'm interested in the following comments: "In the previous three transfer windows, we've always lost key players. We're hoping this will be the first transfer window where we don't lose a key player. That is our aim. In the summer, we lost Alex Woodyard [to Peterborough] and Luke Waterfall [Shrewsbury] while in the January before that we lost Sean Raggett (to Norwich]. The aiming going forward is to not lose any of our key players. If we can manage that it would be a massive achievement in itself."

He goes on to say that everyone has their price, but as the August article I've linked above proves, the players who have had their price in recent seasons have been subject of bids that activate release clauses. The general feeling is that few (if any) of the current squad have such clauses. therefore, I wonder what is the price for some of our players.

Fans have an unrealistic view of what a player may or may not be worth. When buying a player we tend to undervalue them, but when we've had them on our books we tend to over value them. I remember speaking to someone who said we shouldn't accept any less than £750,000 for Sean Raggett, when his release clause was thought to be less than half of that figure. However, when we signed him we felt Dover tried to have out pants down by demanding too much.

Literally, in the space of a single season his value increased tenfold in the eyes of some. Not all I hasten to add.

I'm an offender too, I believed had Alex Woodyard stayed with us he could have been a £1m player. In reality, I suspect we got around £125k for him and if I was asked to guess, I'd say we paid a similar amount for John Akinde. Danny does speak some truth when he says the money we spend ifs earned and in the main, it's earned by transfer fees.

What I don't buy is the fact losing these players is always detrimental to what we want to achieve. Take Luke Waterfall. I was (and still am) a big fan of Luke, he's a down to earth guy who played with commitment and passion. The partnership he had with Raggs will go down as one of the strongest for many years and he's rightly the most decorated Imps captain of all time with two trophies in two years.

However, was losing him pre-season to Shrewsbury such bad business? Okay, we lost a captain and a presence off the pitch, but anyone watching the Northampton game in August could be forgiven for thinking we got off lightly. Luke sold us short a couple of times on that occasion and had battled hard to even get a first team run out the year before.

Our judgement could be clouded because we see him lifting the two trophies or thundering into tackles, but if I gave you a choice now of Jason Shackell or Luke Waterfall, who would you pick?

Perhaps this is a little tougher, but if selling Ollie Palmer allowed us to bring in McCartan, who would you pick? What about Andrade and Akinde coming in for Alex?

Whenever we've been hit with a 'blow' as such, we've seemingly come back stronger, the only time we've deviated from that path was with Sean Raggett. I think we suffered for having him on loan in a way, because instead of preparing for life without him, we enjoyed his services. The harsh reality is that him being with us in the first half of last season probably ended up costing us Rob Dickie, because the reading loanee didn't play and Raggs did. When Raggs left, his so-called successor had been on the bench and left too. If he'd played regularly, he might still be with us now, not playing every game for Oxford in League One.

It's why I don't feel there's a need to worry in the transfer window. If what Danny said in August is correct and we've not got release clauses in contracts, then our key players will command bigger fees than the past. Some of our top players just won't go. Bozzy wont, we know that, he's settled in the area and moved here for location. He's staying put, as is Jason Shackell, a man committed to the project, not the money. John Akinde is going nowhere, same with Freck and O'Connor.

In fact, as I alluded to in an earlier article, the main worry is loan players going back to their parent club or any bids we might get for Harry Anderson, Bruno Andrade or Matt Green. The latter I believe might go, but the other two I can't see leaving. If someone does want Bruno and there's no £125k release clause, are we really going to let him go cheap? Of course not, Danny is as tight as a parking space at the ground, he wouldn't give Bruno away if it wasn't in the contract. Talking about 'realistic' pricing when we sold Raggs was all well and good, but it was only because we had no choice.

I believe in saying he'll deem the window a success if we hold on to our players, Danny is almost saying something he knows to be the case. Bar the odd one or two our spine is going nowhere, for a variety of reasons. Just in case on of the players I've mentioned above is sold, or Bradford decide McCartan is integral to their needs, Danny has issued a caveat.

"From a football perspective, we wouldn't want to lose anyone, but I'm respectful of the fact the club is a business. Sometimes we have to make business decisions in line with the football decisions. Like always, the club and the board of directors are completely supportive in we try to move the club forward."

This is how I interpret that: the key players aren't for sale but, if I have to sell a player for money before he leaves for free in the summer I will, please understand it. If someone offers me three times what one of our players is worth, please understand when I accept it and reinvest in one of the umpteen players we've scouted, compiled dossiers on and know would come here in a heartbeat, even if you haven't signed them on FIFA yet.

He stopped short of using the words 'our fans are clever and they know....' which is his usual piece of mind trickery. Let's face it, it worked before and I don't doubt if something unexpected happens in January. it'll work again. Our fans are clever and they know that whatever money I get from selling x,y,z player, I can put back into the team to make us stronger still. You know the drill, we're all still doe-eyed at being called clever by Danny to bother what came after that.

Right now though, I just can't see it. Not unless that website Team Talk have linked Andrade with Benfica or Harry Toffolo with Jossie's Giants and Melchester Rovers. Because that lot know exactly what they're on.

Winter Warmer: Imps 3-1 Morecambe
December 16, 2018

Over and above all else, before a ball was kicked, a player booed or a goal cheered; it was cold.

I met my old man before the game to walk up to the ground and even with gloves on, his hands were white with the cold. We had hats, coats, hoods and he had long-johns and gloves and yet somehow the prickly temperature got through those layers and gently froze your bones. He remarked to me as we walked down Scorer Street that today was 'a day for football fans, a day where you'd rather just eff off home and sit in front of the fire watching Jeff Stelling'. I asked him why he didn't and he smiled as said 'I'm a Lincoln City fan'. I liked that moment, it summed a lot up for me.

The middle of December, an afternoon that will be followed by another home game in a week's time, playing against a side who were going to make in an unattractive, stubborn game by virtue of their tenacity and yet here we were, still rolling up all wide-eyed and expectant as if it were the first weekend of August. The TP Suite filled up an awful lot quicker than normal and the poor guy on the German Beer stand in the fan zone is probably still defrosting now, but all in all it was just another Saturday, courtesy of your match sponsors freezing rain and pneumonia.

The team selection was a little worrying, I pondered whether Bruno's absence would leave us looking short of ideas up front, especially as their back four would be deep and not affording Harry Anderson the room to move into behind. Other than that it was to be business as usual, the same nucleus that had seen us settle in the top two all season. News that MK Dons game was cancelled late filtered through too, making this our 'free hit' We've been talking about the game in hand and here it was, at home against one of the strugglers and, as it turned out, comfortably the worst side we've seen at Sincil Bank in a while.

There were two other factors that were going to make this an unpredictable game. The first I've already alluded to, the conditions. The swirling wind, driving rain and ball-shrivelling cold would limit the efforts of the players somewhat and, just in case that wasn't enough, the referee was Seb Stockbridge. There's one thing you can almost always guarantee with Seb, and that is something for the home side. He loves the roar of the home crowd as he makes a decision, so there was always going to be a penalty, a red card or something where he could be the man everyone cheers. I'm just glad we always seem to get him at home.

Straight from kick off it was clear Danny wanted this put to bed early. He always talks about wanting an intensity and purpose, they're two words guaranteed to get you a full house on 'Danny Cowley Bingo'. Sure enough, with a handful of minutes gone Michael O'Connor fired wide when he perhaps should have scored. It wasn't to matter, within seven minutes we were one up. The goal was a finely crafted thing of beauty, something those Stevenage fans labelling us 'long ball' would do well to watch. No Bruno on the left? No worry, we've got Tom Pett. He was part of a three-player move that found Harry Anderson in the box who smartly slotted home from ten yards. The cold felt a little less fatal with a goal to warm us up and once again it was a player who has come in for some stick who got it. That goal did Harry the world of good because for the next ninety minutes, I thought he was excellent. Football is a confidence game and he got confidence from rippling the back of the net.

Things began to ebb and flow and for a short while it had the feeling of an even contest. Jordan Cranston, a former Imp himself, looked lively for them but often made poor choices. He shot from long-range a time or two when a pass might work, but one of those efforts almost caught out Grant Smith. It must have been the conditions that saw our stand-in fumble the shot, but had veteran Kevin Ellison been alert, or maybe twenty years younger, they could have equalised.

We had our chances though, a wicked cross from the right could have been nodded in by Akinde and should have been tapped in by Tom Pett, but both missed it. Then, Big John did all the hard work catching a ball forward and beating two defenders, but he fluffed his first effort. When it fell back to him, a ball rolled into McCartan makes it 2-0, but he opted for another effort and the chance was gone. My Old Man tapped me on the shoulder and said 'we'll rue those misses you know'. It wasn't the last incorrect statement made by a Hutchinson in the first half.

Five minutes later, John Akinde was heavily involved once more. A ball out on the right was seemingly set to be cleared, but his persistence kept the move alive. He fed in McCartan who wound his way into the area, only to be floored by a crude body check. It was the moment our Seb had been waiting for. He paused, only momentarily, and then blew the whistle. For the third game in a row at Sincil Bank, he awarded us a penalty. We shouldn't complain, not as this one was stonewall. It was a stupid challenge to make and McCartan doesn't need half as heavy contact to go down.

After a bit of theatrics on the edge of the area where one of our boys went down too easily from a push, John Akinde got his chance. I said something on the pod this week about him and penalties and it proved (again) to be right. It was as calm as you'll see, the sort of strike that set aside the conditions, the pressure of the moment and the earlier miss that could have left us susceptible to a goal. It was languid, looking half-hearted but in truth anything but. At 2-0, the game was over.

Three minutes later we were forward gain, looking to take advantage of the momentum that had swung our way. The performance had turned from competent into controlling, the Imps laying passes from left to right, front to back and leaving Morecambe chasing shadows. The elements hadn't helped, but when McCartan was once again brought down outside the box, we had another chance to test our dead ball skills. We know the Bradford loanee can hit a ball, Harry Toffolo likes a free kick and I believe Tom Pett can curl one to. Jason Shackell though, he's a centre back. As he lined up to take it I sniggered and said; "Jason Shackell taking a free kick? This is only going to end one way..."

As I said the word way, it left his boot and before I'd concluded the 'y' it was rippling the net.

I've always lamented our inability to take a decent free kick, right the way up until 2016/17. We've seen some belters since, Sam Habergham, Maguire-Drew and now, to top them all, something from a 35-year old central defender that would have Neymar fans foaming at the mouth.

At 3-0 a rational person thinks 'game over'. Danny Cowley's sides are not prone to taking a lead and failing to defend it, we've conceded three or more on one occasion this season and that came against a Championship side with half of our fringe players playing. Defeat, even a draw, would be incomprehensible for anyone at that stage, except me.

The problem I have is I cannot seen the rational through the haze of fear at a game. At 3-0 up I'm thinking 'If they get two then they're back in the game, nerves will get shattered. The conditions are going to play a part..' it all goes around in my head until I'm convinced as opposed to be 3-0 up, we're on the back foot.

It wasn't helped by going down to the Stacey West at half time for a smoke. In the relative comfort of Upper 3 I was dry, if not even remotely warm. However, once we ventured into the elements I realised what a lottery the second half was going to be. I feel for you poor sods who sit anywhere in the first ten rows of the lower tier. It wasn't just bad weather, it was grotesque.

I thought the second half was odd, it felt from kick off as though both teams just wanted it to be done. The atmosphere was dulled purely through the cold, the Block 7 boys were in good voice, but it rarely spread across the ground. When a chant did reach us it was lost quickly as people chose to expend their energy on shiver and huddling together, rather than signing. It wasn't hard to spot those with their beer coats on.

When Eardley got a knock and went off, everything changed for us. James Wilson is a centre back, he'd tell you he's a centre back and although he does a decent job when he comes on, we lose our shape. The pace slowed, at times we were walking with the ball at our feet, the Morecambe lads sitting back not wanting to concede more. If we'd asked everyone in the stadium, fans, players and staff, I reckon almost everyone would have happily ended the game at 4.10pm and gone home to get the heating on.

Grant Smith would certainly have wanted the day over, he fumbled Jordan Cranston's weak free kick and let them score what I thought was a perfectly good goal, only for Seb to rule it out. I'm giving the keeper the benefit of the doubt, swirling winds and heavy rain must have made holding things a nightmare. Their keeper barely held a thing all game, our shots went wide, over or in, but Grant had similar struggles. He made up for it with a good save from Vadaine Oliver though, a player enduring another miserable return to his former club.

It's hard to write too much about a half of football everyone wanted over. Harry Anderson had a good header flash just over, Morecambe probably shaded the chances but didn't offer anything serious to threaten us. Their goal was a bad one to concede, a ball angled across the box found the one man who was almost guaranteed to score, Kevin Ellison.

A word on Kevin, the figure we all love to hate. He's like our Rheady, a wind up merchant of the highest order. These days he does it with a wry smile on his face and I for one love to see it, especially now he's not quite as effective as he once was. Any young kids out there wanting a role model, in terms of fitness and approach, ought to look at him. The day he made his debut for Altrincham, Ronan Keating was at number one with 'You Say Nothing At All'. Lou Bega hadn't even charted as yet with Mambo Number 5. Basically, Ellison is old and a credit to the profession, even if we do love to boo the bald-headed bugger.

Seb was enjoying himself, he found five minutes of extra time from somewhere, but by the time Matt Green was (rather suspiciously) throwing his shirt into the crowd, half of the 8,000 (ish) crowd were already listening to Thommo and Michael in the car. People had been streaming out from about 80 minutes onwards and I couldn't fault them. It wasn't an afternoon to stay put, I'm not even sure Danny would begrudge people getting off early on such a horrible afternoon, not when everything we needed to do had been done by 40 minutes. That game was the equivalent of doing all your Christmas shopping in the first week of December, but still being dragged round the bloody shops in the last week because it's Christmas.

There were plenty of stand out performers. Jason Shackell got the vote on the club's Twitter and I can see why, him and Bozzy were brilliant again, but the former Derby man did score that unreal free kick. I personally thought Harry Anderson was excellent, he tired a little late on but never once gave up the chase and frightened the hell out of their left back. Had Bruno been playing we'd be lauding him too, Morecambe are not a side who defend well and we exposed that time and again in the first half.

I thought both Freck and Michael O'Connor were excellent too, always willing runners and driving us on where they could. McCartan had a quiet game on the ball, but was fouled for the free kick and the penalty so was clearly doing something right. The ball didn't run for John Akinde in the second half, but I thought aside from the chance he created and then wasted he had a good game. It's funny because when he tricked past those two defenders and then missed the chance, one bloke above me was saying he was shit for missing the chance, but to my left they were praising his hard work to create the opportunity. Glass half full, glass half empty and all that.

After getting home and warming up (by about 10pm) I decided not to write until this morning for a reason I'm not going to explain anymore. When I got up this morning I'd seemingly suffered from being out in the cold and felt like I'd been caught in a challenge between Ellison and Akinde, which is why my match report is being brought to you in the middle of Sunday afternoon. Apologies to the boys of Stacey West FC too, I was due to go see them in action this morning, but as a snivelling mess I ended up staying under the duvet. I feel marginally better now (thanks for asking).

As I did, I wasn't thinking of the FA Cup third round, I wasn't even thinking about being clear at the top once more with a better goal difference. No, I was thinking about the 35-year old centre half who scored one of the most powerful free kicks I've ever seen with my own eyes, wondering how the hell we ever convinced him to drop into League Two to play for Lincoln City. The next time you're doubting our club, if indeed you do, ponder that yourself. If a man earning (at a guess) well over £20k a week last season can be convinced to drop into the basement division for 10% of that, a man with nothing but Championship and top flight experience, a man who organises a defence like a general and pulls free kicks out of his locker like Ronaldo, surely we're doing something right off the pitch.

'Always worked so hard for the team' – These Imps fans react to Matt Green's departure

December 20, 2018

It's been in the pipeline for some time and now, just before the festive period, the news has finally broken. After 18 months as a Lincoln City player, Matt Green has moved to Salford City.

It's not a surprise at all, maybe the timing has caught one or two out, but the deal itself is a no brainer for everyone involved. As much as we like Matt Green and as much as he likes the club, he's been offered a good deal elsewhere. I feel I write these words most transfer windows, whenever a player leaves who we would like to have kept.

The problem here is Danny wouldn't be thinking of offering a two and a half year deal to Matt, certainly not at the level that Salford will be wanting to spend. That isn't because we don't rate him, but Danny has never been extravagant with spending, nor has he tied up squad places unnecessarily. Whether you agree with it or not, Matt wasn't a starter this season and when we're offered a chunky fee and the player secures his immediate future, everyone is a winner.

Everyone except Danny Cowley, the man who has had the final say on the deal. He loses a good player, albeit one used sparingly, and now has to replace him. That isn't an easy task either. Laughably, I'm still seeing people talking about Macauley Bonne as a replacement. The money Orient would want rules it out, as does the fact he wouldn't play a role in the first team given his style. Danny has to attract a player that fits the requirements of the squad, whatever that might be.

One thing he does not have to do is make a statement signing for the fans. No James Norwood, no Macauley Bonne and no Christian Doidge.

One thing is certain, nobody is glad to see Matt go. He was a great player for us last season, some of us even thought that before the Port Vale game in which he scored. Had he been used in a 4-4-2 all season, and not a wide player in a 4-3-3, he would have scored 20 goals at least. He leaves with a decent record and I personally wish him all the best.

Sadly, I now have to change my banner image, another job to do before Christmas.

Mark Churchill
@church197
Really gonna miss your impact on games Greeny. Always worked so hard for the team. Thanks & good luck

Rob
@Jacobma34309505
Good luck Greeny, can't blame you. Great attitude and work ethic. You will be missed but you deserve to be playing. All the best

A slightly merrier Christmas than most: Imps 3-2 Newport
December 23, 2018

When I was a child, my Dad used to be going about his business around the house signing a song that went along the lines of 'Jingle bells …. oh what fun it is to see, Lincoln win away'. Of course, we never seemed to actually win away at Christmas. For many years, we never seemed to win.

My Dad has a habit of singing inappropriate songs, I'm not talking about German bombers or whatever else we think is wrong these days, but he could be found chanting 'we are top of the league' away at Crewe last season when we were in fact eighth. It means little to my Dad, actual league position, he's been watching City since the late sixties and has seen his fair share of crap. If we're top ten, then we're top in his book.

Only we're not just top ten now, are we? We are top. We're also away on Boxing Day so hopefully, my Dad gets to roll out both of his favourite songs and for once, they'll both be relevant. Events elsewhere meant that whatever we did against Newport, we'd be top at Christmas, but thanks to our endeavour, resilience and a little bit of luck, we'll be top after the Boxing Day fixtures as well.

Thankfully it wasn't as cold as last week and thanks to a few people being missing, I had two seats to myself in the stand. It meant for the first time this season I couldn't feel the person next to me shuffle when his phone vibrated. Last week being unusually close to another man was life-saving, yesterday I enjoyed the leg room.

I was concerned going into the game. Bruno being missing is a big blow and whilst I like Tom Pett a lot, he isn't the same threat out wide that the former Woking man is. That's not to say I would drop Pett, he's been exceptional recently and when we need that little bit of quality, he can bring it.

Other than that it was 'as you were', with the line up taking on a familiar feel. It's odd that we've settled into a favoured XI so easily when at the start of the season we tried three or four formations and different combinations. The only notable absence was, or course, Matt Green. He's still on our header image though, I guess we'll need to rectify that soon.

I often joke about playing Danny Cowley bingo, bankers being the phrases 'start with intensity' or 'start with a real purpose'. What he means, in technical speak, is get at them early and let them know they're at the bank. Get in their effing faces and hit them early. That's what the old school coaches would say, but however you choose to articulate it, that is what we did.

What better way to get in their faces than by grabbing an early opener? A corner from the right found Tom Pett on the left, he took his time to deliver a cross and John Akinde went into double figures for the season with a scruffy finish. Still, penalty, superb strike or scrambled effort, they all count and despite his header not getting anywhere, he was alert enough to hook the ball home via a heavy deflection. With that early goal came a spell of football from Lincoln that should have been gift-wrapped and put under every fan's tree on Tuesday.

For twenty minutes I was convinced I was watching the future Champions of League Two, we were that good. Our passing was excellent, neat little triangles were exchanged as willing runners found gaps in behind. Harry Anderson impressed me most in the opening few minutes, as Danny keeps saying he is only a young boy despite having played 79 times for City already. In all of his matches for the club he might not have scored a better individual effort than the second on the seven minute mark. He pressed down the right hand flank, dropping a shoulder and then dropping the other to try to get past his defender. When he couldn't do that he angled an effort across goal and into the bottom left hand corner of the Newport goal.

At 2-0, most football fans would have glanced at the scores and gone 'Lincoln are winning again', but that's not how it works when you're the Lincoln fan. After getting two my reaction was 'we need three to be sure', but I laughed it off. Last weekend against Morecambe two first-half goals would have been enough to win us the game, so I tried to remain comfortable with the fact we'd be fine at 2-0. Keep it tight, nick one late on.

There was a flash point I didn't particularly like, a clash of heads led to one of our players going down and what looked like an elbow then flattened one of our lads. I didn't have my glasses but I think, possibly, it was Toffolo. Maybe the lack of glasses had me asking for a red card prematurely, certainly some people around me thought it warranted one. Mind you, a female voice behind me claimed at one point that 'Matt Rhead would have run for that' after John Akinde opted not to chase down a lost cause. I'm not sure she's been before.

Once our spell wore off, once the two goals and neat passes had been soaked up by Newport, they came back into the game. I chuckled at their manager's post-match reaction that they were the better team, but they're certainly a side with lots to offer going forward. Antoine Semenyo is a Bristol City youngster on loan at Rodney Parade and he looked to have a bit about him, megging Neal Eardley like the skilful kid in the playground used to do to me, before pulling a good save from Grant Smith. Smith was called into action a few minutes later to make a finger-tipped save from a Robbie Wilmott drive. It might have been 2-0, but the next goal was crucial. If we got a third, we'd be secure but if they got back into it, we'd all be wishing the game was over.

Just before half time, the latter happened. We've been solid enough at the back all season, but have a habit of letting in sloppy goals and this was no different. It was a simple goal from a corner, one perhaps the keeper might have wanted to do better from, but one that the bigger lads might have wanted to get clear too. Up until that point I didn't think we'd put a foot wrong, but as Padraig 'bloody' Amond slammed the ball into the back of the net you just knew the game wasn't over.

Here's my honesty shout; for a few minutes at the start of the second half we looked crap. The fast-flowing passing was replaced by a nervousness, not brought on by a hostile crowd either. Maybe Newport decided we wouldn't like the game brought to us, but that is exactly what they did. We misplaced passes, hacked at clearances and generally looked a different outfit to the first half.

It wasn't the case all the time, we played some nice balls across the back four, looking to slow the game down and keep control, but Newport have the players to push and probe. Jamile Matt is another I like and he was causing us no end of problems. They were very good in the air, but the balls kept coming from long to our defenders and on too many occasions, we didn't win the header.

Credit where it is due, when our fans tried to lift the noise level and give our lads a boost, the small contingent in the corner from South Wales did exactly the same. They proved you don't have to come in big numbers to create an atmosphere and I'm always one who will acknowledge good supporters. Fair play to them, they drove their team on.

It was a pulsating fixture, Newport always looked like scoring but when we did try our luck in the final third, we did to. Shay McCartan wanted to 'do a Shackell' by scoring from a free kick, but drew a good save instead, whereas at the other end a lobbed ball from Fraser Franks was nodded just wide by Semenyo. There was plenty for a neutral to be impressed with, but I'm not neutral and with 25 minutes left to play I feared a draw. MK Dons were losing, which made it worse in a way because a win would give us that four point cushion we did well to throw away in November.

From out of nowhere, the game was won. Newport had been on the attack, we hadn't had a spell of pressure but a big ball into Akinde was nodded on to Tom Pett who scored the pick of the goals with a lovely left-footed finish. It literally came rom nowhere but from being on the rope we seized the initiative. It was just reward for our earlier efforts, but a little harsh on Newport. Still, you have to defend well against the bigger teams in the division and they switched off.

Talking of switching off, it was 3-2 on 77 minutes. Bloody Amond as I'm sure he should be called was the scorer again, but the architect was Grant Smith. My Dad isn't convinced about Smith and I'll be honest, these last two home games he's looked nervy. He pulled off two good saves in the first period, but his sloppy pass into Matt lead to Amond banging in their third. In truth, there was still opportunity to stop it after the bad pass, but we've gone from being comfortable at 3-1 to struggling to hold on at 3-2.

The ten minutes before the goal we were back in the ascendency but those final fifteen minutes or so were nervy. Newport poured forward, we lost Michael O'Connor through injury and ended up with Bruno Andrade on through the middle with Rheady and Scott Wharton in the centre of the park. Wharton created a good chance to make it 4-2, surging forward on the break only to be wiped out by their player. When he didn't get the free kick he got up and wiped their lad out in retribution, only to be penalised. Danny didn't like that and told the fourth official so, but Thomas Bramall didn't like that and sent Danny off. Well, what's a Christmas fixture without a little touch-line drama?

We hung on and after seven minutes of the five minutes added time, the ref blew his whistle and the game was over. Sweet Caroline, not the most popular of songs, rang out loud and proud as we departed the Bank from a very testing match against a solid and exciting Newport side. Micky Flynn felt his side were the better of the two, but you get noting for thinking you're better but coring fewer goals, harsh realities of life.

There were some big performances from Imps' players too. Lee Frecklington did a lot of running and led by example from start to finish, something that might not be noted in the popular press. Tom Pett was outstanding and got the sponsors Man of the Match, a better shout than John Akinde who got Thommo's Man of the Match. Akinde had a good game, when you et a goal and an assist you have to take some of the plaudits. I thought Bozzie was the best player on the field, always dependable and never one to shirk a challenge, header or a bone crunching tackle.

It wasn't convincing for 90 minutes, but it was for thirty-five or forty. We didn't look unbroachable for the whole game, but both their goals should have been dealt with better. We didn't create a lot of clear-cut chances, but we scored three goals from open play. Looks can be deceiving, and in the end I think we were good value for the win.

I'm this league, there's little separating the very best and the very worst. Every side can, on their day, beat any other team in the division. Look at MK Dons, they were the benchmark, or so I was told, a few weeks ago. Now they've lost four of their last seven in all competitions and look to be rocking a little. For the record, we've lost five in all competitions all season, one of which was against a Championship side, away, with a handful of reserves playing.

I know the mantra, never too high when we win, never too low when we lose. That's great, but I wanted to end on something which is a little bit of a retort to some fans chatting what I can only describe as garbage after we drew at Oldham. Back then the train of thought was we were 16th in the six-game form table and I was asked was that reflective of where we were as a side. I declined to answer because it wasn't up to me to do so, it was up to Lincoln City.

We're second in the current six game form table, level with Mansfield at the top on 14 points from a possible 18. we're the only team to have won three in a row and we're currently on a ten game unbeaten run in all competitions, excluding penalties.

Since that game, of the players who came under fire, Harry Anderson has scored two in four, John Akinde has four in four. Words are not always the best way to answer critics, results and goals are.

Merry Christmas.

'There are no corners cut' – Lee Frecklington on intense Christmas schedule
December 25, 2018

I recently caught up with Lee Frecklington in preparation for the Port Vale programme, but got a chance to talk to him about the punishing Christmas schedule which sees the Imps play five games in fifteen days.

We played Newport this weekend, followed by Crewe tomorrow. On Saturday we face Cambridge, whilst New Year's Day sees us host Port Vale, before a match against Everton you might have heard a bit about.

For a team such as Lincoln and a manager such as Danny Cowley, it presents a challenge. The level of preparation that goes into a Lincoln game is no secret, but with such an intense schedule it heaps a lot of pressure on the players. There's the video analysis, individual work on opponents and patterns of play and in the case of some players, different positions to work on.

Tom Pett has to look at a winger's game, as well as his usual midfield role. That will apply to other players too and I asked Lee how they'd go about facing that challenge. He revealed that by hook or by crook, the hard work will be put in.

"The games might come thick and fast over the festive period, but it won't affect the amount of work we put in off the pitch. It'll be tough to squeeze it all in but rest assured, we'll get the work done."

"There are no corners cut at our place, the gaffer might keep us there late at night or he'll get us there early in the morning, but there's no way he'll let us go into a match without the same level of preparation we have for every single game at any other time of the year."

"No stone gets left unturned and we'll make sure the level of preparation is the same for the busy period games just as it will be for the first game of the season, or the last."

Lee was chatting to me after a busy day, training ahead of the Newport win, then off to the press conference before attending a child's party at the club. He squeezed me in quickly before going about his father duties at home, but we chatted not only about the Christmas period but also the transfer window, new year's resolutions and his favourite moment of the year, not only as a Lincoln player but also as a Leeds fan.

Boxing Day Blues: Crewe 2-1 Imps
December 26, 2018

Firstly, there's not a lot I can tell you about the game that you don't already know. I wasn't there, I've spent Christmas in Cambridge and we travelled back today, before going back there this weekend. I wasn't at Gresty Road so the usual level of analysis is either to be omitted, or fudged.

I won't pull the wool over your eyes, so this is to be a single page assessment of the game through the eyes of fans who were there, followed by a few thoughts from me. The general consensus is we were utter tripe. Danny more or less said it and we can credit Crewe all we want, but it doesn't reflect all that well on them. If they were that good, David Artell might be asking why they don't do it every week. It might just have been we were so bad, they looked good.

It does make me wonder how much the mindset was wrong today. Danny mentioned that in his post match interview, as well as saying he wasn't going to applaud them fighting until the end or something along the lines of 'I won't thank them for running around a bit at the end'. That may not be verbatim, but it was pretty much the crux of his comments.

My problem with today comes from the response. You know, that whole 'never too high when we win, never too low when we lose' thing? It just doesn't seem to ram home. The inane comments I've already seen baffle me. 'We need a response against Cambridge' - of course we do. if we're utter shit there, we'll get beat too. However, failure to win at Cambridge won't rule us out of promotion either and we have to remember that.

I read one post saying all the promotion rivals were catching us, absolute garbage. We've pulled away from everyone bar Mansfield Town and whilst I'm sure those posters would argue the exception proves the rule, it does not. Everyone has a spell of form, everyone crumbles a little too and we've just been in form. Unlike the Stags, we haven't had to resort to watering pitches to get games called off, we take the hands we're dealt rather than trying to stack the deck.

Still, none of this masks we were poor today, as were MK Dons who have lost two on the spin (something we haven't done all season), as were Colchester and Bury too.

It also pains me to see the anti-Akinde brigade out in force before the final whistle was even blown at Gresty Road. There are some people who will simply never like Big John, even though he has scored ten goals this season, even though he's had a hand in a further ten. They have their reasons and if pushed, in a non public forum, I'd have a stab at what they might be, but believe me we didn't lose today because of John Akinde, we lost because all the players on the field, bar Josh Vickers, were poor.

I'm going to keep my head, we're still four points clear and after every one of these games that have had fans in uproar we seem to bounce back. After drawing 2-2 at Oldham the world was caving in, losing 1-0 to Tranmere had us down as a mid table also-ran and even I wasn't brave enough to delve too deep into the psyche of the moaners after the Cambridge and Carlisle draws at home.

Yes, we were bad. Yes, we need to be better, but the promotion assault is still on course, it's all still in our hands. Our players, they played badly but they've not suddenly become shit overnight, certainly not as alarmingly as Crewe's seemed to have improved overnight. We'll go to Cambridge this week and give them a decent game but do you know what? I think we'll draw there. I fear we will, not because it will make us play-off hopefuls at best, not because it'll see our lead pegged back to a point or two, but because the very small minority of slathering morons wanting Akinde sold, Ollie Palmer brought back in and Danny fired will once again be given a platform to mouth their views.

Social media has a lot of positives, without it I wouldn't be a writer, I wouldn't get paid for talking about the Championship and I wouldn't have time to indulge my Imps passion on here. I wouldn't have met half as many cool people, many I class as close friend now but who I first interacted with on social media (Neil, Chris and Ben spring to mind before I even have to think about it). However, it also accentuates the noise those with the inclination to make silly, outlandish statements make. It gives people with agendas a chance to further their cause, to undermine others and to generally acts like pricks whilst pretending to be the ;voices of reason' or to be offering 'genuine criticism'.

Nobody is above criticism and today we were poor. I won't hide from that, it's why I've come on here quickly to write about a game I didn't attend, but perspective is important. A football season is a marathon, 46 individual stages that go into making up success or failure. Sure, we've just lost a stage but right now, we've won enough to make me think we'll be on the podium at the end of the race and let's be brutally honest: third would be good enough for 95% of fans.

I will stress we should never be accepting of defeat, we shouldn't have the attitude 'oh well, on we go', but it is not up to us as fans to put it right by getting angry on social media and abusing each other, is it? It's up to Danny and Nicky, the two guys who gave up their Christmas only to have it ruined by our players not bothering to turn up, or not approaching the game in the right manner. Rest assured they'll be given the run around, as per Lee Frecklington's interview yesterday, which you may have missed.

Please, do remain grounded and remember that we've no God-given right to win and that as things stand, we're still in a great position to be promoted to League One next season.

How are we faring? The Imps half season review
December 28, 2018

It was never going to be easy, battling away in a League Two packed with strong teams and good players, but as the halfway point passes us by, it's fair to say the Imps have fared as well as anyone could have hoped.

There's a few out there who'll have you believe we could be seven points clear, or ten, or fifteen and they're right, we could be. However, we could also be six points shy of MK Dons, or we could be like Notts County and have imploded despite the pre-season excitement.

What we have actually done is risen to the challenges we've faced and adapted when we have needed to. The main focus this season is surely on the league, a fact demonstrated as early as August when we effectively binned off the trip to Ewood Park by playing players who later couldn't even get in the side to face Accrington. This season is all about League One football and right now, we're on course for it.

Let's not be arrogant about it, there's a long way to go and no matter where you are in the league, a trip to Cambridge is never going to be easy, nor is a trip to Crewe. We might be doing well but nobody is giving us promotion on a plate, this isn't 2005/06 when we were handed a top seven finish despite being guff. This is all of our own doing and if we're top three in May, it won't be thanks to anyone other than ourselves.

From the outside looking in, we are the team everyone thinks will go up. I went to MK Dons as you know and from inside the camp, they think finishing above us gives you promotion. My good friend Pete is a Manchester United season ticket holder and he continually tells me we're going up. The stats suggest we are too, top at Christmas usually means automatic promotion. Usually.

The problem is as Lincoln City fans we're used to failure. Fans of a certain age will talk to you about 1982/83, when we looked set for Division Two football, only to end up with nothing. My era remembers 2006/07, the season we came alive before Christmas and died after it. We've got form when it comes to throwing away a good hand and whether that was under Danny and Nicky, Schoey or Colin Murphy, it's been done.

What we tend to forget is 2016/17, in an odd way. We're happy to talk about our rise, to use it as 'perspective' when we lose and of course to rejoice when key dates come around, but we forget what resilience and fortitude we showed that season. We forget that Danny's side blasted through more than sixty games and still ended up on top of the table. It's easy to forget, but I had a read of my Season in Blogs book the other night and the same comments I read this season emerged every so often then. Uncertainty. Lack of belief we can go all the way and, when we won, a confidence that only set us up for a fall.

History will not get us into League One this season, nor will it guarantee our collapse. Everything will be defined by what happens when the players step across the paint, wearing the red and white (or grey and black) and going to do battle with whoever or whatever stands in our way. The FA Cup tie will be a nice distraction, but thank God we didn't have to get to the quarter-final for our pay-day this time around. By the time we enter the second week of January, we should simply have promotion to concentrate on.

There's plenty of big games we've got to get past, trips to Mansfield, Bury and MK Dons stand out as big matches. Tranmere and Colchester won't relish coming to the Bank and our form at home will be the deciding factor. I rubbished someone who said you have win your home games and draw your away games, but a point against the Dons, Stags and Bury will be just reward for our endeavours. Killing sides off at home, like we did Newport and Morecambe, will get us promoted. Might be nice to defend a bit better though.

Therein lies our Achilles Heel, the one area of the field I believe we could suffer. There's plenty said about us going forward, how we don't score enough and all that, but we've scored 42 goals compared to 31 on the same date last season. We've played a game less too.

I recall Danny saying to me pre-season that he had to find ten more goals this season. If he succeeded in doing that then he felt we'd be in the automatic promotion spots. It doesn't matter if ten come from John Akinde, it doesn't matter if all ten are penalties, the simple analysis Danny conducted said ten more goals equals automatic promotion. In the first half of the season we've done just that, although a woeful Port Vale might be thanked for six of them. Hopefully they defend as well on New Years Day, a fixture that isn't often kind to us.

What is interesting is the fact we've conceded three more than at the same stage last season, having played a game less. That's where our problem is and yet despite the numbers telling us it's the case, I can't put my finger on exactly why it happens. Shackell and Bozzy are a good pairing, dominant in the air and always there with a tackle. The full backs are very different, Harry Toffolo is a classic wing back but not an old-style full back, whereas Neal Eardley is the other way around. They've both quality players at this level.

Josh Vickers is (by Danny's estimates) a Championship keeper and I'd be inclined to agree to a degree. He is certainly one who could play League One football with little effort. His injury record worries me but in Grant Smith we have a decent replacement, even if his performance against Newport had a few worrying. So to sum up, we have a good centre back pairing, good full backs and a decent keeper, yet we're conceding more than we did last season. Was Paul Farman just that good?

The obvious answer for the year on year change is the set up. this season we don't have the two midfielders screening the back four, something which certainly made us stronger last time out.

When Bozzy and Alex Woodyard paraded in front of the back four it offered additional protection, but it left us shy going forward. the fallibility at the back is a symptom of our slightly more adventurous approach further up the pitch. Nobody is to blame as such, sometimes there is no blame. That'll disappoint a few.

You see, in pointing out that Achilles Heel I am not saying we're going to be brought down by a bad defence, not at all. I am merely pointing out an area which may be of concern. We may sign additional cover, Danny might feel that he wants another left back to come in, or someone capable of playing both sides. I think lots of us would like to see that, especially as we don't have genuine cover in either full back position. Kellan Gordon isn't a right back, James Wilson isn't either and Sam Habergham has disappeared from view, sadly.

That is where I feel we are right now. We're in a great position and every instinct tells me we'll be promoted at the end of the season, but the Lincoln City gene in me tells me not to be so bold. It's pertinent to point out that in 2006/07, after 23 matches we only had 44 points and were third in the table, having scored three more than we have now but conceding seven more. That season we'd thrashed Barnet 5-0 and Rochdale 7-1 too, adding to the goal tally. We finished fifth with 74 points.

In 1983, the year we should have reached the second tier, we had to wait until the middle of January to complete 23 matches, but back then we had 49 points and had scored 52 goals, conceding one fewer. We finished sixth with 76 points.

That isn't a barometer of how we might do this season, nor is it intended to worry anyone, but there's a lot of work ahead of us. On our day, we've proven we're as good as anyone in this division and with the right moves in January, as well as a consistent and well-planned approach to matches, we should be just fine.

Many more outings like Boxing Day and we won't be.

Character Tested: Cambridge 1-2 Imps
December 30, 2018

On a surprisingly mild winter evening, City turned in the sort of performance that has both horrified us and delighted us in equal measure this season.

It's been 21 years since Lincoln last scored more than a single goal at the Abbey Stadium, Phil Stant, John Robertson and an own goal cancelling out a Michael Kydd strike in 1997. In the interim period we've own just once, in 2004 and regularly made the short journey home unhappy.

That didn't happen yesterday but after 45 minutes of action, it might well have been the case.

Thanks to my mate Dave we didn't get to the ground until twenty minutes before kick off. A planned beer in town was scuppered by him being an hour late (it's not my fault he protested…) which meant a late arrival at the game. There was some benefit though, the Imps fans were in fine voice as we made our way across Coldham Common towards the away end. I quite like the set up at Cambridge, the away end almost being isolated if you want it to be and funnelling away from potential flashpoints.

That's all I admire by the way; the burger bar situation was no better than last season and I had to pee in the pitch black after half time thanks to there being no light in the toilets. Crewe fans would have been crying their little hearts out on social media this morning, would they not? that's if they've stopped celebrating their Boxing Day cup final win.

Anyway, the football. One I'd not got a burger and not got a pre-match beer, we took our places on a traditional eighties terracing to watch what was promising to be a great game of football. The home side haven't been having a great season, but Colin Calderwood has got them playing a 4-4-2 with lots of width and pace, something we looked to counter with a virtually identical formation.

The big surprise had to be Rhead and Akinde up front together, two monsters likely to batter a defence into submission if nothing else. the key to that working is pace and width, something offered by a returning Bruno Andrade and a resurgent Harry Anderson. The biggest loser in that formation is Michael O'Connor, the industrious midfielder sitting out in favour of Pett and Frecklington. Perhaps, in the absence of Gary Deegan, Danny thought it wouldn't be such a battle in the centre of the park.

For twenty minutes, he was right. we weren't scintillating, we weren't out of the blocks as quickly as we are at home, but we certainly pressed home our intentions with some positive play in the first period of the game. We didn't create anything clear-cut enough to suggest a goal might come of it, Freck's drive from 20-yards the only real test of David Forde.

Slowly, but certainly Cambridge made their way into the game and we faded badly. We got a montage of the sort of errors we've seen in recent weeks, misplaced passes from our big players, 50/50 balls being lost on the deck and in the air and the lack of foot on the second ball. Cambridge, clearly happy at playing in front of a bumper Christmas crowd, thrived. They've got some good players and like Crewe, they've no business in the relegation battle on their day.

At least Cambridge can point to the manager change as a reason for their improvement. David Amoo really impressed me, his movement and control was excellent and he terrified Harry Toffolo on more than one occasion. Javid Brown is a decent player too and Ibhere up front would be custom-made for our forward line, although his contribution to them is only the same as Akinde does for us. Still, they moved forward regularly and began to get a foothold in the game.

They finally made their pressure count with a goal that was wrong on so many levels for City. A lost tackle in the middle of the park set Ibhere off, he shrugged off the challenge of tom Pett and laid the ball out wide to Brown who teased a cross over. Ibhere, marked by two players, simply nodded into the net. Even his connection was poor and should perhaps have been dealt with better by Grant Smith. There were so many chances to stop a simple attack, but we took none of them. Another game, another goal conceded.

After that we folded like a recently washed duvet cover. Cambridge were backed by a vocal 4,000 home fans, rather ironically chanting 'where were you when you were shit' when they usually have at least 1,000 fewer at the Abbey. Irony wasn't winning them the game, but it was something else that stuck in my throat in that first 45 minutes.

I get pulled over for criticising referees as well, but I didn't think Carl Boyeson had the strongest of matches. He should perhaps have pulled a card out a little earlier than he did, but I suspect he was swayed by the big occasion. He's an experienced referee, but there were two or three challenges that warranted a card, not only from Cambridge. It was a hotly contested game, but as it wore on he looked likely to give them a decision. One such choice, a free kick dead central of Smith's goal, could have given them a further lead, but Smith saved well.

The keeper quickly redeemed himself for any perceived notion of him doing better with Ibhere's header. He got the merest of touches on a drive that ended up rattling the bar, another great chance for the home side to go in 2-0 at the break. They should have done, by the time the whistle went for the break we'd been well and truly taught a lesson. The first ten or fifteen minutes seemed a long way away and I was wishing, more than ever, I'd got that pre-match pint.

After pissing on my shoes in the dark, I checked the latest scores to find MK Dons winning. I begrudgingly went back to the terraces for 45 minutes I feared held little more than broken promises for the Imps, trying to fond solace in the fact we'd still be top as we welcomed in 2019.

One player who had impressed me in the first half was Harry Anderson. Not so long ago he was being pulled up on his end product, but he deserves huge praise for his attitude and his bullish aggression. He's not like normal wingers, he doesn't fly past full backs with grace or poise all the time, he fights. He battles and bullies and in the first half, he'd been our main aggressor.

John Akinde had a decent game too, putting in a strong shift leading the line. I wasn't convinced that him and Rheady would make a good pairing, but we won a few aerial duels even if it hadn't resulted in anything positive. It does make us a little more long ball though, but no more so than some we've played this year.

The early stages of the second period were scrappy. They'd identified Anderson as a threat and seemingly looked to target him, with Reggie Lambe scything him down in front of our fans. It was the sort of booking a players gets secretly applauded for by his own fans, 'taking one for the team'. I rated Lambe too, he'd had a good game, but when he committed another foul a few minutes later I thought he was lucky not to walk.

A sickening clash of heads on 56 minutes led to a long stoppage, then oddly a yellow card for Harry Anderson. He jumped into an aerial duel he was more than entitled to go for and yet when the two prone players eventually got back on their feet, he was carded. He came back on with a bump on his head, but he'd also got more motivation to get something for the Imps.

On the hour I thought John Akinde was felled when through on goal too, a simple punt up field from Smith into the channel found the big man who got involved in a simple race with the defender. For my money, he was pulled back, but had it been the other way around I might not have seen it the same way. City were asking questions though, the home side were showing some mental fragility, maybe because they were defending the corner dominated by red and white shirted fans, maybe because they've been poor for so long they feel it's always going to be tough to close out a game.

When we finally got the break our first half performance barely deserved, it came thanks to Harry Anderson. He collected the ball in the middle of the park and found the energy to surge towards goal, all the while being pulled and pushed around. only when he got within yards of the penalty area was the attention enough to take him off his feet, earning us a free kick 22 or so yards from goal.

Matt Rhead performed his usual trick of blocking the keeper's view, much to the ire of the easily irritated Forde, but when john Akinde joined in too it looked, albeit briefly, like an emerging double act. Surely Matt Rhead, written off more times at Lincoln than any other player, couldn't be the man we end up relying on to partner John Akinde in the second half of the season? Could he? As he blocked the keeper's view and did his usual routine, a pang of nostalgia stabbed me in the gut. He's a legend you know, our Matt. An unorthodox one, but a Lincoln City character we'll never forget.

I have a habit of saying things like 'we never do anything from free kicks', something I said once more, probably in hope more than anything. As Neal strode up I didn't for one second think it's fly high and wide, but I couldn't have called the precision with which he beat the keeper. Could Forde have done better? some on social media think so but I suspect it was perfectly placed to beat him. The crowd erupted and I suddenly felt there was only one winner.

Checking my phone alerted me to MK Dons taking the lead, meaning a win was going to be crucial and within five minutes we'd sealed it. The move started again with Eardley, another of his pinpoint deliveries found Matt Rhead to nod down in the area. His ball landed at the feet of Big John with his back to goal, be he turned and scooped his effort into the back of the net. It wasn't a classic, but it did give us a 2-1 lead.

What it highlighted to me was how dangerous Akinde is when he's not just the target man. With Matt Rhead doing to nodding down, we got to see the poacher in action, a man happy battling for possession in the six yard box. His goal against Newport was similar, this one perhaps a bit more convincing and measured. It isn't one you'll see again and again, but he showed a true striker's grit to not only turned in the area, but also finish despite the attention of defenders and a keeper.

That's five in six now for Akinde and the arguments about our forward line seem to have abated.

The best was yet to come as the thrilling final fifteen minutes turned into almost half an hour. We had eight minutes of injury time allocated, of which I timed us playing almost 11, meaning there was 26 minutes of football to be played after we scored. Cambridge looked like they might get an equaliser and at one point a game of pinball in the area should have brought them joy, but in the end Grant Smith made a superb save to bring the phase to a close. Smith then superbly tipped a free kick onto the post too, proving his credentials as a keeper and giving him lots of confidence going forward too.

Cambridge weren't laying siege as such, but they were fighting for their lives and those final 26 minutes could have seen us draw 2-2, or even win 3-1 as we looked to get away on the break. Our biggest travelling support of the season, 2,276, watched on in agony and ecstasy as a miserable opening 45 minutes were washed away.

Someone who was laying siege to an opponent was Northampton and as we played past five o'clock for yet another week, they snatched a late draw from being 2-0 down. Junior Morais, sent off against us in the last-minute of our FA Cup tie, turned from Imps villain to hero as he pegged back the Dons meaning as the final whistle finally blew at the Abbey Stadium, we'd not only won 2-1 but opened up a six point gap at the top of the table.

What more is there to say? The clear Man of the Match was Harry Anderson, but John Akinde was certainly second and after that any one of three or four for their second half performances alone. If we win the league, we won't win it by sweeping teams aside and bagging four or five a game, but we'll do it by fighting, scrapping, competing and demonstrating the character we have, both in the team and as a club, time and again.

We won't get carried away but thus far over the festive period we have six points from nine, with Port Vale the visitors on New Year's Day. That won't be easy, but it shouldn't be as tough as the last two matches and coupled with the fact a resurgent Cambridge visit Stadium MK, you wouldn't bet against us still having at least a six point lead over them as we travel to Goodison Park.

January

Sucker punch: Imps 1-1 Port Vale
January 1, 2019

I hate leaking a late goal in a game like we did today. It feels like a defeat, especially when you look at the other results. It's also easy to forget what we've gained over Christmas and how we're still very much architects of our own destiny.

There was a bit to talk about today, but certainly not as much as Cambridge or Newport. The team selection raised a few eyebrows, but I'm going to start with a little bit about the fanzine. We've upped the run, saved some for internet sales and a few for the Grimsby game, but on the whole it sold very well indeed. Thanks to our 2018 profits and to our print company resolving the complaints, we're able to put every penny of today's sales into the club and still have the next print run covered.

That means that give or take a few pence, purely from today, £250 will be going directly to the club courtesy of the fanzine. It's going in via sponsorship of a player, be it a youth team lad or a first team player, we'll keep you posted on that as the week goes on. Remember we're also part of the Mattadores group that sponsors Matt Rhead and donates to charity every time he scores, assist or does anything remotely noteworthy.

Today, his mere inclusion was noteworthy. I wonder if perhaps there was an element of 'it's Port Vale, Rheady will be up for it'. As a Stoke fan there's plenty of needle there and he does seem to do well against the Valiants. It seemed harsh on Big John to me, he's been great the last couple of weeks, so maybe it was merely squad rotation.

Other than that there's little surprise in the team selection and that does point to the need for incoming players this January. For the avoidance of doubt, we are not one of the clubs bidding £750,000 for Jayden Stockley, but MK Dons are. That's what we're up against in terms of the promotion challenge. We do not have that money to fritter away, they do. It might be hard to take, with the huge complex some of our fans have about being top in everything, but we are not one of the really big players in this league, not financially.

That was also underlined by the sale of Matt Green, something Danny commented on post game today. His comments were interesting and whilst we're on team selection and options, I want to pick it up. He said that he backed the sale of Matt Green given the sums involved. He did not say he made the decision, he said he supported it. Interesting? Perhaps. Maybe that's just something I picked up on and read too much into.

It didn't matter which XI started, they started badly. Port Vale went at us early doors, forcing a succession of corners and having some good possession. For the first ten minutes or so we looked really poor, as we did in the first half against Cambridge and all game against Crewe. The points haul over Christmas has been good, but the performances have been bang average. Danny knows it too, but this isn't a division you win based purely on performances. points win prizes.

It didn't look to me like we'd get many points in the first ten minutes, but I thought after that we took control of the game. We found our stride with the passing and looked to break down a tight Port Vale back four, or back eight at times. They were solid, but they began to sink deeper. Our joy all came from the right hand side, Harry Anderson never stopped running and offering the out ball, him and Neal Eardley have looked excellent in recent weeks. On the left we looked decidedly average.

I wonder if Bruno is still suffering the effects of his injury, or if Harry Toffolo isn't quite 100% either. Neither looked to have the same penetration, pace or endeavour that we saw in the early section of the season. Then again, they've had four games in such a short space of time and that has to take its toll. If they've gone into that period carrying knocks, it's not going to be made better by such an intense schedule. that's the same for both sides, but it might offer a reason why we've lost our edge on the left.

Or, other sides might have done their homework, seen how effective we are on that side of the field and moved to combat it, moving attention away from the right as much. I'm not as naïve to think that they would ignore the threat on one flank, but when they're doubling up on Rheady and crowding out Toff and Bruno, there has to be a bit of space left over somewhere.

It's hard to think of what to write about in too much depth in the first half because although I thought we controlled it, we did so without ever really looking like breaking the deadlock. We got some balls into the box, sure. We got a couple of headers off, but did we test their keeper? One save I counted came from a Rheady header. We're back to the centre forward looking isolated and when that effort was parried back into the six yard box, I couldn't help wondering if someone might have gambled with a run. It would be Shay's job, but he was lurking elsewhere.

We also had a decent opportunity from a free kick, but having been spoiled in recent weeks the easily-saved shot on target didn't exactly get my pulse racing.

The other incident of note has to be Harry's injury and the Port Vale reaction to it. Everyone got a little bit heated didn't they? Most were hoping that the ref would stop the game, hoping Vale would kick it out. The ref didn't bother, nor did Port Vale and that, I'm afraid to say, is the right call. Harry was scythed, the ref should have blown for a free kick but if he deems there to be no foul, which he did, then the injury is irrelevant, especially as it's not a head injury.

Then we had the dust-up and again, that was handled in a manner which shouldn't raise too many concerns. The issue was the involvement of Anthony Kay. He had been booked early for a bad challenge, got away with at least one more and then made himself a target by getting involved in the handbags. There's an argument he could have seen red, but the referee chose two other targets and kept Kay on the field. It would have been harsh to dismiss him, but those with rose-tinted glasses might feel differently.

Half time, 0-0 and in fairness, I thought it would stay that way.

The second half was as inspiring as the first, Vale never looked like a side in the bottom six, but they didn't give me cause to believe they're a top half side either. They chased, harried and harassed, we did the same and neither side really got into any sort of rhythm.

Some will say John Akinde coming on was to blame, those people will not be correct. It's right John offers a little less than Rheady in terms of aerial threat, but he's more mobile. The thinking, one assumes, was Matt played 90 minutes against Cambridge and was getting involved a bit too much with their lads. John Akinde certainly did his part, but it wasn't his best display in an Imps shirt. Not bad for someone who ended up bagging an assist of course.

Our six goal hammering of Vale earlier in the season came almost exclusively from corners, so it was disappointing to see us fail to force one until the 57th minutes. True to form, the ball was whipped in, Big John got on the knock down and Shay McCartan bundled home. It seemed to be a big moment, everyone let out a sigh of relief and cheered the three points. Port Vale had retreated since their super start to the first half and surely they were there to be put to the sword. Surely.

That didn't happen though, did it? For whatever reason we switched off, stopped stretching the play with passes, or at least slowed it right down. The ball went from side to side, occasionally back to Grant Smith, but on the whole we seemed content that we'd done our job, the work was complete. After 57 minutes of football.

Don't get me wrong, we weren't incredibly poor, but we looked a little sloppy, maybe even tired. When Kellan Gordon came on for Bruno and swapped wings with Harry, our threat from both flanks essentially faded away. Without that outlet, Port Vale found more of the ball and began to edge closer and closer. We had chances, McCartan had a drive saved as did Harry, but they were flashes in what I could only describe as a lukewarm performance. It was made tougher by having the TV on in the box and seeing MK Dons hit Cambridge for six, the same Cambridge worthy of a draw against us a couple of days ago.

As the minutes ebbed away there was only going to be one side scoring the goals. Some might say if we'd had Matt Green to bring on things would have been different, I'm not sure they would. The players looked to just want things to be over and only a fine display from Jason Shackell and Michael Bostwick prevented Vale getting the equaliser. They began to show real quality, linking nice passes and stretching us. Obviously, they hit the bar and then Grant Smith pulled off a great save too. The signs were ominous.

I would moan about a corner they got just before their goal, but only in a desperate attempt to divert attention away from the failure to see the game out. Their boy went through, slipped or tripped and landed on the ball, pulled it in with his hands as if he'd been fouled and saw the ball squirm out for a goal kick, but the ref gave a corner. They didn't score directly from it (I don't think) but it should have given us a chance to alleviate pressure. Instead, Oyeleke got another stab at the long-range drive moments after and this time the bar helped him, not hindered him. 1-1 and that was that, two points dropped.

Was it a travesty? No. After an hour Port Vale deserved nothing from the game, but after ninety minutes they deserved their point. I won't start saying things like 'packed Christmas period', because it is the same for everyone. This wasn't a defeat and although some might tell you otherwise there isn't a huge issue we need to deal with at the club, certainly not on the pitch. You win some you deserve to lose, lose some you deserve to win and sometimes draw when you deserve to. We're still top, we're still clear of the chasing pack by four points and last time I checked, we're still on course for League One football. No team ever wins every game, no side ever plays well every week but if we don't turn up for ninety minutes we'll get punished.

It was disappointing to see a group of Port Vale fans spoiling for a fight both before and after the game. All the time we've had the Fan Zone I've seen no trouble, but six or seven dickheads shoved their way through signing Vale songs ahead of the match just looking for trouble. After the game the same idiots came out into the stream of Imps fans heading the other way, doing exactly the same. Mind you, if my local rivals had smashed my ground up whilst I sat at home not doing my homework a few weeks earlier, I suppose I'd be out looking for some sort of small victory, even if it comes via a 1-1 draw 100 miles from home. Think I'll have some vinegar with my salt.

It's a disappointing finish to the festive period after the joy of turning around the Cambridge game and that's a measure of the standards we've set. We're unhappy at a 1-1 draw, a point that sees us remain top not only into the Everton game, but after it too. In the grand scheme of things we know two points from every game between now and the end of the season will see us finish top three, but for some that won't be good enough. Some will want the title, something we're clearly competing for, but others will be perfectly happy with third. Me? I wanted the title, but I think right now if you offered me third I'd take it. Not because I fear we'll finish lower than that, but because I don't want to have to face the fact we might finish below Mansfield Town, or that a team with £750,000 to spend on a striker might also be above us in the table.

If they're the only two we end up behind then we'll be promoted, if we're above either of them it'll be down to hard work not spending £5k a week on a loan striker with crowds of 4,000, or spending the sort of money that would keep Morecambe solvent for a couple of years on a single player.

Yeah, can I get some chips now to go with the vinegar and salt? Cheers.

Another departure as Joan Luque leaves Sincil Bank
January 2, 2019

The Imps have today allowed Joan Luque to leave the club, becoming the second departure in recent weeks following on the heels of Matt Green.

Luque was signed from non-league Heybridge Swifts, but ended up making just four senior appearances for City. One of those, against Blackburn in the EFL Cup, resulted in a senior goal.

Since then he's struggled to make an impact and a poor showing in his loan switch to Bromley may have sealed his fate. His move is unlikely to be popular with fans though, who hoped to see more of the technically gifted midfielder.

The main issue with Luque was where he could fit in and whether he could achieve the levels of fitness required for the Football League. He was seen training on the astroturf shortly after he signed, pre-match. Clearly, he worked hard, but did he ever convince Danny he had what it takes?

Also, when he did play, he looked a little raw and what we don't need right now are projects. Positionally he looked wayward, like the talented kid at school who chased everything just to get on the ball. He's clearly got something, but not what is needed for our football club.

It's a huge shame, I rated Luque and felt there was a player in there who could have benefitted the side. There's likely to be plenty of reaction from this later in the day, most of it focused on him not being given a chance, but we don't work with the players every day.

He'll likely end up in the National League South or below again, having represented two sides this season.

Luque thanked the club for the chance to play in the Football League in a tweet released earlier.

Everton Build Up: I'm not excited at all and it's a good thing
January 4, 2019

This is the bit where I'm supposed to put some sort of rabble-rousing speech on about David and Goliath, talk about excitement, about it being our time and all that sort of stuff, right?

Lincoln City, heroes from 2016/17, back in the game, back on the big stage. Everton are out of form and likely to play a weakened side and that surely plays into our hands. it's a chance to put ourselves on the map (again) and if we lose, we've lost nothing. I should be talking about memorable days out, visiting a majestic stadium steeped in history and maybe, just maybe pulling off a result.

Balls to that.

The truth is, I'm not excited at all. Not even a little bit. I've spent zero hours thinking about the game and the only time I've mustered up anything close to an opinion has been for the various media people who have wanted a chat. There's nothing in tomorrow's match that has grabbed me by the short and curlies and screamed lifelong memory. Nothing.

I sound like a right miserable sod, don't I? I agree, so in order to work myself up into a frenzy I read back over the blogs I wrote in 2016 and 2017, the emotional stuff pre-Burnley and of course, the excited pre-Arsenal rhetoric. I soaked myself in those magical times and if I'm honest, I enjoyed it so much I read some twice. My favourite has to be the post-Ipswich stuff, reliving that through my own words was almost emotional. Almost.

I then settled back into my seat to recreate that magic for your viewing please and got nothing. Zilch. Nada. The truth is, I'm not excited about tomorrow one little bit. The result doesn't matter at all. If we win, great. If we win I'll change my tune and it will indeed be another great memory for us all to mull over in years to come. I don't actually think that will happen and if it does there's the thought that we'd 'only' be in round four. Been there, done that. We'd only have beaten a Premier League team on their own patch. Been there, etc etc.

There's lots of chatter about it being a great day out for the fans, something to cherish as a reward for the loyal support. That's all well and good if we win, but if we don't it won't be a great day out. I enjoyed Arsenal to a degree, but was it a day I'll remember for ever? Not for the right reasons no. We got beat 5-0, remember? I don't enjoy things like that, whether it's Oliver Giroud scoring the goals or Ollie Banks.

One thing I did like about Arsenal was the 'sesh' as we like to call it these days. There's nothing better than getting mortal with the lads, right? Taking over a big city, singing a few songs and all that. Right now, that's not for me either. I like a drink, but I can do that in Lincoln on a Saturday if I like. It matters little to me where I get together with the Imps fans and my own personal preference is to take over somewhere like Notts County or Mansfield, somewhere they actually give a rat's ass who we are.

Everton won't care tomorrow; they'll smile fondly at us and praise our support like Ipswich did. We can all come away thinking we're the best of the best, but what does it actually matter? We know our support is the best there is in League Two, personally I don't need Everton to tell me.

I'll enjoy the day, of course I will. We're going on the rustic minibus and I'll be with my Dad, Dave, Neil and the gang, so it is all good. I just can't get nervous for a game that has little riding on it. If I just wanted a day out, I'd join the National Trust. I follow Lincoln to watch us be successful and frankly, I don't think we will be tomorrow. I could get that little snippet of hope in my heart we might grab something, but I'll save it.

All of this is going somewhere, I'm not laying on the miserable twat routine for no reason. I realise exactly why I'm not as up for it as I was in 2017. I realised it as I read the blogs from the week before the Ipswich game, or the week after the Burnley game. It's because right now, we're on a different path.

Two years ago, we were only just emerging from the cloak of the National League, peering out from behind and letting the world know we were back. Lincoln fans have a chip on their shoulders, me included, about being noticed. Why aren't we on TV? Why aren't our players picked for this award or that accolade? Why aren't we on the football map? Up until 2011, we were. Keith Alexander's play-off teams were noticed. Colin Murphy's eighties heroes were noticed. Graham Taylor was noticed. We're not invisible, or we weren't until the fifth tier enveloped us.

That is why 2017 was so magical, not only what we achieved but because we were coming back. reading those articles I saw it, each week a little bit more pride returned to our great club. As the season unfolded so did the belief and the cup run magnified all of that. from the 2629 who watched us draw with Guiseley in the qualifying rounds to the 8942 that went to Arsenal, or rise could be charted through the cup run. We could be proud once more and we announced it in the greatest possible way. I'll never forget those days, but let's not forget that it was all a precursor to the real job in hand: promotion.

Right now, we're back. Everyone knows who we are and all the media coverage has centred on our run of 2017, the plucky National League team breaking records. That is not us, not anymore. In six months' time we could be in the same league as Ipswich Town, a club we marvelled at travelling to in that previous cup run. Financially, we're alright now too. The money coming in will be of great use, but we've got a decent budget and a good set of players right now. We can always have better and always improve, but as a club we're so far removed from two years ago it is unreal.

That's why I'm not as excited, because tomorrow's match isn't life changing like it would have been. Win, lose or draw we have a bigger fish to fry; promotion to League One please, ideally with batter and a bit of red sauce. The FA Cup income was vital two years ago, giving us the boost to bring in players such as Billy Knott who helped push us on to success. With or without success tomorrow we'll be challenging for promotion in May. That's why I can't get up for it, because football is all about emotion for me and tomorrow is as much of a free afternoon as any game we've played during Danny's tenure, bar perhaps Southport and Maidstone at the end of the National League season.

I'll reserve my worry for MK Dons away, I'll keep the sicky feeling in my stomach for our trip to Mansfield or the apprehension for Grimsby's visit. I really couldn't care less what happens tomorrow and I wouldn't have it any other way.

That said, if we win, I will cry worse than I did at the end of Watership Down.

It was special after all: Everton 2-1 Imps
January 6, 2019

I don't know what came over me with Friday's article, but to all intents and purposes I stand by my points. I wasn't looking forward to yesterday, the prospect of a big result hadn't entered my head and I'm so anxious about us being promoted I felt it was an unwelcome distraction.

Assembling in the square and singing the songs means little to me, I'm delighted everyone who went there had a good time, but I just wasn't feeling it at all. Even when the so-called Goodison roar greeted the players, I hadn't quite immersed myself in the day. Call me grumpy, call me focused, whichever side of the fence you sit my views will be seen differently.

After ninety minutes of football, I knew that it would be a day I would remember far more fondly that Arsenal in the FA Cup quarter final. It was a day when I got a reminder of what Lincoln City Football Club is, what we can achieve and what potentially lies within the red and white striped shirts, the Michelin men jackets on the bench and the several thousand vocal fans who made the journey.

I'll start at the beginning, eight o'clock in the morning in a Wragby café with the motley crew I've made a habit of travelling with recently. At that point the day was purely about the boys on the bus, my Dad and my friends, one of whom might soon be called family due to his indulgent with my niece, but that's another story entirely.

I wasn't happy even then. Up at 7am on a weekend, not smoking due to a bold New Year's Eve promise I made to my partner, not drinking due to the medication I'm still on for my back and worse of all, enduring the second-best (or worst) breakfast in Wragby due to the best café being closed. As I munched through badly cooked bacon and mediocre hash browns, we discussed results. '4-1 to Everton', '3-0 to Everton'... 'I think Lincoln will win' said nine-year old 'Little' Shane. Bless him, children are so naïve.

We clambered aboard the rustic minibus, some full of nicotine, some contemplating a good few cans and me. I'd cheered up a bit, Chris had brought me a match worn Shane Clarke shirt he didn't want anymore and it's always good getting together with the lads and having a bit of crack.

We wound out way across the country, stopping to get Little Shane some headphones, some say to stop his incessant chatter, others to stop him hearing the borderline banter being shared be the other passengers. A little further along the way we pulled in at the services for a wee and got the first taste of the 2019 Impvasion.

The services were packed, the queue for the gents came past the entrance to Burger King, necessitating me going over the footbridge to the other side of the road. It was remarkable to see some many Imps, some buses had just stopped for a break which didn't help, but for the first time since the draw I got a bit of the 'Ipswich' feeling. we saw Bob Dorrian in the loo queue, Ben my podcast co-host was there as were several hundred other faces I couldn't put names to.

Back on the bus the mood lifted as the drink flowed and I confess I managed a few sneaky shots of a Sloe Vodka I'd put in my hip flask 'just in case'. That warmed me through and by the time we were entering the city of the Liver bird, Jennifer Ellison and Curtis Warren, I was happier.

I've never been to Liverpool, never seen Stanley Park nor realised how close the two grounds are. Like many we parked near to Anfield and walked across to Goodison from there. The number of Imps fans excited me even more, even though many were wearing half and half scarves. one disappointed fan told us that the vendor had sold out. Tragic.

The quest for a beer ended in a pub called the Thomas Frost, but it was heaving and genuinely uncomfortable to be in. We did get a beer, in actual glasses no less. Our Wetherspoons should take note, I didn't mind a lager from a pint glass, but from a plastic beaker it tastes much worse. I could have had a second beer, blog reader Becca brought me a bitter over but given how much I'd already consumed, and the fact Dad wanted to get into the ground, I refused. Sorry!

Getting in the ground was carnage. Everton don't usually have that many away fans, they'd been very generous with the allocation but not so with organising how to get us in. They wanted to search everyone, but had no idea where the queue started our ended. We went up one side and back down another, whilst some were cutting the queue. Eventually a Lincoln fan opened a gate and pulled us through to jump in ourselves. I'm not proud of it, but some said they'd queued for minutes whereas we'd spent the best part of twenty getting nowhere. Aside from that, the stewards were very good, laughing and joking with us.

I've heard comments that their ground wasn't up to scratch behind the scenes, but what do you expect? Goodison is an old ground and certainly never built to modern standards, so the toilets will be a bit aged. My Dad loves to call everywhere a 'shithole', from Wycombe to Grimsby and everywhere between, so he was in his element.

I got a coke, bottle top firmly in place, and took my seat. I have the lid removed at Lincoln in the fan zone, yet at a top flight ground I can keep it on in the stands? What I that all about? Anyway, never one to complain (you know me) I settle back and waited for the game. Bubs popped over, the guy responsible for most of the photos on this article and gave me a team sheet. I laughed to my Dad as I'd opted to buy a programme after the game on eBay to save carrying it, but a kindly fan heard and passed me his; 'I've read it mate' was his response. Top bloke.

That was that. I was in a traditional English stadium for an FA Cup third round match I hadn't been looking forward to joined by four times as many fans as we got for home fixture three years ago. As the famed 'Goodison Roar' turned out to be piped in music turned up loud to drown us out, the players came out and the excitement levels went up a notch more. it was match time.

It was a strong Everton side, packed with flair and ability. Lookman and Calvert-Lewin are both players we'll hear more of in the future, Sigurdsson is a world-class talent and Bernard is slippier than wooden decking in winter. All over the park they had names we recognised and as the teams were read out my mate Dave gave me a sideways look. I didn't need words to read his mind, it was something along the lines of 'shit'.

In the first few minutes we looked to acclimatise well, of course we didn't threaten the goal particularly, but we weren't going to be over-awed. They then flashed an effort over from twenty yards and gave a glimpse of their class. Before quarter of an hour had gone, we got two more.

The first goal came as a consequence of Leighton Baines getting too much space on the right-hand side, whipping in a great ball to Lookman who headed over Josh Vickers and into the net. Bozzie tried a cheeky handball to deny the goal, but it was clearly over the line anyway. The homes fans rippled with a cheer, but they were sat down and quiet by the time Lookman was embracing his team mates. As the ball left the centre circle to resume play it was all Lincoln noise once more.

They did their best to shut us up with a second goal, once again carving their way through the defence before Bernard slipped a cheeky little lob over Vickers. there was nothing our keeper could do, not for either goal, but with 15 minutes on the clock we were 2-0 down to a slick and cultured footballing side. My dad looked at me and said; 'this could get embarrassing'. I responded by joining in with chants of 'we're gonna win 3-2'. Deep down, I feared another Arsenal, another 5-0, another day in a nice stadium I'd do my level best to forget. Basically, my miserable predictions were coming true.

I wasn't going to sit down and shut up though. I hadn't gone all the way to Liverpool with a face like a slapped arse to just lie down and take a thrashing. The Imps' fans were loud and proud and no matter what I felt about the importance of the game; I was going to make sure I did my part. If I felt guilty at letting Danny down in amongst 5,500 fans, how must the players feel? Luckily, they responded just as we did. They fought, the harried and they scrapped and as they did, my mood lifted entirely. Completely unconnected to Carlisle going 2-0 up against Mansfield, obviously.

From that goal onwards Lincoln City did themselves and their fans proud. It would have been easy to defend at 2-0, to sit deep and hope to hell it didn't get worse. It would have been just as easy to let the heads drop and see the top flight side gobble up seven, just like Tranmere. There was none of that, instead there was fight. There was desire. There was a 'f*ck you' attitude that typified everything we've become, a never-know-when-you're-beaten belief surging through the players.

Who led the charge? for me, Harry Anderson was excellent, barging and bashing his way through whenever he could, chasing the ball like a greyhound chasing a stuffed rabbit around the dog racing track. Michael O'Connor was brilliant too; he broke up play whenever he could and kicked everything that needed kicking. you could see we were League Two and they weren't, but we never let that get us down.

There were chances at both ends, they always looked dangerous when given the time and if we ever sat off them, they had the skills to unpick the defence. In League Two we can get away with giving teams possession thirty yards from goal because often they do nothing with it. Give a big six side that grace and they're going to put the ball at your keeper.

John Akinde ran himself into the ground, always a willing outlet but ploughing that lone furrow he's used to by now. The main issue was every ball into him saw two defenders pick him up, one of which was £12m Kurt Zouma. The other was Colombian World Cup star Yerry Mina, himself worth around £27m. I had to defend John on the way home to someone who claimed he'd done nothing, but when you're sandwiched between players who cost more than your entire club, there's only going to be so much you can do.

It was the Colombian who brought down Akinde on the left flank to earn a free kick around the half hour mark. This was our chance, a set piece. We're known for getting balls into the box and putting a head on it and my pre-match bet had us to lose 2-1 with Jason Shackell to score any time. As the ball came in, I saw Shackell rise and briefly I saw pound signs. I soon forgot about those as his header was saved and Big Bad Bozzie slammed the ball home. We had our goal.

That moment was when everything I'd thought about the game went. I later realised much of my dismay was the Arsenal game coming out. I couldn't leave Arsenal disappointed because we'd come so far and achieved so much, but losing 5-0 hurts. I feared we'd have no such hiding place this time, no great run to mask the pain of a heavy defeat, but as Bozzie wheeled away to celebrate you just knew it wasn't going to be like that. We weren't here for a hiding, I had no reason to fear a long drive home. This was to be a day to remember and for the first time since the Port Vale opener, I smiled.

I did more than that, I screamed, cheered and sung. I had been doing it all match, but every word got louder and prouder. It's fair to say the final 15 minutes of the half were ours, we laid siege as much as a League Two side can against a side worth several hundred million pounds, but we did. We got corners, we got throw ins in good positions and we earned every moment of our time on the ball. When the half time whistle blew at 2-1, Everton we happier to hear it.

Little Lincoln City had been stung, but we'd bitten back and were in the ascendancy.

If there was ever a moment that summed up the difference between the two sets of supporters it was the moment the whistle blew. 5,500 Imps fans sat down, at least those who were going for beers or the loo, whilst the quiet majority stood up. I know it's a home and away thing, but it felt like a signal of intent. Everton had one of those though, bringing on Gomes and Tosun at half time. That's Andre Gomes on loan from Barcelona, a player who cost them 350m including add ons, and Cenk Tosun who cost Everton £27m. We stuck with the same eleven who looked entirely capable of slaying goliath.

In the second period we looked on the cusp of creating a good chance without doing so, but Everton were always dangerous. Josh Vickers ensured he'd have a memory to take away that didn't involve picking the ball out of the net, pulling off a wonderful stop to deny Sigurdsson on the hour mark. As the game wore on we saw less of the ball, but without conceding any serious chances. When we made a change it was bringing on Matt Rhead, Shay McCartan and eventually Ellis Chapman, all of whom cost us the grand total of nothing. Everton had £50m Richarlison to fall back on.

Bozzie had to stop Idrissa Gueye getting away and Vickers pulled off a great stop from Tosun, but Everton looked to be out of ideas and perhaps content with their 2-1 win.

As we entered the final ten minutes, City got a second wind. The set pieces were the one area we looked like scoring and with ten minutes left Jason Shackell got on the end of a corner and beat Jordan Pickford. Richarlison, with a mouth full of Andrex, cleared off the line and earned his wages alone in saving them embarrassment.

We weren't done yet though, a masculine looking Ellis Chapman, seemingly aged three years over the Christmas period, flicked a wonderful ball into Shay McCartan. Was he fouled? Some say yes but he wasn't. Moments after City got a corner, but it fizzled out and almost as quickly, so did the game. The final whistle wasn't met with much enthusiasm from the home fans, but little was all afternoon. Instead, Goodison rang out to songs and chants from the visiting supporters, loud and proud.

There's no more for me to say, not really. Everyone one has their memories of the day, not one of the players had a bad game and I left with something I never thought I would; joy and pride. Like many, I'm emotionally invested in promotion, it means so much and along the way I lost sight of what yesterday could have been about. Tranmere trouncing didn't help, but as we funnelled (slowly) out of Goodison Park my team had come to my rescue. they'd shown me that it isn't all about promotion, that there are moments that transcend a league win.

Moments where you stand in one of the most recognisable grounds in the country and watch the home fans applaud your efforts as a club more than their own team.

Moments when a sold-out ground has to play loud music to drown out the chanting of a League Two side.

Moments when you realise that whatever happened against Port Vale or Crewe, this group of players are good enough and those nagging fears of collapse are entirely unfounded.

Moments when you know that your football club isn't just 'on the way back', but going somewhere they've never been in your three decades as a fan.

That is what Everton meant to me, it just took actually being there for me to see it. Plus Mansfield lost. All in all I was still smiling when I finally walked through my front door at 11pm. I'm still smiling now. Up the Imps.

Showing what we have: Swindon 2-2 Imps
January 13, 2019

It's hard to say too much about a game I wasn't at. Usually I'll watch back on iFollow or something, but aside from the highlights and a few things people have messaged me, I'm writing this blind.

Whilst many of you were at Swindon or watching by whatever means you could, I was picking up a rescue dog and turning into one of those annoying childless men who treat their dog better than they treat most people.

I listened of course, swore along with you when things went against us and of course, cheered when I thought ten men would win the game. For the record, I'm not sure ten men would have won the game.

Let's deal with two sides of the coin shall we? There's been some who have said 'ignoring the red cards, let's focus on the positives'. I understand that, why would Danny blast a player or go too deep into the referee's performance when he had players who performed over and above all expectations. They did too, those who did not get sent off were excellent and even Shackell was until the card.

However, there were two red cards and that cannot be ignored if I want to be balanced and fair. Yes, Bruno Andrade's was something of nothing. Quite how the Press Association report suggested he'd 'raked his foot down the Achilles' of Kyle Knoyle is beyond me. I've seen it, he did no such thing. He did stamp down though and whether there's contact or not, there was intent and petulance. That has to be addressed.

Danny addressed it straight away didn't he? Off down the tunnel to (and I forget his exact words) give Bruno some advice on not repeating his mistakes. In my language that is usually classed as a 'bollocking'. It's silly, it's needless and whatever your feelings on the referee overall, it is the right call.

Shackell's red card is one that troubles me a little more. It isn't the fact he got it, dissent is dissent and that's final, but it is the general indecision around what it came from. The BBC report had him down as booked in the first half. Michael Hortin had it as a straight red, Danny thought both yellows came in the one incident. Whatever the facts of the incident are, it's clear the officiating was unclear. Was he deserving of a red? If it was a second bookable, yes. Probably. Some referees we've seen would try to keep men on the field, especially when they've already dismissed one, but Ben Toner was well within his rights to send Shackell off.

Oddly, when Toner took charge of our play-off semi-final with Exeter, I had reserved praise for him keeping his cards in his pocket. Maybe our rather 'intense' touchline style has made an enemy of that particular official, or maybe that 1940s haircut has turned him into a strict card-happy flasher.

Look, I won't go on about it anymore, but anyone hiding behind a dodgy ref or something equally as absurd is wrong. He was strict, he had alternative choices but he was also within his rights to do what he did. He just needs to be much clearer when showing yellows and reds.

That aside, from what I can gather the first sending off galvanised the team. I've seen both goals and obviously one will overshadow the other, but nothing should be taken away from Shackell's technique at the far post for his goal. If they didn't have a calamity keeper in the sticks maybe it would have been an easy save, but it was still a decent finish for a veteran centre back to be making.

That brings us to Shay's goal, doesn't it? Was it as good as Charlee Adam's striker against Grimsby? I think possibly it was. Typically, when down to ten men, teams go to route one and we're more than comfortable in that style, so a big punt by Josh Vickers was flicked on by Akinde into the channel. Calamity keeper comes rushing out, defender hooks it to Shay and what happened next will likely get six figure views on YouTube. It was exquisite, a volley of the finest quality, caught as sweet as any I've seen in a long while and lopped on the angle into the net. The keeper was misplaced but I'm not sure he would have saved it if he were stood on his line.

At 2-0 you expect to see the Imps come out and defend, but the penalty turned things around even more. Michael Doughty is a great player, but I was told he's gone off the boil in recent weeks. He certainly started bubbling again when he came on, slotting home a penalty of which there was little doubt. Whatever did or didn't happen after that, we're down to nine men for 35 minutes against a resurgent home side.

This is when we saw Lincoln City, stripped back of tactics, game plans and transfer window plans. This was a club ripped open and exposed, just it's beating heart and substance on show and my word, what a heart we have.

You see, there's two sides to football. There's all the elements which add to a good team, big players, different approaches, training, spying, sports science and whatever else you can think of. Then, somewhere hidden away, is a team's spirit. There's the one element you don't teach, you don't buy and you don't create on a blackboard. It's there, it grows and develops from the manager and through his carefully constructed group of players. It comes through shared experiences and can be fuelled by great support and belief. Richie Wellens won't have it yet, Paul Tisdale's side don't have it at all the way they throw leads away, but we do.

We have it.

We saw it last weekend against Everton, battling to the end against hundreds of millions of pounds worth of players and coming out with our heads held high. Goliath won the fight, but David's lion heart won the praise of the world. The trick is taking that into the league. Grimsby didn't, they raised their game against Crystal Palace and then let Macclesfield slap their arses, but Lincoln are not like that. We showed our minerals at Goodison and when called upon at the County Ground, we showed them again.

If you look at their second goal it demonstrates exactly what I mean. Hunting in packs, chasing the ball, keeping everything compact and closed down. Swindon should have gone on to score a couple, but they didn't. They tried, but our remaining players refused to lose. You remember that mantra from 2016/17? It's still there. It's still probably pinned to the dressing room wall and if it isn't, Danny probably gets the players to tattoo it on the insides of their eyelids.

Refuse to lose.

That's what we did. For nigh on 41 minutes, we bared our souls once more, not in front of Match of the Day cameras, not when the national press were hunting the story, but in typical League Two action. Right when it mattered. Their 88th minute leveller was harsh on our players, but even at that point we could have collapsed. There was eight further minutes to play, but did we collapse? Did we throw away our lead? No, we pulled further away from MK Dons.

Sure, Bury are closing in on us, but with two games in hand we've got opportunity to extend our lead over them. MK Dons lost, Mansfield lost and yet Lincoln City, nine-man Lincoln City, brought a point away.

Who knows how crucial that point might be come May? Who knows how crucial that performance might be in galvanising us even more, in fuelling the belief in the squad even more. They've had two chances to collapse in the last eight days and on both occasions we've shown why we're top and why, in my opinion, we'll be playing League One football next season.

Imps closing in on first transfer deal of the window
January 16, 2019

The Imps are thought to be closing in on the first deal of the transfer window, with Cian Bolger allegedly in advanced talks with Danny and Nicky.

The Fleetwood defender has also been targeted by Bradford City, having expressed his intention to leave his current club at the end of his deal. He's out of contract in the summer and has not been included in either of the last two matches Joey Barton's side have played in.

Journalist Alan Nixon states that we've moved into pole position, despite interest not only from League One Bradford City, but also Tranmere in our own division. If Bolger does chose to come to us, it would be a significant coup given that both the other suitors would be closer to his current home.

The Blackpool Gazette are convinced he's coming here, reporting yesterday that a deal is expected to be tied up this week. Knowing Danny, it wouldn't mean him being included in the first team straight away, but he's bound to be around the action as the second half of the season progresses.

It's seems that the giant centre back has taken a decision to leave Fleetwood for nothing in the summer, which is going to prompt us to swoop and pay a fee. Joey Barton spoke of his upset at the situation and of being forced into action by Bolger.

"From my understanding, he is intent on running his contract down and going on a free transfer, which puts him in a limbo position. I said to him I cannot have a player who clearly wants to leave the club involved in the first team."

"I'm not saying Bolger is not 100 per cent committed but he has made it clear he does not want to stay at the football club. That was made clear before I got here and since I have got here nothing much really has changed on that. Players who do not sign contracts and again he is in that weird stand-off."

"It was probably fostered last January, when there was interest in him. I don't know what went on because I was not at the club but that is something that has not been revolved since. How do we resolve it? There has to be a desire by both parties to do so. To be honest I'm not sure there is. I only want players at Fleetwood Town who want to be here. If you do not want to be here, then do not be here."

Only a year ago it seemed as though Bolger was destined to move up, rather than down the divisions. In 2017 he was earmarked by Bristol City as a possible recruit for them, with Hull City amongst the suitors in the summer. It seems that Barton is suggesting the player was denied a move in the last window, which has caused some anger with the club.

Who is Cian Bolger? He's a 26-year-old centre back from Ireland who has represented Eire to Under 21 level, but not made a senior appearance for his country. He came through the ranks at Leicester City and spent time at Bolton, but made most of his appearances during loan spells with Bristol Rovers and Colchester. He later joined Southend where he played 51 times before being signed by Fleetwood.

It would be an odd acquisition in terms of position, with several centre backs at the club it seems to be one position we do not need recruits, but perhaps with one eye on Shackell's age and Wharton's loan, we're thinking ahead to a possible League One campaign. There's little doubt Bolger has immense quality, but the value will be if he arrives as the first of three or four new faces of the same sort of quality.

He's back: Danny Rowe signs for City once more
January 17, 2019

The Imps made it a triple-whammy of new signings this afternoon by adding Ipswich Town wide man Danny Rowe on a loan deal until the end of the season.

Rowe had a spell on loan with the Imps last season, but struggled for fitness in the latter stages of the campaign. When he was on it though, he was sensational. His goal against Exeter in the 3-2 win in March will take a long while to forget.

In total he played 16 times for us, including the Checkatrade Trophy Final against Shrewsbury. That consisted of nine starts in the league and four in the cup. His last appearance was the disappointing 1-0 defeat at Port Vale. he came off after 52 minutes of that game and wasn't seen again.

He underwent surgery on his ankle in the summer, but regained fitness and looked to be a part of manager Paul Hurst's plans at Portman Road. He came off the bench four times, once in the EFL Cup against Exeter and three times in the Championship. Sadly for Ipswich, they lost every game and sadly for Rowe, Hurst was replaced.

That meant the third manager of his short stay with the Tractor Boys and Paul Lambert was impressed with the former Macclesfield man, but only his ball control. He gave him two of his outings from the bench, but mainly limited his football to Under 23s. Lambert spoke of him needing to be a bit fitter, whether that was in terms of an injury or physical fitness was unclear, but it seemed to close the door on a return to the first team there.

When one door closes, another one opens and in this instance, it's the door leading him back to Sincil Bank.

I really liked the fit Danny Rowe. He's a mix of Andrade and Anderson for me, maybe even a different proposition altogether. He's perhaps stronger than Bruno on the ball, fewer tricks and more direct but with an eye for the spectacular. In some instances I could see him playing the Shay McCartan role too, if the need arose.

I'm writing this ahead of the announcement, so I won't have Danny's reaction at all, but I'm convinced he'll be utterly delighted. We've needed cover in the wide areas, certainly with Bruno out for three games and Rowe will be able to drop in to the first team knowing some of the lads and how we work.

I'd be surprised if he started against Grimsby though, he does lack game time and with Kellan Gordon and Tom Pett raring to go there's no need to rush him back, but once he's been with us for a week or so we're going to see him in action.

This is one of the signings we've been waiting for. Cian Bolger is massive, but we've not desperately needed a player in his position. James Brown is a good signing too, but Danny Rowe is another attacking element, a man who we know well, who can make a difference to the last 20 games of the season.

I'm not greedy, but perhaps now a striker and one more in the attacking midfield role and I think our January business will be complete. It's like Deja Vu though isn't it? Signing Danny Rowe, a centre back from League One and waiting for a striker.

Is it still 2018?

Joey Barton Issue Contradictory Bolger Statements Following Imps Deal
January 18, 2019

Fleetwood Town manager Joey Barton has had a bitter rant about the recent transfer of Cian Bolger to the Imps in Fleetwood's local press.

Seeing as you're all such big Barton fans after he got owned by Rheady in March 2017, I thought it prudent to report on what he understands to be the Fleetwood side of the story. or, as you'll find out, what he blatantly does not understand at all.

Bolger joined the Imps yesterday on a two and a half year deal that should see him remain an Imp until we're top six in League One. Or the summer of 2021. Whichever is closest.

It's a capture that's raised a few eyebrows, with reports of a Scottish club bidding £500,000 for him in the summer, as well as rumoured Championship interest. Barton doesn't believe there was a bid for him, but in a rather confused collection of comments, he suggests he probably wouldn't know if there was as negotiations are not his job.

He began by refuting the claims that a deal had been on the table in the summer.

"I'm telling you now, if someone offered £500,000 for him in the summer he would not have been here until now."

He reacted with some surprise at the claims of a free transfer, but then oddly admitted there might not have been a fee. he also lamented Danny for talking about his business when, just a few words later, he admitted it wasn't his business.

"I'm surprised Danny is talking about my business," he started out by saying. "I'm very surprised in terms of how he knows so much and I know so little seemingly."

He then claimed that no player comes for free, suggesting that Danny made out Bolger wasn't being paid wages. Which he didn't.

"He has done fantastically well then because, as far as I know, you do not get any player for free. Everybody is paid a wage and, if he has managed to do that, it is an incredible deal; I take my hat off to him. No transfer is a free transfer."

He then offered some insight into why Bolger left the club, but oddly went against his first statement by admitting he didn't know if there was a fee and he wasn't involved in any negotiations. So technically, it wasn't his business.

"For me, he (Bolger) had to leave the club in terms of he was running his contract out. I did not handle the negotiations; it is not my job, my job is to manage the team. My job was to answer the question 'is he going to play?'

"I don't know whether they have paid a transfer fee; there might be a thing on there of promotion which I don't know but I'd be very surprised because our chief executive (Steve Curwood) does not give anything away for free. If he has then that is a seismic moment in his career and he should be congratulated because I am constantly talking to him about freeing up money and he is not particularly great at giving anything away without getting value for it."

To summarise, Danny shouldn't be talking about Barton's business, even if it isn't his business and he definitely didn't come for free. Well, not definitely, Barton doesn't know that, but probably. or, because Danny doesn't lie, he did come for free and Barton isn't entirely happy at letting such a good player go for nothing. Not that it was his business as manager of the football club.

He finished by contradicting his opening statement. Remember, 540 odd words ago how he said there wasn't a £500,00 bid in the summer? Well...

"Big Cian, for whatever reason, they had not sorted a contract out with him. There were bids rejected and certain things that had gone on before I took over."

Bids Joey? Not £500,000 though as you clarified that even though a; it wouldn't be your business anyway and b: you weren't at the club at the time.

Glad we've got that cleared up.

Kind of.

We've won the battle, on with the war: Imps 1-0 Grimsby
January 20, 2019

A season is a series of little battles making up a whole war. From August to May every season we're involved in warfare, battling on a weekly basis for points that will ultimately leave us victorious.

Sometimes we're battling familiar foes, sometimes the enemy are strangers. On some occasions the battle is one-sided, it can be won on the pitch or it can be swung on the terraces. Every so often a battle comes along that means more than three points. What we must remember is that a win only ever brings three points, whether it is 6-2 or 1-0, home or away, against an old foe or new faces.

Yesterday was one of the battles we'll remember for a long while, not because it was particularly thrilling, but because of the opposition. Games against Grimsby always take on an edge, they're always a little bit more important because of bragging rights and local pride. The rest of League Two see we got three points and an extra goal in the 'for' column, but we feel like we've taken a major step forward.

We haven't. Let's be grounded and remember we've won a game against a League Two side who have lost three on the spin and had a horrible start to the season. Take away the fact they're local rivals, this was simply a routine game in which we were expected to win.

Few mid table teams will come backed by 1,500 fans though. Few away attendances of that size will make such little noise all through a game. I'm not saying that out of spite, but I've seen matches at the Bank where the travelling fans have been loud and proud. Aside for an angry mob at the front I thought they were relatively quiet, although aside from our own vocal group in Block 7, we were too in parts. Maybe it's the early kick off that does it. Only the hardcore fans have fuelled up on ale or whatever else they use to power themselves these days.

The rest of us sat in the car with the engine running before the match to make sure we kept warm and got a parking space.

In terms of team selection, I got it spot on with my prediction on Football League World on Friday. Cian Bolger started, a towering ginge at the back, with Danny Rowe on the bench. I didn't think Rowe would play a part as he's been lacking in minutes recently, but he was there nonetheless.

There was a real atmosphere as the teams came out and for a while it felt as though it might continue through the game. Both sets of fans were at each other which is how it should be. They have one song they like, where were you when you were shit? We tend to applaud that these days, not least because of crowds during the Keith era only being a couple of thousand shy of where we are now. I wish there was a song that went 'why haven't you capitalised on National League promotion like us?' but it doesn't flow off the tongue. Mind you, neither does the Bruno Andrade song, not that we heard that yesterday.

The first ten minutes were frantic with both sides looking dangerous. I'm an admirer of Elliot Embleton in their midfield and I called out Wes Thomas too, he's a live wire with a nice touch. He reminded me a bit of Matt Green the way he approached the game.

At the back Grimsby looked unsure, but by the seven minute mark both teams had corners under their belt and referee Mike Dean had made his first booking. Michael O'Connor was the recipient of the card and that could have left him walking on eggshells all match. As it was, the sponsors eventually gave him Man of the Match which is testament to his ability to play under caution as much as anything.

Freck gave them a nice scare too, I thought he had a good game all afternoon, always looking to break through the middle. One complaint I've had of us recent is a lack of penetration around Akinde. The big man has look isolated, we need to see support popping up on the overlap.

Freck's stinging drive didn't find the target, but it was refreshing to see us having a pop from distance. Given how well McKeown has been playing recently I wondered if it might be a fruitless task. A few minutes later I found out it wasn't.

Usually, I find the delight at getting a second corner leads to disappointment, but on this occasion it decided the derby after ten minutes. From our second delivery the ball came out to Harry Toffolo who rifled in from the edge of the area. It was a nice clean strike by the left back, there's little doubt the keeper saw it late but it didn't matter. Somebody pressed the mute button in the away end as the Imps' led.

Overall, the game suffered because of the goal. As a spectacle it changed instantly, we seemed a little more content to spread play and let them try to pick us apart, whereas they didn't show the sort of reckless abandon they might have done had we bagged an opener on 65 minutes. They stuck to their game plan, we retreated a little and the neutral, if there was one in the ground, saw the game shrivel into itself.

It wasn't helped by a finicky display by referee Mike Dean, pulling out cards like it was still Christmas. He wasn't making fundamental mistakes, that would be unfair to say, but the game didn't flow. It favoured us of course, we were 1-0 up, but again as a watch it didn't help. Coupled with the early kick off and it felt like the goal had poured water on the smouldering fire of the Lincolnshire derby.

Occasionally there was a spark of something at both ends. Cian Bolger's only real mistakes in the game came within seconds of each other, once failing to find a teammate in attack and then not clearly adequately from the resulting break. The fact he even got back was impressive though and thankfully when Grimsby worked the ball to Embleton he should have done much better. From there we broke, Harry Toffolo teed up John Akinde but he scuffed a weak effort at the keeper.

As the half wore on the visitors did look like getting back into it. We were resolute in the last line of defence, but retaining possession further up the field looked difficult. John Akinde wasn't looking his usual self and the wide players couldn't get on the ball long enough to create anything. Grimsby were wasteful when they did get a chance, our excellent back four and holding midfielders kept them at bay. Behind them, Grant Smith was in fine form too.

A couple of bookings really got me angry at the end of the half. Firstly, a Grimsby foul didn't draw a card from the top flight referee, but Toffolo got one for allegedly time-wasting at the free kick. It seemed disproportionate to the misdemeanour, as did John Akinde's booking for the ball hitting their lad in the face. If we're being honest, we were probably lucky not to be punished for a nasty aerial challenge in the first half though, so it evened itself out. In the heat of the derby it's easy to be less objective, especially when everyone around is yelling at Dean before he's even blown for kick off.

I did wonder at half time what could change the game. We'd looked great for fifteen minutes, but by the time they went in for the break I thought the visitors had edged the balance of play. The stats didn't back that up, but sometimes they don't tell the full picture.

The visitors lacked that killer instinct, but approaching the box and in the middle third they looked alright. I didn't rate the full back Ring one bit, but he did provide Dave and I some light relief as we thought up a series of derogatory one-liners around his surname. The two centre halves dealt well with Akinde and on the whole they gave a good account of themselves all afternoon.

Whatever was said at half time certainly fired us up and we came out looking more likely to double the lead. Michael Bostwick flashed a header over whilst at the other end, Bolger and Bozzy were both in fine form. I felt after ten minutes of the half as though they wouldn't score and leaned over to tell Dave as much. I thought better of it, tempting fate and all that.

We did have the ball in the net after ten minutes of the second period and we were all off our feet celebrating McCartan's 'goal', but Mike Dean had other ideas. He felt Akinde had fouled their lad in the build up, but it looked weak to me. If it were the other way I'd be delighted of course, but on second view I'm not sure there was a foul. The second goal might have settled a few nerves, but as the half wore on the visitors just retreated.

Akinde came out a different player in the second half and his work rate began to cause real problems. He might be a big man, but when the ball goes into feet or into the channels he comes alive and one run in particular stood out. He bundled their lad off the ball on the flank, strode inside and was smartly denied by McKeown. It's funny how different people saw the incident, I thought he'd done well to create himself a chance out of nothing, others were asking why he can't hit the target. It's all about perception I guess.

On the hour mark we sewed up the game, not with a goal but with a change. Shay McCartan had worked hard with little joy, but as soon as we brought Danny Rowe on it all changed. The train of thought around me was that we'd put Rowe out wide and bring Pett in the middle, but Rowe took up the hole behind Akinde. His energy almost immediately swung the balance in our favour and for the last 30 minutes we were by far the more dangerous side.

We were always going to retreat as the game wore on, meaning legs up from were important. For a player with four sub appearances to his name this season, Rowe looked incredibly lively. It took him five minutes or so to get up to speed but as soon as he did I think we got a glimpse of the next few weeks unfolding in front of us. His first real involvement came from our well worked free kick routine, using him as the outlet in the channel. It didn't bring a goal, but it was another chance for us to extend the lead.

That leads us to the inevitable Mike Dean red card. I went for a toilet break and as I emerged from under the stand I saw them have a free kick from the left hand side. I walked up the stairs with my back to goal and as I turned, we were breaking. It happened so quick, defence into attack thanks to a long ball, but Rowe's pace caught McKeown out. He came to meet the ball, met the player and Dean flashed the red card after a brief hesitation.

Was it a red? In real-time I thought yes, but a second glance has me wondering. McKeown got to the ball, unlike Scott Brown when he pole-axed Freck against Port Vale, or the Carlisle keeper when he did the same to Akinde a week or two later. Of the three incidents, it was by far the weakest. If it had been the other way around I might have accepted it at the time, but watching back I'd feel aggrieved. Of course, going down to ten men blunted their threat even further. I guess when people said after the Carlisle game that these things even themselves out, this is what they meant.

The only way they were going to score was an Imps' mistake or a late set piece. Bolger had settled in quickly and formed a strong partnership with Bozzy, whilst Rowe was now offering the sort of support John Akinde has wanted all season. On the 84 minute mark I thought the was a better shout for a red card as Akinde was hauled down inside the area, but the offence had started outside and all we got was a free kick. Not even a yellow card for the offender. The dead ball was wasted and we still had to nip our bum cheeks for the final ten minutes.

Grimsby had nothing left in the tank though and smart game management by Pett, Rhead and Danny led to us closing the game down. When the whistle went I think it was a feeling of relief as much as anything, not because we'd been under the cosh but at keeping the lead for so long. Whenever you bag an early goal in such a high-profile game there's always a chance that you'll end up conceding, but aside from the half hour period after we scored, It thought we were in control and kept ourselves in check.

We also did well to keep players on the pitch given the number of cards shown. It wasn't even a dirty game, but somehow there were eight yellows and one red. It was disproportionate to the balance of the play, but in the end it didn't affect the outcome.

Filtering out of the ground was interesting, with a number of players being put forward for Man of the Match. I thought Harry Toffolo deserved it, not for his goal alone but his wide play as well. He linked well with Pett, dealt strongly with threats at the back and fought for every ball. Some felt Bolger and Bozzy could have won it for commanding displays, Neal Eardley got mentioned as allegedly 'he does what he always does', but both central midfielders got big shouts too.

Not one of those players will be bothered too much about a bottle of champagne, because whatever they drank last night will have tasted twice as sweet. We've only lost once to Grimsby in five years now, even that came from having ten men for an hour. With Scunthorpe in League One we're not the Pride of Lincolnshire just yet but rest assured, if we keep fighting for each other and get Danny Rowe fit and firing, I'm pretty sure we'll get a chance to claim that crown next season, having won not only this battle, but also the war of 2018/19.

Plastic Fantastic: No shame in the rise of Lincoln City
January 20, 2019

It's the sort of title I know will delight our opponents in League Two. Our recent success has had them calling us plastics recently, none more so than a few Grimsby fans in the aftermath of our derby win.

Unlike John Smiths, they are bitter. Bitter that we're in the ascendency, bitter that the decisions went our way yesterday and most of all, bitter that their club officials couldn't capitalise on their success whilst ours did.

For a few short moments yesterday the usual chants of 'where were you when you were shit' began to ring out from the away end. Harry Toffolo's goal soon put paid to that and if there as any further chanting I couldn't hear it over the 617 lads who, for those who don't know, formed around 2012 to improve the atmosphere at a dying club. Funny then how a video of them doing their thing in a side street at the Bank drew the accusations of plastics.

That's a favourite of football fans isn't it? The rise of the Premier League and the prawn sandwich brigade has left anyone finding the game late, or following a club as they rise from the ashes, labelled as a plastic. It's a derogatory term for those unawares, pointed at us because our average crowd was 2,000 in 2014/15 and it's near 9,000 now.

It's implied that the 1500 or so who follow Grimsby are 'real' supporters, whereas our own support has only come out of the woodwork because we did well in 2016/17 and when we start to flop it'll fall again. The suggestion is our support, the very best in the division right now, is based solely on success.

That sort of thinking should win a 'stating the bloody obvious' award. When a team does badly, their attendances go down. When they do well, those attendances go up. That is football, that is exactly what happens to virtually every other team. Grimsby fans seem to think their support remains the same because they're loyal and we're just a bunch of glory hunters. The hilarious thing is that they're no different to us. Genuinely, the only thing that stops them getting bigger crowds is winning matches. They're local fans supporting their local club. Amongst their number are two team supporters, just like we have. They're virtually identical because our towns are thirty miles apart, average wages are the same, the culture is the same. We're the same apart from one salient fact: we're top of the league.

In fact, 99% of the teams we play are exactly the same as us, from towns and cities used to lower league struggle, sometimes climbing the ladder briefly and other times falling down it. Oxford and Luton in the division above are the same as well. They're getting good crowds now, but were they getting the same numbers when they had to play Histon and Kettering? Of course not.

Grimsby even had the 'plastic' effect themselves. In 2010/11, the year they went down, their average was 3,072. During their first league season, it went up to 5,259. I make that 2,200 plastics, or as I like to call them 'new or returning fans'. If there's any shame in that it is the level of growth being so low. That low growth can be seen during their Championship years though. Between 1992 and 1997, in the second tier, they only got around the 6,000 mark even with the increase of away supporters. Cue chanting: 'our plastic fans, are better than yours, our plastic fans are better than yours.'

Many of our current fans were not watching when we lost 4-0 against North Ferriby in the FA Trophy. That's absolutely true. That's not because they're fair-weather fans, some hadn't even discovered the club at that point. What has happened to us is the result of the FA Cup run and our success in the National League. our club grabbed the chances provided and marketed themselves perfectly. Who recalls the FA Cup run of 2016/17 being cheaper entry through to the Brighton game? That helped.

The PR from our management team, both the football side of the club and those running at the top, has been excellent. There's been a few bumps along the way, but the remit was always to ensure that the fleeting success the FA Cup run can brought had to be seized upon. The club had to retain the returning fans, those discovering the club and those in the city who had previously dismissed us. I don't care what the background of the fan is, they're here now and their money spends the same.

I know it's jealousy on the parts of others. I know that Grimsby have to console themselves in one way or another, having conceded local pride to us for far too long. They missed their chance at pulling away when they came up, never gelling with Paul Hurst and having a board that seemed to want to piss supporters off rather than get them involved. If they'd stormed to the top of League Two would their attendances be the same as they are now? No. they might have been as high as 6,000.

If they were to be the same as now, the joke is surely on them because there's no expansion potential for their club. If they believe their support wouldn't grow by winning a few a games and getting a promotion push going then they're in a sorry state of affairs. Surely the entire point of football is for your club to get better, on and off the pitch? Grimsby missed their chance and that's why they rock up at ours and moan about our big attendances, because they wish it were them. If they tell you they don't and they'd rather have 3,000 hardcore over 9,000 in total, then they're utterly deluded.

Do we have new fans? Yes. everyone starts somewhere and even those hardcore Grimsby fans must have been unawares of the club at some point. They had a first game, just like the 8,100 home fans yesterday. everyone starts supporting a club at some point, some of our fans started in the last three years but why should that matter?

I can tell you this though, as a city Lincoln is growing. The university is bringing investment, new houses are popping up all over and people means more potential fans. As the city grows, the club grows. In truth, the expansion of our fan base should have happened around 2010 as the city truly sparked into life, but we were crap and few other than the lifers want to watch a crap team. Grimsby as a town is not growing and that possibly means their potential for getting new and returning fans into Blunder Park is much smaller. They're scared Imps, because they think we might leave them behind.

Now we're good and the people of Lincoln are building an affinity with their club. Grimsby, Cambridge, Mansfield can all come and give us stick about it, but you know deep down when they're in their half empty stadiums (or half a stadium in Mansfield's case), they'll secretly be wishing they were us, attracting big crowds and winning matches.

PS: Scunthorpe United, we're coming for you. It's called LINCOLNshire for a reason.

Sorry to disappoint you League Two: Yeovil 0-2 Imps
January 22, 2019

Bury blogger 'Bury Me in Exile', an informed League Two blogger, commented on Twitter this week that the rest of League Two would be watching the Imps result this evening, hoping for Yeovil to do everyone a favour in the quest for the title.

A Macclesfield fan on twitter also asked if Danny Rowe would be so kind as to help out the struggling Silkmen by keeping the Glovers within reach at the foot of the table. One of those requests was fulfilled in emphatic style but sadly for the other teams hunting the title, there were no favours.

If we're honest, there wasn't even as much as a whimper from Yeovil was there? They didn't trouble a comfortable Imps side one bit, with us in control of the game from the minute we kicked off until the last blast of the whistle. Mark Whiley commented on the radio it was a champion's performance and he's not far wide of the mark.

If you want to win trophies, you win games like these. Whenever a team has games in hand their fans imagine the gap: two games in hand means you could be six points better off, but you have to win those games. Not picking up the points from games you have over other sides feels like a let down, psychologically there's something damaging about seeing extra games gobbled up by weak results.

No fear of that, not with this Lincoln City.

The big surprise was the team selection, Danny Rowe dropping into the ten role and Bozzy moving into midfield at the expense of Lee Frecklington. Freck had an injection in his groin this weekend and that's kept him out, but the depth of our squad means we're flush with top quality players.... sorry, wait a minute. The depth of our squad?

That's right. We've got the smallest squad of players in the division and yet we've got the strongest squad according to Steve Thompson. After the game Rob Makepeace and Mark were talking about the squad depth and even Danny Cowley spoke of how intense the competition for places were. How can that be? How can we have the best squad and the smallest? I'll tell you how; excellent recruitment.

None of our incoming players have been panic buys and in my opinion, we do not have gaps in the squad as such. Yes, we need cover but I firmly stand by my article yesterday about a striker. We do not need a direct Matt Green replacement, not when Danny Rowe has equalled his goals tally of last season on his first start.

The depth in such low numbers is frightening. The bulk of our squad consists of experienced players, footballers who have won divisions, played in higher divisions or at the very least, been here before. Where we have youth it is not experimental like some clubs, it is Harry Anderson or Harry Toffolo, young players of a certain calibre. The blend is superb and although we're only one or two injuries away from trouble, I can't think of us ever having such a strong match day squad.

That showed from the first minute to the last. Bolger and Shackell were brilliant this evening, both winning everything they could. At full back both Harry Toffolo and Neal Eardley were excellent. Eardley has been all season but because of the standard he set last time out, he's almost having to be a nine or ten just to get noticed. As for Toffolo, his development has been incredible in the last few months. I have to say though, he was very lucky indeed not to be sent off for his high boot. If it had been against us I would have screamed bleu murder.

Shall we be harsh? Yeovil are a bad side. Their defence looked ill at ease with us, Akinde was able to bully them and they needed fresh underpants whenever we ran at them. If Andrade wasn't suspended they'd have had even more reason to be terrified, but they offered nothing. They had no clue going forward and no answer at the back.

Our midfield controlled the play, whether it was the behemoth Bozzy kicking anything that moved, or the cultured boot of Michael O'Connor looking to spread the play. We were men and the boys couldn't handle us.

We still had to be committed and apply ourselves and both goals were examples of us playing good football, not the so-called moon ball we get labelled with. I'm quite happy to be called direct if teams think they can double up on Big John and nullify our threat, because that's not going to stop us. The delivery for both goals was superb, Neal Eardley doing what he does for the first and a truly sumptuous ball from O'Connor for the second.

On the end of both was Danny Rowe, a man who looks to be fitter and sharper than the player we had last season. He's slotted into the ten role superbly and maybe, just maybe Shay McCartan was watching on fearing for his immediate Imps' future. After all, Rowe got closer to Akinde than Shay has managed to and provided a little more energy pushing on. Mind you, McCartan coming off the bench is another fine example of that quality in the squad.

Rowe was unlucky not to get Man of the Match, but on the radio Steve Thompson gave it to O'Connor and it would be hard to disagree. He didn't 'bottle it', there's nothing to bottle. Thommo calls it as he sees it and in O'Connor we have the player who does the unseen work, just like Alex did last season. The difference, maybe, is O'Connor is experienced enough to know when there's a good forward pass on, which he provided with aplomb. We talk about Adam Marriott's ball to Nathan two years ago, O'Connor's to Danny Rowe was almost in that league. Almost.

Into the second half and both teams settled for the result. We asked questions and controlled the tempo of the game, but we never needed to hit the higher levels. We've got a huge game this weekend, one in my eyes that will either rubber stamp our automatic promotion credentials or keep us hanging on a little more. There was no need to bust a gut for four or five goals, Danny will tell you it was a shame we didn't get them but rather win 2-0 and come through unscathed than 4-0 and pick up an injury. I'm not saying we took our feet off the gas, nor did we sit back, but we managed the final 45 minutes with consummate ease.

The win leaves us six points clear of Bury with a game in hand. If they want to be considered as title challengers, they have to beat us this weekend. If they fail to take all three points, it leaves us in an incredible position going into February. If we were to win, opening up a nine-point gap with a game in hand, it would begin to look very ominous for everyone else.

It promises to be a cracker. They've won more games at home than any side this season, but only one team have scored more away from home than us (Forest Green) and we've conceded fewer on our travels than any other side. Bury have scored more at home than anyone in the division by a big margin though. We've lost one in 12 in the league, they've lost two in twelve, but they've won six straight matches in all competitions, including big wins against MK Dons and Forest Green. They even beat a virtually full strength Oxford side this evening 5-2. It's fair to say that right now, we're the best two teams in the division, although the form table has Carlisle between us.

Tonight's win was important, massively so, but let me tell you this: if we win on Saturday I predict we go on to win the league. If we get anything there it will be a fine result, but a win would be a big statement. It's and exciting time to be an Imp and all with a squad of 19. For now.

All the talk of Saturday's game is fine, but the reason we go there confident, the reason we will be top no matter what the outcome on Sunday morning, is because each and every game we approach in exactly the same meticulous manner. Yeovil will testify to that as they lick their wounds and look nervously below them in the coming days.

Two more join the fight: City strengthen even further
January 24, 2019

When Danny once said 'I'll only bring players in who improve the group', I laughed a little. I thought it was a nice soundbite, but eventually he was going to have to sign cover players.

Okay, James Brown is a cover player so it isn't entirely the strategy of the manager, but the last 24 hours have provided us with more proof that in the main, Danny is right. Let's start with the first of our new faces, Jordan Roberts who joins on loan from Ipswich.

I'm assuming to some degree that Danny Rowe, for now, replaces Matt Green. That means that Roberts is a replacement for Mensah, given that Kellan Gordon came in as a right back. If that is the case, we've swapped a League One reserve player for someone who, at the start of the season, was a Championship regular.

Before we look too deep at Jordan Roberts, let that sink in. Ipswich Town and Paul Hurst believed at the start of this season that Jordan Roberts could compete regularly in the six or seventh most competitive league in Europe. He's now at Lincoln City and not even guaranteed a start, such is the depth of our squad.

Roberts started six matches for Ipswich, making 12 Championship appearances in total. The feeling from their fan base is perhaps he was out of his depth, but that at League Two level he's a big player. Crawley fans certainly rate him, they would have loved to have him back. Plymouth fans are pretty hacked off too, because up until a few days ago he was nailed on to go there and boost their survival hopes in League One.

We've also allegedly beaten MK Dons and Bradford City to his signature. Let that sink in again Lincoln City have beaten two League One clubs and MK Dons who are probably considered a 'bigger' club than us. Roberts chose us. Whatever happens between now and then end of the season, it is going to be very important to remember that.

He's primarily a left winger, but he can operate as a striker too. It's an interesting swoop because he gives us a couple of options up front. I listened to the NTT20 Podcast with former Bristol Rovers manager Darrell Clarke earlier and he spoke of having flexibility as one of his great assets when they won promotion a couple of years ago. well, Roberts gives us just that.

Then we were hit with the new Mark O'Hara had joined from Peterborough. It had been suggested by Darragh MacAnthony that the deal was finished last week, but O'Hara attended the game on Saturday and has been around the lads for a day or two and has finally been convinced to come here. There's an undertone to this move I feel, Danny didn't say as much but it sounds like O'Hara regrets the move to Posh in the summer and needed time to be convinced Lincoln was the right place for him. There's all manner of factors as to why a player doesn't sign straight away, so to finally see this one over the line will delight the manager.

O'Hara's capture is really interesting because he's a box to box midfielder just like O'Connor and Frecklington. There's young Ellis in there too, we've got Tom Pett been playing that role and Bozzy has been touted as shifting up the field too. Where on earth is Danny going to fit these players in? we're a squad of 20 now, according to the manager, but that's probably 20 who could seriously start for any other League Two side, certainly any outside the top three or four.

What also interests me about O'Hara is his interview, or specifically the first few words he says during it. You can watch it on the OS here, but he cites the atmosphere against Grimsby as significant in getting him to Sincil Bank. that's a great sound bite and has obviously been seized upon by the club, but it was another thing he said that made me smile: 'I've had many conversations with the gaffer and Jez'.... Now I've heard a lot of negativity from Cambridge fans about Jez George, but under no circumstances underestimate how important he has been in the last couple of weeks.

Michael Hortin tweeted that this is the strongest squad he's seen at Lincoln City since he started covering them. I can't help but agree, but we say it every window. Every time Danny promises improvement, we get it. These players have to perform, there's little doubt about that and of the new arrivals one or two will surely disappoint, just as one or two have in every window. That's not the point though.

In terms of giving us the very best chance to finish in the top three, something that is surely the only aim of the season, our recruitment has been terrific and give or take the odd incoming player as cover between now and next Thursday at this time, all the rest of the work is to be done behind closed doors.

A great advert for League Two: Bury 3-3 Imps
January 27, 2019

Sometimes I find it very hard to be objective. I'm a writer, yes. I write objectively about 71 other clubs without an issue, but Lincoln City is in my blood. I see the world through the eyes not of a football writer, but a Lincoln City fan who writes about football.

It makes things difficult at times. This week I'm going to Cheapside, amusingly the name of Grimsby's training ground, to interview Elliot Embleton about his PFA Player of the Month win for December. I'll be objective and won't be visiting a bitter rival, but simply on a job. Will a part of me want to scratch 'We are Imps' in the toilets? No. Of course not.

Still, it's hard and after watching last night's game I felt I needed time to digest the action in order to be fair. I was disappointed, once again a late goal has cost us a big win. Think Mansfield and Swindon, two points gained under the circumstances but almost certainly also four additional points we could have on the board. Now, thanks to Will Aimson's all-too easy header, there's six points we don't have that we could have.

That was how I felt immediately after the final whistle, having felt genuinely worried we would collapse in those dying stages. We didn't, as you know and when I woke up this morning I realised 100% that we'd got a good result. If we'd been 3-0 down and drawn 3-3 I'd have still be out celebrating now, the manner in which the result occurs shouldn't matter.

As you'll know from my erratic pre-match predictions (win on the pod, draw on the Bury Me in Exile piece and lose as I got to Dad's) I wasn't sure how it would go. I'd heard a lot about Bury, but not seen enough to say for definite what would happen. In those early exchanges, I felt we were perhaps overstating the threat.

As always, we started with the 'intent and purpose' that Danny loves. In horrendous conditions and backed by a great travelling support, we certainly looked to be the better side. When we had the ball we looked to move forward quickly and having Danny Rowe helped that. I've seen enough in the last three games to convince me that he's the best signing of the transfer window, maybe harsh on Bolger, but that's what I think. He's become the player that Shay McCartan should have been.

That's no slur on Shay, he offers a threat that's real enough, but Danny's raw pace is impressive. He's like a focused Harry Anderson, an adaptable figure able to add versatility and most crucially, goals.

His goal was the sort of stuff our critics dream off. A long put up field towards the Bury left, Rowe comes away free when maybe their defender should be dealing with it and it's 1-0. It wasn't an easy finish, angled across goal not dissimilar to Terry Hawkridge's goal against Macclesfield on that final game of the 2016/17 season. It certainly set my mind at ease a little because of the stats; we've not lost a game this season in which we've taken the lead. Surely then, at least a point in the bag?

Not the case, because as poor as I thought Bury looked in the opening ten, they made up for it in the next section of the game. It's easy to single out Mayor as a player who carried a real threat because for me, he stood right out. He was allowed to carry the ball far too far for their leveller, but even then a tremendous long-range effort from Jay O'Shea should have been stopped. It took a nick off Shackell to beat Grant Smith, but in slow motion it looked a weak one from the keeper's point of view.

I wouldn't want to dwell too long on the so-called stamp by Lee Frecklington. Again, slow motion does nobody any favours and in real-time there's no malice in it at all. The Bury fans without an objective view seem to think we're a team of thugs intent on causing injury and harm, but you'll not catch Lee Frecklington charging at women and children outside of a football ground and you'll never find him deliberately stamping on a player's head. It looked nasty and it serves to underline the negative rhetoric against us, which I suppose is a cross we'll have to bear.

At 1-1 I thought we responded well, never giving in to their wonderful attacking play. Danny said afterwards they're the best team on the ball in the division and he's not wrong. They attack at will, using the wide players to cause real problems. When they found space on the flank and entered the box you always felt they might score. Similarly, whenever we delivered into the area, you thought we might do the same.

Our second took me by surprise, but it shouldn't have. When have we not been a threat from set pieces, and I don't mean shots from free kicks? The answer to that is probably since Port Vale away, but with Danny Rowe delivering and Cian Bolger on the end of them, we're certainly a threat once more. Both Stacey West sponsored players were involved, but Big John was in the middle of it too. Was it a foul? No. Was he offside? Possibly, yes. It's evened out those horrendous decisions in the Cambridge and Carlisle matches hasn't it?

I know Danny will be gutted to take the lead again and concede again, but when they're in full flow this Bury side are irresistible. There are things you can do to make sure they don't score though, like track a runner into the box. From a defensive point of view, their second equaliser is a horror show. Harry Toffolo got drawn towards the man in the middle and Tom Pett arrived far too late to deal with the danger. You perhaps have to ask if Toff should have dealt better with the situation and you have to ask if Grant Smith should have done. Still, it's easy to criticise and Mayor once again proved to be the architect of our downfall.

When the curtain was finally brought down on a scintillating first half, a draw was perhaps the fair result. It had made me much more comfortable with City though, I think Port Vale, Crewe and Cambridge over Christmas knocked my belief we're the best team in the league. Seeing how we coped with Bury made me wonder if my belief should have been a little stronger.

The second period went exactly as I expected it too. I thought we'd come out of the blocks quickly again, we make a habit of doing just that, but as the game wore on we were always going to find ourselves under increasing pressure. The key was to get into the game once more, grab another goal and then do what we do best; frustrate.

When the goal did come there was an air of controversy over it. Harry Anderson broke free and showed his usual direct running to get into the area. He went down and the referee pointed to the spot. This incident is one that changes depending on the angle you see it from. There's a GIF going around (forwarded to me by a Grimsby fan.... why so interested in us?) where Harry looks to take a dive. I'll tell it how it is, he seems to do a jump and have the referee fall for it. At first glance, I thought he dived.

My Dad didn't, but then he does have a picture of Harry Anderson and him on his mantlepiece. My Dad said it was a clear foul and when you see it from behind, there was contact. The defender takes Harry's trailing leg, not intentionally, but he clips it enough to send our right winger off-balance. To the letter of the law, it's a penalty. If it was against us I'd be saying the same thing, no matter what a short clip shows.

John Akinde does one of the things we pay him to do in the minutes after, staying cooler than the Fonz and more collected than a Lincoln City programme in my filing cabinet. He strides up and sends the keeper on holiday. 3-2 to City and we're back in control.

That's more or less where my article could end, because from that point on until the final whistle it was all about Bury. That's me being objective. It might have been when Danny Rowe came off a little afterwards, but one of those two incidents basically caused us to go into our shell and invite them on to us.

They moved it about well, probed and battled, but our rear guard held firm. Jason Shackell was obviously immense and I felt with O'Connor in midfield we found more mobility than in the first half, allowing us to repel the Danny Mayor threat a little more. I know Bozzy is a huge favourite but for me, he's a centre back. He doesn't have the same industry as O'Connor, he's a brute strength man, a player who kicks what moves and then goes back into position to do it again. O'Connor plays the ball and darts about more, which helped us in the second period.

It also helped that Bozzy was back in the middle kicking balls away. He thrived back alongside Shackell and both Harry Toffolo and Neal Eardley were excellent in those final thirty odd minutes.

Bury knocked on the door time and again, but at no point did they get anything too clear-cut. The XG data (Expected Goals, the NTT20 lads love that) will doubtless favour them, but data only shows one side of a performance. There's no numbers for grit, resilience and fortitude. If there was, we'd be top of all the charts and not just the one that matters.

The two changes didn't help our rhythm at all. Mark O'Hara didn't get a touch to my knowledge, but it was a difficult game to get dropped into to. The same goes for Jordan Roberts, he did see a bit of the ball but wasn't able to use it effectively. They'll both be improving once they settle in, but my gut feeling would have been to bring on a player up to speed with our tactics. I wouldn't have brought big John off though, he was blowing on 75 minutes but he still fought for the cause. yes, he unorthodox and I grant you we haven't got the clinical finisher we saw at Barnet, but he was an important figure in those dying moments. With three centre halves, we had to have the mobility he offers, even if he was running on empty.

Eventually they did get the goal they wanted and when it came it was as disappointing defensively as the second one. Their lad has got a free header, unchallenged by any of the players around him. Could our lads have dealt with it better? Easy question to ask after 86 minutes of our lads running their bollocks off. I saw enough criticism on social media last night to believe we had crumpled and folded, but we didn't. We got asked a question that we usually have the answer for and we forgot that answer. 3-3.

I genuinely thought they'd go on to win 4-3 at that point, such was the size of the blow, but it didn't happen. Game management, call it what you like, but there was ten minutes of football left to be played and in that time we ensured the best footballing side in the division didn't get another chance. MK Dons couldn't do that. That's why we're top.

The end brought lots of smiles from those in attendance, despite us conceding late. Objectively, it was a superb point and if we take the same from trips to Mansfield and Forest Green, we'll be in good shape for a top three finish. The race for the title is going to be close but if it were a race, we've just negotiated one of the toughest legs and are still out in front.

Now we have to go and do it against teams we should be beating, but seven from nine is a good haul and if we keep that up over the next nine games we'll be in a tremendous position for a trip to Ipswich next season. Only a fool would bet against Bury joining us.

Welcome back to Sincil Bank: Lee Angol
January 31, 2019

The League One striker we've been in contact with all day is none other than Shrewsbury Town's Lee Angol.

He's well-known to Imps fans for scoring a hat trick on his debut against Braintree as well as helping us towards National League promotion. Without glossing over the obvious, he's also well-known for then moving to Mansfield Town on big money.

That didn't work out for him and this season he's been at the New Meadow, where he's had decent impact. He's not been prolific as the shrews have struggled, but he's been involved in the first team set up. They've moved for Stefan Payne today and that's freed up Angol to come here.

This is going to be a deal that divides the fans, but whatever happened in the past is to be put to one side. He's a 24-year-old with a decent future ahead of him, someone who adds value and depth to our squad. He's not a £1m striker from the Championship, but he is someone deemed good enough to feature regularly in a League One side this season.

I think talk of Mo Eisa, Danny Hylton and the like has clouded the judgement here. We were never going to get a replacement number 9, it's why we paid big money for John Akinde in the summer. It was always going to be about adding to the group as a whole, which is what I wrote about a few weeks ago. it seems that fell on deaf ears though.

I can't understand why there is negativity towards Lee as a player, just his contribution on the field being considered. He did well here, he helped us to the 3-1 win against Forest Green almost two years ago that turned the season around, that coming after we'd gone 1-0 down early doors. If we'd lost that we might not be where we are today. Sure, he then went off somewhere on more money, but why is that a bad thing? Would you?

If someone offered you more money to change jobs right now, would you go? If you did, would it be fair to call you a money grabber or cash motivated? Of course not and it's not fair to label Lee as the same.

He won't go into the first team, he'll be on the bench looking to stretch defences in the dying embers of a game. He'll work hard, he has to after seeing two moves not work out. He's been an exciting talent and maybe he needs loving back to life. Danny and the team can do it off the field, but he will need motivation on the field too.

I just hope we're not about to find ourselves another scapegoat here, although I suppose if we are it takes the pressure off 12-goal John Akinde for a while, doesn't it?

Second signing of deadline day is complete
January 31, 2019

The Imps have moved to allay fears over Josh Vickers' current injury issues by bringing in Matt Gilks, a former Premier League keeper.

The former Scotland keeper played for Blackpool in the Premier League alongside Neal Eardley and is arriving presumably as cover for Josh in the event of further injury. Grant Smith has deputised of late, but 36-year-old Gilks will now provide additional support to those two.

Gilks has also played for Norwich City and Rochdale and arrives from Scunthorpe United. Whether he'll feature regularly is another question, but he replaces the outgoing Sam Slocombe who went back to Bristol Rovers.

Hopefully, there's nobody with an axe to wield with Gilks because poor old Lee Angol is getting it all.

February

Opinion is one thing: The Lee Angol situation
February 1, 2019

I'm all for opinion and believe it or not, when it comes from an educated and well argued point of view, I respect it whether I agree or not.

I respect the fact people are unhappy with Lee Angol signing for the club. I remember that moment I saw him smiling away in a Mansfield shirt, gripping the Joker's Carolyn Radford's hand with a forced smile on his face. I was angry because I believed he was a good footballer and I felt he would have added to our offering.

To fully understand this situation I think we have to go back further than his decision that summer. He did polarise Imps' fans opinions pretty soon after scoring a hat trick on his debut. I remember penning an article about a pair of fans behind me in the stands calling him every name under the sun as we beat Forest Green. We were promoted that season, Angol's goals and efforts helped and yet he wasn't universally popular then. He bagged 5 in 11 for us, which would even out at 20 over a season.

Then there was the summer, the move to play for Evans. It wasn't as much Mansfield being the problem then, it was Evans. Few have forgiven Angol for that, I've seen him called a turncoat tonight, a money grabber and all sorts. Take a deep breath and consider this: let's say you're offered £60k a year more to do the same job you're doing now somewhere else, even if you like where you are now. Would you go? Don't lie now, would you go?

Few of you will earn anywhere near that figure and as I understand it, that was the difference between our offer and their offer. Lee Angol liked it at Lincoln, he spoke on the bus journey around Lincoln about wanting to stay and yet when the bigger offer came in, he took it. Imagine that, a 22-year old lad taking a lot more money despite his heart telling him something else. At 22, I wouldn't have hesitated and neither would you. To now call him a money grabber with a questionable attitude is repugnant.

The problem here isn't all about that move, it isn't all about being unimpressed with him before, it's a combination of that and one other thing. Expectation.

I said on the podcast way back in December we wouldn't sign Mo Eisa. Luckily, loads of people in the know on the internet knew better and said we were doing, so that raised expectations. It was never going to happen, but I heard it so much I thought there might be something in it. Mind you, I heard Rheady was off to Grimsby, that Harry was off to West Brom, that Ellis was off to Port Vale. It was all guff of course, fuelled by former agents on Twitter, mystery kitmen and blokes who know a guy who worked with the club's doctor's bit on the side.

These rumours circulate and grow though. When we signed Danny Rowe and Cian Bolger it got people thinking. Maybe we are big players. Maybe we can secure the talents of a £1m striker.... wait a minute though, have you forgotten we're Lincoln City? We don't have the money for a player like Eisa and neither do Mansfield or MK Dons. No, but why let that get in the way of things?

Then, when we unveil Lee Angol, the bad feelings from before are amplified because he isn't Mo Eisa. "We wanted Eisa and we got a half-interested turncoat" is the general feeling. Take Eisa out of it and those ridiculous feelings of entitlement and think again. We signed a player whose contribution helped us out of the National League, who has scored goals in League One this season and who can cover a variety of positions.

"But we only sign better than we have" I hear. Really? James Brown is better than Neal Eardley is he? No, of course he isn't. It's just another hiding place to retreat to when the disappointment of us not signing a player we were never going to sign kicks in. What we've done is brought in cover so we don't go into the final period of the season with three strikers, you know, like last season. One year ago I was listening to people saying we should have signed a striker, any striker, just so we had cover. Now we've done it, it isn't the right striker.

We were NEVER going to replace Akinde and again, some of the people getting angry now are the ones who don't rate Akinde. They're mad not only because Lee Angol isn't Mo Eisa, not only because they didn't rate him before, not only because he took a much better offer elsewhere, but also because it means we're 'stuck' with John Akinde. Akinde having scored 11 times and is routinely named by opposition fans as one player they'd love to have. That John Akinde, the one involved in two of the goals against Bury, a great point we earned in tough conditions.

I'm going to bed now because I've been sat here for virtually 16 hours. It's been a long, hard day at times but I'm not disappointed at the end of it. In Lee Angol we have a player Danny knows and trusts, a player who can offer cover in key areas and who is looking for a chance to build up his reputation. He is still young, has played a lot of senior football and is certainly better than an empty space on the bench. He's not Matt Green, sadly Green's contract was expiring and he got a better deal which the club allowed him to take. I'd have loved Green to stay, but that's football. I certainly won't hold that against Lee Angol.

I implore everyone to get behind Lee when he pulls on a City shirt and for every one of you to get behind the team. I know I'll get called something ridiculous like a Cowley convert for this article but you know what? I am. Before them we were 15th in the National League and signing the likes of Craig Hobson in a transfer window. Now we're top of League Two and please, do excuse me for putting some belief in the decisions they make and the people they choose to have around them.

I once cheered a Ben Hutchinson goal after he'd called us the worst fans in the world. You know why? Because he wore a Lincoln City shirt. I seriously hope you'll all do the same with Lee Angol and you never know, you might actually realise there's a very good League Two striker in there.

58 Hours: Notts County 1-1 Imps
February 3, 2019

It might seem an odd headline for some, but it's been 58 hours, more or less, since I last wrote anything about Lincoln City.

A frantic Deadline Day saw me accrue as many views in a single day as I used to get in a whole month, covering the events of the day and the fall out from it. I got up on Friday morning and read through some of the comments and thought processes and felt very low.

Our manager has got us to the top spot in League Two and kept us there certainly for the longest period of time I've ever known us to be there. His decisions and transfers have won us two trophies in as many seasons and look on course, bar a catastrophe, to earn us League One football next season.

Before he arrived we'd do well to take 700 away to our biggest game of the season, now we average 1,200 on the road. Before he arrived we'd be lucky to get 3,000 at home, now we can sell 4,000 to travel to an away game. Before him our transfer window used to be a case of rolling dice, picking up players like Nathan Blissett, Paul Turnbull and Paul Robson. Still, it didn't matter then did it because few actually cared enough to bother.

I left it 24 hours because of the Lee Angol fall out and because I didn't want to get a reputation for being someone who rubbishes other people's opinions. That spread into Saturday and past the County game and I chose not to write last night because I was so utterly ashamed of a portion of our fan base for their continued persecution of John Akinde. I even told a woman to fuck off on the internet and I never get involved in that sort of exchange.

I can't comprehensively digest the game itself and deliver you the usual report because I'm angry and upset. I'm trying so hard to respect opinion and other people's right to have an experience but I'm struggling.

Yesterday was always going to be a tough game. Michael Doyle in the midfield is an inspired signing for them, he's won promotion from this division and played lots of international football. Enzio Boldewijn has been out injured since November but is a £100,000 player with pace, creativity and trickery in his locker. Mitch Rose, another new signing, brought stability to a fragile back line and Craig Mackail-Smith is another with experience to galvanise the side.

They were at home too and as we said before the Grimsby game, these local derby matches often throw up results that buck the trend and form book. As it transpired, had we not given away a soft early penalty we might have won the game.

It was an enthralling match, frustrating as we didn't hit our levels and yet engrossing all the same. County didn't look like a side at the bottom of the table and I believe they'll make a great fist of staying in League Two this season. When we did settle into our rhythm just before half time we had them on the ropes and Bruno bagged a great goal, but the whistle came at the wrong time and after a regroup, County were able to dust themselves down and go again.

There wasn't a standout performer for the Imps, nor was our game plan helped by losing Michael Bostwick during the game and having Harry pull up in the week either. Still, that is what you battle with as a team and that was something we worked around. The terrible referee I've seen widely lamented on social media was poor, but for both teams. I'm sure there's an assessor somewhere circling a time and a place in his diary right now to talk to Mr Coggins, but on the whole his erratic behaviour didn't lose us the game.

Actually, and this may surprise you if you've been looking at fan reaction, we didn't lose the game at all. We got a point and have now lost just one in 14 matches in the league, We're top by two points and have a game in hand over our big-spending rivals Mansfield who won their game courtesy of goals from two very, very special players in Tyler Walker and Jorge Grant. I suppose our fans see that and think we've got some sort of duff hand, that's the only way I can begin to explain the utter insanity I've been digesting over the last few hours.

It wasn't a good day at the office for the Imps, but it wasn't a terrible one either. Last year we went there and had an erratic referee and some things go against us and we lost 4-1. We stood as a group of 4,000 travelling fans and gave a grand account of ourselves though and came home bolster even further by mishandling by the police. Yesterday, the only thing dividing us was ourselves.

My Dad has come home thinking seriously about not renewing his season ticket, not because we drew and not because he's angry with the team, but because he was dismayed with the comments and attitudes around him. New Harry Anderson wasn't playing was met with a round of complaints, when Bozzy came off it was labelled madness and Danny was the villain, picking Akinde was a bad choice, signing Angol the same. For 90 minutes all he got was complaining about the club, a club top of the league and as close to an automatic promotion spot as at any time in the last 20 years. Even when we went up in 1998 we didn't have this level of success sustained over such a period of time.

It's why I struggle to write anything coherent about the game because I'm getting drawn into the web of negativity and feeling inclined to respond, hit back and get worked up. I've always embraced the swell in crowds and the push its given us going forward, but were these people lashing out all over the place really following the club closely when we signed Craig Hobson? I can't think they were, I certainly never remembered him getting such abuse as John and he scored far fewer goals both from the spot or from open play.

I'm also sick of defending John, much the same as other League Two defenders are but that's something most fans miss. I chatted to a County friend last night who was delighted with the job they did on the big man. 'We put two on him at all times' was his response when asked about him. 'It kept him quiet for most of the game but he is always a danger'. That doesn't mean a goal danger all the time, something some seem to think is what it is all about, but a man who can keep the play in the final third, a man who can create a goal too. Remember, he's been involved in more of our goals this season than any other player, yet you'd think he's actively hindered our progress.

I'm getting to a point where I am beginning to question the motivation of some people in disliking John. I'm not saying everyone who has a negative opinion of him has an underlying issue with him, they don't. People can dislike a player and back it up with reason. I chatted to James Bride this week, a former DF editor and someone who is not an Akinde fan. He has his reasons why and I respect his right to that opinion, but he doesn't just go online and write 'Akinde is shit,' or something equally as insightful. Some people were criticising him in the fifth minute of yesterday's game; you tell me that's purely based on performance and I'll tell you you're wrong.

The classic exchange happened for me on one of the internet sites last night and it typified the sort of moronic follower we've got right now. if this was you and you're offended with what I say, I make no apology. In fact, if this was you and you're reading this, please log out because you're not welcome on my site.

"Angol to start next game? Akinde is awful and doesn't deserve the shirt."

Wow. Firstly, John Akinde was not awful. Like the other 11 players, he had a tough afternoon but anyone understanding football properly could see he was marked tighter than most. In that respect, his back yup striker should have been far better and wasn't. Shay was just as ineffective as John and he didn't have the constant attention of two players. Why is he not being singled out? At least the first comment had Angol down as a viable alternative, but the second guy claiming Angol was shit needs to take himself off to a darkened room for a while. Lee Angol got five minutes. Five minutes.

We talk about being fans and supporting the club but there's an element that simply don't do that. There's an element that still turn up to shout their abuse and generally get mad at the team they're supposed to support. The sad thing is, fans are now identifying that element as the new support but that's not the case. Remember Altrincham in the FA Cup a few years ago? Before Ipswich and Oldham, before 8,000 fans at home, before routinely taking 1,00 away? No? Go back and have a read. The sad, repressed element of our support was as evident then as it is right now.

I've now written 1600 words on the state of the response to our result, a draw which might not seem decent right now but could be important at the end of the season. We're into 60 points, we've lost one in 14 and we're top with a game in hand. Everything is still in our hands and Danny Cowley has not let us down in his two and a half years in charge of the club. Our playing squad has got better every transfer window, our league position has got better every season and we've grown into a club to be proud of once more.

My fear is this destructive element within can begin to derail the season. The fans who buy in the signing section only to sit down and try to sample the atmosphere, they're wrong. The ones who think 'I've paid my money so I'll call Akinde shit' are wrong. Those arguing with other Imps fans in the terraces, posting rubbish on social media as the game goes on, are wrong. That's how it is. We're top and for 90 minutes fans should be supporting the team, not going there prepared to get angry at a player before he's kicked a ball.

Danny said in his post match interview he knew John would get stick on the internet for missing his penalty and lo and behold, he did. He couldn't win either could he? Score it and he only scores penalties, miss it and he's got nothing to offer (apart from leading the line). Within the club, John Akinde is seen as one of the key reasons we're top, one of the main players in the current set up. He allows us to play the way we do, his mobility and strength gives us options going forward. It allows us to sit deep as we did in the game against Swindon, it allows us to break at pace as we did away at Exeter. He occupies defenders and when everyone is fit he'll form a deadly partnership with Danny Rowe. If he stays fit, we go up. If he doesn't, we might struggle. In my opinion and, I'm led to believe' the opinion of people within the club as well.

Still, Linda from the burger bar knows better doesn't she? Or Jack, the year nine with a profile picture of himself with fucking bunny ears and rosy red cheeks. Not Danny Cowley, not Nicky Cowley, two men who have brought unprecedented success to the club in a short space of time, two men who have revolutionised the Mighty Imps. What do they know?

It wasn't a good penalty. I won't defend it. John didn't have a great game, nobody did. Why single him out though? Why make our manager believe the first thing he has to do is damage limitation, not just for John Akinde but also when we sign Lee Angol? How long before the dross, not the honest informed opinion, but the utter dross, drives players away? How long before it drives the managers away?

I'm not saying it'll happen, but I do ask some 'fans' to get some perspective.

£1m loss – Why the figures don't give cause for alarm
February 5, 2019

The Imps have recorded a £1.09m loss for the financial period ending 30th June, a seemingly huge figure given the recent successes on the field.

It certainly isn't as bad as it sounds, with few football clubs running at a profit. Our previous season was incredible and allowed us a platform on which to build, but to accumulate a club must speculate, sensibly. That is one of the reasons behind the loss this season, despite the Wembley run, the charge to the play-offs and the 70% increase on average attendance. Those factors might have an ill-informed fan believing we have made a huge profit, but that is not the case.

There's been investment off the field, not in players but in Danny and Nicky's new deals, in the training ground and some of the backroom staff. it all goes towards the success we're experiencing on the pitch, even if at times it frustrates those who wanted to see another big name striker come in because they don't rate the one we got in the summer.

That won't happen. We're not going to put all of our eggs in one basket, Mansfield style. The club have still got to work within a strict budget, one that does seem to be top three level this season. The numbers only reflect on last year, but even then our budget certainly wasn't bottom half.

What is interesting is that even without the FA Cup run, the club's turnover increased by around £600,000. That's due to the increase in season ticket sales and of course, the additional payments made to League Two clubs. It does go to show the imparity between non league and Football league and only serves to further highlight the job Bob Dorrian and the board did in the wake of our relegation.

All of this will be of little interest to a layman though. They're likely to see losses of £1m and wonder if we're in trouble? The ill-informed might start asking where the money has gone, but fear not. we're not in trouble, the club's official statement on the website ended by saying: "The balance sheet remains strong with cash resources of £2.36 million. This was supported by strong season ticket sales for the current season as well as further equity injections."

The key here is 'further equity injections' doubtless a referral to the ongoing recruitment at board level that not only brings fresh faces and ideas to the club, but also fresh money to further strengthen our future. It's true that with every announcement people are expecting huge spending, but that won't happen. Clive Nates won't put the future of the club at risk and he's outlined his thoughts in an open letter, released at the same time as the accounts.

"We are at a pivotal moment as a club. We have momentum thanks to a remarkable two years of success and progress.

"We believe this represents a rare opportunity to transform the running of the club and attempt to establish ourselves higher in the football pyramid.

"We recognise that we are in a development and growth phase requiring significant investment in assets, systems and people, which will have a negative effect on the income statement in the immediate future.

"It is critical however that we ensure that these investments deliver their expected returns in order to ensure the long-term sustainability of the club.

"We believe that the structure of the board and diverse ownership allow us to seek out like-minded individuals who together with existing investors will continue to fund this growth phase.

"We are also committed to searching out ways to make us more than just a football club, by giving back to the community and making lives better. The recently rebranded Lincoln City Foundation will play a critical role in developing our community strategy."

The loss we've discussed today is sustainable and the club has cash reserves on which to draw, meaning we're living within our means. we're not propped up by one company or individual who, if their interest wanes, could leave us broke. We're spending for the future, investing in the infrastructure and the staff to ensure we're not just at the top of League Two for a season or so, but that we have a long-term future that looks rosy and ethical.

By ethical I don't mean we use recycled horse manure on the pitch or serve or food on bio-degradable trays, but that we're operating as a business should, not making grand outlays we can't afford and not making promises the cheque book is unlikely to back up.

Ellis heads out on loan: Reaction
February 7, 2019

Danny has described it as lending his favourite toy to someone, with Ellis Chapman heading out on loan to struggling Chesterfield this afternoon.

There's always been a suggestion he would go out, perhaps not to Port Vale as one rather errant account described, but certainly to a side where he'd get game time. The National League is one Danny knows well, having had several players on loan during his time as a manager in the division.

Ellis is very well thought of at the club, he's a player with a lot of potential but like any young man he needs games to impress. You see it at all levels of the game, one team loans its youth out to the division below and so on. Chelsea give Villa Tammy Abraham, Villa give Cambridge Rushian Hepburn-Murphy, Cambridge give Kettering Town Tom Knowles.

It's a food chain and the players at new clubs have a chance to get regular games and hopefully come back with a wider experience which they can add to their game. it'll certainly be a change for Ellis, his last outing in an Imps shirt came against Everton, his next match will be against Halifax. Those sorts of jumps in stadium and level of opposition will serve him well.

There's always a danger a loan can go badly. If Joan Luque had been at Bromley, bagged six goals and looked the business, he'd still be with us now. He barely got a look in and I believe he's now at Concord Rangers, but I don't think that'll be the case with Ellis. I think we can look to Sammy Szmodics as a fine example of what we hope happens.

He's the insanely talented Colchester player who should, and will, grace higher levels of the game at some point. He's a homegrown hero but he spent a short time on loan in the National League, namely with Braintree. He went back to Colchester and thrived, using the experience as a huge positive. I suspect Ellis will do the same.

Why? Why will Ellis do well when someone such as Joan Luque struggled? Simple; Ellis has a great support network. His parents are very involved in his development and Danny Cowley, a man renowned for getting the best out of players and spotting talent, has him close to his heart as well. The only way the kid could fail is with a bad attitude and let me tell you, Ellis doesn't have that at all.

Nope, this is a good move all round. With no EFL Trophy games to worry about, no more cup involvement at all, Ellis just wasn't going to play. He might have got on the bench, but with Mark O'Hara adding to our offering and Bozzy getting game time in the middle, it has all got too congested for our local boy. He's best served going to a 'proper' club like Chesterfield, Football league in all but status, and getting game time there. Home crowds are decent, away matches are varied in terms of level and setting and he'll come back richer for the experience.

At least that is the plan.

Put the anger to one side: Let's remember what made us strong
February 8, 2019

It's been a rough few weeks hasn't it? The team are top of the league, we've been to Everton and run them close in the FA Cup and had a strong transfer window.

Aside from all that terribleness, social media has seen lots of vitriol flying around, with players coming under fire, the club's season ticket announcement backfiring when I'm sure it wasn't the intention and someone even accusing me of being sycophantic to the managers who have given us two trophies, a Wembley trip and our pride back. Imagine that!

All the sarcasm aside though, we're in serious danger of missing the point here, as fans and as a club as a whole. What got us here? Aside from Danny and Nicky, aside from investment from the board? I'll tell you what got us here; we did.

We cheered the side on when they went 1-0 down to Torquay in the 80th minute on Good Friday. We stuck with the team when they went 1-0 down at Gateshead a couple of days later. We roared them on at Portman Road, out-singing the Championship side and we did the same at Arsenal, even though we were beaten.

We rallied round to fund a player in the summer of 2016. We bought season tickets in their thousands upon returning to the league, helping the club evade the mistakes of those lot up the road. We seized on the success and built a fortress at Sincil Bank which has seen us lose once in the league at home this season and only six times throughout Danny's managerial reign.

That's what our strength is. We are one, whether you like the hashtag 'Imps As One' or not, it is true. Some people might not like having it served up to them in that manner, but there's a reason the club picked it. We were as one.

Now, I fear we're not, not entirely. I fear that some have a sense of entitlement, some believe we're going to turn up and win games just because we have done before. That never happens. Football isn't just a great game, it is a cruel mistress and the wrong attitude, on and off the field, can backfire badly. We were once the club's greatest strength, but we're in real danger of becoming its Achilles Heel.

Are we in danger of becoming the architect of our own downfall? Is what made us great in serious danger of making us weaker? Surely, we cannot allow this to happen. There's enough hate for us as a club out there right now without us generating some of our own from within.

Two years ago we faced a torrid time in February and early March before turning things around and surging forward as one. We were united off the field, focused entirely on the task in hand. I understand the furore over the ST announcement, but are we going to let that overshadow our first serious chance of lifting a Football League title trophy since 1976? Are we going to let a seething anger at a perceived injustice detract from the task in hand at the club we love?

I believe (aside from trolls and fishermen) that the posts on social media are born from a passion for us to do well, but that can't just be expected of Danny and the players. He tells us so often how important we are that some forget. Some want to shoot this influential manager down, who knows why. We're not all Tom Duggan though, are we? We don't all revel in acting up on the internet and making an infamous name for ourselves.

I get the dissent, I understand where people are angry about the ST announcement but would you let that get in the way of supporting the team, through thick and thin? I've been going to Sincil Bank for over 32 years now and this is the closest we've ever come to finishing top of one of the four divisions in the Football League.

We could play Ipswich next season as equals. It was out big day out two years ago, a match that fans were attracted to based on stature. We could be the same division as them, as well as maybe Sunderland, Charlton, Bolton, as well as being given a stab at finally being the Pride of Lincolnshire.

You want that? Yeah? Me too.

Put down the keyboard, put aside the ST anger and get right behind the lads this weekend and next. When things don't go well, fuck it. Sing, shout and cheer, let the lads know that there's a belief in the stands and a desire amongst supporters to see them get over the line and become a third-tier side next season.

Let Danny know you love him and let the club know that despite the faux pas, despite the outpouring on negativity on social media, that deep down you still love them too. You still bleed red and white, you still hurt when they hurt.

Most of all, lets come back together as one and rediscover what made us great.

We are Imps and once more, it's our time to shine. This journey can only be stopped from the inside and I don't think we're about to let that happen.

Together Again: Imps 1-1 Northampton
February 10, 2019

On the face of it, a draw yesterday afternoon wouldn't seem like a good result. Northampton had been talking about relegation before picking up four points in two matches, they should have been put to the sword.

A Lincoln City side with eleven men on the field could have done that, but things are not that easy at Sincil Bank these days. We made it one defeat in 15 league matches, or two wins from eight in all competitions. Stats, eh?

Let's start by me apologising for the lateness of today's work. I've had a few issues with the site that have ended up costing me a fair bit to solve, but we should be fine now, back up and running as normal. I've also had a shift to do the FLW, where you lot made a Lincoln City story one of the biggest of the day!

Anyway, the real focus pre-match was on a togetherness. The fan base has felt fractured in recent weeks, even articles asking for togetherness brought about a certain negativity. You can see comments on my rallying cry from Friday, both on the blog and social media, to see that there's still an element who want to be vocal in their negativity. It isn't easy, before the game my mate Dave and I spoke about being positive, but within half an hour he was criticising aspects of our play. It's natural of course, when you want something so bad to become frustrated.

Aside from missing Bozzy we were pretty much at full strength and I thought we started quite purposeful. The tone of the afternoon was set inside the first minute or two when Lee Frecklington was pole-axed in the middle of the park. Michael Salisbury, a referee already earmarked by other fans as rogue, gave nothing. It led me to think perhaps there was going to be a talking point or two.

If you watch the challenge it can be interpreted two ways, either he gets lamped in a 50/50 or he's cleverly taken out by the defender. Without my rose-tinted glasses on, I think it's the latter. He was walloped and the ref did nothing. It wasn't a red, but it was a foul. Still, we're Lincoln City and right now, we get very little at home.

Frecklington went off not long after. Our PFA Player of the Month nomination had been targeted and taken out. Mission accomplished and the referee hadn't seen it as a foul. Keith Curle would have been delighted.

The tone of the match was set in a scrappy first fifteen minutes or so. There's going to be a lot of talk about poor old David Buchanan and his bloody shins, but on 13 minutes he scythed Harry Anderson down in front of the dugouts and got a booking. It's clear that their early game plan was to intimidate and be aggressive. I think that was intended to get Danny on the ref's back immediately and eventually, turn his decisions against us. Keith Curle admitted they had a plan to combat the intense home atmosphere and I firmly believe that was it.

If you need evidence, count how many yellow cards we had in the game. Tell you what, I'll save you the time. None. You know why? because we're not thugs and bullies like other fans would have you believe. We're not aggressive and dirty either. Northampton had four and that was with a referee who, in his spare time, has a Cobblers season ticket. Probably.

Northampton made the odd foray into our half, but I thought we were comfortable enough and when Bruno bagged for us it seemed as though the game would only go one way. After a tetchy and niggly half an hour, a bit of class from John Akinde and a touch of composure from Bruno brought us a goal worth watching over and over again. It was great play by both and the goal instantly lifted the supporters. I took the opportunity to go to the loo along with perhaps fifty others who had all been holding it, waiting for the spark.

Within minutes we got another glimpse of the referees uncertainty as he gave a foul against Bruno as he went through on goal, despite the Cobblers man slipping. Danny Rowe was then fouled (in my opinion) as he went through and got nothing given. Danny was getting angrier, the crowd were too and a couple of minutes before the break it exploded. A ball forward went beyond Anderson and he launched into Buchanan. There's little doubt it was a red, I couldn't argue against it.

After that it felt as though the referee lost us and the grip of the game. He signalled four minutes injury time, but played six. A minute after time he awarded a dubious free kick on the edge of the area, two minutes over the time Northampton scored a goal from a badly defended corner. it meant the team went in level at the break.

I was across the other side for a cheque presentation and saw the referee come off the field. He did so to a volley of abuse, one man in the Selenity Stand reserved some very hateful spite. Michael Salisbury smiled, slightly smug if anything, and turned away. I couldn't help but feel that sort of anger swung him further against us in the second half.

It's not all about the referee though and with ten men we still had a job to do. I don't want to sound bitter, but with ten men on the field it would have still be 1-0 at half time, maybe even more. We'd started to get joy down the flank, Bruno had looked comfortable and exciting and having someone in the ten role left John less isolated.

He didn't care about the isolation, a particularly languid and lazy-looking run in the first minute or so of the second half almost brought is our second. I can see why people get frustrated with John because his style looks so ungainly, but he frightened those defenders and could easily have bagged. I thought he had a great game and was a contender for Man of the Match.

The game never got going after that. With ten men we remained compact, but it essentially leaves us hoping to get out on the break, rather than pinning the opposition in. We got a glimpse of why Northampton have struggled, they're a counter-attacking team who were expected to seize the initiative and in truth, they didn't. It wasn't exactly tepid, but it wouldn't be classed as a classic either.

What I was heartened by was the togetherness in the stands. I think as we had a perceived common enemy, the referee, the usual bile started to disappear. The songs were sung loudly and in block 3, where I sit, it was loud at times. It felt like us against the world, us against a conspiracy or against a team of bully boys favoured by the ref. That's not the reality of it, but when you have that sense of injustice, it pulls you closer together.

The shouts weren't at Akinde, Angol or whoever else has had stick. They were at the referee, his linesman and the occasional Cobbler. Whether that game was badly managed or not was irrelevant, it distracted fans from the regular stuff and worked in our favour. Despite having ten men, I felt we were more likely to score.

They were going for the game and Timo Elsnik came on, a player I liked at Mansfield. I expected us to be backs against the wall, but they're clearly not happy having to control play. They came forward, usually Jason Shackell cleared and it all started again. When we did get the ball we played it from left to right and looked to find the channel. It was predictable, but I found that comforting.

I never felt they'd score, but I thought we might. My phone kept telling me Mansfield were losing, MK Dons were losing, Forest Green were losing and it all made me smile. It meant that the draw wouldn't be a bad result, despite the situation. Dave next to me, in a moment of doom and gloom, said 'just because we draw with ten men doesn't make it a good result'. I replied; 'No, but if everyone else loses it is'.

There was an incident when Cian Bolger was clearly held down in the area, a penalty on 99% of other occasions, but that wasn't given. Not long after, I thought Elsnik was lucky to stay on the field too. He got a booking for pulling John Akinde back then not five minutes after committed the sort of foul we'd see bookings given for. In my eyes, whether he's on a yellow or not shouldn't matter, but it did demonstrate that Salisbury wasn't looking to even things up. I suppose that's a sign of a good ref, although in this instance it would be a red herring.

For the last six or seven minutes we laid siege to their goal. The crowd lifted, the chanting started and the belief we could win the game oozed through everyone in the ground. It should have been the eleven men looking for the win, but instead we seemed to start pouring forward. It hadn't been a classic performance, it wasn't easy with ten men and having our captain nailed in the early minutes, but it felt like we might actually win the game. We got a couple of corners which came to nothing then, with three minutes injury time on the board, it happened.

By 'it', I mean the injustice that had everyone together when we came out of the ground. The so-called ball to hand when a defender had said hand extended out like a keeper. The clearest handball you'll see all season was waved away. He might not have realised it, but Michael

Salisbury had been got at. The anger from our fans, the ear-bashing from the bench and the sense we were the enemy had surely been drilled home, because other than that there can be no excuse as all for not pointing to the spot.

Would we have scored it? Who knows. That doesn't matter, what does matter is had it been at the other end I feel he would have given it. We were never getting anything rom him as early as the first minute, but it took until the 90th for him to show his colours. Within seconds we had a second, less obvious appeal which again he didn't go for. He soon blew the final whistle and rightly received a round of boos.

After that, the lads were applauded off. There was a unity again, a feeling that we had been done by the man, done by a bad referee and opposition with a vicious and pointed game plan. It was us against the world again and maybe, just maybe it could be a big boost.

Was it the right assessment? The penalty was as clear as you'll see and the ref saw it, later claiming ball to hand. If his assessor hears that he'll be forced to fill in paperwork, almost certainly. The other decisions were perhaps debatable, Freck was fouled but was he going to give us a penalty in the first minute? Of course not.

He got the red card spot on, but do we see the game differently because of that early incident? Did Michael Salisbury actually have a decent game, get one big decision wrong at the end but be perceived to be poor? Or was he just a proper melt who shouldn't be given a whistle next weekend? You decide.

What matters is nobody came out of the ground around me calling Harry naïve, calling John Akinde everything or even criticising our performance. Up until the sending off we'd been okay, but not brilliant. After it we fought well and the man advantage made a very average Northampton team look half decent. Was there any complaining about that? No. Why? Because we were together in our anger at the referee.

There's the odd voice of 'reason' on the internet wanting to take the focus off Salisbury and his dodgy decisions, but not me. Because while we're complaining about him and his inept display, we're back on the same side, Akinde lover or not. We're back in red and white as one, not divided, facing the injustice together. We're little old Lincoln City again, always being done and hated for no reason.

If we stay that way, this might just be the most important game of the season. Stay together, stay loud and stay focused and we'll be off to Portman Road next season. It's that simple.

Smells like team spirit: Why the Imps are still promotion favourites
February 13, 2019

I couldn't help but smirk as Michael O'Connor did his post match interview this weekend. Aside from having the sort of alluring voice my missus would like to have me tell her tales of my day in, he signalled the start of the business end of the season.

During the interview he made reference to enjoying it and I was taken swiftly back to the National League. Danny urged us to enjoy it then and to be fair, I did. Retrospectively. I enjoyed it the minute the whistle was blown at Macclesfield and I've enjoyed it every single second since. Up until then, not so much.

I'm the same this season, constantly looking down the table, always believing those tipping us to go up don't know the full story. Sure, we're top but Bury are on fire. Mansfield made good signings and there's dark horses in the play-off spots. Forest Green did look good until recently and MK Dons can't be written off entirely.

Part of the worry comes from my own raging insecurity. It comes from knowing we blew it in 1983, knowing we were in the automatic spots in 2007 too. It comes from seeing us battle our way into the top three in 1998 playing ugly, ahead of teams who'd been there all season. Collapses happen.

They don't usually happen under Danny Cowley and there's usually a hint of the collapse by mid-February, but my conscious mind doesn't register that. No, as far as I'm concerned a little assurance goes a long way.

Whilst waking my dog this afternoon I came up with an assurance in my own mind that grew into the idea for today's article. I believe we have something in our favour that only a couple of other sides in the top six have got, something that ultimately led us to the title in 2017 and that hopefully, can do again. The clue is in the title.

Everyone talks about team spirit don't they? There's always a great bunch of lads in the dressing room, whether that's right or wrong. I was catching up with Sunderland Till I Die last night and heard Chris Coleman talking about a great bunch of lads and bringing in the right characters. Turned out well.

It's easy to trot out how good a dressing room is. The Lincoln City lads of 2013/14 had great spirit apparently, but then when the likes of Ben Tomlinson and Sean Newton left, it emerged that maybe it wasn't all that great. Giving the media a little soundbite is one thing, actually having a good dressing room is something else entirely.

I don't think that spirit, the sort that earns you unlikely points and surprise wins, can come overnight. I look at Carlisle and I worry that the chance of manager has affected the dressing room dynamic. The work that John Sheridan and maybe even Keith Curle put in has been set back and perhaps that was reflected in their defeat last night. I'm not saying a manager can't come in and instil it straight away, look at Michael Flynn at Newport in 2016/17, he managed it.

To change things though, they have to be bad in the first place. Grimsby have seen that too, Michael Jolley has built a good spirit in their camp and slowly but surely they're climbing the table. It isn't the be all and end all, there's no use having spirit without quality, but if you've got it, you're at an advantage. Look at Morecambe. They consistently perform well above their means, why? Team spirit, them against the world, all for one and one for all. Kevin Ellison typifies that, the worst kind of arse to opposing fans, but the best kind of teammate to the Morecambe squad.

I watched the Bury team play the other week, holding us to a 3-3 draw and I saw spirit. I saw fight and anger, determination and a refuse to lose attitude. I saw it in the white shirts of Bury and in the grey shirts of Lincoln. That's why it was a classic and it's why the early season match at the

Bank was entertaining too. Two teams with spirit and quality. It's a deadly pairing for the rest of League Two and it's why come May, I believe the two of us can be in the top three.

When I look at the other teams around us, I'm not sure there's enough of that unseen quality in our opponents to make them something we should worry about. Forest Green have quality and I've tipped them to surge up the table, but luckily it's been a kiss of death. They've lost two on the spin and immediately Mark Cooper starts calling out his players. Any positive vibes the dressing room accrued during their good run will have been shattered as the world's worst man manager once again plays a good hand badly. They have spirit all right, it's the spirit of Christmas past, present and future, all urging Dale Vince to get a manager whose go to response isn't 'my players are all shit, good job I'm an ace coach.'

Mansfield are an unknown quantity, they've been openly talking about their great dressing room and the togetherness they've got. I would have believed it before the transfer window, but some of those big signings do make me wonder. If we'd brought in a replacement for Akinde and another for Harry Anderson, would it have broken the spell of camaraderie we have? Could that discord have reflected in our results? Mansfield have lost three of their last eight and their inability to turn draws into wins in the early part of the season has, so far, cost them.

I'm not saying they don't have that special something, they're clearly a decent side packed with quality, but in these final stages you get tested in ways other than skill. You have to scrap, you have to fight adversity and as we showed in 2017, you have to refuse to lose. We did it against Swindon with nine men, but could Mansfield do the same? I'm not convinced.

Colchester I like, but they're another side who might be a character or two away from full strength. They've got ability, yes, and they've now won their last two matches by an aggregate score of 7-0, but their 4-0 drubbing at Carlisle raised questions. If you've got that magic, that spirit, then when you go 1-0 down, or maybe 2-0 down you don't fold like a napkin.

MK Dons are another side I don't think have quite got there yet. My guess would be a blend of good players and the odd bad character. Chuks Aneke shouldn't be in this division and at the start of the season he didn't want to be. Danny Cowley says you can have one bad egg in a squad, but is there another lurking in the Dons dressing room? The got a win last night, but their collapse has been startling.

That brings us to Lincoln City. We had a spirit in 2016/17. We had that togetherness, on and off the field, but in particular the playing squad fought for each other. Remember Torquay and Gateshead, remember the 1-0 wins against Bromley and Chester that few do. It wasn't all headlines and glamour, but we ground out results.

Honesty shout, I don't think we had it as much last year. I believe one or two of the players were not the right characters and although we fought hard on the pitch, there didn't quite seem to be that unison at all times. You'll all have a player in mind who you think wasn't a team player and I guarantee that there will be at least three different names in people's heads. If you think one stood out, put his name in the comments, you'll be surprised to see someone different appear below your choice. I'll be surprised if it doesn't.

That's not to say we were poor or set back, but last season was transitional. We won at Wembley and made the top seven, which only serves to underline what might have been achieved if we'd landed the right players at the right time.

This season is different. This season I see a fight and determination once more. Case point, Notts County away last year. We had a man sent off at capitulated, losing 4-1. It was partly because Danny went adventurous, but maybe because something in the squad was lacking. In 2016/17 we won 1-0 with 10 men against Wrexham and survived Alan Power being sent off against Chester. This season, we lose two men at Swindon, lose one at home to Cambridge and another at home to Northampton. Did we lose any of those matches?

That's why I think we'll still go up, even though Mansfield have signed big players, even though we've drawn three on the spin and even though I convince myself in the deepest, darkest depth of the night that we won't. As I lay there, my dog snoring at the end of the bed keeping my mind active and imagining a bloody play-off game against Grimsby, I should remember the spirit of '17.

It's alive and well and this year, it's hopefully taking us to altogether new levels of success.

Two more points dropped: Imps 2-2 Stevenage
February 16, 2019

I had to sit down for a second when I first got home tonight and compose myself. Three times in conversation with my other half I referred to us as having lost the game. We didn't, we got a point, but rarely has it felt that bad to get a point.

On the face of it, from the outside looking in, this was always going to be a tough game. They're hunting a top seven spot and recruited well in January. They're slowly building something themselves and always should have made it a hard game. From the inside looking out it's different and I've seen them referred to as 'nobodies' on social media this evening.

I'm not going to defend everything I've seen this afternoon, but to call Stevenage, a top ten team, 'nobodies' is one of two things. It's either disrespectful to them or its gross arrogance from our fans. I make no apology for saying that either, us being top has given some of our fans a superiority complex. I heard someone behind me, possibly my Dad, say that 'we've not played like a team that's top of the league all season'. You know what, I'd rather be top and not play like it than fifth having played like champions.

I want to start my analysis by thanking Terry Brown. You might not know him, but he gave me a suitcase full of programmes before the game to sort through. As a regular blog reader he knows they're my passion and there's some crackers in there, so cheers Terry. I appreciate it immensely.

Having met him, met with Maria and Martin about the upcoming Cowley v Cowley 2 and then had a Supporter's Board meeting, I was really enthused for a game of football. These people, the different projects and groups all come together to form a community but it is always about one thing first and foremost; the game.

On paper, I fancied us for this one. I was surprised at the team selection, I expected Andrade and Rowe and the flanks with Shay McCartan starting and I would always have Michael O'Connor in the side. I'm not a fan of Bozzy in midfield, I know some like him there but I feel we miss the mobility in front of the back four when he goes there. He's a centre half in my eyes and for some reason since Bolger arrived he's just not looked as comfortable at all.

Then again, I don't work with the players all week, I don't see the patterns of play. One pattern did catch my eye in the first five minutes, Danny Rowe and John Akinde linked up nicely to force an early corner. I thought we were going to be on our way early doors, but instead from five minutes to thirty five there was only one side in the game.

We seem to be nervous playing at home and that came through immediately I wonder if we're beginning to suffer from the same symptoms as other clubs with big crowds, in that the support turns quickly It happened today, as much as the singing was excellent, there were plenty of moans and groan within the first twenty minutes. Freck came in for some stick around me, with the game 0-0. Before the half hour mark I was hearing stuff like 'we should be putting this shower of sh*t to bed'. This, when Stevenage were clearly the better side.

They wanted to get long efforts in on goal and Chair was a real handful. He was probing and pressing with the ball constantly. His crosses were teasing, his efforts got closer and closer. Even in the first half I'd marked him down as the one to rave about on the NTT20 Sunday Scouting report tweet!

It wasn't as if we made life all that hard for them. I thought big John had a good first half, running the channels and trying to flick the ball on, but it looked very disjointed. They looked more likely to score, until the final ten minutes or so. Then, in typical Lincoln style, we piled forward and could have taken the lead. Farman spilled a cross, Akinde reacted and headed towards goal and they hacked it off the line. There were plenty of appeals in the stand, but from my angle it looked to be a good clearance.

Within ten minutes it happened again, this time it was definitely not over the line. It was John again, connecting with Pett's cross but not seeing the net ripple. By the time the half time whistle went the thirty minutes of average football had been forgotten thanks to two John Akinde headers and a couple of set pieces which promised a lot but, like most of our set pieces recently, delivered little.

What is it with our set pieces? We used to be a real threat, but in recent weeks our free kicks have been poor and our corners worse. We were the set piece kings, but I think we used all of our corner magic up at Port Vale. What we wouldn't do for a sloppy, ill-prepared defence like that again.

After a half time without a drink because the machines serving Coke was broken under the Coop Stand, we were back underway and soon in the lead. I had to chuckle a little as Bruno Andrade scored with his head, it seemed to be fate. The last time Paul Farman played against Lincoln, Ali Fuseini bagged with a header at the Stacey West end and Andrade seemed less likely to score a header. It was a great cross from Rowe and it made me wonder even more if we might have started with him out wide and McCartan central.

The goal really set the tone for most of the second half, because I felt it stopped Stevenage in their tracks. Bozzy had a long-range drive that went over, but we began to control the tempo a little easier. We kept Chair off the ball as much as possible and despite the odd errant pass and stray touch, we were largely in control. it's easy to forget that now of course, knowing what we know, but until they hit the bar on 66 minutes we looked like the team at the top.

When Andrade bagged the second the game seemed done and dusted. I thought bringing Michael O'Connor on gave us some mobility in front of the defence and the tempo changed even further in our favour. Having said that, it was a Bozzy tackle that saw the ball end up with Bruno, who waved that wand of a left foot at it to conjure up another magical moment for City. The worry of letting the lead slip .lifted and dreams of a four point gap with a game in hand seemed close enough to touch.

Behind me I heard a comment that it was going to be a big win and I said, half jokingly, we hadn't won it yet. Unlike the Grimsby game I could see Stevenage scoring, but two? Hardly. Three? Not a chance. We'd have to be really unlucky or really sloppy to let a two goal lead slip, wouldn't we?

I thought Akinde was brilliant all after and had it not been for Bruno's brace he would have been a contender for Man of the Match. He was back making clearances in the 75th minute. Ilias Chair hit the woodwork just to let us know we were still in a game, but twice Akinde made chances for those around him. Bruno slipped when it seemed easier to score thanks to a Big John pass, then a swift break again from Akinde fed McCartan whose effort was blocked. Say what you want about Stevenage, they've got a real spirit. They defended doggedly and put their bodies on the line.

Just moments after McCartan's effort, it all started to come crumbling down. You could see them getting a goal and when Chair whipped in a superb strike we'd had enough warnings. I think Danny hinted that the midfield hadn't reacted quick enough to Eardley pushing him inside, but there's little accounting for that sort of strike. It should have been a case of once bitten. twice shy.

Six minutes of injury time brought a gasp, if fans had known we'd play closer to nine there might have been a riot. We retreated and that refuse to lose attitude didn't kick in. Jason Shackell had to head a Chair effort off the line before Grant Smith was deliberately clattered for a third time in the game. I didn't like the early challenge where he was battered into the post, it was 'robust' to say the least and a blatant foul at worst. The third knocked the wind out of him, but the longer he stayed down, the more the pressure increased on us. That six minutes suddenly became an unknown quantity.

Still, their goal was perfectly fair and came within the initial six minutes. The fact it was a carbon copy of the first was utterly criminal from our defensive point of view. Danny didn't condemn anyone of the radio, he's not Mark Cooper, but the message will doubtless be received by whoever should have been doubling up on Chair. The worst thing was the fact we could have nodded the danger away earlier in the move, but once again we found a bank of blue shirts 25-yards from goal with no red amongst it. Inviting pressure.

Should their gaffer have been sent off? I don't think so. he got lost in the moment, he shared that joy with his fans. He asked for a hard referee and the only evidence of that came when he got sent off. I'd prefer to let stuff like that slide and stuff like our keeper being barged into a post on purpose go punished. Maybe I'm just old school.

If being caught out twice wasn't bad enough, we gave the kid a third strike which Grant Smith was equal to. It could have been a whole lot worse although I doubt very much anyone feels like it could have got worse than it did. When the whistle finally blew it felt like we'd been beaten.

We hadn't been beaten. we haven't lost at home since Crawley and we still haven't lost a game we've led. We're still top, we still have a cushion and we've got a game in hand. They're the positives.

Negatives? I'd by lying if I said I didn't see any. I don't think we have the same verve and vivacity to our play we did in the early part of the season. I think one or two of our first team regulars were cruising a little today, one or two looked as though maybe, just maybe they need a spell on the bench. I can't see how Michael O'Connor doesn't start and if I'm honest I think maybe a rest might be in order for Freck and Tom Pett. I like both players, but Pett is nowhere near as effective on the wing and today I thought Freck looked lethargic.

I'm not going to start claiming there are fundamental issues. Those who are saying we haven't looked like Champions for a few weeks are right, but aside from Bury nobody else has either. Our wobble included too many draws, not defeat at Notts County, not slipping to sixth or seventh in the table. Although I thought there were too many moaning fans around me, in the main the support was very good today, the 617 never stopped and the atmosphere remained ramped up. No, today the fans didn't contribute to the defeat (oops, sorry we drew didn't we. Hard to tell on social media) but one or two players did.

Danny admitted it, not everyone brought their 'A' game this afternoon. Bruno did. John Akinde did. Who else did, genuinely? Which other players put in the sort of performance they could be happy with? Maybe Jason Shackell. When you consider that maybe six or more of our players were below par today, it's an achievement we were even 2-0 up in the first place.

I don't see a crisis. I see a blip. I do fear for our title credentials and unless we get a win or two, I fear for our top three spot. Maybe that's what we all need, a dose of realism. we're still in a fight, we're still leading the pack but the next 14 games are going to be hard to watch at times.

Enjoy it? Did someone ask why we can't enjoy it? Come ask me again at the beginning of Mat because until then. I'm a bloody bag of nerves. We could have this division wrapped up by now, if we'd won just three of the six we've drawn recently we'd be eight points clear with a game in hand. Instead our opponents are breathing down our necks and I feel like crying whenever I go on social media.

Promotion hunts shouldn't be like this, should they?

'Very intelligent footballer' – Chesterfield boss delighted with Imps' youngster
February 21, 2019

Chesterfield boss John Sheridan has been lavishing praise on Ellis Chapman after the youngster impressed in his first two outings for the Spireites.

Danny is looking for the 18-year-old to get 10 appearances under his belt in the National League and judging by the praise from Sheridan, that won't be a problem at all.

His side are embroiled in a relegation battle, with just two points separating them and Havant and Waterlooville in the final relegation spot.

It's a tough situation for them to be in having dropped out of the league last year, but with versatility on his side as well as intelligence, it sounds as though Ellis will be a key figure in their upcoming fight.

Sheridan, who began the season managing Carlisle, has praised the youngster's versatility having played him as a left wing back this weekend.

"His position is left midfield, he'd like to play in the middle of a three, that's his preferred position and I know that," Sheridan told the Derbyshire Times.

"I saw him when he was at Lincoln City and he played against us the other week. But because he's so cultured and has a calmness about him in the way he plays, I wasn't too concerned whether I played him left-back, left wing-back or left midfield. He can fill those areas."

He also praised Ellis' maturity and intelligence in the report.

"He's got a very old head on his shoulders for a young player. He's 18 but the way he speaks, the way he acts, the way he plays you'd think he was in his mid 20s. Very, very intelligent footballer."

Ellis, who only turned 18 last month, has impressed for the Imps this season. Having made his debut last season in the EFL Trophy, he started against Bury in what we now know was a key promotion match. In total he has five league appearances to his name this season, as well as a cameo in the FA Cup against Everton.

Both of his outings for Chesterfield have resulted in victories. He made his first appearance for them in a 1-0 win against Halifax, before helping them overcome AFC Fylde this weekend in a shock 1-0 win.

He's linked up with former Imps' trialist Lee Shaw, who has bagged once for his current club in 21 outings.

On Track: Morecambe 0-2 Imps
February 24, 2019

After a week of self-induced panicking and uncertainty, the League One promotion hunt got back underway with a vital three points against lowly Morecambe yesterday.

It's easy to say 'lowly Morecambe', but they'd won two on the spin in their hunt for a finish outside the bottom two, so it was never going to be 'easy' as such. No game is, there's no match left between now and the end of the season that you could say will be one we're expected to win.

However, with one defeat in 18 matches in the league, there's few teams going to be upbeat when we pay a visit either. I heard a Bury fan yesterday claiming to be the only side in the title race unbeaten in all competitions since the start of the year. Yup, great stats, but remember our only defeat in 2019 was against Everton, at Goodison.

What's in the past is largely irrelevant, apart from the 33 matches that have put us on top of the table, but what happened yesterday and what is to come is not. We're entering yet another of those periods I mentioned in my article on Friday, the ones that are impossible to enjoy afterwards. I'm going to amend that slightly, they're easy to enjoy a little at 5pm on a Saturday when we've won.

There's a certain relief once another game is done. Okay, everyone won yesterday but when we win it doesn't matter does it? we're just one game closer to Portman Road, one game closer (maybe) to the Stadium of Light. If we match everyone else's result between now and then, it'll all be fine. In the hours after a win I feel much more relaxed. Maybe, instead of a medication cabinet with bottles labelled 'tramadol' I should have a bottle labelled 'Andrade', because he seems to do the trick just as well.

More on that little beauty later.

I think all eyes were on the team selection yesterday. There wasn't anyone doing anything particularly 'wrong' in the last couple of games, but something needed shaking up. Sometimes when a fine wine is fermenting you're meant to shake it up, get the sediment mixed in with the liquid in order to get a finer flavour. Danny did that yesterday, the sediment being Matt Gilks and Mark O'Hara. They've been brought in to do a job and in the shake up, they found themselves in the action.

I know calling up Gilks caused a few to feel sorry for Grant Smith. Grant's a nice lad and a decent goalkeeper, but he's not a League One stopper. That's my opinion, as is the fact that had Josh Vickers been in goal against Bury, we win 3-2. I'm not saying Smith has been bad, far from it he's made some good saves, but I'm convinced that a League One keeper is needed for a League One promotion push. Gilks, a former international, is definitely that.

As for O'Hara, I'd toyed with putting him in to my final XI on Football League World this weekend, but instead plumped for Jordan Roberts. I guess that was the only bit I got different to Danny though. In my eyes O'Connor has to play, he brings a zest and energy to the middle of the park. I feel hugely for Bolger, but he has to understand Jason Shackell likely won't be with us next season and his time will come. It's not a sprint being a Lincoln City player, it's a marathon. Tom Pett knows that better than anyone.

I'm never one to be arrogant or complacent, certainly not when Lincoln are concerned recently, but you felt that when we bagged after just ten minutes there was going to be little to worry about. I mentioned about needing a bottle of Andrade to settle nerves and relax me and he came up trumps with yet another wonderful strike. It was heartening to see Mark O'Hara involved too, the big Scot had been lively in the opening exchanges.

It wasn't a simple goal though, just like our strike at Notts County, it involved some lovely intricate play as we swept forward. I know the accusation has been levied that we're not playing like champions, but if you watch a highlight reel of our goals recently, you might be inclined to disagree.

I thought we might run riot after that, Andrade having another effort going just wide after Akinde's work too. Big John doesn't score enough goals, that's not really something anyone can argue, but his contribution can't be faulted either. He's such a handful and while defenders are occupying him, they're having to leave players elsewhere. Like Andrade. Like Rowe.

Aside from a brief moment on the half hour mark, and the Jordan Cranston free-kick just before half time, it looked like top against bottom four. City played possession football, comfortably moving the ball around and creating chances on a relatively regular basis, six in total with four on target and two off target. Danny Rowe had a super half, as did O'Hara, Andrade and Akinde and we might feel a little anxious we weren't further ahead at the break.

Being a 'score watcher', half time brought much more joy. If we win, it doesn't matter what the others do, but Bury were losing and Mansfield were drawing. Those sorts of results could make three points feel like more, if they came off.

The second half started much the same as the first, with a confident looking City side largely on top. It's not that Morecambe were poor, they just don't have that extra quality that a budget like ours brings. Sure, they fought hard but when they had the ball at their feet the choices weren't right, the threat wasn't quite there. When we got possession we looked lively, dangerous even and that comes from loaning players like Danny Rowe and Mark O'Hara, instead of bringing in players like former Boston man Zac Mills.

It took Bruno ten minutes of the first half to settle the nerves, but his second dose was doled out slightly later in the second half, albeit by two minutes. Just when thoughts of 'we need a second here' entered my head, the Portuguese magician conjured up a second moment of magic for us to enjoy.

It wasn't one of those gasping moments, not a goal out of the top draw, but it certainly came from the box marked 'typical Lincoln goal'. It came from John Akinde's persistence and from Bruno Andrade's foot. He's bagged six in four now, a couple of which have been laid on by Big John.

I remember when I was thirteen (this is going somewhere). I was a striker for Wragby Juniors and my Dad had asked a local guy, John Skepper, to take me down the pitch and give me some striker training. John told me that a striker's job was not to score goals, but to lay them on for the midfielders. I thought Skep must just not like me and took his advice with a pinch of salt, but only now 27 years later can I see his point. Without John Akinde, we don't bag the second yesterday.

After the goal we managed the game superbly and I know that's not what everyone wants to hear. At 2-0 there's a thought we should go for three or four and if the chances came we would, but we play a different brand of football with the cushion. We retain possession across the back four more, we make them come out a bit further and if we can, we pick off the rotting carcass of the opposition. Last weekend, that rotting carcass had a dagger in its boot and we ended up drawing, but there were no hidden surprised with Morecambe.

The changes unsettled the game a little, Aaron Collins looked lively for them, we brought on Matt Rhead to do exactly what he does. He began to hold the balls up in the corner, our pacey players looked to get closer to him. It became about protecting the win. If anyone is going to criticise the approach, which they will, they'll say we could have bagged more.

Had it not be for Matt Gilks, the clean sheet might not have been in the bag, but with ten minutes to go he produced the sort of stop you expect a League One keeper to produce. It sent out a clear message to me, that this wasn't to be another Stevenage. We went on to simply see out the game, little in the way of chances coming after Bruno's goal, but little in the way of genuine scares either.

There weren't many player who could be criticised yesterday, if any. Andrade had to be Man of the Match, his goals alone earned that, but O'Hara was excellent too. he reminded me of what Lee Frecklington was for us before he moved on in 2007/08; probing and energetic. O'Hara also has a combative edge and it wouldn't surprise me to see him start every game between now and May. Danny Rowe was excellent, John Akinde did everything asked of him and at the back, Bozzy dropped effortlessly back alongside Jason Shackell.

The win wasn't even tinged with sadness that Bury came from behind and beat Oldham. If we want to win the title I'm sure we want to win it on our merit, not the errors of others. The 2005/06 season is till the year we got into the play-offs because Peterborough were so bad, 2018/19 has to be the year we go up because we're good. Bury will push us all the way and it seems as though MK Dons and Mansfield are pretty set on doing the same.

We've led League Two for 905 of the season. we're still out in front, two points clear and have a game in hand which will be played this Tuesday. After that it is a straight race, a twelve game sprint to League One. There's a title on offer, there's promotion as a second and third prize and, for the first time ever in the basement division, there's the booby prize of a play-off spot.

Right now, in the warm light of Sunday morning, I'm enjoying it. By tomorrow the fear will grip me once more and I'll be looking at Exeter with trepidation and worry but, if I have a couple of doses of 'Andrade' during the game, my nerves will be settled and hopefully I can focus a little more clearly on the end game.

Maybe, just maybe, we all can. Here's to one defeat in eighteen matches, here's to two points per game between now and May and finally, here's to that incredible little Portuguese winger with the Midas touch.

96th minute goals don't happen by luck: Imps 1-1 Exeter City
February 27, 2019

I think I've made my feelings on this run in very clear indeed. Enjoyment is not entirely a part of the experience for me, not until I know where we're going to finish.

Maybe I care too much, maybe I'm missing the point, but I struggle to enjoy games we're not winning. I'm not fickle, I just have a sick feeling in my stomach at the thought of failure.

I know where it comes from, it's the years of dirge we were served up between 2008 and 2016. It's the stench of struggle, the insane fear of watching the club that I love so dearly ever fall into decline. I once said something along the lines of hope being integral to everything. every season you start out in August with hope, but ultimately it is that hope that kills you.

I've only watched us a third-tier side once and I so desperately want that experience again. In the dying embers of last night's encounter I looked to the skies, searching for one of the Imps long since departed to give us a helping hand from above. I used to do it when we were in the National League, asking a higher entity for help. Never God, he wouldn't give a toss about us and if he did, why favour us over anyone else? No, I've asked my Grandads (both of them) as well as my Uncle Jeff who I think came once to the Bank.

Last night in the 90th minute of a tough match to watch, I asked Pete Newton. Like those before him, he came up with the goods.

These equalisers, these moments that make a draw feel like a win, or a loss, they don't happen by accident. The probably don't happen because of long since departed fans either, but I like to think otherwise. They happen because a side fights, even when things are going badly. They come about through belief, something Stevenage had ten days ago and something our side had last night.

Launching long balls into a box filled with six-foot players helps too of course.

Let's not beat around the bush, nor dress it up as anything other than what it was. Lincoln City were poor last night. We started well, in the first ten minutes I thought we were by far the better side, looking threatening and alive. How many times has that happened in recent weeks though? The players come out all fired up then one misplaced pass, the crowd groans and like a house of cards, it all comes tumbling down.

Is it confidence? I'm not sure it is. The 617 boys were loud and proud and I thought the stadium reacted well when we went 1-0 down and intermittently throughout the second half too. For some reason though, the players lost their composure and once it had gone, they couldn't get it back.

Here's something I've not said in a long while: few players can bring any credit out of the game from a technical point of view. Passes went astray, decisions were made that invited pressure and players looked on completely different wavelengths. I can recall too many to mention, but how about Matt Gilks playing the ball to Harry Toffolo, who failed to trap it and let it go out for a throw?

How about Neal Eardley slicing so many balls out of play he'd look more at home in a butchers slicing ham? Mark O'Hara got caught in possession more times than Snoop Dogg and Tom Pett looked as comfortable on the wing as a centre half. It was disjointed, uncomfortable to watch and it made Exeter look much better than they were.

I heard someone say they were one of the better teams to come to play us this season, I can't let that go unchallenged. They had a couple of decent lads, sure. They played the ball around nicely too, but the space was there for them to do so. Our shape allowed them to look better than they were. Don't get me wrong, they're not a bad side, but were they worthy of a win? No. Newport were a better side, Stevenage were a better side and Forest Green certainly were.

How many times did Gilks have a save to make? Aside from the free kick, how many big moments featured the Scot? Very few. When they did get decent chances it usually came through our own lapses in concentration, much like the goal. It was a great free kick by the way, nobody was stopping it, not even an eight foot keeper with hands like chopping boards parries that.

Bruno felt he might have had a penalty in the first half, but I imagine looking back he will feel the warm Cowley breath on his neck as he's politely advised not to go to ground so easily again. We're not getting penalties when a 13st, 6ft forward is hauled to the ground so we're certainly not going to get one when a light weight winger blows over in the breeze, or at least thinks he has.

Were they worthy of their lead at half time? Yes, they had found neat patterns of play and some penetration, but in the main it was because we were worthy of very little that they deserved the lead, not because they were the best of two good teams.

The mutterings of discontent went on all around me at half time. My mate Dave has gone and shacked up (for want of a better phrase) with one of my relatives down in Bletchley (not Milton Keynes he wants you to know), so I don't have him to bounce off. Instead my Dad, fuelled by six pints of beer, let his disappointment out to anyone who wanted to listen. He felt let down because he thought we'd win 3-0, yet after 45 minutes we hadn't looked like getting one. He lets his disappointment out by getting angry. I stay silent.

I perused my phone, hurt. Not because of a lack of effort from the players. They don't go out to play badly on purpose, but the anger aimed at red and white shirts upsets me. Why? Partly because their efforts weren't good enough, partly because after 34 games we are the best team in the league in terms of points accrued. It hurts that the anger directed towards Tom Pett out wide doesn't take into account his PFA Player of the Month award from earlier in the season, because around 72 hours earlier the same XI had looked so confident and composed against Morecambe.

It's different away though, isn't it? Teams have to come and get us and when that happens, there's more space to express ourselves. When sides come to the Bank they shut up shop, just as Exeter did. They sat deep, inviting us on to them. When that happens we're in danger because our centre backs have to step up, leaving gaps in behind. Quick players will outpace all four of our defenders, so they still remain a little deep. That leaves spaces in the middle of the park and Exeter filled those spaces better than we did.

I hoped for a second half filled with expressive football and goals, but instead we got a slightly better version of the first half. I say 'slightly better', for a while it was much of the same. Wild passes, lack of understanding and failed technique. This isn't the Lincoln City that have got to the top of the table, is pressure beginning to show? Or rather, is the pressure of playing at home starting to show?

Something had to change and although I heard the rhetoric that the subs changed the game, I don't buy that. Maybe I missed it, but I didn't think McCartan changed very much at all. No, everything changed when Matt Rhead came on.

It isn't Rhead as such, he's certainly one who gives the fans a lift, but it's the change of emphasis. What amuses me is when I hear something like 'bring off Akinde for Angol'. I like Angol, but if we're failing with one approach, why would a different player in the same role have any joy? As a collective, we were poor last night. The approach we used didn't work. Whether it was O'Hara or Frecklington in midfield, Pett or Roberts out wide, it failed. The individuals weren't entirely to blame, although they didn't play well.

No, the system changed. We went back to what we know, diagonal balls onto the big man's head. His flick ons found Akinde running the channels and only then did we look a threat. Let's face it, if the foul on Akinde in the area is at the other end of the field with one of our 'monsters' hauling back their forward, it's a penalty. I didn't make a lot of it, but something similar happened against Stevenage and we didn't get it. Right not, we're not getting penalties. Maybe it makes up for the soft one we 'earned' at Grimsby earlier in the season.

Danny suggested the referee admitted he made an error of judgement which was refreshing to hear.

Only when Rhead came on did we seem to be a threat, but by then the players have been burdened by the misplaced passes and shoddy technique. It meant a frantic final fifteen minutes or so, with us launching things into the box, appealing everything and getting nothing. When we did get a decent free kick, it was wasted. When we did get a corner, it was wasted. Technically, our players were not at the races but they never gave up.

It would be easy to come on here and give the social media view, we were poor and deserved very little, but we weren't poor all over the park. We kept fighting, kept trying to knock down the door and eventually it became incredibly tough to watch. After our 3-3 draw with Bury I heard pundits purring over what a great advert for League Two it was. All I'll say is this; it's a good job that wasn't televised.

Still we kept on knocking and eventually, six minutes into four minutes of added time, we got our stroke of luck. I know Exeter fans are not happy at the added time, but when you make a change in that period you've got to expect the worst. A referee will add 30 seconds on for the change, but he's going to stop his watch too. That's another minute or so going on the clock so if you're going to do it, make sure it's before the board goes up.

Shay, who grew into the game which isn't perfect when you're on as a sub, had an effort scrambled off the line and as we all watched the ref to see him bring the curtain down on only our second home defeat of the season, we scored.

After the game Rob Makepeace asked John Akinde how it felt to score with a shot that didn't go where he intended it to. John's answer? 'It went exactly where I wanted it to, in the back of the net'. I think that sums up the finish perfectly.

It was a great moment and walking away from the ground it felt like we'd won the game for a while. I was still angry at the performance, but again felt it best to wait until the a warm sunshine came flooding through my office window and I could apply a sense of reason to my words. I never want to be a sycophant, if we're bad I will say we're bad, but when we're top there has to be some saving graces. When we've not lost a league match since Boxing Day, when we've lost once in eighteen matches and are undefeated in eleven, that has to mean something.

We refused to lose last night and you know what? It might just be that point which secures League One football at the end of the season. It might be that dropped two points that costs us it too, but until we know there's no point in getting angry, upset or indeed overjoyed.

Just enjoy it, or something.

Dispelling the myths: Why these common-held fan opinions are not accurate
February 28, 2019

It's been a tough month has February. It always feel like the calm after the storm, the furore of January and the transfer speculation dies down and you're left with a tough period.

It's not close enough to the end of the season to be truly nerve jangling, but it's a time when the league has taken shape. Fans see the end game and feel it's close, but there's a lot of football to be played. Pitches are still heavy, but the nights get lighter and fans think spring is in the air.

It's been tough for us. We're unbeaten of course, top of the league, so it's a tough we can get used to, but it's not easy. Some of those teams in the middle of the pack are making a big push up the table, the teams at the bottom fight for their life and traditionally, the leaders do fall away. We haven't.

We've stumbled, maybe grasped out for the bannister rail to hold on to, but we've not fallen. We're still top, words that offer comfort every week as our lead is reeled in and teams get closer and closer.

I think February is the toughest month of the season, I genuinely do. For a football writer it's a nightmare, the transfer window has gone and there's little to write about. I don't put lots of importance on my page views but they drop in February. August and January are the best months by far, February is the worst. Nobody is talking players, everyone is just focused on the matches.

I've felt flat, the site has felt a bit flat and across the country fans and teams have felt, well, flat.

I could sense it a bit in the stands this week, which brings me to the point of the article. I could not only sense a certain malaise, but also I heard some rhetoric rolled out that I've felt compelled to rebuke. Things like 'Angol on for Akinde', things like 'Tom Pett isn't a winger'. These are untruths being spoken and believed across the Coop Stand.

Not for much longer. Here's my attempt to dispel some of the popular myths around Sincil Bank right now.

Lee Angol should replace John Akinde up front

I see where this comes from, the Akinde doubters are often out in force. I heard it this week, people behind me saying that 'Angol has to be a better option' in the dying stages of a game.

Let me ask you this: would you replace Matt Gilks with James Brown? Or Jason Shackell with Harry Anderson. No.

Angol is a striker, Akinde is a striker so those comparisons might seem odd, but in terms of what they bring and where they fit into the method, they're like chalk and cheese. Angol is a player you only play into, giving it to feet or in behind. He runs the channels and presses defenders, much like Matt Green used to.

When you're chasing a game, losing 1-0 and wanting to get somewhere fast, the play has to go from front to back quickly. That means diagonal balls into Rhead, Akinde or whatever other behemoth we want in the box. It marginalises Angol admittedly.

There's a dilemma though. When we're looking to see a game out the ball has to stick up front. That's when Akinde comes off for Rhead, but where does it leave Lee Angol? In the same place it left Matt Green for most of the season, sadly.

On the bench.

The Cian Bolger sub made no sense

'We need to win, not defend,' 'He's lost it.' Definite comments I heard when Cian Bolger came on against Exeter.

I didn't comment too much myself, I try not to at a game. There's a real pressure and passion about football that affects the ability to think clearly and to articulate with any sense of reason. I was baffled, but when I saw the resulting game plan, it made sense.

Bolger has been unlucky, dropped not because he's been bad, but because we want to accommodate Bozzy and Shackell without losing legs in the midfield. He has a big role to play for us, but perhaps not right now.

That said, what good would a winger have been in the dying minutes? Jordan Roberts may well 'get at them' down the flanks, but not if he's stood out there like a lemon while the ball is being pumped from left to right into Rheady.

We have to acknowledge that sometimes, the manager knows best.

Grant Smith has been hard done by

Grant is a good keeper, worthy of a place in most League Two squads. At Swindon, Newport or Port Vale, he'd be number one choice.

We're not a mid table side though and we need something more. We've got former Premier League defenders, players with 500 outings in the Football League. they expect a certain level of organisation and communication from a keeper and whilst I'm not saying Grant doesn't deliver, he's not Matt Gilks.

Josh Vickers is young and perhaps lacks that, but in terms of commanding his box and stopping shots, Josh is a different level again. Football is sentimental when you're in the stands. Former players are loved, popular players are seen through rose-tinted glasses whilst those who are not so warmly received can do no right.

On the field, it is a business. It's ruthless and if we want to go to the next level, we need a ruthless manager. Grant Smith is not as good as Matt Gilks, so Matt Gilks plays, Doesn't matter if Smith's done nothing wrong. The fiver in my wallet has done nothing wrong, but if you offer me a twenty for it I'll swap tomorrow.

We should play Rhead and Akinde

Do you know what? Maybe we should.
That's hardly me dispelling myths is it? Maybe we should stick the big man up top, get Akinde to run off him and start pumping balls forward. Nobody studying video evidence will have gleaned that approach as one we use and it worked well against Exeter.
Or, to rephrase it, it worked well against Exeter in the last twenty minutes, against tired legs with lots of brute force pushing forward.
I'm not convinced we'd play it from the start. It might work, but the lack of mobility in the front two would be a concern. John Akinde is mobile is a blundering, battering kind of way. Matt Rhead is mobile in an immobile kind of way. they've got strengths and for the last twenty in any game they're a great option, but from the start?
I'm not convinced.

We play it back too much

It's another groan I hear all the time. Why do we play it back so much? It's always going across the back, why don't we go forwards?
Anyone who has played Pro Evolution Soccer will know football isn't all flair, shooting and lofted through balls. Sometimes, it's a grind. Sometimes, it's about patience and probing.
When we play a ball from side to side, we're moving the opposition, pulling them in different directions. It tests their movement and awareness and gives us a chance to maybe find an opening. If you have a woollen jumper and you keep pulling it in different directions, eventually it will snag and a hole appears. That's what we want to do with the opposition players.
Usually, teams come to us with two banks of four, meaning two walls to break down. That's why we can't just probe forward because they'll defend it well.
Think about us away at Bury. How many times did Bury actually get away through the centre? Very few, you know why? Because we're best in this division without the ball. I laughed because I was told you don't score goals without the ball, but that's not right. When team look to shift play and open us up, we're the best in the division at not having holes pulled in us.
If we're the best, it make sense to assume the other 23 are not and that's why we play from side to side, retaining possession and waiting, almost like a wild cat stalking its prey. If that doesn't work then after 75 minutes we bring on Rheady and attempt to smack our prey in the face with a battering ram.

March

Questions? Answered: Forest Green 1-2 Imps
March 3, 2019

Sometimes I wait until midday on a Sunday to give a measured and balanced response to the afternoon before, whether it is the referee who has riled me or whether I'm in danger of offering a reactive statement to a late incident.

Stevenage is the perfect point. Those late goals knocked the stuffing out of me and everyone in the ground, but it paid to be measured in our responses. Exeter was the same, with lots of reaction to the performance seemingly missing the bigger picture.

It's too easy to offer immediate reaction these days, grabbing your phone before the referee has stopped blowing on his whistle to write words such as 'woeful' on Twitter. In a game based heavily on emotion, it is understandable. As the ground disappears into the distance and you settle down at home, it seems less severe when you do badly.

When you get a big win, the importance doesn't fade. I let my emotions run away with me last night with a post straight after the game, because rarely does it feel so good. I have to admit, of all the wins we've had this season, that one will stick with me. That one will be remembered beyond May, just like the 3-2 at their place in November 2016.

Not because of some perceived rivalry between the clubs either. I've made it clear why I don't like them, but I don't see them as rivals. The media build it up, Mark Cooper has his little digs but they're no more of a rival to us than Colchester, Cheltenham or Yeovil.

Anyway, lets rewind back to 2.30pm yesterday, a time when things seemed a little less certain. Our recent run (unbeaten in 11) had seen us reeled in by some of the clubs below us. They all had winnable home games and we had a real banana skin. A result, an acceptable result, would have been to draw and still be one point clear at the end of the match.

Walking out of the ground on Tuesday I told my Dad I felt we should go with Rheady and Akinde up top and hit Forest Green where it hurt. They can't deal with the big men and although some consider it to be anti-football, I think we play it in the right way when we do. We're not a long ball side, not usually, but against Forest Green it makes sense.

In the week I even discussed it, pointing out the positives and the pitfalls before arguing I wasn't convinced Danny would roll with it. This is Danny Cowley though and second guessing him is very, very hard. When push came to shove, the big man got his run out.

It was a bold move and it's easy in hindsight to say it worked and we should do it more often, but it was a roll of the dice. Danny gets paid to do these things, to make these decisions and he will feel vindicated this morning.

It didn't feel that positive after the first ten minutes did it? Some looking through miserable eyes would say we didn't get a grip of proceedings early doors, but in fairness Forest Green just did what they're good at. They got on the ball, played some neat football then managed to get a goal, albeit a horrible fluke from a nasty deflection.

It could have been the goal to make it 2-0 as well, had Matt Gilks not been in fine form to stop Shawn McCoulsky early doors. The signs were ominous and McCoulsky is a player I like, his switch from Bristol City raising some eyebrows in January.

The last place you want to be is 1-0 there early, especially with the weight of recent results on our back. Those results by the way, the ones that we seem to think constitute a bad run, include zero defeats in two-and-a-half months. That's not a bad blip to have.

Still, the reality was that the Imps had eighty minutes, give or take, to underlines our title credentials. It was a season-defining eighty minutes, the sort of afternoon that not only makes a difference, but is critical to the entire season.

Eighty minutes.

The response was pretty instant, as we now know. A Harry Toffolo long throw was flicked on by Rheady to big John, who had to try to get pace and direction on his header. He got direction, but just not enough pace to beat their keeper. The partnership had begun though and within six minutes of going 1-0 down, we were level.

Watching the goal back, it's classic Lincoln. The returning Harry Anderson looks to surge down the right, checks and feeds in back to Neal Eardley. Putting his Exeter performance behind him, he whips in a wonderful cross and there's John Akinde the poacher to nod his 14th goal of the season. The cross allowed him to simply use direction as leverage, because the pace was in the inch-perfect delivery.

That just spurred us on even further and for the remain half and hour of the first half, we were rampant. They couldn't cope with the aerial threat posed by Rheady and John, with the former almost putting us 2-1 up not long after we levelled. They wanted to stick by their principles of playing out from the back, but our high press and their limited capacity meant it looked shambolic at times.

I can't enthuse enough about those front two, who worked the game like a classic partnership of old. They have everything between them, brute strength, brawn, aerial ability, excellent technique and an eye for goals. I know they can't play together every week, unless we alter the style to suit, but on this performance there has to be a call for it to be considered.

Every ball into the area caused havoc. Who did the defenders drop on to? Akinde, the deadly League Two marksmen they all know and fear, or Rhead, the very best header of the ball in this division? They panicked and we looked likely to run wild for a spell. The switch in emphasis caught them on the hop and they looked terrified.

I'm not going to dissect every shot or save from the game, it wouldn't be in keeping with what I usually do, but here's a stat for you. We had ten efforts at goal in the first half, five on target and five off. The home side had four, all on target, with Matt Gilks excellent when called upon. It was a great advert for the game at our level though and a million miles away from Tuesday night's game of attrition.

Nathan McGinley went off at half time, he'd been one of those defenders who simply didn't look capable of playing out from the back at all. That was something their boss, Mark Cooper, must have been keen to change. They'd been battered in the first half, that's the truth of the matter and were it not for some good stops and a few efforts off target, we could have had three or four.

The second half didn't quite bring the same number of chances, but it was another great performance by City. John Akinde was putting in not just one shift, but two or three simultaneously. He ran the channels, held the ball up and linked up fantastically with Matt Rhead. The way we play means they'll not start every game together, but with Rheady being the best in the business at flick ons and holding the ball up, Akinde looked to be a free man.

They weren't the only ones impressing though. The flanks kept on providing a source of chances, with Harry Anderson making a triumphant return to action with a rampaging display on the right. The full backs ably supported where they could and Bruno Andrade did what Bruno Andrade does. The Imps commanded the game, dictating the pace of play and always looking to be on the verge of taking the lead.

At the other end, the home side looked tepid. I'm told on of their strikers moved in the summer for £1m, only to return to League Two recently. I'm not sure you'd be able to tell which one, although Jason Shackell has bossed much better players during his times at Derby. Cian Bolger might feel hard done by of late, but the return to a Bozzy / Shacks partnership has seen us look more stable.

I have to pay homage to the keeper too. I hate to sound negative about any of our players but in my mind, Grant Smith just isn't in the same class as Gilks. He's an organiser, a man who commands and dictates how the back four should play as well as making the big stops. He proved that on 67 minutes with a truly world-class stop.

Right up until the deciding goal, you felt we'd get it. Akinde looked dominant and dangerous, with an effort flashed over displaying all of his attributes. he controlled and turned, creating a chance for himself from nothing. His drive just missed the target, but he looked hungry and he looked motivated. A clip on Harry Anderson might have given him a chance from 12 yards, but a lenient referee saw no foul.

Just as we were lamenting our luck Bruno got away down the left, made yet another box entry and was bundled to the floor. He didn't look for the penalty, he didn't play for it and he drew the foul. The referee didn't hesitate this time out and pointed to the spot.

What happened next was a break that seemed like ten minutes. Their players went down, one even kicked the ball away as they desperately tried to put Akinde off. His last penalty, against Notts County, drew some criticism from some quarters (not here), but this time was different. He'd been unplayable all afternoon and when presented with a chance from 12 yards, he took it with aplomb.

We could still have added more, Shay McCartan offered a different dynamic after replacing Rheady and drew a late save, as did Mark O'Hara who formed a great partnership with Michael O'Connor all afternoon.

After a spell of injury time in which Forest Green still didn't really offer a threat, the curtain came down. we won the game.

Danny was clearly delighted, letting the façade slip in his pre-match interview by stating maybe John's performance would 'shut a few up'. It was uncharacteristic, but it showed his passion and delight. The recent run hasn't been easy and as a manager I'm sure he's felt the pressure. This morning, he'll be feeling a whole lot better.

Of course, everyone won around us so it's as you were, but one of those tricky away games has now been chalked off with three points. There's still big matches to play, there's no hiding from that, but every time the 'games played' column increases by one, there's less chance of sides catching us.

Last night, at the White Hart in Nettleham, every bite of steak tasted juicier and more flavoursome than the last. I slept like a log and woke up this morning to an overcast sky still brimming with the delights of spring. A defeat leaves me down overnight, but a win stays with you until the next game.

This win might just stay with us for ever, sat in the annals of history as the moment our title push regained the momentum it deserves.

Breathe with me: Imps 1-0 Yeovil

March 9, 2019

Business end, squeaky bum time, the period all fans should enjoy; call it what you will, we're well and truly into it right now.

In an incredible display of hindsight, Danny's Friday night match has handed a major advantage back to the Imps, not just in the hunt for a place in League One but also in the race for the League Two title.

The midweek fixture between Bury and Cheltenham certainly helped, one struggling team at home is a different prospect to another away. When the Shakers missed the chance to go top, albeit temporarily, they missed the opportunity to score a major psychological advantage. Last night, we didn't miss our chance to do the same.

The gap between us and Bury is now five points, with a further three the difference between us and Mansfield. We know, whatever happens between now and 10pm Tuesday, we'll still be top at that point in time. Of course, results could swing our way today but it would be hard for them to go against us because we kept our end of the title bargain up. What Bury do at Stevenage, or what MK and Mansfield do is irrelevant to a degree.

Won't stop us watching on though, hoping for more to cheer about.

There's been a lot of call for Rhead to start alongside John and that was the case last night. I guess after such a richly deserved win over Forest Green, Danny found it hard to change the first XI. I can understand it, especially when he warned of changes to the side ahead of the match. Is there anyone in football who reveals so little to the press and gets away with it? He misdirects over team selection, dodges injury news and yet somehow still hold an interesting press conference.

His surprise for Darren Way's side was two big men up top and an element of direct football. Before anyone says it didn't work, which on the face of it, it didn't, you have to consider the wider picture. In recent weeks at home we've tried the neater approach in the final third and got nowhere. Last night, the game plan looked very much to me like 'batter them for an hour' with the big lumps then try the original plan against tired legs.

In fairness, Yeovil looked ropey at the back at times, but their right back certainly had the measure of Bruno and I think that makes the long ball approach seem more obvious. They were prepared to stifle us out wide and frustrate us all over the pitch, although they also had Rheady wrapped up too. I heard a comment on the radio coming home saying he won almost all of his headers last night, I assume the caller thought he was the chap in green and white, not red and white.

That's not a criticism, but it's proof Yeovil played well without playing well. They kept a shape, they frustrated us and did what they had to do without the ball. It wasn't always pretty, neither was our approach, that's a bi-product of having John and Rheady up top. The referee had a sound grip on the game though, but how embarrassing is it when you're booked for time-wasting three minutes into the second half? I understand game management, but their 150 odd fans have driven what, 600 miles all in? Just to be treated to that.

What I mean by them playing well but not playing well, is when they had the ball they didn't truly have a clue how to break us down. Occasionally they strung a few nice passes together and there was a spell in the first half where I thought maybe, just maybe we might be in trouble. When your armour is as solid as ours across the back, it's a fallacy to believe that though. Yeovil can pass sideways as much as they want, just like FGR did, but when it came to penetration they had little.

I did like their number seven, Rhys Browne. I thought he delivered some telling balls, as well as having our wide threat weighed up nicely. Sadly, the rest of his side weren't quite up to the challenge.

Losing Shacks was a big blow, but as soon as Bolger strode on to take his place you knew it wasn't going to affect us too much. Danny called Bolger a 'top League One defender' after the game and you know what? He's right. Bozzy is the same and together they didn't look like being breached.

Harsh truth moment: we should have gone in 2-0 up at the break. It's hard to be too harsh on Harry after what he did later, but he had too much time to think when he went one on one with the keeper. Most FIFA players would have been desperately crying out for a succinct lob over their keeper as he broke away, but instead he fluffed his lines. It's easy in the stands to be critical and it showed awareness from Harry to get the ball away from the defenders in the first instance, but it was crying out for a better finish.

Then, maybe, John could have had one or two. One drive into the box looked even more lumbering and languid than usual and his tame shot was saved, before a wicked Neal Eardley ball evaded everyone and took the big man by surprise at the back stick. All it needed was a touch, off his arse, ankle, nose, whatever. The key was getting into those positions, although trying to tell my Dad that is fruitless. As far as he was concerned, we weren't playing well.

It didn't look like we were, but under the conditions we were doing okay. Yeovil without the ball looked alright and Lincoln with the ball looked pressured. I don't buy the fact 9,000 home fans is a disadvantage or that we're the reason the players look nervous. I think it's the situation, the desperate need to break resilient teams down when they come to do nothing but defend.

When the half time whistle went it did feel as though there was more to come, but quite where it would come from I couldn't see. Rheady hadn't been as effective as the weekend, John had subsequently not been on fire either. Bruno was taped up on one flank, Harry flagging a little on the other. I liked the combination of O'Hara and O'Connor, but it looked functional rather than productive. Mind you, I have to admit Michael O'Connor is quickly turning into one of the contenders for Player of the Season in my opinion, he's been industrious and energetic whenever we've seen him.

Didn't help after 45 minutes last night though with the scores poised at 0-0.

I enjoyed listening to the Prodigy at half time. Losing Keith Flint this week felt like a bit of a gut punch, it's a stark reminder of how fragile not only life is, but also your own mental state. We're all only one jarring incident or bit of bad news away from a big fall. It should put football into perspective, but what it did for me was to remind me to enjoy the things I enjoy because you just never know.

Back to the game and the lyrics of my favourite hit, Breathe, never seemed more apt; "Breathe the pressure, Come play my game, I'll test ya." We were being tested and I'm not sure about breathing the pressure, but I'm damn sure I was excreting it through several damp areas of my body.

I did think the first two minutes of the second half could have brought a penalty after Bolger was bundled over from an early corner. The linesman had a good view of it but didn't make the call, but had we done it at the other end I would have breathed a sigh of relief.

From there we began to exert our own pressure, Harry came out like a man possessed and finally started to get some joy down in front of us. He's an instinctive player, give him time to think and he doesn't do as well as when he just has to run with it. His smart drive brought a decent save, with Michael O'Connor's header also bringing a stop. We were edging our way in, tentatively and not exactly rampaging, but you could sense something would happen.

It was the change in the 67th minute that switched the game. Rheady came off after drifting out of the match and Danny Rowe came on, instantly bringing the change of emphasis. That wasn't by accident, the game plan all along was surely to tire them for an hour or so and then hit them with pace and direct running. As soon as we did that, the game changed. Yeovil couldn't cope with our attacking threat, not after the gruelling time the big man had given them, whether he won his headers or not.

67 minutes, change. 69 minutes, 1-0 City.

Rowe was involved, his neat ball to Harry set the 22-year-old up to deliver another teasing cross and finally, someone got their head onto the ball. Mark O'Hara, who'd had a decent game in the middle of the park, glanced the ball into the back of the net.

The place erupted, like taking the lid off a shaken up bottle of Cherry Pepsi Max. The pressure had been building, the atmosphere bubbling under the surface and threatening to break out one way or another. The moaners and groaners had their time, the vocal support had theirs and everything teetered on the brink of tipping, one way or the other. As the net rippled thanks to the Scot's goal, it went to way of positivity and relief.

That immediately prompted Yeovil to bring on forwards Alex Fisher and Francois Zoko. They knew now all the time-wasting and negativity was in vain and they had to get at us. Sadly, for them, they just don't have the quality we have and it was a futile gesture. Now, it was our turn to drag our heels, our turn to gesture to ball boys to leave the bloody thing alone, to let it roll under our feet when knocked back for a throw in.

It's an amusing aspect of the beautiful game, watching a team who have been dragging their heels all evening suddenly up their game, but similarly it is fascinating to see our game management mode kick in too. Bruno goes down and all our lads went to the dugout. Their lads stayed away from the manager, geeing each other up. Was that somewhat symbolic of the two club's direction? One manager stood watching on as his players get together themselves, the other smack bang in the middle of the red shirts giving instructions.

Not a lot happened after the goal, not really, We had chances, Bruno could have bagged a couple. I was gutted, I had him to score anytime and Lincoln to win for a possible £25 return, but had selected Mark O'Hara at first for £55 return and bottled it. Bruno could have perhaps had a brace late on, half chances at best of course, as could John Akinde. The lads started playing with a certain freedom, the shackles had been cut off after the goal and Yeovil didn't have a response.

That's the difference between top and bottom, or at least one of them. Yes, there's the quality element and although Yeovil are not a bad team, they certainly don't have the quality in all areas that we have. They've got a couple of good lads, one or two who might fit into our squad somewhere. What they didn't have was a plan B and I think that is what sets us apart from the rest.

Bury like to be labelled as a passing side, slick in attack, as do Forest Green. Other teams are direct by nature, some like the high press, others like to sit deep. Us? We do whatever the moment dictates. How high did we hold our line late on? Much higher than usual, almost penning Yeovil back. We can go long, but if we need to we can switch up to hit with slick passing on the break. We can control the pace of a game, keeping it fast when we need the goal, but slowing it down when we don't.

That was obvious in the final five minutes, certainly when Harry Toffolo took his booking to stop a counter. With the high line they had to get in over the top, but they didn't have the pace up top to do that. The only way they'd get a goal was a quick counter and even in the final minutes, our attacking full back had the awareness to commit an obvious, cynical foul. It's not something everyone would admire but you know what? I did.

That relief when the final whistle went was worth it, reminiscent of us beating Bromley and Chester two years ago. We'd ground out a result, finally coming up against a side determined to defend and finding the answers we needed. Our strengths, certainly in recent weeks, have been against the top teams who want a proper game, but we've struggled against eight or nine behind the ball. We didn't dominate with free-flowing football, but we probed and even when things didn't run our way, we kept on at them.

I would also like to mention referee Scott Oldham who I thought had an excellent game. He let it flow where possible and although we didn't get all the decisions I felt we should, a neutral would certainly have given him a nine out of ten. How many times have I mentioned him in the article? very few and that is the sign of a good referee. Can we have him every week?

Anyway, on Tuesday all eyes were on Bury and they missed their cue. Last night all eyes were on us and just like DHL, we delivered. It might have come a little later than we'd have liked, but we delivered and right now we've got a five point cushion to enjoy.

At least until 5pm.

The mysterious case of the transfer window 'invisibles'
March 10, 2019

At one point this weekend, before Mark O'Hara's header and certainly before Mansfield fell out of the top three, there was a feeling of anger somewhere behind me.

It came from behind my Dad, who sits one row back from me in the Coop. I'm not sure where it was from exactly, but it went along the lines of 'why the French Connection did we sign Roberts and Angol?'

I suppose there's a fair point there in someone's eyes. Football is a game in which we see between eleven and fourteen players at a time, usually the same ones every week. There's a reason for this, certainly when we're top. You don't need to experiment and play around with the faces you have out because those in the team have done well so far.

There's a feeling that maybe Danny's late business is always underwhelming. You know what I mean, waiting for Simeon Akinola, but not getting him. Bringing in Angol when some deluded fans thought we might get Mo Eisa. Usually, the big business is tied up relatively early.

Look at Danny Rowe. He was intended to be a key player last season and in fairness helped us to Wembley, but he was in the building early. Lee Frecklington, another who was a huge coup at the time, was in Sincil Bank long before the last day shenanigans. To be fair, even Tom Pett arrived the day before the curtain came down.

No, Danny doesn't wait until the last minute to get his main man, at least not in 99% of instances. He knew he needed a striker this transfer window, but was it going to be one who replaced John Akinde? Maybe if we'd signed the rumoured Joe Nuttall on loan, there might have been competition. It's the same with Jorge Grant, if he'd come in then somewhere across that bank of three behind Akinde, someone would have missed out.

That's not going to be the case though with Angol and Roberts. Look, both are good players who would play for 90% of the other teams in this league. Angol, who I believe could be a big player for us given the chance and the system, isn't going to get that opportunity when we play as we do. Think about it, if we play the 4-4-1-1 that we like, the runner behind John is likely to be a midfielder such as Rowe or Pett. Maybe, Shay McCartan gets the nod, but if it's Angol then we go to a 4-4-2. If the 4-4-2 is the favoured option, it's going to be Rhead and Akinde.

Never underestimate the importance of Matt Rhead to the squad. He wasn't at his best this Friday night, but he was still a presence, working as hard as ever and always willing in the aerial challenge. John looked happier after Rhead went off, but that's not the case. It's just that he's ploughed a lone furrow up front for 34 matches and this week was asked to do it differently. It wouldn't take long to see the John that we saw at FGR at the Bank.

There's the problem for Lee Angol though. John Akinde plays both roles and whatever your individual thoughts on him, he's been a significant figure this season. Plenty of assists, key passes and goals. I think we have to be careful how we label assists, the figures coming out of the club have him assisting double figures, but those official ones through the likes of whoscored, or Google search, do not.

A word on that; Harry Anderson got a lot of plaudits for the cross for Friday's goal and rightly so, but what of the ball back to him by Danny Rowe? Rowe wouldn't get a so-called assist as he didn't have the last touch, but he was just as involved in creating the chance. We should always be careful when talking assists because sometimes, the pass that creates the chance is just as important. They call that a 'key pass' on whoscored, but then a pass that leads to a chance but not a goal, in otherwise a missed assist, is also a key pass. Stats eh?

Moving on to Harry and Bruno, where would you play Jordan Roberts? Serious question. I heard someone behind lamenting the fact we'd not see him and I'd love to know where we want him to play. This isn't FIFA, you don't always swap like for like on 70 minutes and do the same things for the final spell with fresh legs. We'll change shape if we're 2-0 up and usually, Stevenage aside, it works. If we're chasing the game we'll do the same, as we did at Exeter.

Even when we're drawing, as we were this week, a change will bring about a different approach. Just doing the same things with different players suggests the first players weren't good enough, to a degree. I buy they might be tired and all that, but that's not been the case through February. We've had to change things, chase games and Roberts has been the unwitting victim in all of that as he's not fitted the patterns.

There's plenty of reasons why we haven't seen them yet and it's not to say we won't, but Danny works with these players every week and genuinely knows best. It would never be said at the time of capture, but some players are brought in 'just in case'. There's no plan to drop a first team member, no need to break up the current squad, they're just there if we get an injury or suspension.

As for James Brown, if he wants a game he's going to have to lock Neal Eardley's electric gates from the outside or slash his car tyres or something. Sorry lad.

Please, do bear that in mind if you're the one voice in Block 3, row L, M or No seat's 76 to 84, ish. Cheers.

Playing like Champions: Imps 2-0 Oldham
March 13, 2019

There's been a criticism around the club that we haven't played 'like Champions' during our six month tenure at the top of the table.

We might be top, we might have a good lead and we might have won more games than everyone else, but apparently as fans, we've not always been entertained. I've seen it said, you'll know if it's you that said it.

We've ground out results, often getting ahead through endeavour and process, not that slick, magical football we think we've seen at Luton and Bury. Apparently, we're functional. We're process orientated. If last night is anything to go by, we're also going to League One.

For me, last night was crucial. It was Exeter all over again, the game in hand that could put us five points clear. Only this time, there's fewer games left to play, fewer opportunities for those wanting to catch us to do so. Whilst we're all hoping to see the title delivered ready for that final day against Colchester, third place is where it's all at.

Finish third or above and we're going to Portman Road, we're going to Peterborough as equals and maybe Bolton or Millwall. Finish third or above and we're going back to where my Dad thinks we belong, where we certainly made our name in the early eighties. I was brought up on a diet of 'Lincoln City are not a fourth division team', yet for three decades it's virtually all I've ever known, or worse.

The gap between us and fourth is ten points, but in real terms it is 12. MK Dons and Mansfield meet on the final day of the season and one of them will drop at least two points. Technically, we're 12 points clear with nine games left to play.

To put it another way, we're five wins from League One, or fewer if we beat MK Dons or Mansfield.

That's exciting, isn't it? Sit there for a moment and forget the fear, the cloak of darkness that we all throw over ourselves at times. We're five wins from being a third division side.

How has that happened? After the run of draws we had you'd be forgiven for fearing the worst and for ten minutes of last night's game, I feared the worst.

Pre-match was a little different for me. I had the pleasure of being invited into Running Imp's box once more, something always welcomed and never more so than on a cold night! I got to meet Val too, the fan who penned the now famous 'plastics' piece. It was her first time in a box, something she didn't think she'd enjoy as much as being in the throbbing masses of the Coop Stand.

After ten minutes, I was inclined to think I was in the best place, behind a sheet of glass and next to a heater. The game started with Oldham looking to be a terrific side, stretching the play and laying the ball about nicely. We had an air of nervousness about us, a feeling that an error was only ever a second away.

My Dad, who as you know is never the most positive of fans, was immediately worried, but I allayed his fears. I thought the start went exactly to our favour, because it showed they'd come to get at us. Do that, and we'll get right back at you twice as hard. It also looked to be taking a lot of energy out of a side who, in recent weeks, have lacked energy in the latter stages of the game.

It didn't mean they weren't a threat and two smart Matt Gilks saves stopped the pressure mounting on us. Gilks was one of the best signings we made in the transfer window and three clean sheets from five proves that.

Fifteen minutes in and they were done.

After quarter of an hour the game ceased to be a contest, not because Oldham were so bad, but because they played into our hands. With the swirling wind behind us we began to press forward and soon became the dominant force in the evening.

You have to feel for big John, he's such a focal point of our attack but he missed a real sitter didn't he? I watched him sky something similar in the warm up and when Bruno whipped that low ball in from the left, it just needed a tap in. Barnet fans would place their house on John Akinde scoring, but Lincoln fans wouldn't. He blazed over the bar but, to his credit, the miss didn't affect him at all and he went on to put in a decent shift.

The breakthrough came minutes later, Harry Toffolo popping up (out of position joked Danny afterwards) to play a one two with Mark O'Hara before scooping the ball home. The atmosphere, which had been terrific before the goal, went up another notch. As the Oldham players looked at each other as if they'd had their pants pulled down, you knew it was our night.

We weren't rampant, but on 43 minutes we were handed the chance to show what we could really do.

My view of the Jose Baxter challenge was blocked by a girder, but everyone told me it was a sure-fire red. I've watched it back and my first thought was 'FIFA tackle'. You know what I mean, FIFA players. You lose the ball and angrily tap the 'O' button, realising too late that you're getting sent off. Baxter knew as soon as he connected it was a red and Cian Bolger's reaction told you the same story.

Ten against eleven, 1-0 up.... there was only one outcome after that.

Don't let anyone tell you that playing ten men is easy. We've seen both sides of it against Oldham. Earlier in the season, around the same time as last night, Ishmael Miller was sent off for a bad challenge on Josh Vickers. That evening we laboured to a draw, unable to break down a resolute Latics side who had Sam Surridge as on outlet to take away the pressure.

Last night, they had no outlet but we still had to break them down.

I suggested to Neil from Selenity in the box next to us that it'd be wise to take off Matt Rhead, bring on Danny Rowe and look to stretch them as much as possible, especially with the wind behind us. I guess Danny overheard me, because that's exactly what happened.

What followed, in my opinion, was the best 45 minutes of football we've produced at Sincil Bank this season.

I know the mantra, never too high, never too low. That starts to go out of the window when you're so close to the prize you crave, especially when you look to be hitting some real form. We won't always have ten men to face, we can't be as dominant as that away from home, but my word, we were good.

Danny Rowe was an obvious catalyst, that boy is very, very special. His control of a football is incredible and he seemed to drift inside and out at will. He started running the channels as Big John dropped deeper and Oldham didn't know how to cope. If they plugged a gap on one side, we shifted play across the field and simply went down the other. They tried to stay compact, but when our main threat is from out wide it simply isn't the right approach.

They couldn't get out to the wide areas though because if they did, we loaded the box with the likes of O'Hara and Akinde. It all flowed so nicely and both Harry Anderson and Bruno Andrade were excellent, back up by their full backs. Last night was the first time we've seen both flanks be as effective as each other for the full game.

The goal was something very special, started by a tenacious John Akinde pass and finished with aplomb by Danny Rowe. The whole sweeping move was a sight to behold, Harry's little flick to make Danny the room was as subtle and effective as I've seen all season. Alan Partridge talked about 'liquid football', utter nonsense of course, but for a moment I could have said that myself. in fact, I will.

Liquid football.

Oldham simply didn't threaten at all. Bruno was incredibly unlucky not to get on the score sheet with a rasping drive from Big John's knock-down. The keeper didn't have a clue where it was going and thanks to the wind, neither did Bruno. I was right behind it watching it swirl with such ferocious power that I was convinced it would give us (at the time) a second goal.

Tom Pett was back to his best after a couple of months out on the flank and he played a Lee Frecklington type of game. Mark O'Hara was excellent too, the pair of them giving Danny even more cause for sleepless nights with O'Connor on the bench. When my favourite Irishman did come on, he was unlucky not to score with a point-blank volley from a sumptuous ball over the top of the defence.

I'm not being biased when I say we could, and should, have scored four or five. Oldham stuck to their guns and fought hard, but they were never able to find a plan B after Baxter's red card. At 2-0 against Stevenage you felt we were likely to concede but, if we'd kept playing all night right up to the point you're reading this, Oldham wouldn't have scored.

They brought on Chris O'Grady, an experienced player who should have been able to hold the ball up and buy them some time, but the wind made hitting him virtually impossible. Every time Daniel Iversen delivered the ball forward, it came back either down the left, down the right or down Big John's head.

Referee Paul Marsden knew the contest was over, he added on an obligatory three minutes and no more. There was no point in drawing things out any longer than absolutely necessary, the Imps had done what they needed to do and in truth, Oldham had simply turned up, played patsy and then gone home again.

News that Mansfield had continued to bottle their automatic challenge with a draw was warmly received, just as MK's demise at Morecambe warmed the cockles on the walk back to the car. We had the benefit of Sky in the box and they went from 3-0 down to 3-2 quickly, before fumbling the comeback and losing.

By the way, Morecambe have won four of their last six, beating MK Dons and Forest Green as well as giving Bury a huge scare before that. Makes our so-called comfortable 2-0 win look even better, doesn't it?

We're not promoted yet and doubtless as my Dad put his head on his pillow, the fear came over him once more. He's not usually one for emotion, but over a pre-match pint he admitted it kept him awake at night, worrying that we might blow it. Even now, seven weeks and nine games before the end of the season, he sees the ghosts of '83 coming back. Me, I was still on a potty then, but I think the spectre of '07 has been put to bed by now.

Here's the reality: we have one foot in League One. There's still the nagging doubts, the grounded fear and realism that comes with sitting on the inside looking out, but few on the outside looking in would bet against us getting promoted one way or another. It's easy for them, they don't live it. they have the clarity of perspective and see the division emotion free.

No team battling for promotion has the same lead as we have over fourth place. No team has led their division for as long as we have. Nobody in their right mind would back us to be in League Two next season.

We're on the cusp of history. We can almost touch three trophies in three years, unprecedented in Lincoln City's history. We can almost dust of the guidebooks to Ipswich, bought as a laugh for the FA Cup tie when we were nobody. We can almost taste the burgers at Peterborough.

Almost.

But not quite.

Danny Cowley praises squad players as Imps enter final stages of title chase
March 15, 2019

Imps' manager Danny Cowley has been praising the recruitment in January and the motivation of his fringe players as we enter the final straight in the League Two title race.

City are five points clear of Bury at the top of the table, with a ten point gap to third place. With a free Saturday to watch other results come in, the pressure is off tomorrow.

Ahead of Monday's huge clash with Mansfield, Danny Cowley has been speaking to press about his recruitment in January, something that has been crucial in the recent run. Danny Rowe has come in and scored four goals in seven starts, with Mark O'Hara and Cian Bolger also playing key roles.

Danny revealed he was delighted with the business conducted in the transfer window.

"I think we've been really pleased with the recruitment we've done this year, credit to all the staff and the amount of work that goes on behind the scenes in that process and that area.

"You want a squad of 20, 22 players and we've managed to have that. We have more depth than we had last year, definitely. We've had more competition for places. What people don't realise is that players can have a real impact without actually playing 90 minutes on a Saturday or on a Tuesday.

"The competition that we have in a number of different areas drives the players on that are playing. Look at John Akinde's performances and consider that he has Matt Rhead, Lee Angol, Jordan Roberts, Shay McCartan and Danny Rowe all vying for those positions it can really drive the standards."

Two notable absence shave been Jordan Roberts and Lee Angol, both with little more than a cameo or two to their names since moving from Ipswich and Shrewsbury respectively. Whilst they might not be having an impact on the pitch, Danny hailed their input off it.

"When we planned the recruitment in January, we knew the position we were going to be in at this stage of the season and what we wanted to do was make sure we cover all eventualities. We've certainly done a good job of covering all of the outcomes in a 46 games season.

"I think everyone wants to play and we sign players that love football. When we look at recruitment one of the first things we look for is the love of the game. We know if they love the game, they're going to have an enthusiasm and a willingness to learn.

"But with that, when they're not playing and you're the one starving them from doing what they love there can be a natural frustration. Ultimately, we sign good people and good characters and I think they see the bigger picture. We work really hard with 12 to 20, we probably spend more time with 12 to 20 than we do one to 11 because we know it's really important that we influence those boys and keep them focused and motivated."

Danny concluded by admitting he was as proud of the players on the fringe of the squad as he was those in the side.

"I've been really proud of the boys who have been on the periphery. When you're top you tend to have less personnel changes than when your mid table or near the bottom. They've had to be really patient and had to stay really focused and motivated as we know there's still a lot of football to be played and we could need them any moment."

All eyes will be on Ryan Lowe's Bury tomorrow as they host relegation-threatened Cambridge at Gigg Lane. MK Dons, ten points below the Imps, host Stevenage. Fifth-placed Tranmere might be 14 points behind the Imps, but they're hot on the heels of both MK and Mansfield and host managerless Oldham at Prenton Park.

One Step Closer: Mansfield 1-1 Imps
March 19, 2019

270 minute of league football has now elapsed between Mansfield and the Imps without a clear winner.

Two EFL Trophy games and the opening league encounter of last season saw clear victors, but in the crucial stages of last season and all of this, there's been nothing to separate us. We get late goals, they get late goals and yet we're till deadlocked.

Last night, the draw was certainly more valuable to us than them. They're fighting for a top three spot but, bar the shouting, we have more or less secured ours.

That's a bold claim I know and I'll come to it in a bit, but first the game.

This write-up will be different to most because of the fact the game was televised. There's been plenty of punditry available, whether it's our own beloved Michael Hortin, Sky's Lee Hendrie or the studio guests. Everyone has a view on the game and I suspect my view is very similar to theirs.

Firstly, we were poor in the opening exchanges. Certainly their goal was very unlike us. Danny will have fumed at conceding early, our game plan would have been something like contain them as long as possible and slowly break them down. I imagine it surprised them too, they're a great counter-attacking side but I doubt they expected to get such an early opener.

They started with a great pace though and we were seemingly caught cold. Danny said after the game the players are not robots and the first half wasn't as they were programmed, but I think that Pearce header affected us more than usual. Maybe we knew what was at stake, maybe the fact it was a high pressure game replicated some of that worry we've seen at home.

Whatever the issue, passes went astray and we didn't offer much going forward.

It wasn't on the scale of the Exeter game, we showed more cohesion than that. What we didn't do was deal with Gethin Jones down one flank, something that I found surprising. They played something like a 3-4-3, which meant our wide players could have tried to overload those areas, but it was Jones getting all the joy.

I wouldn't have picked him out of their side as the main man at the start, but Hamilton, Walker and Grant didn't get the breaks they were looking for. They created plenty and should have gone in at the break two goals to the good when Walker drove wide from eight yards.

We weren't without our chances, when the patterns of play came off it looked good. Harry and John combined nicely to give Danny Rowe a decent chance and that wasn't the only one. They'd retreated after their first goal to a degree and when we got it together, we certainly threatened.

There's not a lot more to labour on in the first half. We weren't entirely at the races and the better team took the lead into the break. I suspect they will have been disappointed because they had chances to inflict more pain on us, but despite not being at our best we matched them toe to toe. In terms of clear cut openings, there was little to shout about, but we did compete.

I tell you something, I like Neil Bishop in the midfield for them. He's one I thought might be a bit old for this game now, he's 37 and that's veteran by any standards, but he played with a real confidence. Whereas at times their attack was hurried and lacked that clinical edge, he grounds their other players and must surely be one of the main reasons they've done so well this season.

Also, while I'm unusually doling out praise for Mansfield, the lad Sweeney at the back is a class act. We're spoiled with our central defenders but if Cian Bolger is indeed upper League One quality, Sweeney is exactly the same. He'd fit into our back four with ease and there's only a handful of defenders at this level I'll say that about.

Honestly? I was worried at half time. I had a sicky feeling sat on my stomach and it wasn't the reheated rice and curry I'd had earlier in the day. It was 'the fear', the ghosts of '83 and '07 all surrounding me, laughing that we might fall once again.

For ever bit as bad we were in the first half, I thought we were good in the second. I know it wasn't 'Oldham second half' good, but we weren't playing ten men and a disinterested manager, we were playing eleven men and a surprisingly genial David Flitcroft.

I don't like Flitcroft, I don't like Mansfield but (contrary to what some feel) I do try to be fair. They're a good side, nice and compact and they stick to the game plan. It was like a home game for us in the second half, not just because of the noise. We had to go and break them down, they were clearly happy with the one goal lead.

It was almost as if we were playing Pontoon and they'd got 19. They chose to stick, fearing all out attack could see them conceded. They bet on us not being able to break down their resilient bank of three and four. They dropped deeper too, happy to simply soak up the pressure and see what we had to offer.

Our own approach remained constant, but it began to pay dividends. Those who think we're long ball (various calls of 'hoof' every time we went long proved that's what the natives thought), ought to look again. We can go long, but we didn't do that constantly last night. When a chance came to get it into big John, we did. However, we also played some nice, patient build up play.

The usual route is to go down one flank, full back to winger, back to full back. The winger peels off but if the runner tracks him, we come inside, usually switching sides and trying the same on the other flank. It can be tedious for those who want constant chances, but it's patient and measured. It was never more evident than last night, us probing carefully but deliberately, them snuffing out where they could.

The difference always seemed to be Danny Rowe for me. He's the 'wild card', the one who doesn't conform to the rigid process. He's clearly got license to carry the ball, to duck and weave and make something happen. Harry Toffolo, excellent again last night, fed Bruno on many occasions. They like the neat interplay, the little knocks around the corner. Neal Eardley is more direct with Harry, he plays it over the top for our own bull-in-a-chins-shop Harry to batter his way onto. It's planned, they get away, often lay back for a cross.

With Danny Rowe, it's different. He gets the ball and the pattern becomes unpredictable. He might look for a channel runner, he might go outside himself or look to the feet of John Akinde. Of all the players, he was the one I thought might get a chance.

Arguably, Bruno's long-range drive after cutting inside was the closest we got. Mansfield's back three was superb, checking runs, blocking passes and may I say, blocking runs too. No complaints from me, we do it but one corner in particular showed them at it. Logan came out for a ball and their lad never looked towards the keeper or the swirling cross, he eyed our player and got right in the way. Sure, I could moan about it but it's be hypocritical. We do it, it's part of the game.

The referee, who looked like someone had just drowned his cat, had a good game too. Plenty went on from both sides, blocks, nudges and afters. If a weak referee had got the game it would have been punctuated by free kicks and fouls. He let it flow, miserably, but he did. He had one big decision he needed to get right and he got it spot on.

Little moan time: Bruno goes down to easily. I love Bruno, he's exciting on the ball and often gets a cross is from impossible angles, but the slightest touch and he's on his arse. If he did it a little less frequently, maybe it'd pay dividends, but when it doesn't come off he looks a bit foolish. He went down last night on a couple of occasions when I'm pretty sure the contact wouldn't have floored your average six-year-old.

Harry Anderson though, he's different. Because he's bullish, stocky and strong, when he does go down referee's tend to believe him. I'm thinking Bury as a fine example. Last night there can be no complaints at all about the foul.

Oddly, after a game in which our other chances came from a patient build up, this was route one. Gilks down the middle, flicked on by John, hooked on by Danny Rowe and Harry raced clear. There wasn't any real danger, yet Conrad Logan had a rush of blood and we're back in the game. No arguments from Stags' fans, I'm sure.

If there's one player you'd want to take a penalty in that situation, it's John Akinde. I don't care about the Notts County miss, he's as cool as you like from twelve yards. After the game he had me chuckling with a typically direct answer. He was asked if he always felt confident at penalties, to which he replied 'it helps when the keeper falls over'.

That's John. I've spoken to him a couple of times and he's a man of few words. He's to the point, but he won't furnish a conversation with adjectives and description. You ask a question, he answers it. Last night he was asked a question again, one involving big penalties and bottle.

He answered it with aplomb.

After the goal Mansfield's second half tactics were laid bare. Oddly, Flitcroft took off Jorge Grant, booked for diving and only showing flashes of his talent, but surely one of their most creative players. Their one decent chance had come on the break with CJ Hamilton, but he'd been forced wide enough by Harry Toffolo not to be a threat.

For the embarrassment of riches they have in their attack, they offered very little in the second 45 minutes. Of all the loan players on display, Grant, Walker, Rowe and the rest, Danny Rowe stood out. Tyler Walker looked dangerous at times, uninterested at others.

I never thought we'd lose the game after the goal, which is exactly what happened. It was classic Lincoln City, fighting through a few loose touches and an early knock to come out on top. I think it's why the Stevenage result hit us hard, because it's the exact opposite of what has made us strong.

Mansfield now go into a foot race with MK Dons and Tranmere for the final automatic promotion space. I can see the Stags getting it by virtue of being well organised at the back, but Flitcroft needs to look at the keeper situation. He could also do with exploiting some of the wonderful attacking player he has. I've not seen MK Dons recently, but both sides look likely to draw a lot of games.

Maybe, just maybe James Norwood might have a big say in who finishes in the top three.

Enough about them. We're 15 matches unbeaten now, encompassing a run of draws everyone thought would be damaging to us. Three of the four so-called tough matches away; Bury, Mansfield and Forest Green, have been dealt with. We have a six point gap, still a twelve point 'real' gap over fourth place and now just eight matches to play.

I barely dare utter the words but, in my honest opinion, we've got one foot in League One. I know the huge points gap makes it obvious, but there's always that nagging doubt, there's always those ghosts of the past ready to remind us of what happens to complacent teams. I just can't see us throwing away such a big lead in such a short space of time.

I can't see Danny Cowley's Lincoln City playing anywhere other than League One next season and I'm as excited as hell about the future.

Eight more games, but I'm backing us to have it wrapped up in five. Carlisle on Good Friday? Maybe. Tranmere on Easter Monday? Book the Tuesday off, that's my advice because we're painting the town red and white that night.

Red and white.

Reasons to Relax
March 20, 2019

Admit it, as an Imps fan you're almost certain we're heading for League One.

It's not been rubber-stamped and having Danny tell us a thousand times that we shouldn't be complacent makes us nervous, but surely we've got the minerals to pick up another four wins this season, haven't we?

I'll be honest with you, it keeps me awake at night. My dad too. We're not together at the time of course, but we chatted the other day about the fear. He's not an emotional man and most of my heartfelt stuff gets written rather than said, but we're so close to touching something we never thought possible three years ago.

League One, or for those with a little more grey in their hair, Division Three. Once upon a time we were a staple of that level, even higher during the fifties. Lincoln City never were a Fourth Division club, but time is a cruel mistress and a generation of fans today don't know anything of life outside the bottom division, unless it's non-league.

I've been alive 40 years, but been coming to the Bank for 33 this season. That's 33 opening days full of hope and, in most cases, 33 times March has come around with either nothing to play for or relegation still a fear.

Only once have I known us to be promoted out of the Fourth Division. Once. I remember it well, my last days as a fan before taking up Poacher. I remember the joy, tainted a little by the fact we played awful football, but it didn't matter a great amount. Ask a selection of fans about that season and it's either a happy memory, or a stain on our history.

I eat, breathe and live Lincoln City Football Club. As you know, I write about football for a living and find immense joy in penning articles about us, both on Football League World and this site. I do the podcast, I have pictures on my wall and have written books about us. Like me or not, my existence is fuelled by the club. When we lose, it hurts. When we win, it matters.

If we get promoted, it'll be as memorable as the birth of a child, a wedding day or graduation. It will be a life moment I'll look back on and reference as one of the happiest days of my life. I'm sure you'll be the same.

Still, we're not there yet, are we? We've got matches to play and despite that ten-point cushion (twelve in real terms), we're still not certain. Do you lay awake at night too? Does your mind wander to 1983, for those who remember? Do those who can't remember fear another 2007-style collapse and a failed play-off assault?

If so, here's some tonic for you.

I've gone back 42 years, looking at the Fourth Division league tables as of March 20th of every season and compared them with the sides that ended up being promoted. I've done this for my own peace of mind but, as I've found some solace in the figures, I wanted to give you a chance for a sound night's sleep too.

Only once in my lifetime has a team who leads the table on March 20th not gone on to be promoted automatically. History can tell you anything, stats can too, but the fact is that just one team in 42 years have been in our position and not gone up. Ironically, that one team were prevented from going up by us.

The year was 1992 and the league leaders were Blackpool. In a division of 22 teams, or 42 matches, they were top after 33. They had nine to play, one more than we do now, and were joint top with Mansfield. Burnley, eventual league winners, were third with two games in hand and one point to make up. The fourth placed team were Rotherham, six points shy of the Seasiders.

All Blackpool needed to do was better Mansfield's result on the final day of the season to go up, albeit in third. They came to Sincil Bank, Matt Carmichael scored two penalties and they had to go into the play-offs, which by the way they won.

So, in 42 years of teams being top on March 20th, every single one has gone up, with just Blackpool needing a play-off win.

Happier? How about this as well. Only once in the last 42 years have two teams in the top three on March 20th not gone up automatically. That again involved the Imps.

In 1998 we never truly looked like being in the automatic mix. we hadn't been top three all season and on March 20th we were six points outside the promotion spots. Notts county were runaway leaders, 16 points clear of Torquay in second with Barnet four points below them in third. The gap between us and Torquay was ten points.

By the final day of the season we'd closed that gap and overtaken the Gulls, as had Macclesfield. The Silkmen finished second, us third and Colchester ended up winning the play-offs.

Happier? I suppose the only worry is patterns. Patterns emerge in football and perhaps we should be cautious that the only time a team who were top have failed to finish in the automatic promotion spots, we stopped them. Then the only time two of the top three have not been promoted it was us that stopped them again and we overturned a ten point gap in doing so, the same gap we have over the chasing pack!

The one difference was we'd only played 37 matches. By the time we played the 38th, leaving eight to play as there is now, the gap was down to eight points. Still....

Finally, to deal with the big collapses of the past, those ghosts that stand on the edge of our dreams with foreboding looks on their faces. They're not exactly relevant in our worries right now.

In 1983 we were top at Christmas but had already lost four matches by that point, as many as we've lost all this season. Also, we only had a seven point gap after eighteen matches. By the time game number 38 had been completed we were sixth, 11 short of the top spot and six outside the promotion spots. We blew it long before the final straight.

In 2007, with eight matches left to play we were fourth, eight points shy of the leaders. Although we'd been top at one point, it was for just a couple of days and not the whole season, like this year.

Sleep easy tonight, unless there's a cataclysmic collapse the like of which hasn't been seen in 40 years we're going to League One, the big question is whether we go as Champions or not.

Disclaimer: If it all goes tits up now, don't blame me. Cheers.

The Perfect Away Day: Crawley 0-3 Imps
March 24, 2019

At 3pm yesterday I was in a rather unusual position of standing on the terrace, relatively inebriated, full of hope and excitement.

Anyone who follows me regularly will know I haven't had a drink since New Year and that I'm not the most optimistic of fans. I often struggle to enjoy our matches as I fear falling away from the top three. I felt the same in the National League and have spent many an afternoon since January sat trying not to bite my nails, wishing it was 5pm.

It was different yesterday. Since I've stated that automatic promotion is secure in all but fact, I've felt comfortable. The black dog on my back telling me 'It's Lincoln, they'll bugger it up', has been silenced. The darkness has lifted and its coincided with the boys doing the business on the pitch.

For a short while I wondered if draws might be out undoing, I cringed through Northampton and Stevenage at home, but that' in the past. This is our promotion season, just where we finish in the top three is the question to be answered. That isn't arrogance, it's belief.

I enjoyed the drive to Newark train station yesterday. I relished the chatter between Pete, Dad and I on the way down. I thoroughly enjoyed picking up Dave meeting my good friend Roy and his crew at the services. No sick feeling in my stomach, no real worry of collapse. I thought we'd draw, but never did I feel I'd be making the same trip next season.

I wouldn't be upset to travel there in terms of hospitality though. The ground is very nice, perhaps reminiscent of the National League more than anything, but it's adequate for League Two. The people are friendly, car parking was free, the home bar was good and the food in the ground wasn't terrible either. In my opinion, we won't be back at Crawley but it's not the worst away trip I've been on in the last couple of years. Thanks to the result, it might be one of the best.

Anyway, this isn't a ground guide nor an assessment of my mental state before games. The focus is on the field and the quest for three points. I felt they'd look for a response after the 6-1 defeat last weekend, maybe not play the ball out from the back as much, but that didn't happen at all.

Instead, for the first ten minutes, we looked excellent. The opening exchanges belonged to us and it quickly became evident why they struggled with conceding goals. The keeper look sloppy, the defenders looked scared and a couple of early corners could have proven to be damaging, had we got into the right positions.

After that, the game tailed off a bit. We weren't bad, not by a long shot, but one or two passes went astray. They began to find a bit of build up play and in one area of the pitch looked promising. Just in front of our back four they played the ball nicely, left to right, hoping to isolate one of our full backs. Our game plan involves Eardley and Toffolo getting forward, but it can leave them open to attack. The home side tried to get through that way, but it always broke down when they looked for the centre forward.

No comment.

They offered a bit, a tepid shot from Camara and a 'mazy' (read cumbersome and aimless) run from Palmer drew a corner, but aside from that you could tell it was top against lower half. I turned to Pete and said 'one goal changes this.'

One goal then changed it. Neal Eardley delivered yet another wonderful cross into the box and Bruno, cutting across goal, stroked the ball home with ease to make it 1-0. If this was a boxing match, the underdog had just been floored for the first time and right then you knew this was only going one way.

What baffled me was their lack of answers to the same question. The madness definition, doing the same thing over and over expecting the same result, has a flip side. The definition of stupid is having the same thing done to you time and again and not stopping it. How many times did our quick free kick routine work in the first half? Three I think I counted. Crawley's defence just didn't learn and even after the goal, we could have gone 2-0 up using that routine.

Elsewhere the Cods were drawing and Mansfield were drawing too. The half time whistle brought proceedings to a close with us edging ever-closer to the automatic promotion spot I believe we've already got in the bag.

What I felt we had to do was come out and keep having a go at them. There's been a tendency, for whatever reason, to sit on those one goal leads, but this Crawley side are not a patch on Kewell's of last season. They're not organised, the threat up front is minimal and I fail to understand on yesterday's showing how they're the only side to beat us at home so far this season. They're not the worst I've seen, but they're in the bottom four or five.

Still, you have to beat what is in front of you and to a certain degree I think they dragged us to their level in the first half. I'm not saying we are Brazil, far from it, but it all felt a bit disjointed and scrappy without us actually playing badly. It wasn't Exeter bad, it wasn't second half against Oldham good. At least not until the second half.

I might be over enthusing, the red wine is perhaps still in me from last night, but I thought we were utterly dominant in the second period of the game. Shooting towards an unbelievable following of over 1000 fans, the lads seemed much livelier.

By the 50 minute mark we could have been 3-0 up. Danny Rowe's whipped free kick from the right was closer than it looked, then Bruno was fouled in the area but the shouts ignored. I thought referee Craig Hicks had a good game on the whole, but I was right behind the challenge and Bruno was fouled. It's that simple. Sadly, when he goes down easily as he did against Mansfield, he sets a precedent. We can't complain though, we get a decent amount of penalties and when we do, John usually scores them.

Plus, I'm not calling Bruno at all as he was having a typically electric game. He'd already bagged the goal and minutes after the penalty shout he was driving forward again, a deflected effort ending up not being turned in by Harry on the right, who was also excellent all afternoon. Bruno then just curled a free kick over as he looks to move into double figures for the season.

It has to be said, Bruno has probably been one of the biggest signings of the summer. John's been strong all season and the other boys have all added value, but there's a special vibe about Bruno. He has that little bit of something else, that unpredictability that can't be measured or trained into a player. When something magical needs to happen he's one who can provide.

The same can be said for Danny Rowe, but he's not usually providing with his head. He put in a hell of a shift and was the unlikely recipient of a headed chance from a Harry cross. He nodded over, but the goal was coming.

Crawley hadn't had a chance in the second half, but they had a little spell. I still like their forward Camara and he did have a couple of half chances as they looked to get back into the game, but after Danny Rowe came off for McCartan we went back on the offensive. Rowe had played well, but McCartan brought a different element and he brought a goal.

The official site said it was 'ridiculous', but it's actually a goal born of perseverance and bad defending as much as anything. He picks up the ball and beats two men in a twenty yard run. How has nobody else challenged him in that time? He gets a bit of luck with a bobble, but there was no doubting the quality of the finish. Second knock down for the home side. Game almost over.

One of the biggest cheers (from my internal monologue) came as Ollie Palmer went off. I had been a little concerned he might score but he never looked like it, not really. That's the Ollie I remember from last season, the one who started against Crewe away and looked utterly lost. I was still laughing (in my own head) when Cian Bolger gave me a reminder of another away trip.

Anyone else at Port Vale? We won 6-2 and scored four or five from corners defended as badly as an under 11s team would against the Imps. It was that all over again, a corner gets whipped in and Bolger just wanders across unmarked and stoops to head home. Call the police, that defending was criminal.

Three knockdowns. Crawley were out.

Not long before the end of the game Michael Bostwick, a big contender for Man of the Match (as always) showed them how defending should be done with a vital clearance off the line.

That was that. It took 7000 man hours, give or take, to provide the support, but it took just 90 minutes of controlled, committed football to move us closer to the Holy Grail of League One football. Grimsby did us a favour, our county cousins (little bit of sick in the mouth) holding Bury 0-0 to extend our lead over them. Game in hand or not, eight points is a big gap to close. They still can, I'm not as confident of the title as I am promotion.

Promotion is, in my opinion, now simply there to be coloured in and completed. Mansfield are seemingly bottling it once more, their defeat by Crewe not entirely surprising. If we were in this division next season, I suspect Crewe would be one of the teams to watch. MK Dons' win wasn't a huge concern, not if we just want top three. I'm more worried about Tranmere now, but if they're winning games against the likes of Bury, it still leaves us in a great position.

There wasn't a truly bad player on the pitch yesterday, not in the grey of City. Tom Pett grew in stature as the game went on and in the second half his industry was certainly vital. The wingers were brilliant once more, their full backs worked hard too. Toff didn't always get the rub of the green, but he never stops trying. He was the first over to the fans at the end and I see something really honest in him. All our players have it, but he's come from a top academy and dropped into League Two, yet he carries himself as if he's stepped off the terraces to play for his home town club. I respect that.

I thought Bolger had his best game in a City shirt, the centre back pairing of him and Bozzie only gets stronger. That's our first choice paring next season, without a doubt.

I felt a tinge of sadness in the second half as I watched James Wilson warming up on his own in the corner, the forgotten man of a whirlwind season. He's a nice lad, or he was when I spoke to him, and I feel desperately for him, but right now I can't see his future as being with us. I might be wrong.

Worth mentioning Matt Gilks too, he's kept four clean sheets in seven matches. He commands his area excellently and although his distribution is sometimes a little off, he's had a huge impact. Before he came into the side against Morecambe we'd kept four clean sheets in 26 matches. Make of that what you will.

When betting companies stop taking bets on you being promoted, you know you're close. When you win 3-0 away at a team you've never beaten, you know you're close. When you're eight points clear of second place, 13 clear of fourth, you know you're close.

We're close. Close enough to smell the burgers at Portman Road. Close enough to touch our tickets against the automatic readers at the Keepmoat Stadium. Close enough to wish we didn't have to drive to effing Plymouth on a Tuesday night in February for a fixture that is bound to be rearranged for some reason.

The permutations confuse me. The different possibilities are concerning, not knowing whether we'll need to haul ass up to Carlisle if we want to see them lads promoted, or perhaps it could be wrapped up against Cheltenham.

I believe in fate, patterns and the like. You must know that by now and if you don't, you'll find out when you buy my new book later this year. In 2016 we watched Cheltenham get their title trophy, in 2017 we lifted the title. In 2018, we watched Accrington get their title trophy....

There's still twists, turns and surprises to endure, but with only 630 minutes of football left to play (more for Bury and Tranmere), time is running out for everyone else.

You never know, I might even enjoy another drink or two before the season is over.

EFL Team of the Year 'snub': Let's keep our hair on
March 26, 2019

The EFL League Two Team of the Year has been announced and apparently, the Imps have been snubbed.

Despite being top of the table, our manager hasn't won the award and we have just two players in place, Jason Shackell and Michael Bostwick. Oddly, Bozzy is in the midfield, a position he's perhaps played twice for us this season.

The usual outpouring of anger has ensued, something perhaps once upon a time I'd have gladly indulged in. You know the drill, we're all angry because we're top and we're not getting the recognition we deserve. Boo hoo.

Firstly, and this is a salient point, the awards are voted for by other managers. These are not votes open to the fans, if they were we'd likely win more places as we have more fans. No, these are awards in which managers vote for their favourites over a season. Let's face it, we're not exactly flavour of the month with other clubs, are we?

Let's deal with Danny first. We know how good Danny is at his job. We know he's the best manager in the division because he's put us on top of the table, Ryan Lowe is second in the table by playing good football, but they're still in with a shot of the title. The truth is there's little to separate the two men this season. I get that we're top, but not everyone appreciates how we get there, nor does this award take into account us coming from the National League to get where we are. It's a subjective snapshot voted on perhaps eight or ten weeks before the season ends.

Danny is a winner and when the boys are on the grass, he fights for everything. He falls out with other managers, he puts himself in the fourth official's face and when he doesn't, Nicky does. Do we honestly think that a manager of that ilk is going to win an award voted for by the very people he's trying to get at?

Plus, footballer managers like to see football played the 'right' way, as if there is a right way. I say the right way is whatever results in you being top and if negative tactics were hugely successful, Pulis would be top of the Premier League. We're not only top because we sometimes play a long ball, but that's the perception. We know, as fans, that some of our passing and patterns are excellent, but when we need to mix it we will. We're adaptable, but that doesn't always win us style awards.

It fits for the likes of David Artell to believe that we're aggressive and angry, because he can claim to do things the right way and be downtrodden. A vote for Danny is an admission that actually, Lincoln aren't as bad as the stereotype suggests and in fact we are good at football.

Heaven forbid, why would anyone suggest that?

On to the players. I've seen it described as 'outrageous' that some have not been picked. I've seen Bruno's name mentioned as someone who might have got in, which is a decent shout. Today, I presented him with an award voted for by the fans, the PFA Player of the Month for February. If this had been voted for by the fans, maybe he'd have got in.

It isn't though, it's voted for by the managers. Looking at the list, there's a couple of contentious inclusions. I can accept Tyler Walker and James Norwood based on their goals, I can accept the Bury pair too as they've been class. We've already got Bozzy in there, that leaves the only available slot having been picked up by CJ Hamilton which could be contentious.

Holding off our own anger, how do you think Colchester's Sammy Szmodics feels? Or MK Dons who have nobody in the side? At the back, there's two more from Mansfield, Jason Shackell and the Oldham full back. Nobody from Forest Green gets in, Reece Brown for instance, or Exeter who have had Nicky Law on top form all season. Nobody else from James Norwood FC either. Only two from Bury, same as us. From 24 teams, only 11 players can be voted for.

If you're voted as the best keeper in the division by the way, your defence have done something wrong.

Voted for. Not picked, voted for. League Two footballer managers believe that the four Mansfield lads are four of the best players in the league up to the beginning of March. What does that say about their team as a whole, down in fourth?

We have to shed this sense of entitlement we seem to have that our players are the best. They're not, our team is the best. So what if Mansfield have four players in the selection? They're fourth. that tells me more about their team than it does ours. Four players generally regarded as the best amongst their peers and they're 13 points behind the leaders. Either the rest are utter rubbish (not the case) or something else is amiss.

Once upon a time I used to get uppity about this sort of thing, but anyone who thinks we don't get recognition needs to look again. Danny and Nicky on Football Focus is testament to the fact we do. Two televised matches in the last few weeks proves we're a big draw. There's no overlooking us, no conspiracy by the authorities.

We're not well liked. I'll take that. Fans of other teams don't particularly like us, other players don't and there's nothing wrong with that. Being liked and being a success is not the same thing.

You know what I really love? I see the comments on the EFL's post about Lincoln City and Danny being arrogant and disliked. I love that. I saw a similar comment on the Romford website too. Danny is an ogre and we're abhorrent for allowing him and his brother to get away with the things they do.

In fact, his team are so bad they've had second fewest number of bookings in the division. Danny is such a bad person that this afternoon, when I turned up at the training ground in an official capacity, he came out of his office to shake my hand and show me a video from the weekend to explain a point I'd made in a blog to me. He's so awful that last week, in a meeting with someone who has nothing to do with football, I heard a tale of how they'd witnessed him speaking to a star-struck child in a supermarket, open, friendly and approachable.

He's so hated by other managers that Arsene Wenger, one of the finest ever to manage in England, took time out to record a congratulatory video after our National League triumph.

So what if that's not recognised in some panel voted for by a few managers? Do you think Danny would prefer to be given something they'd voted for, or the freedom of a city he has been pivotal in waking up to its football team? Would he have more pride in being given a civic award for his services to the city as whole, or the other thing?

Today's news isn't a snub, it is something only a small portion have people have voted on. Those included will be delighted and fair play to them, but those not recognised shouldn't feel snubbed, nor should we. At the end of the season, as far as I'm concerned, individual awards are meaningless if we've been promoted.

5,000 to MK Dons? The Imps remarkable support could break new ground
March 27, 2019

I always feel a little reserved when penning something about our support. That terrible word 'plastic' always comes to mind doesn't it?

It's something we've addressed internally, but from the outside other teams think that's what we are. The whole 'where were you when you were sh*t' thing is popular with some fans, whilst others think our huge resurgence is all about the FA Cup games again Oldham and Ipswich.

It's not though, is it? We talk about home support, we look at the numbers and point to those games but the truth is something happened before that. this club was woken up before the headline-grabbing FA Cup run and promotion. Here's something I wrote about the travelling attendance for our away trip to York City on November 22nd 2016, before we beat Oldham.

"1068. Let that sink in. That is more than seven National League teams average at home, and if you take away following into account it's probably more than ten or twelve National League teams' home support. Dagenham get 1500 on average at home, and most of their visiting fans are within a thirty mile radius. 1068 is better than League One teams expect to take away. It is three times as many as Scunthorpe, top of League One, took to Peterborough tonight."

1068 seemed, at the time, a phenomenal number to take away. Remember, it's more than a play-off hunting Scunthorpe took to Peterborough on the same night. It seemed that every hardcore Lincoln fan of a certain age was rediscovering their team. A thousand away, the cheek of it.

It's seemingly the norm now, with more than that going to Crawley, a full seven hour round trip, this weekend. When we go to MK Dons a week on Saturday, the numbers are likely to be higher than that.

Not just higher, but five times as many.

That's right. As of a few minutes ago sales of tickets for the trip to MK Dons were almost at 4,400, with more promised if we sell out. Our initial allocation has gone. Our secondary allocation, has almost gone as well. We're on course to take more than 5,000 fans to Stadium MK next weekend, swelling the crowd to a five-figure number.

There's going to be a whole host of people from outside Milton Keynes and Lincoln who shudder at this fixture. Them, a so-called franchise club. Us, the plastic fantastic who couldn't get 3,000 a couple of seasons ago. This weekend, two of the most unpopular clubs in League Two will get as many fans at one game as any other two, maybe three fixtures in the division combined.

I'm not going to get into the MK debate, we all have different feelings on them as a club, but I am going to praise our support. Look, it's easy to take 9,000 to Arsenal, or 5,000 to Everton because you're attracting a certain type of fan. Little Jonny, no interest in the Imps at all, will be roused by a trip to Goodison Park. Your sales rep mate who supports Liverpool would surely be tempted along to watch his home town side go to Arsenal.

Milton Keynes though, with the greatest of respect, are not the draw here. The opposition is not the draw here. A combination of proximity, importance and allocation has opened up a unique window for us to write our own story.

Fulham in '82. I know we drew the game, but I hear about that all of the time. Huge numbers travelling down to an important fixture that defined the era. This weekend there's not quite as much riding on one result, but it's the same sort of seminal fixture that you'll hear about in 25 years time. I was at MK Dons the day we took it over.

I don't do rallying cries very often. I certainly don't do the fan shaming that seems to mark out so 'real' supporters over others. Not everyone can make Carlisle away, or the long trip down to Crawley. Financially, it isn't always an option. Sometimes, families and girlfriends (and boyfriends for those who are PC and want to find a fault with every word I write) play a part in deciding to make a trip or not.

This one though, this one you'll remember. These next few matches could see us become a competitive third-tier side for the first time since I've been coming as a fan. In 1998/99 we went up, but were we competitive? No.

If we go up next year, would we come back down at first time of asking? I doubt it.

Bittersweet Point: Imps 1-1 Macclesfield
March 31, 2019

I know why you usually pop along to read my articles, the thrilling insight and balanced opinion, right?

Those who go to the game like to see if their view matches mine and debate the salient points, those who do not go like to understand from a fan's perspective what the Imps looked like. I'm pretty sure that's the case, apart from the odd one or two who like to pull me up on spelling or hope for some perceived injustice they can message me about.

Today, I fear some of you will be disappointed (not the spelling guys, they'll find something).

The last time I missed an Imps' home game was courtesy of having spinal surgery. This weekend, as my beloved Imps' were hunting points in the league, I was walking around the island of Lindisfarne with my partner and dog. I can't even pretend it was booked out of season or without prior knowledge of the fixtures. It was a decision I made consciously as it was the only fitting weekend in our schedules, despite the football.

It didn't mean I spent the afternoon oblivious to proceedings, of course I didn't. However, being out of BBC Radio Lincolnshire's range meant I wasn't privy to the dulcet tones of Messrs Hortin and Thompson. Instead, I relied on the club's Twitter feed and the different posts from people during the game.

It was an interesting way to follow the Imps and it wasn't one I'd be keen to repeat. Seeing pictures from the ground, the warm sunshine bathing my place of worship in light, made for a difficult morning. Don't get me wrong, I thoroughly enjoyed my time on the beach with the dog, but a little part of me knows I belong at the Bank on a home fixture. Seeing people there, life going on without my attendance, stung.

I perhaps bored Fe a little too much ahead of the fixture, posting about not being there, telling her about the strengths of Macclesfield and how they'd look to sit deep and soak up pressure, Using my trait of linking previous holidays to football, I told her the last time we visited the beach we were on was the day Elliott Whitehouse signed for Grimsby. I'm not sure she was impressed.

What did I make of the time between 3pm and 5pm? Not much if I'm honest. Refreshing a Twitter feed is all well and good, but there is a certain bias towards the home side. It's natural, but the suggestion was we were utterly battering them and should have been out of sight. Their goal knocked the stuffing out of me a little bit, but I never truly felt we'd get beat.

I found myself spending an insubordinate amount of time looking at the other fixtures too. Mansfield springing a completely surprisingly result away at Exeter, MK Dons clearly indulged in a tough fixture at Forest Green and Bury's home tie with Swindon. Their results became almost as important as our own.

We're at the stage of the season now where it's impossible not to look at other results. In September and October, it doesn't matter. You get your points on the board and let everyone else do what they need to do. Now, we're at the sharp end of the season and anyone other than Danny who says other results don't interest them are surely fibbing.

Instead of being nervy at our performance, I found a certain calm as the afternoon wore on. Neal Eardley bagged a sumptuous free kick which, courtesy of several fans on Facebook, I watched within seconds of him scoring. I found it easy not to fret about our result, because the Twitter feed made it look like we were doing well. It's amazing how a half chance that fails to convince a fan at Sincil Bank looks like a glorious opportunity when condensed into a single tweet.

The worrying times are when you go five or ten minutes without seeing a message, I likened the experience to playing Championship Manager as a kid, watching the updates easing through on my phone. The Imps had a corner, so you wait. Hit refresh.... nothing. Hit it again... nothing. The excitement is palpable, before finally the update arrives and you find it's been gathered safely.

There's none of the fear that they might break and score because there's no tweets highlighting their possession in the middle of the park. The official twitter feed never says 'Harry Anderson is struggling' or 'Macc look good on the ball'. It was football like I've not known it for years, without fear.

It wasn't without expectation though and as the clock wound round towards 4.45pm, I began to panic. It was still 1-1, as you know. Macclesfield Town, exactly the sort of team we struggle to beat, were holding us to a draw. The teams who were meant to struggle, MK Dons and Mansfield, were flying. Tranmere, another promotion contender, were doing the same. Only Bury were fluffing their lines, meaning a win would take us a big step closer not only to promotion, but to the title.

The dying minutes were painful. Not being there, not seeing pressure being applied, felt agonising. Those five minutes seemed empty, void of the passion and excitement that they usually bring. It's never occurred to me before how heightened our levels of expectation become in those final few minutes, not until you have it taken away. Whereas watching text updates made 80 odd minutes bearable, it took away the very essence of the game in the final ten.

Finally, like a huge anti-climax, we'd drawn. One minute I was anxiously refreshing, hoping for something to happen, but like a crap end to a subtitled film, the credits just rolled.

The opinion started flowing immediately, as if the final whistle was a blow to the head with a rock and it were the claret running down the face of Twitter. The usual doom and gloom merchants were out in force, some of which is opinion just as respected as those claiming it was a good point. My Dad surprised me, asking how we could play so well and not win. The same old names criticised the same old players and I reacted much stronger with the block button than usual.

I did have the pleasure of receiving an update from Lewis Kelly, contributor to the blog and fanzine in the past. I respect his opinion and find it as balanced as my own, so felt he'd offered me decent insight into the game. For those who rely on this article for their own news, I've added his assessment on the next page.

At 5pm, once I'd told Fe we could go out again, we took a walk up to Lindisfarne Castle in the warm spring sunshine. The dog (predictably) was an arsehole, barking at anything that moves. As we tried to rein him in I tried to balance the outcome of the afternoon's football in my head. Never too high, never too low. I was high as anything last weekend and yet I found it hard to hit a low.

Sure, we'd drawn and messed up a thousand accumulators, but anyone betting on top against bottom doesn't deserve to win anything.

Sure, we'd lost ground on the teams all double-digit points behind us as well, tightening things up a bit.

We'd also taken another step towards the title, not just promotion. Bury getting beaten is huge and they're beginning to look like they might be freezing on the final straight. Danny Mayor being sent off is massive as well, hindering another of our rivals.

The optimism and belief have perhaps ebbed ever-so slightly, but I still firmly believe we'll be playing League One football next season. That being the case, despite missing the chance to go further ahead, we did actually strengthen our title credentials. Other teams will have looked at the results and perhaps found a glimmer of hope in our draw, but games are running out and our lead isn't being significantly reduced.

At least that's what I told myself to enjoy my lamb tagine at the Ship Inn yesterday evening. It worked, proving that in actual fact, you can kid a kidder.

Normal service to be resumed next weekend.

Lewis' view
They came for the draw, obviously, but not the worst team when they got it down and played. Thought Fiacre Kelleher was impressive. O'Hara continued his form from the game at their place- he made 2 cracking saves from Akinde. Sloppy goal for us to concede, O'Hara cleared and Bruno was just too short for good contact with the header, and the contact he did make clipped it back over Toffolo to Elliott Durrell- he squared for Wilson, and to be fair it was a decent finish from him.

We responded well and were undoubtedly the better team, actually playing some really nice football, with Pett pulling the strings. Andrade picked up the ball and danced through a few defenders before being taken out on the edge of the box. Eardley stepped up and put it in via the post. We looked a threat for the rest of half and Gilks had nothing to do.

After the poor kids in the half time match were once again drenched by sprinklers- we had the second half. Perhaps played at a slower pace as Macclesfield sat even further back- notably a back 3 throughout the game-

we struggled to get in behind as much. Gilks did have make great save, mind. McCartan had our best chance of the half with about 5 to go, but he miss hit from about 10 yards.

All in all not a 'fair' result. We played some great football and I'm not worried, especially with Bury losing and Mayor being sent off. Eardley MOTM.

April

Another remarkable night of League Two action – what it means for us
April 2, 2019

It has to be said, even the most optimistic of fans couldn't have hoped that both Tranmere and Bury would drop points tonight.

Just a fortnight ago it looked likely to be MK Dons and Mansfield missing out this season, with Bury set to challenge us for the title and Tranmere almost certainly looking like dark horses. I called Bury as possible champions a couple of times, not least because of their superb attacking threat.

Many have called them the best team in League Two, perhaps as much for their football as anything. Now, after 40 matches, only one side has lost just four matches. Us. Only one side is top, clear by eight points. Us. They'll be handing out the best team award in a few weeks time and that will go to whoever is top of the table.

After the weekend's draw I feared perhaps we had missed a chance to seize the initiative, but did we actually make good a tough situation? As he season draws to a close, are the tougher matches against sides fighting for their life?

Tranmere had won eight of their last nine matches before this evening, setting League Two on fire and seemingly staking a real claim for a top three finish. Who could have envisaged Oldham, so woeful after fifteen minutes against us, as beating them 2-0? Well, of those eight Tranmere wins only three have been away from home and prior to that they'd won one in eleven on their travels in the league. Maybe, just maybe that defeat wasn't such a surprise.

Oldham weren't exactly fighting for their lives, but at Boundary Park earlier in the season they were resolute against us. They're not a bad side, they've got decent players but off the field turmoil has set them back. They are still fighting for a top seven spot and perhaps feel that tonight's result justifies their endeavour in recent weeks.

Then there's Bury They were my title tip a few weeks ago, as we drew with Stevenage at home, they were on a collision course with the top of the table. Cheltenham kept them off the top and since then they've floundered whilst we've pushed on. Cambridge have moved on to the 45 point mark and having seem the U's twice this season I'm baffled how they're not top half. In both matches against us they were strong, hard to break down and offered pace going forward. Jevani Brown is, in my opinion, a hugely talented player with Championship potential and George Maris has always been quality too. Their win might have been eyebrow raising, not least as it was away, but it wasn't an impossible result. On their day, Cambridge are as good as anyone. They were certainly as good as us at Christmas, but we ground out a 2-1 win.

It seems inconceivable that Bury are now behind MK and less of a threat to our title challenge. Football, it works in mysterious ways.

That's not strictly true though. In my opinion, this league is very tight. There's only luck, fortune and a bit of quality separating the bottom four and the top four. Look at Macclesfield this weekend. Okay, we could have got a win and maybe should, but were they really that bad? No, yet they're in the relegation mire. We've struggled in two matches against them, not because we're poor but because in truth, they're not a bad side. A couple of decisions going their way and a few more quid to spend on a decent striker or midfielder and they're a top ten side.

On their day, anyone can beat anyone. It's why the consternation at a draw with Northampton is misplaced; any sort of result that carries on a run is good. We've dropped points, but our 'bad' runs have been draws, not defeats. The only side to beat us so far in 2019 had a £50m striker and still needed to hang on in the dying moments.

We're maybe not the best side in the division in terms of passing, we're maybe not harbouring the best striker League Two has to offer in our squad and maybe we didn't get four players in the EFL Team of the Year, but there's no denying we're the best team right now. When we've needed to, we've ground out results. Whenever there's been a situation where we need to turn up, just like there was tonight for Bury and Tranmere, we've done it. Even when we struggled (Exeter at home), we still salvaged a point. Also, we've lost half as many games as 22 of the other sides in the division and three fewer than the team closest to us in terms of defeats.

Tonight's results haven't handed us anything, because nothing will be handed to us. With six games and 18 points still to play for we have to go out and win this League. We've done a great job of getting into pole position with six games to go, but this evening's results have proven that means nothing at all if you take you eye off the prize. I firmly believe there's another defeat lurking in the final five fixtures for us, but three more wins and we're essentially home and hosed.

I'd thank Cambridge and Oldham tonight, but they're fighting their own battles and certainly didn't win their matches on our behalf. However, a word of caution. Five matches ago Bury had beaten Macclesfield 3-0 and were just three points behind us with a better goal difference. In five matches they've dropped six points and seen a ten goal swing in our favour.

The season isn't over, not by a long way.

We're still going up though....

Lincoln City Women's side are back
April 5, 2019

News has just broken that Lincoln City will once again have a women's team next season.

From 1st June 2019, the current Nettleham Ladies FC team will become Lincoln City women, seeing a branded team representing Lincoln City for the first time in 2013.

The original Lincoln City Ladies formed in 1997 and climbed the ranks of the Women's division, reaching an FA Cup semi-final in 2008. They played their home games at Ashby Avenue, but often struggled to get the credit they deserved in the city.

The women's game has developed immensely and finally, after six years without a women's side, The Imps are back in business. The 'new' side will simply be a rebranding of the current

Nettleham side, who play in the fourth tier of the women's game. Under the stewardship of Chris Hamilton, they earned promotion from the East Midland's Division last season after reaching the second round of the FA Cup.

However, Chris left in the summer to take over at Barnsley, with former Imp Richard Cooper replacing him at Nettleham. As it's a rebranding, the current coaching staff, players and committee will continue their excellent work and keep the side on the right track.

Nettleham Ladies currently play against the likes of Wolverhampton Wanderers and West Bromwich Albion in the FA Women's National League Division 1 Midlands League. In their first season at the higher level they've acquitted themselves well, currently laying in seventh place in an eleven team league. They've amassed 24 points, five clear of the team below them and a whopping 21 clear of the bottom two.

Roger Bates, is delighted at the latest development, saying; "As a board at the Football Club, we had it in mind that we might look at introducing a women's team at some point. Richard approached to see if we could help by allowing them to become Lincoln City Women. Bringing women's football to Lincoln City was something that was in our minds for the future, but suddenly as a result of the conversations with Richard and Nettleham it quickly came to the forefront of our thinking.

"The board were very quick to acknowledge it was a good thing to do, we have a significant female supporter base and we're proud to have such a high percentage of women amongst our supporters. Women's football continues to go from strength to strength and we felt it was something that ought to be part of our club.

The future manager of Lincoln City Women and current boss of Nettleham Ladies Richard Cooper said; "We raised the potential for a closer link with Lincoln City FC back in October last year and the prospect of a name change.

"It is imperative that the excellent work and achievements by all concerned behind the scenes were recognised and loyalty shown for getting the team to where it is now. The team is overseen and operated by a passionate group of individuals that are fully supportive of the team flourishing as Lincoln City Women FC.

"This came about due to the progress of the team into the FA Women's National League Division 1 Midlands. For the team to focus on promotion in the near future we had to consider match day facilities that would meet certain ground regulations, that we currently can't achieve. It was felt that it would be a shame if this held back the development and progress of the leading women's team in Lincolnshire and so plans were discussed for the prospect of a Lincoln City Women's team.

"This is a fantastic development for female football in Lincoln and the wider community, which will further create opportunities for women and girls to become involved with the team and Lincoln City Football Club."

The team will follow in the footsteps of their predecessors, by making a home at Ashby Avenue. Their chairman Rob Bradley is also happy to be involved in further links between City and United.

"We are pleased to work with the Imps in several areas already and being able to help in terms of a providing a venue for the women's team hopefully cements that working relationship even more.

"The growth of women's football is a phenomenon and Lincoln United are delighted to play a small but significant part in helping that happen in the city. The fact that the team we'll be hosting is a Lincoln City one is all the more reason to help."

From a personal point of view, I'm delighted. It'll mean we will open our coverage to the women's side too, adding a dimension to our site. It also follows on from last season when I had a lot to do with Chris and the Nettleham side. There's some cracking players in their ranks, Olivia Clark has represented Wales, Abbie Murrell is a proven scorer and Katy Thornley always impressed with her driving runs, as did Tia Johnson.

This is a great move by both Nettleham and Lincoln City to further enhance the appeal of the women's game in Lincoln.

Champions Elect – MK Dons 0-2 Imps
April 7, 2019

"Never too high, never too...."

Sod that. Sorry, but sod it and no mistake. Danny might well be moving on to the next game, process orientated and all that and fair play to him and the lads, they have a job to do. I've tried to write by his mantra towards the end of the season, reserving judgement and trying not to build pressure, but here's something I believe to be fact for you to digest: Lincoln City will win League Two this season.

It seems a pretty safe bet though, doesn't it? Five matches to go, 11 points the gap with the teams in second and third set to face each other. That wasn't the situation at the start of play, had things not gone our way we'd be just five points clear now.

I boldly predicted we wouldn't win this weekend. I recall it clearly, I said I thought it'd be a draw, but that we wouldn't come away from Stadium MK with all three points. I imagined they'd be a potent attacking threat, peppering the goal of Matt Gilks with efforts that eventually would lead to them taking a lead.

I imagined wrong, very wrong indeed.

Stadium MK is an impressive venue, not quite as much as it could be were there significantly more home fans, but nice to look at nonetheless. I've seen it inside and out now and it's a fine example of what a Premier League ground should look like. I imagine it may be a bit soul-destroying to play in front of just 7,000 in it though, even though that's great for fourth-tier football.

I've seen some comments since the game ended that MK should perhaps give less allocation to away fans to keep it hostile, but that really wasn't what won us the game. Of course we sang louder, we made up a third of the crowd but every one of us was fully invested in it. MK had perhaps 2,000 that were as invested, maybe fewer, but they were dotted here, there and everywhere. We had 5,600 fans fully concentrated on singing and creating a home atmosphere away. With 20,000 empty seats every week, I imagine MK create an away atmosphere at home every week.

That didn't stop them putting in a decent shift though, as you'd always expect from a Paul Tisdale side. His team selection does seem a little odd to me; I'm a huge Chuks Aneke fan and like Cisse in the centre too. Seeing both in the bench gave me quite a lift, they're game changers at this level and perhaps one or two who started are not.

It didn't stop them moving the ball about nicely and, like the first match between us, I felt it was a tactical battle. Tis and Danny know each other well and I'd imagine there's a mutual respect for each other's achievements. They say familiarity breeds contempt but in this instance I suspect it breeds respect.

MK had the better of the opening exchanges, but from our vantage point behind the goal it was easier to see their build up play and efforts. Gilks made a decent save, then a corner got nodded wide, but it felt like they were going to keep their side of my prediction. We weren't bad, not by a long shot, but this is one of the best teams in League Two we're talking about and they were always going to offer a threat.

That's where our hard work earns us points. As Ian Holloway later said on the Quest show, we make the hard work look easy and I think that was never more evident than yesterday. We defended like our lives depended on it, never desperate or last-ditch though. We covered the ground we needed to, broke up play and ensured balls into wide areas were always tracked.

Tom Pett and Mark O'Hara were nothing short of sensational, trying to upset the rhythm of MK's attack and spring something of our own. Big John had a tough role once more, but he does it well too. All over the pitch we were working hard to combat them in the first 15.

When we did get away, I felt they panicked a little. Harry Anderson was felled every time he got on the ball, but it gave us opportunities to deliver set pieces. Eardley delivered the ammunition and after one aborted attempt we finally got an effort cleared off the line. Jason Shackell's effort causing the trouble.

This is where the atmosphere played a big part. Their efforts, in the main, were met with a muted applause. Maybe it's because of how spread out they were, but when we had a chance it seemed the stadium lifted. As the noise cranked up, so did we. John Akinde was rather cynically fouled and our quick free kick routine once again almost brought something.

It wasn't a classic at this point, let's be honest. Neither side were bad, but it wasn't end to end. Gilks had another save to make from David Wheeler, but it was what I'd best describe as a measured approach from both sides. Neither wanted to go hell for leather and lose it, neither wanted to give the other a chink to exploit.

Just after the hour mark, Ryan Harley gave us something to exploit. Following a smart quick throw, he fouled Shay McCartan in the area and the ref had no hesitation in pointing to the spot. Was it a penalty? I've seen them not given, normally whenever it's Bruno who is fouled, but I know had it not be awarded we'd be unhappy. It was a foul, it was in the area and for me, it is a penalty.

You know what happens next. John Akinde, that big, beautiful bugger strolls up and looks as calm as Mr Calm from Calmchester and puts the ball into the back of the net. Cue delirium in the away end.

On the balance of play, a draw would have been fair at this point. MK Dons are no slouches and it was harsh on them to be 1-0 down, but it was also testament to our incredible hard work. How often have we moaned about a lack of options at a throw? How often have we taken the time at a throw in to slow the pace of the game down? Rarely do we take a quick restart like that and yet when the opportunity arose, our players adapted quickly to it.

After that MK looked to be winded and Harry caused havoc with a cross that the veteran Dean Lewington hacked clear. Jason Shackell had some similar defending to do before the first half ended though as Tisdale's men regained their shape. By the time the ref called a halt on the first half it seemed to have been a breathless, end to end encounter without any real end to end action. Each team had two shots on target and one-off, yet it felt as though we'd be thoroughly entertained.

I confidently predicted that the second half would remain 0-0 and we'd take all three points. I told everyone that in the drinking area at half time, because I'd seen all I needed to from the Imps. In terms of attacking threat, I felt we were unlikely to carve them open, but the same applied the other way around, These two sides were both stoic and determined in defence and if one was to score, it would take something remarkable.

If 5,600 fans turning up all likely to be content had given us a great atmosphere in the first half, the same number suddenly believing a win was on the cards ramped it up even more. I've been to a lot of away games, some where much has been a stake but I've never known anything like that yesterday. That number is usually associated with big cup games, but for a league game in early April, it was utterly ridiculous.

The game didn't surprise me in the second period either, but I spent as much time looking up at the clock as I did the pitch. It seemed to take an eternity for the minutes to count down and every half chance for them had me wondering if we were going to have that 'draw that feels like a defeat' syndrome on the way home.

That said, when we did come forward there was a slight feeling we could cap the afternoon off nicely. John Akinde was excellent once again, putting in a huge shift and almost giving us that two-goal lead on 51 minutes. That was six minutes into the second half and it felt like we'd been playing 60.

In September against anyone, a match is just the early building blocks of a full season, but this was different. We know what's needed now, we know exactly how close we are. This fixture in particular has always been the one that stood out as key, it was always likely to be pivotal, but leading 1-0 as we were made it even worse. Did I feel as focused as at Turk Moor? Yes, I think so. The result here didn't just matter as a standalone win, it mattered in context of a whole season. It wasn't an 'all comes down to this' moment but it was a game that you knew was the most important we'll play all season.

If it was a game of poker, MK blinked first by bringing on big Chuks Aneke for David Wheeler. They had to chase the game and we know that when that happens, we're at our best. When teams have to come at us, we deliver. Our 'problem', if you can have such a thing when you're eleven points clear, has always been breaking down two banks of four. MK couldn't settle and that played into our hands.

They did play their role well though, with both Agard and Aneke on the pitch they had much more threat going forward. Nothing truly looked like going in, but they were the better side for a good period. Aneke had given their attack a lift and if they were going to get back into the game, this was the phase to do it. Instead our excellent back four remained calm and when needed, Matt Gilks took command.

The little coming together in front of the dugout on 64 minutes finally gave the game some passion, rather than the tactical battle it had been. Big John picked up a yellow card, as did one of their lads, but the game finally had the needle to go with the size of the occasion. Fire up our players and they only become stronger.

It might be an unpopular decision, but I thought MK were the better side in the second half. We sat back, soaking up their pressure like a sponge, but not really offering much of our own. They came through the middle, from the left and from the right and couldn't ever get through the brick wall we've built our successful season on. With ten minutes to go they seemed to run out of ideas and we got our spell.

A few corners here and a deflected effort there signalled the end of the encounter, surely? MK looked tired, finally realising they were going to concede the match. We stood firm, dead on our feet having given everything we had stopping them having anything clear-cut. The board came up signalling five minutes and after what seemed like a week, the clock showed 90 minutes. We were surely home and hosed.

Enter Chuks Aneke. Enter Matt Gilks. Cue the defining moments of our enter season.

A quality delivery into our area would usually have been gobbled up by Bozzy or Shacks, but this one time it wasn't. This one time the ball found the head of Aneke and the big striker got a good header at goal. It wasn't unlike one of Bury's goals in our 3-3 draw and even from the other end of the field my heart sank as he rose. Surely, this was 1-1, the draw that would feel like a defeat.

Matt Gilks, positioned centrally, had little time to react. Good keepers do it instinctively though, they make the right shape and jump as an inbuilt reaction without thinking. That's what the he did, parrying it not back to Aneke, but with such force it bounced off their lad for a goal kick. It was one of those saves every bit as good as a goal. I grabbed my phone to Tweet something along the lines of 'If Matt Gilks calls round mine tonight, he can have whatever beer is in the fridge."

I hadn't typed the word fridge before all hell broke loose. I'd anticipated a slow, protracted goal kick and some game management from our boys. Instead, we got the second goal. It was fitting that Akinde, so often maligned as not being a poacher, provided a superb pass to Bruno Andrade. It was typical Akinde, big and bullish with energy left in the tank despite a gruelling ninety minutes. Bruno, as energetic as the first minute, did what we know he's capable of. He picked it up, went this way and that before finishing with aplomb.

Game over.

In those moments, the ones that you know will stay with you forever, I don't go mad. I can't. I feel that to truly enjoy the scenes, to absolutely get out of them what I need to make the memories everlasting, I watch. Sure, I hug my Dad tight, sure I celebrate a bit too, but I spend a few seconds turning on the spot and watching the people around me. Some, I know. Some are strangers to me. Yet that collective joy, that one moment where anything and everything else doesn't matter, they feel spiritual to me. I'm getting goose bumps writing it now.

I had a tear in my eye, that's the truth. I didn't cry, that'll be reserved for the next couple of weeks, but I had that special feeling in me. That moment, from Gilks' save to Bruno's finish, will be talked about just as much as Nathan at Ipswich or Terry Hawkridge against Macclesfield. It wasn't just special, it was the very definition of ecstasy.

It wasn't the moment we won the title, but it was the moment I knew the title was won.

I'm going to produce another article about the away day from morning to night time, so for now this will be the end of the article. I've dealt with the game, an engrossing encounter that summed up the reasons we're top of the table. I've said it before we've not been the best at going forward and at time we've not even been the best defensively, but we have been the best team this season. We succeed on work ethic, belief and attitude.

We will win the League Two title, our third trophy in as many seasons. We are on the cusp of a new era, one that beckons competitive third-tier football for the first time since I started watching. We are on the edge of a completely unknown adventure, one that will test us as fans and the club as a whole. it's going to be new ground and I feel honoured and privileged that my club is having this journey. It's what I used to dream about as a kid, it's what I saw happen to other clubs, making me feel jealous.

Now, it's happening to us. Now, the dreams come whilst we're awake. This is our time and thanks to yesterday's win, I can enjoy the final five matches of the season. Never too high?

Balls to that.

Imps on Tour – MK Dons
April 7, 2019

I've not done many tour diaries this season, not due to a lack of trips but just because I've always been pushed for time.

Shane's Rustic Minibus has made a few trips this season and as always, the fun never stops. Port Vale turned out to be one of the best, but after only seeing us win away once last season, I've only seen us fail to win once this time out. I hoped that in making what could be the penultimate trip of the season, we'd be a good luck charm.

Shane's minibus tours are unique in that you never quite know what sort of bus is going to turn up. The last couple of trips have been in a seven seater, rust on the side but heated at least. Last season I'd always take a coat for the journey home as I knew it'd be colder in the bus than naked in the Arctic circle.

We've always congregated for breakfast in Wragby, although my preference of the Corn Dolly does cause a few arguments. I'm not sure why, they serve nice, thick bacon. There was a vote before on the Facebook messenger group but, like Brexit, I was going to do what I wanted anyway.

We've seen a huge number of different people come through the bus, but as a new, nine seater pulled into Wragby market place, the group was fairly familiar. I say 'new', it was new to Shane, but not new in any other sense. The interior roof carpeting hung down in places and there was a cam belt on the floor in the back, which could have caused others to worry. If there's one thing I can say about Shane's tours, you know the bus will get you there and back. Slowly, uncomfortably, but you'll get there.

My dad and I were the first to hit the café, followed by Chris and Ryan / Bryan. Shane was soon to follow before the Market Rasen contingent rocked up, usually consisting of Neil and Riegan, but added to by Shaun and his daughter Charlie. That was the group that took to the road, aged between 18 and 65 and certainly a broad spectrum of views and opinion.

Obviously, as drinking on a mini bus is not allowed, we didn't but if we had, Neil would surely have cracked open the first can as we entered Bardney. yeah, you heard that right, Bardney.

Shane decided the quickest route from Wragby to Milton Keynes was via Bardney, Navenby, Waddington, Ancaster and Grantham. I respectfully argue it wasn't and for a short while I wondered if we were the subject of a bold kidnap attempt. We weren't and eventually we hit the A1 services which many felt would be packed with Imps.

It wasn't, because most people would have gone a different way, or as I like to call it 'the right way'.

MK isn't a long drive but in a minibus where smoking out of a partially open window is allowed, it bloody well feels it. Still, it's a good crack with a group of people I probably wouldn't normally get a chance to socialise with. Neil Carlton is one 'football friend' who has made an impression on me in the last year or so; he's one of those fans who I now consider a friend, purely from bumping into him on match day. His long-suffering son Riegan sometimes has to keep him in check later in the day of course, but two nicer blokes you wouldn't find. Unless you met me and my Dad....

Anyway, after what should have been two-and-a-half hours but seemed like eight, we arrived in the concrete jungle of Milton Keynes. I knew a bit about the ground and surrounding area thanks to my trip there earlier in the season and I'd hoped to get an authentic pint in like-minded surroundings, we'd end up meeting Andy's Fun Bus in Newport Pagnell. We didn't, Shane wanted to get parked and decided to chance it at the ground.

Once we'd (predictably) been turned away it seemed like a mile drive to the outskirts of town and a nondescript industrial area for the day's parking. In truth, with 15,000 fans going to the game, it was actually quite easy.

We cut through an underpass on foot and a homeless guy sat on a sheet looking for a few coins. I didn't have any, but instead of actually asking he said; 'Bloody hell, I hope you lot locked the gates to Lincoln before you all left, there are thousands of you'. That felt great. Football is tribal, almost like warfare and here we were invading a new territory. For a random local to make that sort of comment solidified that good feeling about our support.

The walk back took about ten minutes, but plans to meet Dave in Wetherspoons collapsed when we heard they were turning people away.

That's how a bunch of football fans found themselves in TGI Friday's drinking before a game. It seems, on the face of it, the most inauthentic experience you could possible have. Going to watch a team widely regarded as a franchise by so-called proper fans, drinking in a faceless restaurant chain before a game. I imagine fans up and down the country drinking in the faceless Wetherspoons chains would have turned their noses up.

To many yesterday was very much 'plastic against plastic'. We're Lincoln City, once struggling to get 3,000 for a home game but now taking 5,600 away. They're MK Dons, a club formed by ripping (an ailing) club from its home and relocating to a new town to force a new identity. Yet here we were, top against second and about to serve up the most interesting game of the afternoon. Odd that.

Stadium MK has clearly been designed with Premier League football in mind. It's a cracking venue in truth. Some might say soulless, as I'll touch on in a minute, but there's a certain appeal to something that just works. The queues to get in were minimal, the stewards were friendly and helpful and behind the stands the concourse was accessible and service was quick. The little pockets of bars worked well too, so you could enjoy a drink before kick off and pick from a decent selection too.

It seemed that everywhere you went, staff were pleased to see us. It felt welcoming, perhaps something we shouldn't encourage at Sincil Bank, I don't know. Back in the day, you couldn't get beer in the ground and in some places this season the selection of food has made a student's fridge look bountiful. I didn't get any food yesterday but I'm told that, like everything else, it was good.

Getting into the stand was easy too, so after me and Dad had quaffed a few beers and chatted to the usual faces, we were seated within seconds. The row and seat numbers weren't all that clear, but if that's the only thing I can possibly think to pick on then surely it wasn't a bad afternoon? The seats were a good size, not that I sat on it for long, and the leg room was excellent too. I think back to my season ticket space at the Bank, practically sat on the knee of the guy next to me and squeezed in like tuna in a can, it did make me envious.

What did not make me envious was the atmosphere. The trouble is right now, Stadium MK is too big for MK Dons. As impressive as it might be, they would be better served with a Rotherham-style stadium. 12,000 seats might have meant fans missing out, but from their point of view it would feel tighter, maybe even angrier. The clapper things they gave away were an irritant and the cries of 'you're only here for the Nando's' would have embarrassed me if I had been a home fan.

I'm not against club's trying to fill their stadiums. When Notts County gave tickets away you didn't see me giving them stick for it, same with Mansfield. However, calling us plastic because out fans turn up in numbers when we're challenging at the top is a bit rich when 3,000 of your own supporters are only there for a chicken dinner. We're all missing the point when we give each other stick for going to watch the other club; if you're in a stadium watching football and not at home on your sofa, you deserve some respect. Whether it's chicken, hammers or table-topping football that drives you to a stadium it doesn't matter.

A few of our party were dotted around the stadium, so it was Neil, Riegan, me, Dad and Shane in the first half. I've never sung as much, nor as loud. Maybe it was the mix of vodka and lemonade as well as a few cans of Carling, but I really felt it yesterday. I thought the whole Imps' support had an energy and belief. This was our generation's 'Fulham 83'. There was no red card though and the spirited performance brought results.

I've already covered the game, but to hear us vocal throughout, not just around the goal, was excellent. I've heard some MK fans saying they could only hear us after the second goal, perhaps if those bloody clapper things hadn't affected their hearing, they might have heard a bit more. To be fair, their fans tried but they were too spread out and sporadic. We were all in one place, truly 'Imps as one'. Was it the best support I've been involved in on an away trip? Maybe so. I didn't get to Coventry last year and I do think it topped Everton for sheer volume and belief.

John's goal did stop an argument between a couple of fans close to me, I understand someone had criticised Akinde and been taken to task. It wasn't nice to see, but with John scoring whilst the argument raged on, he answered a critic he didn't even know he had. With that a plume of red smoke appeared behind me, something that will undoubtedly earn the club a fine but that I can't say didn't add to the atmosphere.

The ease with which we could get a beer at half time was impressive too. Big double doors opened into a smoking area for those who enjoy a cancer stick, but it allowed for conversation too. I caught up with a few friends again and everything just felt right. It felt like a celebration, although obviously winning wasn't assured. I've said already at 1-0 I never thought we'd lose the game. After all, we've never lost after taking the lead, but we've only lost four times in the league anyway!

By the time we got back to our seats for the second half, Shaun and Charlie had joined us. Such was the room in front of the seats that six went into four very easily and we didn't feel squashed. It did mean I stood right behind my dad, echoing how he used to stand behind me as a kid. Football is as much about the people you go with and the experiences you have as it is winning or losing and I'm so lucky that I'm enjoying the best of times with the man who made me the fan I am today. He's been struggling a lot recently with a bad shoulder, but you wouldn't have known yesterday.

The minutes ticked away and not once did the noise level drop. I can't say I've ever sung for 90 minutes, but I didn't miss one word of one song. I'm told the iFollow feed panned around the ground at one point and settled on me, arms aloft belting out whatever tune we were singing at the time. I'm often pensive at games, keen to study what happens for the writing, not always invested in the moment.

I was certainly invested in a moment towards the end. After Matt Gilks' save I felt I wanted to tweet about him and was busy on my phone, maybe hoping to eat up a minute of that stoppage time, when I heard someone say 'go on John' next to me. I looked up as Bruno curled the ball home and everything went mental. I stood, surveyed the action with a real sense of being there at the right time. That moment will be talked about as much as Thommo's sending off at Fulham, as much as Phil brown's winner against Wycombe in '88, or Nathan Arnold's goals against Ipswich. It's a real 'I was there moment' and you know what? half of Lincoln was.

I remember coming out of Burnley and hugging random people as I did and I felt a similar ambience as we streamed out of the ground. I did finally see Dave, queuing up for a wee as he does half his life. I caught up with Warrs (Matt) too, the guy who will be taking Dave's seat next to me next season. Ric Stephens was outside, a lad I seem to know far better on social media than I do in the flesh but again, when we met up its as if all the computer based stuff was us sitting around a table in a pub chewing the fat. I even gave Chris Ashton a hug, a man who has been as much a part of Lincoln City as anyone during his lifetime.

Predictably, it took us hours to get home. The minibus was blocked in a car park that seemed to empty slower than Sincil Bank after a game. We all sat around, Chris lamenting the fact his singing section ticket had turned into a non-singing section somehow. No idea how of course, nor how my non-singing section one (that I retained) got me in behind the goal. Anyway....

We left the ground at 5pm and it was 8pm before we hit Peterborough services. by then one or two of our party, mentioning no names, were a bit worse for wear. Ryan slept, Chris and Charlie smoked and Neil drank. This time when we stopped we did see some familiar faces and had a bit of a sing outside McDonalds. There were a few Oldham fans in, on their way back from Colchester and they wished us well. A few of them just stood around with their coats zipped up, not quite sure what to make of the 6ft 5in skinhead lolling about with a half-eaten burger in one hand and a can of beer in the other.

That was that. We hit Wragby at 9pm, my lift to Louth was already waiting and I was soundly asleep before the clock struck ten. When I dreamed, it was of writing up the day.

When I woke, with clarity and sobriety on my side at last, I realised I'd witnessed the day that Lincoln City FC showed why they were heading to League One and I'd done it with a great group of friends and, perhaps most important of all, with my Dad.

The Final Comedown; Waiting for Saturday
April 9, 2019

This week feels a little strange if I'm honest. The highs of the weekend have begun to wear off and like any high, there's a comedown to suffer.

It's not the worst I've ever had, coming down from a 2-0 win against your main rivals to find you're 11 points clear with five games to play, but it's a comedown, nonetheless. The superlatives poured over the side from the weekend have drained away and it's back to the hard work.

There's a feeling amongst the fans that this is job done. I feel it in my bones. Four points to secure the title? No problem. One thing we've been good at is drawing at home and that's when we've been judged to be off form. Four points from five games is the sort of return a relegated side will get.

We're not that. We're the champions elect. We know in our heart of hearts that it's all but secure and that when we go to Carlisle next Saturday, we could wrap up promotion. Are we getting ahead of ourselves? The table suggests not, but then until it's mathematically safe there's always the fear.

The fear... always lurking...

The win on Saturday banished the fear somewhat. It began the day travelling with me, every so often tapping me on the shoulder and whispering, 'what if'. Luckily, drinking vodka and lemonade quietens it down a bit, not quite as much as a last-minute Bruno Andrade goal though.

This week it's been hiding under the bed, only creeping out in those moments between consciousness and sleep, just reminding me it isn't won yet. All these words I'm writing could come back to haunt me. I finished off the fanzine yesterday and the opening gambit referenced the fact we 'should' have won the title by the time you read it.

Shoulda. Woulda. Coulda.

That's why this week is an odd one. It looks to be in the bag, but there's still work to do. It reminds me of the final day of the month at my old job. We had a sales target to meet and usually, by the last Saturday, we'd met it. I'd called my boss with the figure, he'd dialled it in to his boss and all that remained was to get the last kitchen out and sweep the floors.

What if the last kitchen cancelled unexpectedly? What if some joker tried to bring a ten grand kitchen back? What if in sweeping the floors I found a delivery note I thought had gone still sat there waiting to be processed?

What if.

It never happened by the way, but the fear was always there. Even when I sent the officer joker out for a McDonald's breakfast and we sat around throwing rolled up post-it notes at each other, the fear was there. Right up until midday when the clock struck, the computers closed down and the result was in the bag.

The not knowing is tough too. We could win the title this weekend, but my partner wants to go out for dinner in the evening. It's booked for 7pm, meaning I'd need to be back for 6pm. Would I really want to leave the ground dead on five if we've won the title? Really?

So, we rebook the meal. Then again, we might not win it Saturday and then I'll be in trouble for our steak not arriving until 8.30pm.

We might not win it at all (says the fear).

That means Good Friday away at Carlisle looks favourable, but I'd made plans months ago. I tried to cancel them, and rather shamelessly because of the title potential. I couldn't make the trip to Cumbria under usual circumstances, not financially nor logistically. Having been to MK and recent home matches, budgets only go so far. However, if we can tie up the league…..

Then there's Tranmere at home, a fitting fixture to do it at. They've followed us up and it fits the pattern. Last year we were the promoted team and we watched Accrington lift the title, so they could come up and watch us do the same. So many possibilities, so much to think about.

The more you think about it though, the more the fear creeps in. Football should always teach you to never be complacent, but is 11 points clear with 15 to play for complacent?

Yes, it's complacent… nothing is in the bag yet….

NewsNow has been quiet for the last 24 hours or so, just the EFL Awards to talk about. The speculation has been quashed by the weekend's results; we're all sat waiting to see exactly what happens. It's the calm before the storm, the intake of breath before the big cheer. It' so still and quiet, you know something big is about to happen.

The League Two title race is flatlining, its time is nearly up. However, until the switch is flicked, until Big John stroke homes another penalty or Bruno smashes a curling effort from outside the box, we're still catchable. I'd say the waiting is worse than anything but, having witnessed some seasons ended before Christmas and others only alive at this time because the trapdoor is open, this is the type of waiting I can handle.

If only the fear would stay locked away for a couple of days. Where's my vodka?

The Imps Are Going Up
April 13, 2019

Long before George Lloyd nodded a deserved equaliser for Cheltenham this afternoon, a song rang out across Sincil Bank.

We've heard it ten thousand times before; "The Imps are going up, the Imps are going up, and now you're gonna believe us..." This time was different though wasn't it? Because this time it wasn't wishful thinking. This time it wasn't us pushing for the top seven, or just winning a game of football prompting the chant.

This time, we really are going up the Football League.

There was a surreal feeling to that second half, a feeling of inevitability encrusted with drippings of 'the fear'. Let us be entirely honest, if we had failed to rubber-stamp League One football it would have been incredibly disappointing. Especially after a first half which we deservedly led, and with other results going our way.

This wasn't about one game though, this was about a whole season. This was the culmination of a journey, or at least the penultimate stage of a journey.

I'll do my usual piece tomorrow, tonight for me looks pretty much like a steak dinner in Belchford followed by Beechams and a long night's sleep, but my 100% killer man flu does feel a little less serious in the cold hard light of League One football.

There's still work to do, but for a few moments at the end of the game we got that buzz, the sneaky little pleasure that's dogged the Cowley's reign at Lincoln City. I'd worked out we were up on the final whistle, as had a few of the lads around me, but it still had to be confirmed. Even though I knew, it didn't seem real.

Then Alan Long, the voice of Lincoln City, made it final. Breaking news; Lincoln City are promoted to League One.

Even though I knew, even though it's been inevitable since Bruno's goal last weekend, even though deep down I've believed it since Northampton away, it still felt emotional to hear it. It wasn't a belief anymore, it was real.

Ipswich. Bolton. At least two of Sunderland, Portsmouth, Charlton or Barnsley. All opponents next season, all playing at the same level as my club, as OUR club.

'Three years ago, who would have thought...' is an easily rolled out rhetoric. It'll form the headlines and opinion pieces across the Football League this weekend. Three years ago, we drew 2-2 at Southport on route to finishing in the middle of the National League pack. Now, we're heading to Portman Road on level terms. Fiction writers wouldn't dare be so bold as to pen a story as incredible as ours.

The title is still to be won, but it will be. Right now though, that's not in my mind. Right now, all I can hear is Alan Long's voice telling me we're playing League One football next season and I can see the watery glint in my Dad's eye as he hears it too. I know he was thinking about his Dad, who passed away 27 years ago this weekend.

League One football, coming to Sincil Bank. As inevitable as it's been for a while, it still barely feels real. It is though. The Imps are going up and you don't just have to believe us; it's fact.

Rubber Stamped – Imps 1-1 Cheltenham
April 14, 2019

I've been sat, staring out of my window wondering how to start this piece. Where do you possibly begin?

Yesterday felt a bit like Christmas as a kid. You ask for a bike, way back in the summer. For the rest of the year, you think you're getting a bike. You're not told you're definitely getting one and every so often you wonder if perhaps your parents might have forgotten and you'll get clothes or something instead.

Then, on Christmas morning, you see a bike shaped gift near the tree. Even then you wonder, is it something else? Is it a bike-shaped chocolate, or some other cruel joke being played by your parents? Finally, after all the anticipation, you unwrap a bike and even though you knew all along, you still cry your eyes out with joy.

Yesterday, we got our bike.

The weekend started badly for me. After being on the radio with Rob Makepeace, I went home and felt like I'd had the stuffing kicked out of me. I slept from 8pm until 11.30am, and by slept I mean tossed, turned, sweated, coughed and dreamed of going up. It was an uncomfortable night punctuated by my partner saying things like 'are you sure you should go tomorrow?'. She knew that was futile.

Even my Dad text and said; 'if you're that bad maybe you shouldn't go'. Give over.

A message from Val, the final proof reader of my book, sparked me into life. She's finished and now all that's needed is for me to put it together and get promoting. It felt quite important to have the story finally complete on this day, almost prophetic.

I was much later into town than usual, forced into paying £8.50 for parking and even then felt badly, but not long after arriving at the ground, I began to forget. There was an air of something, not particularly anticipation, nor expectation, but a subdued excitement maybe. The inevitable is, by definition, always going to happen, but never have we been arrogant about it. Waiting for it isn't easy and I sensed people were supressing their delight. The excellent tunes being played by the Gazelles helped settled a few pre-match nerves, that's for sure.

Even yesterday, surrounded by the usual suspects in the fan zone, there was no pre-empting the events that followed. I don't usually name the people I chat to before the game, but yesterday there was a steady stream of faces that have punctuated my Imps support this season. Skip this bit if you're not interested and sorry if I miss anyone out, but I caught up with Wayne and Fred Raithby, Jimmy Atkin and James Cairns, Terry Ramm, Gareth Virgo, Ben and Rachel Ward, 'Tang' as I know him on Twitter, Bubs, Shaun and Charlie, Chris Cawthorn, obviously Dad and Mo, Andy Pearson, a chap who we see home and away in the smoking area and have done for years who I believe is called Andrew who looks a bit like Smithers from the Simpsons and a host of other people I class as good friends and will feel bad that I've missed out of the list. We all felt the same.

It was a perfect day for football and the weather presented a nice metaphor too. In the sunshine, it was warm and summer-like, but as soon as you stepped into the shade it was bitterly cold. Get the result we needed and it would be party in the sun. Fail, and even though we'd still be favourites the last knockings of winter would pay us another visit.

I'm always looking for patterns in football, always. When we changed ends I noted it was the same set up as when we beat Wycombe in '88 and Macclesfield in '17. Cheltenham were the side we watched lift the National League title in the last game 'BC' (before Cowley) and something about them being visitors again caught me too.

Even the appearance of Mr Lincoln City, the legend that is Grant Brown, felt important. He played the day we last earned the right to compete in the third-tier and as he took the deserved applause and his place in the Hall of Fame, thoughts inevitably went back to that day against Brighton. The scene was set.

The trouble with football is you can't predetermined the outcome of a game, unless you're Delroy Facey of course. Cheltenham, literally the supporting cast, the uncredited walk-on part in the blockbuster of our promotion, hadn't read the script. All the people predicting 3-0 (Dad, as always) or a walkover were grossly under-estimating the excellent job Michael Duff is doing there. even without Luke Varney, they weren't going to roll over and have their belly tickled.

What we needed was an early goal. Against Macclesfield in 2017 we made it exciting by conceding ourselves, but we came out of the blocks looking like a side who wanted it. Cheltenham were organised, efficient and clearly not there to be hammered, but they didn't have a great amount in the final third. In the other areas of the pitch though they looked like a good work in progress team.

I thought big John had a real purpose about him. He got a ball across the area for Bruno, he had a half-volley of his own and put a header over all in the first 15 minutes. Everyone was hungry for it, but him and Tom Pett grabbed me in the first quarter of an hour. Pett, seemingly a lightweight winger when he joined last season, has morphed into an excellent box-to-box midfielder with nice control and a decent tackle. It's remarkable what our coaching team see in some players.

Just after the 15 minute mark, it happened. Shay McCartan, never one to bag an easy goal, cut inside from the left and seemingly missed his cue to lay the ball off for a teammate. He had other ideas though and on an afternoon where his parent club all but rubber-stamped their League Two status, he gave us the first glimpse of our promotion.

Shay doesn't score easy goals, but he does score important ones. The second at Swindon for instance, the winner against MK Dons at home, our 6500th and, as it turned out, the one that sent us into League One. It was a worthy effort too, although the keeper might have fancied doing better. It bounced just in front of him and the Imps were 1-0 up.

The chants of 'the Imps are going up' rang out across the stadium and for the first time it felt real. I've believed we're going up since the summer, but as the furore died down and play restarted, it became so much closer. We'd peeled the first bits of paper from that Christmas present and revealed

We've sung about promotion for years. Under Keith the songs rang out loud and proud, even back under Murph the second time, under Thommo and of course, John Beck. I've sung 'the Imps are going up' at times when in fact, we haven't gone up and whoever we've been singing at would be best served not believing us. Yesterday, they'd better believe us.

For the rest of the first half we gave the sort of performance I expected. It was methodical, probing for chances and getting a few, none really clear-cut. Neal Eardley had a free kick just over, John dragged an effort wide and yet the opposition never crumbled. It wasn't domination on our part, they were playing neat football outside the final third, but if one team was going to extend the lead it was us.

Mark O'Hara was excellent in that opening period. For a big lad he moves with real grace, but when called upon he sticks his head in too. Of all the loan players we currently have, Rowe included, I want to see O'Hara sign for us the most. Tall central midfielders are a rarity, especially ones whose height isn't their gimmick. You can see why he played top flight football in Scotland and why given a chance, he'll be a big asset to us next season.

The other notable performance for me was Bozzy. If he doesn't win Player of the Year I'll be shocked. He's just so consistent, any balls in the air seemed to be gobbled up. he doesn't even have to jump half the time, he takes a step back, gives the forward a nudge and has a clear header.

Bruno was clearly struggling though. I guess the injections and pain threshold has been breached, although he tried to get on the ball it wasn't easy. The visitors had done their homework and ensured there was no space to exploit behind and with him being at 75%, there was none of the unpredictable trickery we're used to seeing. It's not a criticism, but maybe now promotion is sealed he'll get a game or so to recuperate properly.

That was the first half. All around during the break we checked the scores, but did it really matter? If we won, we'd be up. The others can do what they liked, although I did still want to see MK Dons and Mansfield lose. Not quite sure why I'm so keen on Bury to join us, nor Tranmere, but they'd be my picks, along with Exeter in the play-offs.

If we thought the second half as to be a formality, we were wrong. I don't think we were terrible after the break, but it just didn't click. Let's give credit where it's due, the opposition had made it tough in the first half, but they made it even tougher in the second. I never thought they'd score, they didn't look to have anything up front at all, but you could see they were well-drilled.

Things started to go awry when Shay was booked for simulation or, as it should be called, cheating. That's what a dive is, it's cheating. In this instance I think the referee was harsh, there wasn't any need to dive and I don't think he did. When the ball fell to Harry, had he bagged I don't think the ref would have blown for the dive, but with us missing it he did. I've got to say though I thought the man in the middle was excellent again and that was perhaps the only decision I disagreed with from my vantage point.

Minutes later, Shay was lucky not to get a second yellow with a late challenge in the middle of the park. I thought it might be time to take him off after that, he'd had a decent game but it looked like a case of 'head's gone'.

Sometime after that I witnessed a piece of so-called 'shithousery' that I'm still stuck in two minds about. Ben Tozer took a water bottle from the side of the pitch and had a swig. John went over and indicated he'd like a drink too, so Tozer tipped all of the water onto the floor and chucked the bottle away. It made me angry, but John simply got another bottle, drank from it and then either tipped water on Tozer or threw the bottle at him. What I didn't like was Tozer then asking the linesman if he'd seen it.

I'm partly in admiration of the levels he went to with tipping the water out and if it were Rheady who'd done it we would likely have cheered, but to try to get John punished afterwards was a bit off. I decided in the end Tozer was an arsehole, just for the afters.

Cheltenham got their goal not long after (I think, you might pull me up on timelines here). It'd been coming if we're honest, a lacklustre second half had produced little for either side and sub George Lloyd bagged with their only effort of note on target. I immediately went to my phone and did the maths, confidently telling everyone we'd still be up no matter what. I wasn't 100% sure, but I sounded convincing as my eyes desperately searched for Chris Wray, maths teacher and cartoonist, who would surely have bene able to confirm.

After their goal they were happy with a point I think. We had a couple of chances, Danny Rowe did everything right with an effort that flashed wide and Big John had another effort saved as well. In the 90th minute, I thought the fairy tale had been written. Matt Rhead, on as a sub, crashed an effort at goal and knowing how the other results looked, had it gone in we'd have virtually been champions. How fitting would it have been for the big man to put us in League One?

As it was he couldn't manage it. The time began to drain away and John was announced as Man of the Match. He'd had a good game, granted, but Bozzy and O'Hara had too. Harry Anderson was another who deserves a mention, he never stopped running and has truly evolved into a significant player for us this season.

Five minutes of injury time found itself sucked into a vacuum of uncertainty. My Dad asked with around a minute to go if we were getting off, knowing I had a dinner date booked. He, like 90% of the stadium, thought a draw wasn't good enough. I was still convinced as the whistle blew that we'd done it, but as everyone checked their phones, the signal strength dipped and I got nothing. I moved by the exit, climbed up a couple of rows and waited.

As fans poured out I think a few got wind of the fact it might be a premature exit and began to try to get back in. The area in front of me became very busy, people asking each other if we were up, confused in a good way. I wasn't confident enough then to say yes, so we found ourselves watching the pitch, waiting on the official word. That really did feel like '98, when we needed confirmation of Orient and Torquay after we'd beaten Brighton. That day, without mobile phones, good 'ol boys on radios had relayed the information. Given my 4G signal, a wireless might have been better in 2019.

Then, after the sort of pause that X-Factor results shows would have been proud of, Alan said those magic words. Lincoln City are promoted, or words to that effect. I can't recall them specifically, because I was hugging my old man and choking back a little tear. We'd known it for a week or so, believed it for a season or so but when it actually happened, when that last bit of paper came off to reveal a brand, spanking new bike, it became fact.

Lincoln City will be a League One club next season.

It was amusing seeing the 'promoted' board turned around and the flags coming out quickly. I wonder if there is another box at the ground with 'Champions 2018/19' on them that got hurriedly put back in the dressing room for another day? It doesn't matter, our boys celebrated promotion with gusto, people congratulated each other and the phone went into overdrive. Ipswich, Bolton and the like; we're coming for you.

It was only walking out of the ground it all began to feel a little bizarre as well. It was as if we were celebrating winning silver at the Olympics, when we are still in the running for gold. All the champagne, flags and cheers were great and I wouldn't change it for the world, but we'll be doing the same over the Bank Holiday weekend, be it at the Bank or Brunton Park. We will win the League Two title and these players will cement their place in history. It's bizarre to think all of yesterdays adulation and joy was just a precursor to the bigger achievement of finishing top. It felt very un-Cowley like to celebrate when there's still work to be done.

Mind you, for everyone connected with the club, the initial aim has now been completed. Anyone would have taken third at the beginning of the season, the aim was top three. I doubt it was ever first, not officially. Yes, we want to win the league and always have, but the target was promotion. The title, well that's the cherry on the cake, that's finding out the bike you've just unwrapped has got a gel seat, 15 more gears than you thought and a bell that plays 'we are going up' when you ring it.

Despite there still being work to do, despite this being half of the job completed, it didn't dampen the joy and rightly so. It's easy to compare to three or four years ago and say look how far we've come, but it's also incredible at the same time. We've gone from trips to Altrincham, Hayes and Yeading and Welling, to hosting Ipswich and maybe Sunderland, Portsmouth or Bolton.

Let's not forget as well that we're now 19 unbeaten in the league, a club record that's fallen under Danny and Nicky, or should we say another club record. We're also the first team in the Football League to earn promotion, a wonderful achievement for everyone from the management and players to the fans who have travelled all over the country.

Yesterday might not have been the main event, it might not have been the game that won us the title, but it is still one we'll always remember. Not for the performance, not for the result, but for the moment Alan Long announced over the tannoy that we had been promoted to League One. Money can't buy that feeling, it's why we follow a football club, the Holy Grail that 72 teams started out chasing and only seven achieve without the help of a play-off.

This is our time and it's going to get better before the end of the month. Believe.

I'll end this gushing amble through our promotion confirmation with a message. Granddad; we're finally back where we belong, like you always used to tell me. Lincoln City were, according to you, a Division Three team. I hope you get the Quest highlights up there with Keith, Butch and all of the other Imps not around to enjoy what is absolutely the best time ever to be an Imps fan.

Lincoln City in League One. What a time to be alive.

An Open Letter To Staff & Players Of Lincoln City FC
April 16, 2019

Dear Staff & Players of Lincoln City FC,

My name is Gary, I've been following this football club since the dark days of 1986. Fresh from the tragedy of the Bradford Fire, I came to the club when the focus was, quite rightly, not on football. We suffered successive relegations as a result and lost our Football League status.

After bouncing back, we never became the third-tier club my Granddad believed we should be. He'd remembered the days before Bill Anderson when we were a Third Division North club, then he experienced the fifties and the second tier. You may not know it, but for ten years Bill Anderson kept us in the old Second Division. Sadly, Geoff Hutchinson died on 11th April 1992, never seeing us get back to a level he thought we belonged at.

Throughout our history we've flirted with Division Four, but only in my era have we really become a staple at that level. We had one season in the third-tier, as you'll know from the recent news reports. However, in 1998/99 even the bravest, most optimistic fans could only see us finishing 20th. We didn't by the way, we were relegated after a brave, but futile fight.

Since then I've seen my club almost fold on more than one occasion, I've spent nights laying awake wondering if I'd have a team to support. I've cried at play-off failures, bawled at relegation.

I've shied away from telling workmates who I support and I've despaired as we came close to following Stockport, York, Darlington and Halifax into oblivion.

I never thought we'd play Ipswich as equals, not in my lifetime. I didn't ever think I'd see my club lift a Football League title, something I'm sure you'll wrap up in the next seven days. I never thought we'd go to Wembley and lift a trophy there either. I never thought I would feel not just pride, but an intense joy when someone asks me who I support.

You may know this, you may not but in 2016 I had a serious flirtation with stress and anxiety. My route to becoming well again brought me to the written word and seeing as Lincoln City is all I really know, you became the subject of my ramblings. I've written about the Imps on this site since before Danny and Nicky took over and at first, it was a hobby. The success with which the club have progressed has been eclipsed by my own development and today I am a standalone writer, someone who (hopefully) never has to revisit those dark days of selling building materials and hating my life. I sincerely hope the same can be said about the football club, never must we return to the days when losing at home to Welling was met with an acceptance.

All of the progress and achievement of the recent seasons was capped off this weekend when you confirmed League One football. Three years, two promotions and a Wembley final, that is without a doubt the most successful period in the club's entire history. Think about that for a moment, whether you're a key player like Michael Bostwick or one who hasn't featured as much such as James Wilson. Whatever your role, you're at a club creating history and whatever you go on to achieve, you'll always be a part of this. In years to come this season, these achievements will be talked about around family dinner tables.

Growing up, my Dad and Granddad used to talk about Percy Freeman and John Ward, or Gordon Hobson and Glenn Cockerill. Even the fringe players from those successful eras evoke images of success. That's what you've achieved. In the eyes of thousands of fans, you and your teammates are now the embodiment of success. When I'm 65 and telling my nephew about how good this side were, your names will pop up.

From me personally, a thank you. Thank you to all of you who have helped me, be it with interviews, or just by being bloody brilliant on a Saturday and giving me something to write about and talk about. Thank you for bringing me much closer to my Dad too. We always had football, but with this success there's a stronger bond than ever. When you score, when you win matches I know you're creating personal memories for me and him that will last me a lifetime. There will be a time when I have to go to games without my Dad and although I'll be sad, I know the images in my mind will be travelling back from a 6-2 win at Port Vale, or hugging him as Alan Long announced we're promoted. I know this season will be something we cherish together for as long as our lives go on.

I love this football club, whether it's the bricks and mortar of the ground, the various takes on red and white stripes we model each season or the faces I see every week and have done for years. The spirit at the club might not be all that different to any other, but it's ours. Lincoln City isn't just a sports team, it's a community and a way of life for some. I can't claim to go to every away game, but I've not missed a second be it on the radio, iFollow or at the ground. What you do, matters.

When you win, I win. When you lose, I feel like I lose too. When the club makes a big signing, it boosts my life, it makes me feel better.

You, more than any other group of players and staff in my lifetime, have achieved something remarkable. I'm not detracting from the great work Keith Alexander did, nor Colin Murphy's mission to get us out of the GMVC, but the Cowley era has to be the most successful of our entire existence. The constant drive forwards, the unparalleled success and now a chance to compete at a whole new level. It's exciting, invigorating and I wanted to say thank you.

Thank you from me, still the wide-eyed 7-year-old at heart who watched his heroes beaten 4-1 by Hartlepool in 1986 and fell in love. Thank you from my Dad, who feels closer to his Dad whenever we succeed, despite his passing 27 years ago. Thank you from my partner, who doubtless loves me supporting a team that wins because (and I'm sure she'd echo this) my smile is prettier than my scowl. Thank you from every single on of the readers of my site, and from those fans who don't know or care who I am, but still feel that intense joy when you win matches and reach new heights.

So to Clive, Roger and the board, Liam and the office staff, Terry and the media team, Danny, Nicky and the backroom team and Freck and the rest of the lads, thank you. You've done your club, the city and the supporters proud and will surely continue to do so.

This is a wonderful time to be a Lincoln City fan and although I love the club as much when were winning as when we're losing, it's a damn sight easier when you're top of the pile.

Now go and win us the league.

Gary

The not-so Good Friday: Carlisle 1-0 Imps
April 20, 2019

I didn't write last night, but I had plenty of time. I wasn't one of the 2,000 Imps fans who travelled to Carlisle for the game, sadly. Still, I was angry at us losing and felt perhaps it was best I stayed away from the keyboard.

Previous engagements, including a wedding, work and dog grooming, meant yesterday was a bridge too far for me. Believe me when I say I was in a foul mood up until kick off, wishing I was there on a sunny afternoon, surrounded by friends. that stands, whatever the result in the end.

At the end of what has been an extraordinary week, it seems that Carlisle were in no mood to play patsy. To be fair, Cheltenham weren't last week either, but in a straight out eleven against eleven fixture, I believe we would have got a point yesterday. It wouldn't have been enough as Mansfield turned on the style at Field Mill, but it would have given our fans something to cheer.

I'm going to leap straight in to the contentious incidents. I have watched everything back now (you have to love technology) and the first aspect of the game we have got to talk about is Lee 'bloody' Mason. I've given him a middle name, like the singer Kevin 'bloody' Wilson. The reason? He's a danger.

Let me be very, very clear. I am not blaming him for our defeat out right. That would be crass in the circumstances and would do no favours to either Carlisle or ourselves. Both sides had the same ref, although he did appear to lean one way. He'd missed a couple of tasty challenges before the first Jason Shackell booking, but if that first card is a yellow we all may as well pack up and go home.

The mad five minutes that followed were both Jason Shackell's fault, and Lee Mason. You see, the second challenge is a yellow card. Mason had no choice, he'd already made his bed with the first soft card, so to he couldn't possibly let the next one go. He had to send Shackell off. I think the former Derby man has been one of our key players and he's clearly competitive as his game doesn't change when he's on a yellow.

He shouldn't have 'shoved' the fourth official as some wag from Carlisle put it (it wasn't quite Paulo Di Canio), but he was clearly worked up. Sadly, Lee Mason did have to send him off and that was partly due to his own soft yellow minutes early and majorly due to the fact Jason Shackell gave him no choice.

My major issue comes with virtually everything he did after that moment. His display was erratic, inconsistent and bordering on narcissistic. We thought Mike Dean had a chip on his shoulder at Sincil Bank earlier in the year, but Lee Mason looked as though he finds League Two below his level. Booking Cian Bolger was, to the letter of the law, correct. He did enter the field of play with the express permission of the referee and that's a yellow, but how does that happen? The fourth official keeps the player there and oversees the transaction, so why did he allow Bolger on? It was a bizarre yellow card that seemed to be the result of a misunderstanding by the officials and yet punished the player.

The rest of the first half seemed a bit flat to be honest. Carlisle didn't react quickly to us being a man down and we just wanted to get to half time. I could hear the team talk stuck in my car in Boston. 'Don't be victims, be fighters' and all that. Danny ensured none of his players were victims as they came off too, because knowing Mason he was itching to get that yellow card out of his pocket again; just not for a tackle by a player wearing blue, eh?

I know it sounds bitter and you know why? Because the outcome hurts. We lost our unbeaten run in the second half despite a brave and resilient display. No matter what rhetoric you roll out about 'ten playing better than eleven', unless the eleven are crap, or the ten simply shut up shop, it doesn't happen. We didn't shut up shop, there was still a desire to get forward and yet we defended well. Their goal, when it came, was a hell of a strike. Could Matt Gilks have done better? It's easy to say watching in back isn't it?

I'd be loath to heavily criticise any of our players in the second half because the performance clearly warranted something. They worked incredibly hard, for me (from what I've seen), Harry Anderson perhaps deserved Man of the Match for City. Harry's matured this season but his bullish, direct approach is always useful in away matches when we're under the cosh. John Akinde has to take some praise too, his qualities are accentuated whenever we're down to the bare bones too. He works tirelessly chasing those lost causes and holding balls up to buy the other players time.

What truly rankled me in the second half was the challenges that Lee Mason let go. It was as if in the second he'd resolved not to send anyone off and tried as hard as he could to keep it ten against eleven. On the strength of Jason Shackell's early yellows, we could have had one sent off, them too.

What's odd is how much the defeat pissed me off. We're promoted and, barring a calamity, we'll win the league too. We're going to be playing League One football next season and we're in the best shape off the field of my entire life, yet this result still hurt. People on social media were still having a pop at players, not as much as usual but a bit. It proved to me that no matter what a team does, defeat hurts.

I suppose anyone saying 'it doesn't matter, we're still going up' kinda misses the point. It always matters. 2,000 fans didn't make the trip up there to watch Lee Mason, nor to shrug their shoulders on the way home. We can take solace from the fact we are still going up, but losing our unbeaten record in those circumstances is tough. Eleven men wearing grey and black draw that game at worst, perhaps win it given the questions we'd asked early doors. Instead, the unbeaten run is set back to square one as is the proud record of scoring in every game since failing to score at Colchester.

Today, I'm at a wedding in Washingborough, but part of me will be reflecting on the result yesterday, lamenting Mason's performance and perhaps begrudgingly applauding Carlisle who were able to do what so few have done before. Cambridge didn't beat us with ten men, nor did Northampton and nor did Swindon. They did and they should be given the credit for that, even if the red card was, in my opinion, a little harsh.

There's that awful saying in football; 'we go again'. It winds me right up as the stock response to a defeat but, on Easter Monday, we get another chance. We get another stab at creating the golden moment where the whistle could go and we're crowned champions. We get that glimpse once more of success, that opportunity to pour out our joy and share the moment with our friends at Sincil Bank.

Pull it off and we can forget all about Lee Mason for a few months at least.

League Two Champions
April 22, 2019

This is a quick post. Since the curtain came down on our clash with Tranmere I've found it hard to get in front of a computer.

There's been a bit on talkSPORT, the duties that I neglected at home to be away today and (of course) two episodes of Game of Thrones to catch up on. I've done my bit at home but wanted to get something down on record tonight.

April 22nd. It had to be, didn't it? Two years to the day we returned to the Football League in a blaze of glory, we're champions of League Two. It's been on the cards all season, I called it on the site in my pre-season preview but it still had to happen. The boys have still had 44 gruelling matches, highs and lows which have brought concern, worry and delight.

I saw on social media this morning some people were nervous, I wasn't. It was strange, I always felt it'd be today. I said several weeks ago, Tranmere at home would be the day. It felt calm, almost as if it were meant to be. I'm still struggling with this bloody illness, but it was my bunged up ear causing me concern, not fear of failing. When it did happen, some have said anti-climax; that's not the case.

No matter what we thought might happen, no matter what we have believed would become of the season, nothing prepares you for that moment of realisation. Maybe you got it when Oldham went 3-1 up, maybe it was when our final whistle went. For some, it won't have come until you streamed on the pitch. For me, the one moment where I felt it choking in the back of my throat was after all of that.

I watched the game in Running Imp's box, which was a great privilege, but at the final whistle my friend Pete and I made a dash round and into the ground. We were on the pitch, surrounded by delighted faces, people joyous and ecstatic. Still, it hadn't hit me. I took out my phone, typed the word 'champions' into a text message with a kiss and pressed send to Fe.

That's when I got the full force of what we'd achieved. The National League was something different, it was redemption and a return to our former selves. This is the next step, this is what deep down every single fan who saw us beat Oldham 3-2 has believed to be possible. That night in the FA Cup we saw our team match a League One side and I recall a conversation with Pete days later where he said; 'get out of this league and you'll be League One in two years'. He's like Nostradamus that man, I'm telling you.

It was perhaps fitting as I read the text I'd sent to my partner that it was Pete at the side of me. I'd have liked my Dad there too, that meeting came later, but for a second my eyes filled with tears. Visions of '76 came to me, two years before I was born, but I've seen the stills. I've studied those pictures looking for my Dad or my Grandad, wondering if we'd ever win a Football League title in my lifetime. Today, I realised pictures were being taken that will remain part of Imps' history forever.

My moment with my Dad came later, a rather candid and emotional hug. I'd not seen the game with him and we met in the car park behind the Stacey West. It was just a hug, no fist pumps, no songs or cheering. It was a hug, without words. Who needs them? The pain of 2011 had be forgotten in 2017, shrunk to no more than a distant afterthought in 2018 and today, in 2019, it was washed away for ever. We're not just back, but we're back and we're better than we've been ever since my first game in 1986. All the time, every step of the ride, my Dad's been there. That was what the hug said, nothing less.

It was always going to be today. I woke up to a message from Gordon Hobson's son-in-law, a picture of Gordon holding a match ball he once picked up for scoring a hat trick for City, complete with good luck message. I was (very kindly) given a priceless piece of Imps' history before the game too, a copy of 'Cock 'o the North', a 1930's publication that is the Holy Grail of Imps books. The person who gave it to me, who wants to remain nameless, said his Dad would have wanted it to go to someone who will cherish it. History, on both counts.

All of that, the omens, the date, the bits of history finding their way into my morning, that's all part of my experience, not yours. Yours will be different. You might have had your moment as you carried your son or daughter onto the pitch, it might have been bouncing in block 7 knowing Mansfield had lost. You might have sat serenely in the Selenity stand, picturing ghosts of the past and wondering what they'd make of it all.

April 22nd, 2019. Lincoln City were finally confirmed as Champions of League Two. Whatever it meant to you, whether you celebrated in a pub with friends or like me, with a glass of Cherry Pepsi Max and a beef dinner with your partner, you'll always remember it. What occurred today was history, to be written about, talked about and toasted for years to come.

Who knows, with three trophies in three seasons we might not have to wait 43 years for the next. That said, they say wine tastes better with age, so perhaps the fact we've waited so long made it sweeter. Maybe the years in the National League made it feel more powerful.

Whatever you experience was today, hold on to it. Cherish it. We don't get gifts like this often, although the last three years might make you think otherwise!

Just in case the realisation hasn't hit you yet, maybe this will be your moment: Lincoln City are Champions of League Two.

Mission Accomplished: Imps 0-0 Tranmere
April 23, 2019

At times, it's hard to remember we had a game of football to play yesterday. We've secured a league title with a defeat and two draws, but the elation those results have brought means they're not likely to feature high on the list of worries.

Besides, yesterday's 0-0 draw with Tranmere was entertaining, exciting and hard-fought, without the added tension of a possible title win.

Before the game, the mood was great all around the ground. The fan zone was busy before 1pm, people wanting to get to the stadium and just soak up the atmosphere. You live for days like these, or days like we hoped it would turn out to be. Some fans were nervous, others excited and some seemingly nonplussed.

I tried to fall into the latter category. A horrible breakfast at Wetherspoons (40 minutes, then no bacon) added to this dreaded man-flu meant I wasn't soaking up the beer or singing loud. Don't let that fool you into thinking I didn't care as much; that wasn't the case at all.

As I said on another article my day started with a private message from Gordon Hobson's son-in-law, a picture of Gordon holding a match ball he once bagged a hat trick with for Lincoln. It seemingly set the scene for a great day, added to when a copy of Benny Dix's 1932 booklet 'Cock o'the North' was given to me. They might not seem like huge things for the average fan, but they were both huge moments in my day.

They added to the mystique of the date, April 22nd. The day we did Macclesfield, they day we bounced back. Surely fate wouldn't see us do the same again, would it?

News of James Norwood's injury seemed to be premature, although it did pass my podcast co-host Ben by. he passed me his phone proclaiming no Norwood, only to have him pointed out. I won't repeat what he said. I even struggled to concentrate on selling copies of the fanzine, so please do come and find me for your copy against Colchester.

By the time the game kicked off, the atmosphere had reached fever pitch. even in the box with Chris and Josh Illsley, you could feel it. The air was bristling with excitement, the songs pricked by a nervous tension in some quarters and a party atmosphere in others. It did remind me of the Brighton game in 1998 a little, only we didn't need a win and would get another chance.

We could have got off to a dream start. Within minutes, John Akinde had shown great resilience to feed in Michael O'Connor, who should have buried his one on one. They're not easy, especially not when you're a holding midfielder but Mickey did well to get in behind, only to fluff his lines.

The Tranmere fans were in great voice too, by far the best we've had at the Bank this season despite having a smaller allocation than Grimsby and Mansfield. They almost sucked a Matt Rhead volley from 30-yards into the net, but the 'ooohs' from the crowd gave the effort move gravity than perhaps it had.

Lincoln were playing well, but the Tranmere back line were strong too. Monthe in particular had caught the eye, I'd heard plenty about him and was interested to see if he was as effective as everyone says. He was, he's such a big lad he made John Akinde look small and that's no mean feat.

He didn't keep Akinde quiet though and I thought he had one of his best games in an Imps shirt. Was the a coincidence that it came on a rare start with Rheady, giving Akinde license to run at players but with support around him? Maybe, maybe not.

It took the visitors 20 minutes or so to get going, but a James Norwood effort sparked them into life. Matt Gilks held on well, but it was already evident why Norwood has had such a tremendous season. I've been critical of him, partly through jealous and partly because I felt they were a one-man team. They're not, not at all. Norwood is incredible in terms of the runs he makes and his strengths and although we wouldn't be able to afford him, he would make a superb partner for John next season.

He was constantly alive and it gave the game an edge, adding to that prickly heat and slight doubt.

The half hour mark was a huge moment for two reasons. Matt Rhead had a goal ruled out after one of the few mistakes the referee made all afternoon. It should have been advantage to us and the big man would have put us 1-0 up, but instead play was hauled back. Anthony Backhouse has been criticised before but he turned in a very good display in the middle of the park.

Elsewhere, a goal just as important had gone in. Oldham took a 29th minute lead against Mansfield and from that point on, a draw was enough. If Oldham won the game, a defeat would see us crowned champions if MK Dons didn't win their game. It wasn't as complicated as a week ago, but it still left a few nervous fans in the stands.

The exciting first half came to a conclusion with more Imps pressure, Bruno getting an effort away after a smart free kick, before Neal Eardley's follow-up was also saved. It had been a great first half, with Tranmere looking dangerous and organised, but the Imps absolutely the better side.

As things stood at half time, we were champions. Having given up smoking for new year I couldn't settle my nerves with a half time cigar, so instead I paced the box, watching the Sky Sports news feed as though something was going to happen during the half time break. I hadn't been nervous, not for one moment, but as our destiny moved closer it got more real.

Imagine, Lincoln City champions of League Two. We'd be sailing into unchartered waters as far as I was concerned, League One has only featured on our calendar once since I've been watching the lads. The last time we finished in a respectable position in the third-tier was 1985, the last time we competed at the top probably 1983.

The last time we lifted a Football League title was 1976, but there's not an Imps fan alive who couldn't tell you that. At half time, the ghosts of '76 were strong in my mind. 40 years of being brought up on their heroics was about to be eclipsed. If only we could hold on or, failing that, if only Oldham could.

Tranmere made a double change at half time and looked all the better for it. They were creeping into an engrossing game and only a huge tackle by Michael Bostwick prevented a one on one for them. It typified Bozzy's season for me, a crunching, well-timed dispossession that was as valuable as a goal line clearance or maybe even a goal.

James Norwood was getting his sights in though and he missed a big chance himself to give the visitors the lead. Had he been fully fit, I have little doubt his rasping effort would have put them 1-0 up.

We talk about two years ago and Macclesfield, but three years ago on this weekend Bruno Andrade scored for Woking as we lost 3-2 at home. On that afternoon, Jake Caprice was excellent for Woking and he had a big say in keeping the scores level before the hour mark. The wonderful Akinde pulled a ball back to Matt Rhead to write the headline, but his placed effort was heroically cleared from the line by Caprice with the keeper beaten. It was a scintillating game, fuelled by what was at stake but engrossing as a standalone encounter.

I thought we had two decent penalty shouts, one where Rhead was adjudged to have fouled two players at one by giving them a fistful of his shirt and staying on the ground, another a partial block on Andrade as he cut into the area. Had they been given, they would have been soft. Luckily, I didn't have time to lament either as Oldham scored again at Boundary Park.

I knew at that minute, this was the day. Mansfield weren't going to pull two back, not in my mind. We only needed a draw and could even lose, with MK Dons struggling at Port Vale. Their game had quickly moved from 0-0 to 1-1 and a goal for the hosts could have given them a chance of catching us. It wasn't going to happen though.

Connor Jennings disallowed goal had a few butterflies doing aerobics in my stomach, but the linesman's flag was as welcome as a cheque from the Inland Revenue. I didn't see it go up and for one second thought we might win the title by losing at home. would it have mattered? Not really.

That wasn't the point though, back to back defeats don't happen to this Lincoln team, not in League Two in 2019.

As the game wore on it became more evident that we were going to be confirmed as Champions. Norwood had a couple of decent efforts, underlining his potential as a top League One player, but neither troubled Matt Gilks. As we went forward we always looked likely to prise them open, but never created anything clear-cut.

That is until the dying minutes when, spurred on by the rising atmosphere and realisation that we were going to win the league, our game went into overdrive.

Mansfield had pulled two back, but Oldham had made it 3-1 first and that was always going to be enough. Shay McCartan had a late effort, as did Tom Pett.

Then, in the dying seconds, a ball across goal just evaded Mark O'Hara. He saw a shadow to his right and lashed out, believing in to be a defender. It wasn't, it was Danny Rowe, placed perfectly to put us 1-0 up. The chance went, but the title was here to stay.

When Anthony Backhouse made his way towards the tunnel at a dead ball situation and you knew what was coming. I knew anyway, Mansfield's game had ended as had MK Dons, but it hadn't been confirmed at the Bank. The whistle went to his lips and for a minute, everything went blurry.

Mainly because I shot out of the box, out of the ground and in through a gate. I was on the pitch before a smoke bomb had taken hold, the beginnings of a tear held behind my sunglasses. I didn't have a purpose to be there, I wasn't heading for a player or for a photo-op, I just wanted to stand there, being a part of what was a historic day in the life of Lincoln City.

Spiritual? Emotional? Touching? It was all of those things. I was surrounded on the field by present day fans, but all around I could feel the ghosts of the past. Pete Newton was there in spirit, his white hanky firmly in his pocket as we won the league, as was Colin Morton and Dave Mundin. So was my Granddad and whoever you've lost close to you. The players of old were all around in my mind, even those who are still with us. If you don't follow football or support a club, it all sounds ridiculous, but as a part of something it's a unique experience.

I've said before I was brought up on a diet of 1976, I've seen pictures from that era over and over again. I've heard stories about Dennis Booth, Percy Freeman and John Ward and yet here I was, right at the heart of the latest chapter. Not 'just' a National League win. Not redemption, not even a Wembley appearance. This is a Football League title, this is history. I wanted to be there and in my rush to do so I never thanked Chris for his hospitality. I'm sure he understands, this once.

In clearing the pitch the players came out and gave their victory lap. Like in 2017, I made it to the corner of the Bridge Mac stand and the Coop, the corner that inevitably gets cut as the players go around. Even Bubs walked past without pointing his lens at us! I didn't care. I wasn't there to get on camera and my own stayed in my pocket, in the main. No, I just wanted to watch. I just wanted to take it in, the noise (even the overly-loud music), the colour and the utter joy on everyone's faces.

I remember, all too vividly, that afternoon in 2011 when the colours were drained of vibrance and the noise nothing more than booing and sobbing. The tears then were of sorrow, they came as our club flatlined. Eight years later, we're in the greatest period of our history in terms of trophies. Eight years it's taken to not only rebuild the club, but to take it to new heights.

Danny and Nicky get the plaudits and rightly so, but the truth is this title is not down to them alone. Their relentless work ethic and attitude has delivered it in the final stages, but Bob Dorrian and his board kept this club alive when even the city wrote it off as dead. Chris Moyses began to bring the fans and the players back together and by the time Clive Nates came on board, our heart was beating once more. Ever since that day in December 2015 when Clive joined the club, the progress has been remarkable.

The crowd began to slowly disperse and I remained for a few moments. I never want to leave the ground after a win, but yesterday I wished I was part of the stands, forever to bear witness to scenes like those. Did I cry? A little, maybe. I know I had a lump in my throat when I text the word 'champions' to my other half, and I stifled a little sob when I finally got to hug my Dad, but there were no flowing tears. That's not my style, I prefer quiet contemplation and to just soak things up in silence. I didn't go wild at our second goal against MK Dons and I stood rooted to the spot when Raggs nodded us ahead at Burnley that day.

I like to appreciate those moments not by joining in, but by bearing witness. Sometimes, if the mood takes me, I celebrate, it's not a conscious decision I make. Yesterday, with the chanting and delight all around me, I watched with clarity and purpose. Those images will be with me forever.

I did eventually leave, listening to the coverage on the way home and forgetting about my bunged up ear, runny nose and general malaise pre-match. I even forgot that Wetherspoons didn't give me any bacon and you know when I forgive a bacon error, it must be serious day.

League Two? Completed it mate.

A Trio of new deals
April 24, 2019

This is three articles, merged into one as they're all short..

Once upon a time, nothing surprised me at Lincoln. Not really.

Players coming to the end of their contracts eventually left. Top performers moved on and we seemed destined to be a selling club for eternity. By rights, every team is a selling club, but we did seem to bend over whenever someone came in for our players.

Today's news has really shown us to be something very different indeed. I wasn't convinced Jason Shackell would stay with us next season. In fact, I was 99% sure he'd go. I'd heard it all; contracts in America, deals with Nottingham Forest to go as a coach. He wanted a year with the Imps to learn the ropes from DC and then was off.

Instead, he's staying put until the summer of 2020. I'm genuinely shocked, surprised and of course, utterly delighted.

Cian Bolger might not be of course, but competition for places is everything in this side.

I've been putting together my assessment of the centre backs this season and I've pointed to Jason Shackell as a key component in our success. He helps Harry Toffolo with his experience, he's fearless and aside from the odd moment of madness, he's been reliable throughout his stay. Basically, he's much better than League Two.

He's delighted too, telling the club's official site: "I'm delighted, I've really enjoyed this season and getting back to playing regularly. All the staff and the lads have been great, after all the success we've had this year I'm really excited to be staying for another year."

So, there we have it. Another surprise, another key player committed to the cause and another reason to celebrate. Jason Shackell is a professional, experienced and still able despite his advancing years. When you talk to him, you know you're talking to a man who understands the game, not just the media angle but all aspects of being a footballer.

He's a role model for younger players, a great man to have around the EPC offering advice and guidance and of course, he's a bloody good footballer.

I can see us having a quiet summer you know. With the players already committed to the club, I think we'll need a handful of faces to come in, but no wholesale changes.

The debate around which direction Danny is taking with the keepers has led some to speculate that Josh Vickers might be departing following his injury struggles.

That's not the case, with the popular young keeper signing a new one-year deal, hot on the heels of a similar move for Jason Shackell.

Josh has shown himself to be a superb shot stopper with good distribution skills, but injury has blighted his Imps' career. Since taking over as number one from Paul Farman, he's had no fewer than three spells out of the side, the most recent seeing Matt Gilks come in to replace him.

The former Arsenal trainee has made 33 league starts in total for the club, the last of which came during the 2-2 draw with Swindon in January.

Vickers is a committed squad member, likeable and hard-working, but then which of the players can you not say that about? He fits the ethos perfectly and despite being side lined for two spells this season, he was still energetically celebrating the title win on Saturday.

"I enjoy Lincoln. I enjoy working under the staff here and we've got a great bunch of lads at a club that's moving in the right direction and I just want to be part of that as much as I can," Vickers told the official club site.

"One of the biggest things though is the fans. To be part of this here, is like being part of a massive community with them. We are all as one and they play a massive part in getting players here and of course players staying here."

The big question that needs answering is his fitness and I believe the length of his contract means we're going to see an additional keeper come in over the summer. It wouldn't surprise me if it's not Matt Gilks, but Danny won't play risk with Vickers fitness this time around.

Grant Smith might find game time limited and I can see him going out on loan this season, with either Gilks or a loan replacement coming in and covering for Vickers, or with Vickers acting as cover for them.

Either way, the 23-year-old will be delighted to get a new deal over the line for next season.

On a busy day for contract renewals, is it worth asking who is next? Michael O'Connor? Matt Gilks? Big Rheady? or are we done, for now?

He might be 34, he might be appearing with less frequency, but the big man is still a huge part of the squad, physically and in terms of his personality.

He's been with us since it started, seeing the green shoots of recovery under Chris Moyses, followed by Clive's arrival and then that of Danny and Nicky. We nearly lost him that first summer but a deal was struck and he's not looked back.

When he first broke into professional football at the age of 27, he surely can't have imagined by the time he was 34 he'd have three trophies, a Wembley appearance and be a League One footballer. Well, now he is.

"I'm delighted to have signed a new contract. The club is moving in the right direction, and I'm over the moon to be here," he told the club's official website.

"I have loved every minute here, from day one, it's been a rollercoaster journey, but to get the contract signed and be here for another year is unbelievable."

He's become part of the furniture at Sincil Bank, but his presence next season is going to be important.

The supporters like Matt Rhead. Sure, he's less effective over 90 minutes now than he was against Eastleigh and Woking, but he still has a role to play. I thought John Akinde had his best game in a long while this weekend and it's no coincidence that comes when he's running off the big man.

Anyone who thinks League One is a step too far only needs look at Akinfenwa at Wycombe. he's been a part of their League One campaign, as Rheady will be ours. We won't rely on him, but if we need the ball to stick up top in the last ten minutes, he's going to be the 'go to' guy. When we have an EFL Cup game, or need an impact sub and a last roll of the dice, he's the man they'll call from the bench.

Besides, he's a likeable character. he's down to earth and understands football supporters. He's been one of us, he's sat in the stands watching Stoke knowing exactly what he wants to see from his heroes. When he's out on the pitch, he gives his all.

Without sugar-coating things too much, he will be on the periphery. If you want to challenge in the top half of League One, you need strikers who will deliver more mobility than Matt Rhead. That, sadly, is fact. However, his attributes far outweigh the reasons to let him go and again, this is a wise move by Danny and the club.

Don't be fooled into thinking it's a sentimental decision either. Danny doesn't do sentiment, whatever this may look like. Remember Terry Hawkridge? Alan Power? Sean Long? No, Danny isn't a man to hand out a contract unless there's a viable gain. Every single action is done with a gain in mind, be it on the field, in the dressing room or psychologically. Matt Rhead hasn't been given a deal because of what he's done for the club, he's been given one on the basis that he can still do more.

Personally, I like Rheady. He's a great guy to interview, down to earth, dry and witty but also honest and open. he's a throwback to another era, when players and fans were alike. He'll tell it like it is, politely of course, and he offers up more in some interviews than many of our players. he's less guarded and although there's very few I struggle to connect with, he's one player I love to see appear as my next programme interview.

50 goals, closing in on 200 appearances and now another year to add to that tally. Anyone claiming this man isn't a Lincoln City legend is soon going to have to have a rethink.

Season Ticket Announcement: Fears Unfounded Once More
April 26, 2019

Remember when the season tickets were suddenly put on early sale? Remember the uproar and anger, the usual suspects full of scaremongering about 'rip-off' Lincoln City?

I do. I remember it well and I had to hold my silence knowing that discussions had been pointed towards cheap, affordable tickets for everyone, even those unable to commit to the super early bird price.

Today, the new ST prices came out and, lo and behold, the club are not looking to rip anyone off, nor capitalise on the promotion as such. £16.50 per game with a total price of £379. That's all areas remember, we don't have tiered prices either. It's easy to point at one club and say 'their cheapest ticket is £xxx', but you have to remember they charge different amounts for different areas. We don't.

It's tough for the club in some respects. There's little doubt in an ideal world, some seats would come at a premium. I know the Legend's Lounge does, but there you're paying for the stuff before, your seat is the same price as everyone else pays. It's usual for more restricted views to be heavily discounted, or certain areas in a lower tier to cost less than an upper tier.

We can't do that though, because of the number of ST holders we have. Imagine if you were in Upper 5 for instance, suddenly marked out as a level one price and therefore shooting up £50, but lower 5 was a different level and subject to the same in saving. Would you be happy? No, so the club stick to the one price fits all.

The early fears were completely unfounded and although I know I'll get accused of being pro-club, it boils my urine when I read the sort of utter nonsense some were peddling a few weeks ago. I heard figures of £400, £425 and some 'in the know' claiming the early bird prices were to prevent a cash flow problem. You know what; that's garbage.

I don't think the announcement was handled in the best way possible and some information did seem to be withheld which made people's decisions harder to make at the time. The Zebra Finance debacle clouded things too, but at the heart of it all was this notion the club were exploiting us yet again. It's a fallacy, a myth that the club are trying to milk the fans for every penny and I'm honestly getting sick to the back teeth of reading about it.

Take the awards night that's coming up. It works out a costly night and sadly, due to being a poor writer (financially, not bad at what I do...), I can't afford to attend. However, did I attend a reasonably priced one in 2007? No. You know why? There wasn't one to attend. Back then the trophies were presented on the pitch and this year, they will be too. So, why the uproar about a high-cost night at the showground? Resentment that some can afford it and others can't?

Oddly, some of the people who are arguing against the night will happily spend £150 on a coat, or pair of trainers. I would deem that to be rip off, but those people want to be seen in the right clobber. Similarly, some want to spend their hard-earned on this event. Honesty shout? I'd go if I could justify it, but I'm saving to build a mini bar and pool room in my garden. I'm going to call it the 'Get Inn' and have a picture of the Imps celebrating the title win as the sign outside. True story.

The point here is why, whenever the club plan something with a cost pointed at a certain market, are they out to rip of loyal fans? For me, a loyal fan would understand with an extra £1m or so to find next season the club need to find a few more opportunities they can take. However, when it comes to the fan on the street, they're not taking their opportunities at the expense of people.

When I was asked about season tickets, I felt the price we were presented with, £379, was too cheap. The club needed more revenue and a tenner each from 5,000 fans would have been a big step in the right direction, but did the club do it? No. I was one of only a couple who felt that way, but they didn't want to exploit fans and throw loyalty back in their faces. Shock, horror.... fans being treated with dignity and respect!

If you got a chance to listen to our recent podcast with Chief Exec Liam Scully, you will have heard him discussing the fan zone. Recently, the food in there has been superb and throughout the ground, the offering is improving. Liam confirmed in terms of commercial revenue, the current deal is perhaps not quite as lucrative to the club as others they could have pursued, but because it's using local suppliers and the fans have given it an overwhelming thumbs up, they'll continue to work with them. There's a marginal gain there, but not at the expense of fans choice.

The club can't be as honest and open as people expect. They're a professional institution, not a bloke down the pub bemoaning his luck. When they make decisions they can't chew over the fat, explain the ins and outs nor can they please everyone all of the time. I just hope that listening to Liam and seeing the evidence in the ST prices that people start to realise they're working not only to make the club a viable business with League One income, but also doing as much as they can to improve the fans experience, through pricing and on match day.

They don't always get it right, they'll be the first to admit that, but who does? I'm damn sure they've got more right these last couple of years than they have in the past. The deep suspicion surrounding their motives has to end, we are not owned by Roland Duchatelet or Norman Smurthwaite, we're owned, managed and run by people who genuinely have the club's best interests at heart, on and off the field.

Missed Chances: Newport 1-0 Imps
April 27, 2019

You don't lose for the best part of four months, then within the space of ten days two teams beat you. That's football.

It's looking suspiciously like we could have lost all of our matches after MK Dons and still won the title, such is the desire of the chasing pack to throw it all away. Ilias Chair ensured Mansfield's biggest crowd of the season went home gutted, MK Dons can't put their riches to good use and the best result of the day was probably Bury getting their match postponed.

It's crazy, I've started writing about Lincoln's game and as yet, haven't really felt an emotion about it. So, we lost. Meh, whatever.

Perhaps becoming Champions has dulled my emotions when it comes to these final few games, but I can't get excited about records like away wins or fewest defeats. I can get excited about the thought of trips to Ipswich and Sunderland and maybe, just maybe that's why my disappointment really isn't evident tonight.

We've not been playing badly, not one bit. Danny won't be settling for defeats either, one or two players might be feeling the wrath of our ambitious manager this evening. I noted with interest his post-match comments about not wanting consolidation next season... that hot on the heels of a suspiciously long pause after being asked if the board meet his ambitions in the presser. I wonder if perhaps the feeling that getting to League One is the big achievement is weighing on the gaffer's mind a little? He was vehement with his comments about consolidation. His life is too short, he wants promotion again. I love the drive and determination, but there's going to be a huge funding gap next year. All I hope is Danny can address the issues he feels we have with the budget we offer.

I don't want to bring the doom and gloom, in most of our play today I felt we were adequate. It was a difficult match against committed opponents under hard conditions, but at least two of those criteria have applied to every match we've played. It seems we've never come up against disorganised clubs in disarray, not if you listen to the official rhetoric. I'd argue Notts County early doors were a club on their arse and Yeovil were awful both times, but in the main League Two is much of a muchness. It's about desire and quality.

We've got quality, but we're lacking it in front of goal. We missed a host of chances for the second or third match running and I think that's an indication of what the squad needs this summer. John Akinde's qualities have been obvious and even today, I thought he had a very good game. What he needs is a partner, even if it is someone coming from deep to put the ball in the net. Craig Robertson will undoubtedly cry hypocrite when he reads this, but we need a James Norwood.

Genuinely, on today's showing I think we're a striker away from being a top half League One side. Sure, the squad needs peppering elsewhere with some loan players and a couple who can cover, but in the main decisions are being made about some of our players right now. We've made them ourselves, of course we have. Danny will be looking at one or two and wondering if maybe they've got what it takes.

Today will have helped him. The late free kick for instance, should Neal Eardley have grabbed the ball? Shay obviously wants to impress and is eager to earn himself a full time deal but I'm beginning to wonder if it's Shay's role that we're going to work hard to replace. If so, will we be breaking the bank for a player who, with respect, has finished the season on the bench?

I know this isn't the usual write-up of a game, but it's not the usual game. We're champions, over a 46 game season we've won the league. Danny will hurt tonight at the defeat, but I'll be smashing a my dinner in front of a Netflix film tonight with little bothering me. Sure, we're on a bad run of results but a season is the sum of 46 matches, not four or five in a row. It's like when people were saying we were 16th in the form table earlier in the season. I said don't worry and I stand by that. Anyone who thinks our run doesn't bode well for next season is way off as well; when the big kick off comes this form will be forgotten.

We always knew we had a tough run in and believe me, it won't get easier with Colchester next week. We've not faced anybody in the last few weeks with nothing to play for and it's unusual. The truly tough matches, away at Mk Dons, Forest Green and Bury; that's where the league was won. now, in the ones which looked more 'straightforward' on paper, we're finding out exactly how close this division is.

Okay, we lost today, but what did Newport create that was clear cut? One chance in the first half? Credit to them, like us they work hard, press well and defend stoically and it's perhaps why after going 1-0 down we struggled. Carlisle did the same but with 11 men we would have beaten them. Today, we missed decent chances and should have been coming away with a draw, but take nothing away from Newport they looked very good.

In fact, had they not had some distracting cup runs this season, I think they could have been in the top four. That doesn't mask the fact we've lost, again, but come August we know whatever happens, we'll be in League One. It makes defeat easier to swallow.

First of all, I want to commend the excellent travelling support. Even on the terraces there's a party atmosphere and defeat won't have worried many watching the game, nor those who chose to remain in the club bar and have a few drinks to celebrate out title win. It's been 43 years coming, I think people can be forgiven for celebrating. The players could be forgiven too, but that's not up to me, it's up to Danny.

There's one or two I think still have an uncertain future, even those under contract. If we're going to fund a push up the table and someone comes in with a big bid for a player, are we going to say no? If it's a League One club we're unlikely to sell, but I believe one or two of ours are on Championship club's radars. If there's a bid for Harry or Bruno, as ambitious as we are, there's a chance we could cash in and invest. I'm not privy to information and I may be well adrift but it's something to be aware of.

I think we can all agree Mark O'Hara would be a fine acquisition, but other than that I'm not as sold on our loan players staying. I don't mean I wouldn't want them too, Danny Rowe is a very good footballer, but I don't see him as someone we simply 'have' to bring in. O'Hara is different, he's a big midfielder, good on his toes and in the air. If we sign one, it's got to be him and I thought he had a good game today.

I don't think we were particularly awful today, not at all. I also don't think there's anything to learn from today. I know we've lost and I know we're not on a great run, but our management team know what is needed at the next level and the players know what is expected. We were unlucky not to get a point today and maybe a more clinical striker partnering John (not replacing) would have seen us over the line. That's the priority.

I wonder also if the team selection might point to Matt Gilks not getting a fresh deal or perhaps not wanting one. It's interesting to see Josh back once we've secured the title and there's got to be a thinking behind that. I like Gilks and believe that we need two top class keepers at the club. I like Grant Smith, but would I be happy to see him on a ten game run in League One? I'm not so sure. Gilks, yes. Vickers, absolutely.

We go into next weekend knowing it's another time to celebrate, more cheers, more lauding the management team and staff, more reminiscing on fans no longer with us and of course, enjoying the moment with those that are. We'll learn nothing from the result, just as with today's game. We know what we need to know, we know what is expected, what is needed and how big the step up is going to be. Now is not the time to be asking questions, certainly not from the fans perspective. Danny Cowley, he's paid to ask the questions, he's paid to make the decisions, but whether we won 10-0 today or lost 5-4, it didn't really matter.

We're champions, enjoy it and don't let a defeat ruin your evening. On this one occasion, I think you're safe to feel alright at a failure to get three points.

On another note, how sad to see a late Ilias Chair goal ruining Mansfield's day, to see Scunthorpe losing at home to a side already relegated and to see how unpopular Steve Evans is at Gillingham even though he's only rumoured to be their new manager. Then we have Bury up for sale, Yeovil relegated, Notts County still in real danger, Bolton cancelling fixtures and a £4m striker not enough to get a team automatic promotion out of League One.

Think on all of that before you feel a bit mopey this evening.

Matt Rhead reveals his Player of the Year and which opponents impressed him the most
April 30, 2019

Matt Rhead is currently the longest-serving member of the Imps squad, and perhaps one of the most popular too.

The big man, as he's affectionately known, has been fighting for the cause for four seasons now and is widely regarded as something of a club legend. Who else can boast almost 200 appearances, 50 goals and three pieces of silverware during his Imps career?

As well as being a handful on the field, he's a likeable and down to earth character off it. Whenever I have the chance to catch up with him it's easy to forget you are talking to a professional footballer. Perhaps it's the fact he was doing work as a shift manager until the age of 27, maybe it's because he's been a season ticket holder at Stoke City, but of all the players in the current squad he's one of the most relatable.

He's also incredibly dry and he put his charm to good use when I attempted to get to the bottom of a mystery that developed last week. Ben and I attended the training ground to do the podcast and in the course of doing so, uncovered an overhead locker that had a hair dryer in it.

Rheady might not need one himself, but he's pretty sure he knows who is harbouring a need for a quick dry after training.

"A hairdryer? If I could say anyone I'd say Josh Vickers. He's got a big beard hasn't he, his hair is all nice and combed as well. That's what football is all about now isn't it? These young players, they want to look good. Petty likes to have use of a hairdryer as well; it could be any one of them!"

Aside from the jokes, the Imps squad are clearly very tight and that close-knit togetherness is one of the contributing factors in our title success. I asked Rheady who he felt the Player of the Year was, putting him right on the spot. To be fair, it took some deliberation but he didn't just sit on the fence.

"The whole squad have done well this year, it's hard to pick any one out. Defensively though, we've been solid and I think that's a big part of our success. Eards has chipped in with goals too, he's been a big figure for us, but if pushed I'd have to go for Jason Shackell. He's been superb and a class above. He's playing a league or two below where he should, be we don't mind as we love having him here and will have again next season."

"You can see why he's played at Premier League and Championship level throughout his career, he's different class on and off the field."

Perhaps more challenging was when I posed the question which opposition player did he admire most.

"That's a great question! I like the kid at Forest Green who scored against us at Sincil Bank, Reece Brown. I know we won the game 2-1, but I thought he was perhaps the best player on the park that day. Tyler Walker has done well at Mansfield as well, but he's not had the best of times against us! We've done well and kept him quiet."

May

'Consolidate? I want to try to establish' – Danny Cowley dispels any notion of mismatching ambitions at Sincil Bank
May 2, 2019

The first mutterings of discontent began last week, following the press conference ahead of the Newport game.

Danny was asked if the boards ambitions matched his and for a second, there was a pause. That alone would usually be simply the actions of a man thinking of his answer, but twitchy fans saw something else. I wasn't watching the presser because of work, but I got two messages quickly asking if I'd seen it. On its own, it meant little.

Then, after the Newport game, there was an angry Danny, disappointed at losing, mentioning how he wasn't going to be happy with consolidation. The general feeling amongst many fans is that a year of consolidating would be the right way to go about progressing, but the manager seemed to feel otherwise.

Put those two things together and what do you get? The start of a rumour.

Even my Dad asked if I thought it was a happy camp after the two moments. Well, now I think we can answer firmly and emphatically, yes it is.

This afternoon, never one to shy away from the important questions, Michael Hortin asked Danny a very similar question to that of a week ago, but adding in his post match comments. That pause came again and, as I watched live, my bum twitched; here comes the doom…

Or not.

"I think we're going to have a budget that is going to give us an opportunity to be competitive. It'll be a budget that first and foremost we'll have to survive with," he started out by saying.

"I'm not setting off on a journey next year with that in mind for us, I'll be setting off to add value. We've had budgets at Concord and Braintree that were significantly less than our competitors and we've always found a way."

He then addressed the whole 'consolidate' comment, preferring another word rather than being anxious at the club's position.

"For us as a football, club we've come an awful long way in a short space of time. I don't like the word consolidate; I've got a real issue with it. That to me is treading water and I haven't got time to tread water. For me, it's about trying to establish and if it is about establishing it's about trying to put a plan together to get to the Championship because that's the next division.

"Now, whether that happens in one year, three years, five years; there has to be a plan in place for that to happen. We know for that to happen, we'd need significant investment. We've got a brilliant board who are incredibly hard-working and who are working behind the scenes to try to find that investment."

It's not all about money though, it's about people too and once again, Danny found the right words to dampen down those who felt there was trouble ahead.

"We've seen a lot of other clubs suffer because they've got the finance, but not the right people. For us, the model has always been about people. Everyone at Lincoln City can rest easy because the board are doing all they can. In my opinion I believe Lincoln City is the most investable club in the lower leagues of English football.

"I genuinely believe that and I think there will be an intelligent businessman out there who sees the potential in us. Football, clubs are football clubs, it's not the bricks and mortar, it's the people. If anybody has followed this journey from afar, they'll realise we've got some really good people here at every level inside the club."

Even though the board are putting the hours in behind the scenes, Danny hinted that player trading might be one way to bring in better finances for the club in the coming months.

"In the meantime, I'm not just going to wait and hope, I'm going to try to do something about it. The other two ways are football fortune which we've done well with in the past with the FA Cup run and the Checkatrade trophy, and the other is trading players which is maybe something we'll look at as well. We need to find a way to have a competitive budget to keep the momentum that we've got."

As with any good speech, the answer ended with a 'hell yeah' moment as he emphatically stated his desire for the club once more, leaving spine-tingling imagery of us establishing ourselves at a level a whole generation are not familiar with.

"I've said all along, my ambition and my aim for this football club is not just to create a moment in time for people to look back on and say weren't they fantastic years in the history of Lincoln City, I want this period to be a period where we change the status of the club forever."

In terms of putting any mutterings of discontent to bed, I'd say the light's out and they've been well and truly tucked in for the night.

Bittersweet Symphony (Champions Edition) – Imps 0-3 Colchester
May 5, 2019

It's been over 48 hours since I last penned anything for the site. For those who don't know, I now work with the Priory Academies delivering alternative media content on a Friday afternoon and that, coupled with yesterday's game, kept me off the computer.

When I got home last night, despite having witnessed a Lincoln City team lift the first Football League title in 43 years, despite having been able to sing 'Champions', or whatever Spanish sounding equivalent we felt was required, I was still seething with anger. Football, it's a funny old game, isn't it? I poured myself a glass of Pepsi Max Cherry and watched the first series of Line of Duty. That's rock and roll for you right there.

There should have been a carnival atmosphere. The final day of the season should have brought sunshine, singing and celebration. In the main, that was the case I guess. To soak up the atmosphere Dad and I went not just in our usual Wetherspoons haunt, but also the Golden Cross before heading to the ground. Having seen a planning application to turn it into flats had been turned down, we both felt we wanted to show solidarity to a good, traditional English boozer.

Once we hit the fan zone there was an air of celebration, but the intermittent showers seemed to dampen any atmosphere. I envisaged sunshine, singing and celebration and got showers and subdued joy. Of course, there were the really touching moment I shared with people. Andy Townsend almost had me in tears; here's a man who has followed the Imps since the day he slipped out of the womb and when he sees what's happening he, like me, thinks of ghosts of fans who can't be with us.

Weather aside, it was a nice morning. No pressure, no need for a win and eyes on everywhere else. So many people said the result didn't matter and although I said on the podcast it did, I wasn't worried like most home matches. Despite the rain, I enjoyed the morning. I liked the celebratory programme, the gold cover and the names of fans who had passed inside. I bought a 'champions' scarf from the club shop, turned my nose up at the groups hawking their illegitimate wares in the High Street and gave faces I've been seeing for years hugs, handshakes or whatever else was appropriate.

Heading into the ground it began to feel really special, the 617's display always adds something to the incredible atmosphere and when Chris Wray, who I'm sure was worse for wear, came and gave me a hug, I found that celebration within me. Having not partaken of alcohol I enjoyed it all with clarity, but also with restraint. Since I've no been drinking at game I've found myself a little more grounded, perhaps that's my personality as much as anything.

The teams came out, the guard of honour was formed and the display cards went up. This was it; the champions were here. This was our time, our Doncaster '76, our lifetime memories. Whatever happened for 90 minutes, we were about to witness the sort of history nobody could ever take away from us.

We certainly witnesses something in the 45 minutes, perhaps it was history. I certainly won't forget it!

For the first fifteen minutes I thought we looked the better side. They'd come to attack us and that left gaps we could expose. It had the makings of a great encounter, especially with them needing something from it. Trevor Kettle, a referee I usually associate with over-zealousness, had a calming influence on a game that threatened to boil over. He could have sent one of their lads off early on, two bad challenges in succession gave him a decision to make; he made the right one and kept it as eleven against eleven.

Slowly but surely their urgency began to show and their skill players got on the ball. Sammie Szmodics is one I've talked about before and naturally, he impressed me. I really liked Courtney Senior as well, he was tricky and direct whenever he had the ball. They began to get a bit of possession and I nipped down to the loo with the scores 0-0.

By the time I got back, it was 1-0, I took my seat to see a Neal Eardley free-kick zip over before it was quickly 2-0. The following 20 minutes could have seen them go in 5-0 up at half time as we fumbled our way through 25 minutes of misplaced passes, bad decisions and ineptitude. It was the worst period of football I've seen from this side, worse than when we lost 4-1 to Crewe and definitely worse than anything we've seen this season.

Danny talks about not reaching our levels, we didn't reach Notts County's levels yesterday. Hell, we didn't reach the levels my eight-year-old nephew reaches when he lines up against me on FIFA.

25 minutes of truly terrible football from a team who won the league three matches ago, earned promotion five matches ago and have been top of the pile almost all of the season. A team with the highest number of their players voted into the Team of the Year by their peers, a team winning their third trophy in as many seasons and lifting a Football League title for the first time in 43 years and only the second time in 66 years.

As they trooped off the field, they were booed.

I don't know what your experience was. I don't know if you heard the booing, but there was plenty around me. It wasn't everyone, not by a long shot, but for a few seconds it was the loudest noise I could hear. I did also hear someone kicking off about it as well, which pleased me. Elsewhere in the Coop one of what I refer to as 'the Market Rasen lot' heard booing and ended up almost coming to blows with one 'supporter' who allegedly asked 'what are you going to do about it?' when taken to task.

The football had been poor, no denying that. I heard plenty about the home form being awful since Christmas too, but it's not so awful we dropped off the top spot is it? I heard people complaining they drive long distances and deserve better football. Here's an idea.... stop coming. I know of several die-hard Imps, unable to afford a season ticket who didn't get one yesterday.

My fanzine seller, Mike Downs, couldn't get an ST as he was travelling round Australia for half the season. he turned up yesterday, sold the fanzine and then waited outside the ground, hoping to get in at the end to see the presentation. He wouldn't have booed and, in my opinion, he deserved to see it more than idiots who booed.

I even heard of fans walking out at half time.

Not only that, but the 617s display paper began to get thrown onto the pitch, the club had to ask fans to stop, but I watched it carrying on. The referee couldn't deduct points from the club, but he could have stopped the game and it could have cost us, yet I watched kids (some being allowed by the parents) keep doing it after the game kicked off. Again, is this what we attract now? A petulant defiance? Do you think the 617, their volunteers and organisers will be allowed to do another display after that? It left me feeling really jaded at half time, not just because of the result by the realisation that 45 minutes had turned some of the 9,800 crowd inter what I tend to term as utter morons.

I've got to try to move on from the negativity, but I felt a historic day was being ruined. The game didn't help, but if the entirety of our support were genuinely as good as we claim, we wouldn't have booing and a smattering of childish defiance going on at half time. This was meant to be a party and yet it felt more like we were going down. For a short while at half time, I couldn't work out whether it was May 2019 or May 2011.

Oddly, we lost both of those games 3-0.

When the second half kicked off I thought we got a better match. Colchester were happy they could do no more, they'd got ahead of Exeter on goal difference which meant they didn't need more goals. If Exeter scored, they dropped out the top seven. If Newport, losing at Morecambe, scored then the same happened. They had their lead, big enough to go up if things stayed the same and it showed.

They went with two banks of four for us to break down and it led to a rather tepid and flat second half. We could have bagged within seconds of the restart, Matt Rhead's effort perhaps the best we had all game. What we saw was a replay of all those drawn matches at home, a dogged defensive side looking for a break and a Lincoln team perhaps lacking the guile to unpick the defence.

There's already been one cliché in this piece, but here's another; it was a game of two halves. The first was open and expansive but we didn't turn up with our A game, the second was closed and protected. It was nice to see an indirect free kick in the area, you barely see them at all these days and the minor excitement of thinking we were going to score caused a bit of excitement.

The real excitement came from looking at the other scores. I know plenty of fans didn't care what else happened, but I did. For 90 minutes, Colchester were the enemy and I wanted them to fail. I wanted Newport to score and I wanted to know who was going down. Oddly, it was only when one of those scores changed that the crowd's mood turned.

The Coop rippled with a few chants of 'you're not going anywhere', then as Colchester's supporters went quiet it became a crescendo. If we couldn't take pride in our own performance, it seemed we'd be happy responding to their calls of 'champions, you're having a laugh' in the first half. It's tribal and for a brief moment, even suffering a heavy loss, our tribe had something to sing about.

It led to an odd ending to the game. Matt, who has replaced Dave as my match day partner (and who sadly has a much wider leg spread than Dave) commented it felt like an end-of-season friendly. They knew a goal elsewhere was all that could save them, we knew that eight goals made no difference to us and everyone waited for the final whistle.

Let's be honest, the football wasn't great. It wasn't what I'd come for today, but evidently quite a few had. The ground didn't empty when Trevor Kettle blew and left the field, but a few wandered out. I wouldn't call anyone out, some had long drives back, others didn't want to see the trophy. I know it got ugly at the back of the Coop as some left moaning that we were crap and would be relegated next season, but I didn't see that because I stayed put.

I have around a 60 miles round-trip, not as far as some, and often I leave early to beat the traffic. Nothing wrong with that. I'm not convinced missing the trophy presentation because we were 'rubbish' is a good shout though; if we were rubbish we wouldn't be getting a trophy labelling us as the best, would we?

Reflecting on the game, I thought Bozzy was excellent, I thought John Akinde worked incredibly hard and I thought Harry Toffolo put in a good shift. The second half changes surprised me, I did hope to see a couple of fringe players and maybe to see us go a bit more adventurous with our selections, but Danny's the gaffer not me and he's put us on top of the division, so who am I to argue? There were some questionable performances from some players, we certainly missed Jason Shackell's influence in the first half and lost the midfield battle for large parts of the game.

Still, when the game ended none of that mattered to 90% of the home support. Lincoln City were finally crowned champions of League Two. I heard someone say 'we haven't played like champions', but as we did win the league I'd argue we had, just not the conventional idea of champions.

Once the worrying elements of the support had done their booing, left because it was rubbish or whatever else they wanted to do with their pent-up anger, a different mood took over the stadium. The podium got set up, the fans had a bit of a sing-song and to their credit, a large number of Colchester fans stayed put to watch us crowned. I felt a bit bad having been so happy they'd failed to make the top seven at that point, especially as they'd played so well. Sammy Szmodics went over and seemingly said goodbye to them and again, I felt for their supporters. We'd been there before, so close and yet so far and then witnessing our top players leaving.

It pleased me we're in the position we are. None of our top performers were saying goodbye. We didn't have to watch another team handed the trophy. Rather ironically, in the last four years we've seen the trophy presented four times; away at Cheltenham in the National League, then we won it, then away at Accrington last season and now we've won it again. Odd stat I'd say.

It was soon time for the congratulations, cheers and a bit more booing. I wasn't upset to hear Shaun Harvey booed, not one bit, but after that the staff got their moment as they came out to applause, then Danny and Nicky and finally the squad. The players came out as if they were going to board Noah's Ark, two by two. I had some fun in my own head working out the pairs, it took my mind away from the numb feeling in my hands as we applauded for an eternity. They took their medals, took the places and waited.

This was the moment it was all about, the moment that seemed written in the stars the day he signed for the club. Lee Frecklington, born in the city, raised on the pitches of Lincoln and with links as strong as anyone to the club came out alone. I remember watching his early matches, for us, tracking his swift progression and finally seeing him go off into the world to make his fortune. He walked across the turf towards the podium, took his place and after a brief pause, hoisted the League Two title aloft. History.

The reaction was emotional, some cheered, some cried and like usual I simply applauded and took it all it. I have a good mix of people around me, the chap I've sat next to for two seasons introduced himself a 'Stan' and he had a wistful look in his eye. My Dad was obviously delighted and from my right hand side I got a hug from others who share the match days. The booing and anger had subsided, at least in me, and all that was left was joy and relief.

Danny's speech was natural emotive and passionate, invoking images of further success, but also of a chapter ending. I couldn't help but think this is the culmination of the story, the end of the chapter labelled 'redemption'. When they took over, League One was the aspiration and although the Championship is the next stop, it's a big jump. We've done one stage of the journey, but the loco is about to pull off to a destination completely alien to us all.

I did like seeing John Akinde going around all of the staff, one by one, on the lap of honour. The rest of the players rightly lapped it up, but I think it showed a bit about Akinde's character. I see him as a gentle giant, but this promotion means a lot to him. Of course, it means a huge amount to everyone, but there's something in that smile that tells me it's really hit him in the right place. I like big John, I think he's isolated at times, but he's such a handful and the fact other players voted him in the PFA teams shows what he does bring to a side. He's a footballer's footballer, not necessarily always a crowd pleaser but someone the players understand the importance of.

That was that. I wanted to stay in the ground for hours, get down the front and have a few selfies, but that's not what I'm usually about. I'd had the moment I wanted and sadly, as I left, the controversial booing and leaving early seemed to dominate social media. Maybe it's because we won the title weeks ago, maybe we've celebrated this season on three occasions now and it feels routine, but for some reason that ill-feeling spread across some social media platforms.

It's a shame because although we did lose the game, the individual battle if you like, we won the war. We're the champions, the one and only and as Chesney Hawkes sang; you can't take that away from me (us).

Four awards in two days for Imps' stalwart
May 5, 2019

Michael Bostwick has been handed four awards in the space of 48 hours, even before the rest are handed out at the dinner this evening.

Sponsors, staff and some supporters will gather tonight at the Showground to watch the presentations of a host of awards, having travelled the length of the city this afternoon on an open-top bus to show off the League Two trophy.

Even before the festivities, defender Michael Bostwick is having to clear some room in his trophy cabinet, as he's been the recipient of four different awards in the space of just 48 hours.

First up, he was handed a pair of awards at the training ground on Friday morning. He won the PFA Player of the Month for March, which meant a presentation by Snack Media's representative, me, at the EPC. I was joined by Andy Helgesen who was presenting the FPS Player of the Year. Again, the bearded menace won the award to make it a brace.

Then, following yesterdays game, he won the Player of the Year and the Away Player of the Year, both being presented on the pitch following the conclusion of the fixture with Colchester.

30-year-old Bostwick joined the Imps from Peterborough in the summer of 2017, following our promotion to the Football League. His capture raised eyebrows across the EFL as he'd previously been linked with a £750,000 move to Blackburn Rovers of the Championship.

He's gone on to make 104 appearances in all competitions for the Imps, the bulk of last seasons coming in the centre of midfield. He's typically been deployed at centre back this campaign, although he did start the 3-3 draw with Bury in midfield.

He's started 45 of our 46 league matches this season and scored three goals in total, the last of which came again Everton at Goodison Park in the FA Cup.

The First Day of the Summer: Never Forget the 56
May 11, 2019

It's the first day of the summer; at least that's what it feels like for a football fan.

This is the first Saturday on which there is nothing for Lincoln fans to do. For me, the summer starts when the season ends and oddly, ends when it starts. I'm not a man who subscribes to conventional timescales, the football season is how my year is divided up.

For those who wonder, autumn starts when the season kicks off, winter starts on FA Cup first round weekend and spring starts the first weekend that we drive home in daylight. Simple in my world, isn't it?

That means today is the first day of garden centres, trips shopping for furniture, decorating or any number of things you'll do as a family. For the first time some of you might spend some time with your spouse and find out they're not that bad at all. When I was a kid, it was time to head to the park on an all day football bender, stopping occasionally to send someone to the shop for drinks. Nowadays it probably means a FIFA session or an afternoon of anti-social behaviour. Maybe. Maybe that's my age.

It's a long time until we see the Imps in action and traditionally this is also a 'no football' summer. The rise of the women's game means there is a major tournament during the off period, but there will still be fans who follow the men's game and not the female equivalent. That's their prerogative and for them, the summer of 2019 is like every odd-numbered summer ever. No football.

I'm spending my first Saturday off writing this, going to see my nephew who turns nine today and quietly recalling that it's been four years since I got engaged, wondering if perhaps we ought to start looking for a venue. You'll be doing whatever it is fills your life until the team who love gets back into action. It's the first day of the summer.

The summer of 1985 was another that remained football free. Euro 84 hadn't featured England and the Mexico World Cup was a year away. Back then, Lincoln City were a League One club, albeit in what was Division Three. That year was the last time we finished outside the relegation places in the third-tier. Nobody will remember it fondly, nobody at all.

That was the day that 56 football fans went to a match and never got to see the first football-free Saturday of the year a week later. Two were from Lincoln, but where these men, women and children came from is irrelevant. Some were celebrating a title win, just like we were a week ago. Others were taking a last away trip of a dismal season, but still staunchly following their side through thick and thin. All of these people were football supporters who, like you and I today, cared about a club and were facing a football free summer.

There were no garden centres with their partners a week later. No trips into town with their kids or grandkids. No birthday parties, no weddings, no more free Saturdays.

I came to Lincoln City just over a year later and although the full horror and sadness of that day 34 years ago is obvious to me, I cannot for one second begin to imagine what it must have been like to be there and to live through it. I remember it, the TV images and the tears in my fathers eyes as it unfolded, but I only came to understand football and Lincoln a year later. A tragedy like that during my tenure as a fan would have broken me, whether I knew anyone connected or not.

The name 'Stacey West' is now ingrained into Lincoln City as much as that of players, managers and the ground itself. When I took the name for the site I took it as the end I grew up on, the place where I watched my football as a teen and through the Keith years. I wanted to express where I felt was my home, but it has a much wider meaning. As almost everyone knows, Bill Stacey and Jim West were the two Imps supporters who lost their lives that day and it's a fitting tribute that they will forever be remembered at our ground and of course, as part of the Imps history and heritage.

56 people lost their lives. 265 suffered injuries. On a day where our friends from Bradford City were set to lift the title, they suffered the most horrific of tragedies that has defined and characterised our relationship since. Nobody wanted to see them drop out of League One this season because the opportunity to come together with them, to celebrate the lives of the 56 and to remember them once more is always relished. We share a bond with the Bantams, one of grief and strength in equal measure. Both clubs came back from that awful afternoon, supporters who survived the day hugged their loved ones a little tighter and approached their lives with a deeper appreciation of the things they had.

Today, whether you're at a garden centre, in a pub, shopping for the kids summer clothes or like me, celebrating Isaac Hutchinson's ninth birthday, pause for a second and remember the 56, their families and their friends. Give a moment of thanks for your own life, the wonderful things we've enjoyed this year and give those you love a huge hug.

34 years ago today, 56 people went to a football match and they never came home.

Rest in peace

The Squad

Josh Vickers

Before we get started, let me state this as my opinion; Josh Vickers could play top flight football. Remember, he's only 23 and has shown himself to be an excellent shot stopper and to have good command of his area.

Should we expect anything less though? He came through the ranks at Arsenal and will have had lots of top flight coaching as a young man. He may be young with plenty to learn, but at 23 he still has 15 years of football left in him.

An outfield player usually gets until he 32 perhaps, then the decline starts, but a keeper can easily play into his forties if he keeps fit....

Ah. If he keeps fit. Josh Vickers' horcrux, his Achilles heel. He can't stay fit.

It's heart-breaking to witness the struggles the giant keeper is experiencing. He was brought to the club surely with a view to making the number one shirt his own and dare I say it, had he stayed fit all season we might just have had more points than we do right now.

He's struggled though and that's a real shame. Is there a future for him at the club? You'd hope so, but if he can't prove his long-term fitness then it could be a real problem.

Up until Matt Gilks arrived, Josh was the number one. If Gilks remains next season, he might find his football even more limited than he has this season.

Grant Smith

I know I'm going to write this and feel cruel. I can feel it in my bones, but as an independent blog I have to write what I feel, not what I think will be well received.

I don't think Grant Smith is good enough to play 46 games in a title-winning team. I'm not saying he won't be good enough, but right now he isn't. Had we not signed Matt Gilks, I suspect we would have fewer points than we do now.

That's not to say he's a bad keeper, not at all, but if you watch one game in particular I think the issues with Grant are laid bare.

The 3-3 draw with Bury was a thrilling encounter, but I firmly believe that a Lincoln City with Gilks or Vickers in goal win that game 3-2. Whether it was the late header, not unlike Chuks Aneke's effort this week, or whether it was the weak opener, I think a better keeper makes a save there.

He's not been bad, after a couple of worrying showings over Christmas I think Grant bounced back strongly, but in my eyes he's a lower League two keeper at best. The thing is, until you've had better you don't know what it looks like. I was a huge Paul Farman fan, but we wouldn't be top of League One with Farms in the sticks and the same goes for Grant.

He's a worthy back up, but I can't see Danny wanting three keepers next season. There's surely going to be a loan spell, that's if he remains at the club.

Matt Gilks

We all looked to the transfer window for inspiration up front. The usual 'which big striker are we signing' debate went off as the deadline closed, with fans angry that we hadn't aimed higher. It was all pantomime of course, Danny's recruitment has widely proven to be excellent and once again, it proved to be.

Capturing Gilks didn't raise too many eyebrows. Sure, he's played for Scotland and spent time with Rangers, but he was coming in as cover, right? Okay, he'd played for Scunthorpe last season, but Sam Slocombe had been with Bristol Rovers and he was never anything more than back up to the back up.

What we've actually got with Gilks is a wonderful keeper. You'll read about his dedication and application in the programme this weekend, but his overall impact has been unreal. He rarely concedes from open play, that's the benefit of having a good defence, but when he is called upon he's excellent. he makes certain saves look routine, the stop early on against MK Dons being typical.

When really tested though, he's outstanding. The stop from Chuks Aneke was enough to win us the game and he pulled a similar one off against Macclesfield as well. Strikers score goals and get you promoted, but keepers stopping them is often overlooked.

He came in at just the right time and has been a key figure in our excellent form holding off the chasing pack.

Neal Eardley

Ah, 'The Postman' as he's been named by our media team. In case you're wondering, I think it's because he always delivers, but it might be his preference for the top corner of the goal when striking a free kick, the area known as the 'postage stamp'. Either way, he doesn't have a little red van or a cat named Jess.

What he does have is 39 starts in the league, just three games shy of being ever-present. He's started three times as many matches in two years with us as he managed in the four seasons prior to joining. That's a testament to his hard work on the treatment table as well as his quality on the pitch.

It's been a tough season for Neal in that he hasn't shone as much as he did last year. That isn't because he's been any worse, not at all, but he's been surrounded by players who have all raised their game. He's doubled his goal tally this season, from one to two, plus he's weighed in with plenty of assists as well.

Has he been as consistently good? Maybe he's had one bad game, perhaps two at a push, but name me a single footballer who doesn't have one or two bad games a season (apart from Neal Eardley last year).

He's been an eight most matches, his delivery has been terrific, his dead balls have been deadly and he's played more league football than all but two of our players. He also appeared in all three FA Cup matches.

He won't win Player of the Year, but through no fault of his own. This lad is League One quality and next season, he gets a chance to prove it.

Harry Toffolo

We've played 42 league matches this season. Harry Toffolo has played in all 42. We made three appearances in the FA Cup, of which Toffolo played in all three. That's the definition of ever-present. When we've played, Toff has played.

He's been lucky with a couple of tackles, one that sticks in my mind at Yeovil perhaps deserved a red card, but he rode that storm and has kept himself fit. He's not just been fit in the literal sense, he's reached incredible levels.

He's not your average left back. Sam Habergham for instance is a left back in the strictest sense. He can get forwards, but is a reliable figure who won't be caught too far up the pitch. Toff isn't. he's a wing back, strong in attack with a habit of popping up on the edge of the area to bag goals.

He's created and scored, just like Neal Eardley has, but he's stood out more because of that attacking prowess. On the right, Eardley and Anderson have a relationship which focuses a lot on Anderson getting in behind and laying it back to Neal. On the left, Toffolo is just as likely to be getting in behind, overlapping Bruno. They're more dynamic, interchangeable and it's meant he's caught the eye.

I believe Harry Toffolo should be a major contender for Player of the Season. His attitude has always been superb, he is a threat going forward and competent at the back and, if he stays fit, he'll be the only ever-present in our title-winning side of 2019. That's a huge achievement in his first full season with us.

If you're reading this as a non-Lincoln fan, do keep an eye on Harry Toffolo, he's got the potential to go a long way in the game.

James Wilson

Here's a man I feel sorry for. James Wilson is a centre back, but gets onto this list by virtue of starting at right back in the three games Neal Eardley did not. He's been played sporadically and when he has featured, he's been out of position.

Against Port Vale he even came on in midfield, scoring a header, but he's not been able to force his way into the first team picture.

I don't know what it is with James Wilson. He's not a right back, that much is for certain. He can play there, but looks uncomfortable and steady. I'd compare him with a lower League Two right back, yet he's a player with international experience in another position.

He's just not able to get a go at centre half. Michael Bostwick has been ahead of him, Jason Shackell too. Scott Wharton perhaps was by virtue of being left footed and when Cian Bolger arrived, he went into the first team ahead of Wilson as well. It's been frustrating for the player and to a degree for us as fans.

We know there's a quality footballer in there, one with League One potential, but he's not going to play. It's doubtful he'll force a start next season if he remains, which means his short Imps' career is likely to end with more starts as a makeshift right back than in his preferred central defensive role.

He's only started nine games for the Imps in a season and a half, with half of those as a right back. He'll be frustrated with his time here and will probably look back on it unfavourably, which is a shame considering he'll take home a title-winner's medal, should we seal that honour in the next four matches.

Scott Wharton

Let's start the centre backs with this season's Sean Long shall we?

By that I mean the player who would have got more games had it not been for a former Premier League player arriving at the start of the season and scuppering his plans.

It's really simple here. Scott Wharton is a very good footballer, better than League Two. Whatever his meagre appearance total suggests, it isn't a lack of ability. In Scott Blackburn have a young man who is measured and calm, flexible in the positions he can play and certainly one with a good future ahead of him.

Any League Two club would be lucky to have him and, since he moved to Bury, he's made 13 starts to become a regular. Basically, he's a firm fixture in the first team of the side likely to finish second, but couldn't get a kick with us. Why? Jason Shackell.

Taking out the fact he struggled for games, he always showed a great work ethic, he was reliable when called upon and never once moaned, complained or looked like he'd given up. It might seem like a pre-requisite to us as fans, but players struggling for games can lose motivation. He proved that wasn't the case by coming in and scoring at Port Vale.

Sadly, after five starts and six appearances from the bench in the league, he was gone. Blackburn called him back and he's going to now help Bury to automatic promotion.

Top player, sadly the right man at the wrong time this season.

Cian Bolger

You could be forgiven for thinking Cian Bolger hadn't featured all that much since signing from Fleetwood, but remarkably he's start 11 matches, with a further five outings from the bench. It's fait to say he's been overshadowed both in terms of centre backs he's up against, and the signings who arrived in the window at the same time.

This was a coup for Lincoln, there's no mistake there. Cian Bolger is highly rated and was wanted by Championship clubs in the summer. Like James Wilson last season, he's expected to be a first team player in the coming months, especially when you consider the length of contract he's been given.

I would offer a word of caution; we've not seen the best of him so far. he's still travelling back to Ireland I believe to see his girlfriend and as of a couple of weeks ago he was living out of temporary accommodation. I believe he's very much like Tom Pett of a year ago; still setting in.

There's no doubt he's good in the air and has some quality on the ball, but I think he's going to be the sort of player who needs time and a pre-season before we see the best of him. I believed, naively, that him signing meant Jason Shackell would be going. The fact Shacks is staying means Cian has a big challenge next season.

I think he's up for the fight, I believe he has quality and can be a consistent performer for us. I just don't think we've seen the best of him yet and considering he's not put in a truly poor performance as yet, that bodes well.

Michael Bostwick

They don't make footballers like Bozzy anymore, an enigma and elusive to both the media and the club's own PR machine. Signed a new deal? Record a video clip and get off home Bozzy.. I love it.

I tell you what else I love; hard men. Not hatchet men, but players who can put in a thunderous tackle and not get sent off on a regular basis. Sometimes his challenges are so bone-crunching I feel like I've cracked a rib just watching. Then you see him time a challenge as he did against Tranmere, coming from nowhere to dispossess the last man with next to no effort, or at least that's how it looks.

I would imagine to play against, Michael Bostwick is an utter bastard. I would imagine to play alongside, he's a dream. He's uncomplicated, a centre half who does exactly what Steve Thompson used to pride himself on. If the ball is near his feet, he kicks it away. If it's near his head, he nods it away. If the ball is nowhere near then he looks to stop the player.

He's a 100% man, every single game. I can't wax lyrical enough about Michael Bostwick, but then you'll know how good he is. You will have seen him putting his body on the line, making the blocks and tackles as if his life depended on it.

He's grabbed three goals this season too, one at Goodison Park. Not many Lincoln City players can say they've had a £50m forward in their pocket. He can.

I get to meet him this week, I'm at the PFA Player of the Month presentation and of all the Imps' players I've met and spoken to, he's the one I really can't wait to meet, even if he just grunts a few words and buggers off.

Plus, I'm a beard fan.

Jason Shackell

Honesty shout; when we signed him I had to get on Google. I'd been following the National League, not the Championship and the different players who graced the likes of Wolves, Norwich and Derby were a mystery to me. I knew Liam Scully was very excited on the afternoon before it was confirmed, but I felt a bit underwhelmed. 34-year-old dropping into League Two haven't always covered themselves in glory.

I remember Steve Foley, Trevor Hebberd, Kingsley Black and Dave Phillips They were all from further up the divisions, they were all past 30 and they were all complete and utter dross. All I saw when Shackell arrived was more of the same, or rather I feared the same. I suppose fitness has move on, sports science has too and I didn't truly believe Danny would sign a carthorse, but still. 34-years-old? Come on.

I expected someone to play a few games and maybe get into the coaching side of things, but what we got was a defender who still showed all the qualities required to play in the second tier. How we ever attracted this Rolls Royce of a player to Sincil Bank I'll never know, but for 33 matches he's played the calming influence next to Bozzy's raging bull. They're yin and yang, the opposites which complete a whole.

Jason Shackell organises and controls. He reads the game superbly and has rarely been caught out. At Goodison Park, the threat through the centre was very much stifled thanks to both players and to judge one without the other is actually quite hard. They're a great pairing, complementing each other to the benefit of the team.

He's also surprised with a few goals too, none of which have been tap ins. The Morecambe free-kick obviously stands out, but then the Macclesfield finish was clever and the Swindon strike was good too.

The only blots on his copybook have been the red cards, both of which were avoidable. I suppose I should condemn the whole 'pushing Seb Stockbridge' thing as well, but I'll do so with a wry smile as though I'm telling off a child who has done something I would have done myself in the same situation.

To have him for another year is exciting, it's also interesting. Will he keep Bolger out of the side, or will his legs finally begin to show signs of the career he's enjoyed? Who knows, but for now he's been a key component of our championship winning season.

Ellis Chapman

In terms of progression, this has been a huge season for Ellis. he began the campaign a boy stepping up into a man's world and by the time he's back in the fold, he'll be very much a man having played 14 times for Chesterfield in the National League.

He's impressed there and leaves with their best wishes. I'm not here to assess how he has done, but the indications are that if we sent a talented young man away, we're getting the same back but with much more experience of senior football. His return is what prompted me to question the game time others might get next season as he's definitely going to be involved much more.

In terms of his Imps appearances, I think we only got to see flashes of what he can do. The controversial red card against Cambridge didn't help his cause, nor being hooked at half time against Bury in a tactical switch. What it did show was his application and attitude, on both occasions he got his head down and worked hard towards getting back in the side.

His outings were always calm, he sprayed the ball about nicely and didn't look overly nervous when he played. What he needed was minutes on the pitch and through his loan spell, that's exactly what he got.

This might have been his 'coming of age' season, but next year is where he's going to break through properly.

Lee Frecklington

One of the real stories of last season was the homecoming of Lee Frecklington, a Lincoln lad with the club running through his veins. It was always going to be him that bagged the winning penalty in the EFL Trophy semi-final and although Luke hoisted the silver aloft, this weekend it will be Freck having the honour.

In the early part of the season I thought Freck was excellent. He bagged three goals in three matches and against Exeter gave us a look at the Freck of old, the player who left for Posh all those years ago. he was running the midfield, slick and composed and would seemingly play a huge part in our season.

The red card against Crawley, justified I might add, stopped that for a second, but he came back just as strong and impressed at home against Crewe. We then went to Port Vale and he looked sharp again, only to be pole-axed by Scott Brown and put out of action.

I believe since then he's not been able to find the level of fitness he showed early doors. The knock kept him out and although he's been a key player all season, injury issues have plagued him somewhat. He's found his game time limited as the season has worn on and only the strong squad depth has prevented it being a serious hinderance to our title charge.

He's our captain and a big influence off the field as well as on it. he might not have got the goals he would have liked, but certainly in the early stages of the season he had a big impact.

Mark O'Hara

The quality of a January signing can make or break your season. Often, certainly with the likes of Lee Angol, it can look like you've been signed for a reason and neglected. Players come in as cover and are rarely seen, but sometimes one comes in who seriously impresses.

Mark O'Hara has seriously impressed. The Peterborough man has added an energy and physical presence to an already impressive midfield area, weighing in with a goal against Yeovil which settled a few nerves too.

He gone about making the right noises with regards to a prolonged stay at the club and the suggestion is he'll be one we pursue during the summer. It would mean a packed roster in terms of central midfield players, but the 23-year-old is one I'd love to see remain at the club.

The aerial presence is one aspect of his game that is unique to our other crop of midfielders. He has a huge leap and is a threat at set pieces, which plays to our strengths and is something I believe we'll see utilised to good effect again next season.

If we can find a way to sign O'Hara, it would be a major coup for the club.

Tom Pett

I found myself defending Tom Pett at the end of last season. He took a while to settle and find his feet, but even in the glimpses we had of him I felt we'd found a real gem. Maybe it's because I'd talked him up when we first came up, but that final day goal against Yeovil delighted me, not least because I was laid in hospital unable to move and needed something to cheer.

This season I was incredibly surprised to see him deployed in central midfield, even more so to see him succeed. He didn't just do well, he won the PFA Player of the Month at one point. That set him up for a strong season.

Looking back, I was surprised to see he'd only bagged three goals. He often seems to be getting forward and threatening, so to find out he hasn't bagged in 2019 has genuinely surprised me. He's one who may have lost out a bit with Mark O'Hara coming in, as well as suffering when he went out on the flank following Bruno's dismissal.

When he arrived he was thought of as a winger, but the switch to the centre has suited his tenacious play and ability to travel with the ball. He's certainly likely to be seen in matches we need to press home an advantage over ones we need to doggedly defend in, as he's more of an attacking midfielder than anything.

He's a reliable member of the squad though, one who will be relishing the chance to prove himself in League One. He's certainly earned it, an eloquent and well-spoken member of the squad with a community focus, he's certainly very popular off the field as well as on it.

Michael O'Connor

My comments on a previous article were taken by Michael as suggesting he wasn't League One quality. That isn't the case at all.

In fact, only a couple of weeks ago I called him as my dark horse for Player of the Year, something that I stand by now. I've explained my other comments, at no point have I said he's not a League One quality player; he is.

What I've liked about him, and writing this will doubtless appear like me fawning and trying to make amends, is that he's the closest thing we've had to Alex Woodyard. Every team need the industrious midfielder, the player who can do the dirty work but has a bit of class too. Harsher fans than I have said O'Connor is like Woodyard but actually passes forwards. Whilst I won't hear a word against Alex, I do see the reasoning behind those assumptions.

I believe he's bene one of the strongest signings of the summer, a player we didn't know we needed as fans before he arrived, but wouldn't have won the title without now he's proven himself. I'm a little saddened that my other comments were taken in the wrong way, especially as I began the paragraph with the words 'I fear'. I did that because I wouldn't want to lose him, but could see a pathway whereby we could.

You don't make 44 appearances without being a big influence on the side and when you consider the collection of players we've had in his position, it's a testament to his ability and impact.

Now, I just hope he doesn't take it up with me at the EPC tomorrow afternoon!

Harry Anderson

Ah, Harry Anderson. Here's a player I've been waiting to write about, a player who seriously impresses me and frustrates in equal measure. He frustrates me because his potential and skill should see him making headlines every week and he doesn't. I'm not sure why.

He scores goals, he's quick and he is strong and yet for some reason the plaudits go elsewhere. He's young as well, but has over 100 outings to his name in Lincoln shirt. He's lifted three trophies with us and is as much a part of the Cowley era as Danny and Nicky themselves.

He's also a very down to earth lad, focused on his game and sure to increase in value. Maybe, because a more flamboyant Bruno is on the other flank, Harry gets overlooked. His direct style, stocky and strong isn't always as easy on the eye as Bruno's flicks and tricks, but it harps back to a golden era for wingers.

Harry is very old-school in his approach, the sort of bulldozer figure that would have impressed in the sixties and seventies. Opponents can snuff out his threat by playing certain tactics and if he's having an off day nothing works for him. You'll never see his head drop though and he just keeps ploughing on. the 3-0 Colchester defeat was a clear reflection of that, he struggled all game but just kept on doing what he was there to do.

I like that, determination, desire and single-minded focus. As his game becomes more refined and involved, he's going to evolve and impress more and more.

Bruno Andrade

"He belongs to us, Bruno Andrade," is how the song goes, but if rumours are to be believed he might not belong to us for long.

Bruno is a good footballer. He's quick, spots space well and is full of flicks and tricks. Whereas Harry is an old-style player, Bruno is very much the flamboyant wide man of the modern era, full of stuff the kids call 'tekkers' and flair. When he's on song, he's utterly unplayable.

I saw a remarkable comment on social media the other day, surely tongue in cheek, that said he'd had one good month. I had a look back and tried to see if I could figure out which month that was. Was it the explosive September in which he provided assists, into October where his relationship with Harry Toffolo increased, or maybe February when he won PFA Player of the Month?

Sure, he had slow patches in the season, but he did pick up injuries before Christmas and towards the end of the season. People keep mentioning the petulant red card, but seriously.... players get sent off all the time. When you're on the grass and things are happening around you, it's hard not to get drawn in. It's easy as fans to say players should behave in a certain way, but in practice it's tougher.

I thought he bounced back well and was a key player for us throughout the season. Yes, he sometimes goes down easily but then when he's genuinely fouled it gets overlooked.

he got ten goals from open play, making him our leading scorer if penalties were discounted and when you throw assist in as well, it's strange that anyone chooses to comment negatively about him at all.

Here's a fact for you though; he's our most saleable asset and if anyone is to go for a big fee to help fund League One, it'll be Bruno.

Kellan Gordon

Occasionally, someone comes to the club and doesn't get a lot of football, but when they're gone you just know they'll do well somewhere. Kellan Gordon is that player.

We saw Kellan from the bench on six occasions in the league. When he signed, we were led to believe he was right back cover and maybe that was the intention, but when he got on the ball it was clear he was a wing back at worst and a winger at best.

He scored two goals, both in big matches. He won us the game against Forest Green coming in off the right flank, just as he almost had the clash with Mansfield.

It's hard to write a lot about a player with six substitute appearances but I felt with Kellan Gordon, I needed to get it off my chest. One day, this kid will play 40-odd games for a Football League side and at the end of the season, that side will be lauding his input. He's a very good footballer who was the right man at the wrong time.

I wouldn't be disappointed if we signed him next season for six months and gave him more appearances from the bench.

Bernard Mensah

From a man with six appearances from the bench, to one with just four. I was genuinely excited when Bernard Mensah signed, I felt we'd bagged a player who would be a big part of our season.

In truth, aside from a passionate celebration of our late goal against MK Dons, he may as well not have arrived at all.

His first interview impressed me, he came across as reserved and intelligent, a man with a significant amount to offer. Whether he, like Gordon, was the right man at the wrong time or not I don't know.

We barely saw him and when he was on the pitch it was hard to tell. He has since enjoyed a successful National League loan but I think he's got a lot to offer a lower League Two side, something we've not been since 2011.

Jordan Roberts

I remember once, maybe ten years ago, lamenting how Lincoln never signed wingers. I've always loved a wide player, be it David Puttnam, Gareth Ainsworth, Dany N'Guessan and even Mustapha Carayol. There's few sights in football more beautiful than a wide player knocking the ball past a full back and roasting him alive in a foot race.

This season we've had more wide players than ever before and sadly, some just haven't lived up to the hype.

That's unfair on Jordan, he's another talented player who just wasn't going to get a game on a regular basis. He did look lost on his introduction against Bury and after that, he drifted off the scene. Towards the end of the season he did get a few late runs from the bench, but you could probably count his touches on your fingers.

Again, like Gordon and Mensah before him, the right man at the wrong time entirely.

Danny Rowe

Danny Rowe got it right. Come back in after impressing last season, smash goals in your first few matches and convert from being a wide player to avoid the troubling problem of Bruno and Harry.

Rowe is a winger, but Danny had him through the centre and for a short while it looked as though he was going to take League Two by storm. Jorge who? Tyler what? Ilias when? No, the main loan signing was Danny Rowe, at least for three matches.

After that, dare I say, he tailed off a bit. Shay McCartan and him battled for a starting role and I wondered if maybe injury restricted Danny as it did last season. After that explosive start I felt he just went off the boil. He still had those driving runs in him, but as teams retreated at Sincil Bank it became harder for him to impress.

His best games came away from home, Bury and Yeovil certainly two that stand out. Why? Space. Those sides had to attack us and that left green pitch for Danny to run into. It remains to be seen if our inability to break two banks of four down is because of players or the way we approach most fixtures.

Danny Rowe started 12 matches for us, played 17 in total in the league and scored four goals. He's likely to go back to Ipswich this summer and whilst it pains me a little to say it, I do think we can use the squad place in a more constructive manner. I like Danny, we sponsor him, but if we need a versatile player to fill a couple of roles I'd like to see Kellan Gordon back and make a big saving on wages to spend elsewhere.

John Akinde

May as well wade straight into the argument hadn't we? Even sat around the table on Sunday night, celebrating the Imps' first Football League title in my lifetime, we were having the John Akinde debate.

It surprises me that we still have to defend big John, 'we' being those who see exactly what he brings to the side. I think he got better as the season went on, which for anyone who saw him against Exeter might seem hard to believe. The fact is we've played him in a very different role to the one he played at Barnet.

He was part of a two man strike force for the Bees, which meant he was often the runner off a big man. We have seen that used to effect in some matches this season, but in the main he's been the target man and the runner in one.

We won the league this season because our away from eclipsed our home form. Last season we won four fewer away from home and lost three more. My firmly held belief is John Akinde is the difference.

Away from home we need to play a more counter-attacking game. Last year, if we wanted to break at speed, we went long to Matt Rhead and got Matt Green around him. That took up two players and left us less compact at the back. This season, John performed both tasks. We could have ten behind the ball where needed, and get out to John who would be able to carry it away.

How often did he look isolated? Often? You know why that is? He was. Not his fault, but it reflected in his goal tally. However, that isolation was often part of the plan, with his 'partner', often McCartan, looking to occupy the last midfielder as well as get forward.

We conceded five fewer goals way from home than last season and scored 12 more. That's where the league was won and lost.

Matt Green

I miss Matt Green. He did the right thing for his family and for himself, but I was a big fan. In eighteen months at the club he proved to me to be as energetic and aware as anyone we've had since the Keith Alexander days.

It's odd, he was often maligned by our supporters, as many strikers are, for not scoring enough last season. He's not 'prolific' was the accusation levied at him, but then when he was out of the side everyone wanted him in. I guess it's easy to be a football fan, especially when things aren't going your way.

Matt didn't shine this season, but he didn't get the chance. He bagged a few goals early doors, featured on the cover of our printed fanzine and was cast aside. He probably didn't fit the pattern of play we wanted to operate. After all, John Akinde wasn't employed purely as a target man and if Matt Green played, we would use him as the runner.

It meant he often got half an hour or so with Rheady, but never struck up a partnership with Big John. They'd run the same channels and looked to be very similar players, only with John having the added bulk and Greeny perhaps, just perhaps, being too lightweight to play the hold up role.

I still miss him though and his contribution to the season shouldn't be forgotten. He saved us from a draw on the opening day and settled nerves after coming on against Swindon, two results that gave us the foundations of a great season.

Shay McCartan

It would be hard to be too critical of Shay, would it not? He bagged our 6500th goal, he bagged the goal that sealed promotion and he bagged the Goal of the Season as well. In fact, whenever we needed something out of the ordinary, something memorable and uplifting, he was there.

Who can forget that equaliser against MK Dons which set up the comeback early in the season? That's my gripe with Shay; take out the wonder strikes and he doesn't chip in with many the normal ones

It's an odd accusation isn't it? He bagged seven in 43 and I doubt that there's one you'd call 'run of the mill'. He's got a terrific volley and when he's not scoring, he has a driving urgency to his game I like as well. He reminded a bit of Wayne Rooney, able to carry the ball and bag goals at will.

I just feel that maybe he wasn't the exact profile of player Danny wanted behind big John. Maybe he needed a touch more pace or a player with a striker's instinct. For me, McCartan is an attacking midfielder, someone who'll link play and pop up on the edge of the area. I don't recall him sliding in at the back stick on the end of a cross and I can only remember one scuffed effort from six yards (Port Vale).

I wouldn't be upset if he came back next season, he's a good player and with a little more time on the ball might be more effective in League One. If I'm honest, brutally so, I suspect he'll remain at Bradford and help them get back up at a level he's been used to for the last twelve months.

He's certainly got a place in Imps folklore though and he's a nice lad to boot.

Matt Rhead

We finish on a player who does divide opinion but, in the main, is a crowd favourite. In my eyes he's a legend at the club, he's someone who has done enough during his stay to genuinely warrant being called that. Sure, he got one league goal last season (Cambridge at home) and just three in total, but there's much more to him than goals.

He's on 50 (or 49 in some people's eyes) and will top 200 outings by the time he gets into next season. This article isn't about next season though, or the previous three. It's about 2018/19 and Matt Rhead played his part.

He started 12 league matches this season, coming from the bench on 22 occasions. That's one goal in 34 league matches and yet he's still revered by much of the fan base. I know Paperclip Imp won't be happy in the comments, but I believe Rhead played an important role for us.

Yes, he upsets opposition players. Yes, he's an aggravator and a player others love to hate. At times he isn't mobile and his haranguing of the officials isn't something many like to see. All of those factors I've mentioned though are why he's so important.

1-0 up and need the ball to stick for longer up front? He's your man. 1-0 down and need to just keep landing it on someone's head to make a chance? He's your man. Need a player to come on in the dying seconds to add aerial presence at the back? You get the picture.

He is a very good footballer too. He gets pigeon-holed and to a degree it's harder for him to show his skills as the years advance, but he's got a wonderful touch and vision. I sometimes think he'd be better in a mix between football and netball, in that when he got the ball he had to stop still before moving it on. His technique belies his size and the general stereotype that has built up around him.

Do I think he'll start 12 matches next season? No. Do I think he'll score five league goals next season? No. Do I think he'll make twenty or so appearances from the bench and be a right handful whenever he does? Yes.

Most importantly, is he a hugely important part of not just the playing squad, but the club as a whole? Yes, yes he is.

Squad Details

Player	Total Apps	Total Goals	League 2 Apps	League 2 Goals	FA Cup Apps	FA Cup Goals	League Cup Apps	League Cup Goals	EFL Trophy Apps	EFL Trophy Goals
Josh Vickers	21	0	18	0	3	0	0	0	0	0
Sam Habergham	0	0	0	0	0	0	0	0	0	0
Michael O'Connor	44	3	31+7	2	2+1	0	1+1	1	0+1	0
Jason Shackell	40	5	33+1	4	3	0	2	1	1	0
Mark O'Hara	17	1	14+3	1	0	0	0	0	0	0
Tom Pett	51	4	33+11	3	3	1	1+1	0	2	0
Lee Frecklington	29	4	23+3	4	2	0	0	0	0+1	0
Matt Rhead	43	3	12+22	1	1+2	1	2	0	4	1
Lee Angol	2	0	0+2	0	0	0	0	0	0	0
Bruno Andrade	50	11	39+3	10	3	1	0+2	0	0+3	0
Ellis Chapman	12	0	2+3	0	0+1	0	2	0	4	0
Harry Toffolo	52	3	46	3	3	0	1	0	1+1	0
James Wilson	15	1	4+7	1	1	0	2	0	1	0
Michael Bostwick	49	3	45	2	3	1	0	0	1	0
Shay McCartan	43	7	23+15	7	1+2	0	1	0	1	0
Matt Gilks	12	0	12	0	0	0	0	0	0	0
Danny Rowe	17	4	12+5	4	0	0	0	0	0	0
Grant Smith	17	0	16	0	0	0	1	0	0	0
Neal Eardley	47	2	43	2	2	0	1	0	1	0
Cian Bolger	17	1	12+5	1	0	0	0	0	0	0
Jordan Roberts	5	0	0+5	0	0	0	0	0	0	0
Harry Anderson	51	7	39+4	5	3	1	2	0	3	1
Jamie McCombe	2	1	0	0	0	0	0	0	0+2	1
Tom Shaw	1	0	0	0	0	0	0	0	0+1	0
John Akinde	52	17	41+4	15	2+1	1	0+2	1	0+2	0
J Adebayo-Smith	1	0	0	0	0	0	0	0	1	0
Kellan Gordon	10	2	0+6	2	0	0	0	0	4	0
Luke Waterfall	1	0	1	0	0	0	0	0	0	0
Scott Wharton	15	1	4+6	1	0+1	0	1	0	3	0
Matt Green	25	6	2+16	2	1+1	0	2	1	3	3
Bernard Mensah	8	0	0+4	0	0	0	0	0	4	0
Joan Luque	4	1	0+1	0	0	0	1	1	2	0
Adam Crookes	5	0	0	0	0	0	1	0	4	0
Sam Slocombe	5	0	0	0	0	0	1	0	4	0

League Table

Pos		Pld	W	D	L	GF	GA	GD	Pts
1	Lincoln City (C, P)	46	23	16	7	73	43	30	**85**
2	Bury (P)	46	22	13	11	82	56	26	**79**
3	Milton Keynes Dons (P)	46	23	10	13	71	49	22	**79**
4	Mansfield Town	46	20	16	10	69	41	28	**76**
5	Forest Green Rovers	46	20	14	12	68	47	21	**74**
6	Tranmere Rovers (O, P)	46	20	13	13	63	50	13	**73**
7	Newport County	46	20	11	15	59	59	0	**71**
8	Colchester United	46	20	10	16	65	53	12	**70**
9	Exeter City	46	19	13	14	60	49	11	**70**
10	Stevenage	46	20	10	16	59	55	4	**70**
11	Carlisle United	46	20	8	18	67	62	5	**68**
12	Crewe Alexandra	46	19	8	19	60	59	1	**65**
13	Swindon Town	46	16	16	14	59	56	3	**64**
14	Oldham Athletic	46	16	14	16	67	60	7	**62**
15	Northampton Town	46	14	19	13	64	63	1	**61**
16	Cheltenham Town	46	15	12	19	57	68	−11	**57**
17	Grimsby Town	46	16	8	22	45	56	−11	**56**
18	Morecambe	46	14	12	20	54	70	−16	**54**
19	Crawley Town	46	15	8	23	51	68	−17	**53**
20	Port Vale	46	12	13	21	39	55	−16	**49**
21	Cambridge United	46	12	11	23	40	66	−26	**47**
22	Macclesfield Town	46	10	14	22	48	74	−26	**44**
23	Notts County (R)	46	9	14	23	48	84	−36	**41**
24	Yeovil Town (R)	46	9	13	24	41	66	−25	**40**

HERE'S TO THE FUTURE

UP THE IMPS

Printed in Great Britain
by Amazon